# The Guinness Book of Cycling

## FACTS AND FEATS

Jeremy Evans

GUINNESS PUBLISHING

# Acknowledgements

The author would like to thank the following who have helped provide information and ideas for this book:

*Cycling Weekly* – the magazine proved an invaluable source of material on all aspects of cycle racing from early times up to the present day.

CTC – the Cyclists' Touring Club were particularly helpful with information from the early days of the bicycle.

Thanks to the Adventure Cycling Association (USA), Audax UK, the British Cycling Federation, the Road Records Association, the Road Time Trials Council, the UCI and the US Cycling Federation. Thanks also to Guinness Publications and their *Guinness Book of Records* in both UK and USA editions, the *Guinness International Who's Who of Sport* and the *Guinness Encyclopedia of International Sports Records and Results*.

Text design and layout: Mitchell Associates

Cover design: Ad Vantage Studios

Printed and bound in Great Britain by The Bath Press, Bath

A catalogue record of this book is available from the British Library.

ISBN 085112-677-4

# Contents

# ABBREVIATIONS

| | | | | |
|---|---|---|---|---|
| A | Austria | | IRL | Ireland |
| AUS | Australia | | JPN | Japan |
| B | Belgium | | LAT | Latvia |
| BUL | Bulgaria | | LUX | Luxembourg |
| BOL | Bolivia | | LIT | Lithuania |
| BRA | Brazil | | MC | Monaco |
| BS | Bahamas | | MEX | Mexico |
| C | Cuba | | MOL | Moldavia |
| CDN | Canada | | NOR | Norway |
| CIS | Commonwealth of Independent States | | NL | Holland |
| COL | Colombia | | NZ | New Zealand |
| CZ | Czechoslovakia | | POR | Portugal |
| D | Germany | | PAK | Pakistan |
| DDR | German Democratic Republic – East Germany | | POL | Poland |
| FDR | Federal Democratic Republic – West Germany | | ROM | Romania |
| DNK | Denmark | | RUS | Russia |
| E | Spain | | SLK | Slovakia |
| EST | Estonia | | SU | Soviet Union |
| F | France | | SWI | Switzerland |
| GRE | Greece | | UK | United Kingdom |
| H | Hungary | | USA | United States of America |
| I | Italy | | USSR | Union of Soviet Socialist Republics |
| IND | India | | | |

# BIBLIOGRAPHY

**Journals**
*Arrivée*
*Cycle Sport*
*Bike Culture*
*Bike Report*
*Cycling Plus*
*Cycloclimbing*
*Mountain Bike*
*Mountain Bike Action*
*Mountain Biker International*
*Mountain Biking UK*
*MTB Pro*

**Annuals and Handbooks**
*Audax Handbook*, Audax UK
*BCF Handbook*, British Cycling Federation, UK
*CTC Handbook*, Cyclists' Touring Club, UK
*Road Records Association Handbook*, RRA, UK
*Road Time-Trials Handbook*, RTTC, UK
*The Guinness Book of Records*, Guinness Publishing, UK
*The Guinness Sports Yearbook*, Guinness Publishing, UK
*The ROSPA Bicycle Owners' Handbook*, Royal Society for the Prevention of Accidents, UK
*Velo*, Editions Velo, Belgium

**Books**
*Alpaca to Skin Suit*, Bernard Thompson, Geerings (Ashford, UK) 1988
*Cycling on Road and Trail*, Jeremy Evans, Crowood Press (Ramsbury UK) 1995
*European Cycling*, Noel Henderson, Vitesse Press (Vermont, USA) 1990
*Offroad Biking*, Jeremy Evans, Heinemann (Oxford) 1991
*Pocket Guide to Cycling*, John Wilcockson, Bell and Hyman (London) 1992
*The Complete Book of Performance Cycling*, Phil Liggett, Collins Willow (London) 1992
*The Fastest Man on Two Wheels*, Phil Liggett, Boxtree (London) 1994
*The Guinness Book of Olympic Facts and Feats*, Stan Greenberg, Guinness Superlatives 1984
*The Guinness Encyclopedia of International Sports Records and Results*, Peter Matthews, Guinness Publishing, 1993
*The Guinness International Who's Who of Sport*, Peter Matthews, Ian Buchanan and Bill Mellon, Guinness Publishing, 1993
*The Road to Hell*, Graham Watson, Springfield, 1992

# The Dawn of the Bicycle to the Present Day

### Baron von Drais and his Invention

Baron von Drais invented and patented the *Laufmaschine* (machine that you run with) in 1817, and is generally credited as the inventor of the 'hobby horse' or 'dandy horse', a wooden bar supported between two wheels propelled by the 'rider' who ran it over the ground. His *Laufmaschine* was mainly made of wood and weighed about 40 lb (18 kg). Some sources claim Baron von Drais was preceded in his invention by a Frenchman named de Sivrac who invented the *Celerifere* (Celeripede in English) in 1790, which was a success among the smart set of the *Directoire* period.

The 'hobby horse' came rapidly into fashion in Britain, where Denis Johnson of London applied for a patent on his similar design in December 1818. A year later Johnson travelled to New York, where Davis and Rogers of Troy had introduced machines known as velocipedes based on his designs. Not everyone approved. The 9 July 1819 issue of *The Federal Republican and Baltimore Telegraph* reported: 'A curious two-wheeled vehicle called the velocipede has been invented, which is propelled by Jack-asses instead of horses.'

*Baron von Drais looks faintly ridiculous as he takes his pride and joy – also known as the 'Draisienne' – for a ride in 1817*

### 1819

Denis Johnson introduced the idea of the drop-frame cycle which would accommodate women's skirts.

### 1839

The first design for a machine propelled by cranks and pedals with connecting rods has been attributed to Leonardo da Vinci (1452–1519) or one of his pupils and is dated circa 1493. The earliest such design actually built was in 1839 by a Scottish blacksmith named Kirkpatrick Macmillan (1810–78) who lived in Dumfries where he perfected a system using a rear-driven wheel and treadle cranks, so the rider had no need to run and could instead pedal a hobby horse. Some believe this allows Kirkpatrick Macmillan the right to be called the father of the bicycle, but there was no immediate follow-up to his invention. A copy of his machine is kept at the Science Museum in Kensington, London.

### 1845

R.W. Thomson took out a patent for 'a hollow rubber tube inflated with air' in 1845 in Britain and in 1846 in France. No one appeared to notice, and it is believed that J.B. Dunlop knew nothing of this pioneering work when his pneumatic tyre was 'invented' 43 years later.

■ Willard Sawyer began to make four-wheel cycles and became Britain's most successful quadricycle manufacturer over the next 20 years. His machines had wooden wheels with front- or rear-wheel steering, and typically weighed around 58 lb (26 kg).

### Pierre Michaux and the Vélocifère

In 1861 the Parisian coachmaker and wheelwright Pierre Michaux fitted a crankshaft and pedals to the front wheel of a hobby horse that had been brought to him for repair. His invention was a success which transformed the hobby horse into a machine that became recognizable as a bicycle. The early Michaulines, as he called them, came to be known as *Vélociferes* or Velocipedes. The weight of the average velocipede was about 60 lb (27 kg). The method of starting was to run alongside and then jump up onto the saddle, but steps mounted on the frame were later introduced to make this operation easier.

In 1867 *Michaux et Compagnie* developed a new version of the Michauline shown at the World Exhibition in Paris. An order was taken from the Emperor Napoleon III, and a de luxe model in rosewood and aluminium-bronze was supplied to the Prince Imperial.

By the end of the decade France led the world with around 60 velocipede builders in Paris and 15 in the provinces. The brothers Aimé and René Olivier took over the Michaux business, renamed it *Compagnie Parisienne des Velocipedes*, and by 1870 employed a staff of 500 workers producing 200 machines a day at Rue Bugeaud. Most velocipedes in Britain were imported from France until Rowley Turner persuaded his uncle at the Coventry Sewing Machine Co to begin making velocipedes in 1868. The company changed its name to the Coventry Machinists Co, entering the market with perfect timing as bicycling in France was swept away by the start of the Franco-Prussian war in 1870. Pierre Michaux died in a paupers' hospice in Paris in 1883. He had been ruined by the war and his attempt to set up a new business in competition with the Olivier brothers.

## 1866

Pierre Lallement, an employee of Pierre Michaux, emigrated to the United States where he took out the first known American patent for a *Velocipede à pedal* with his partner James Carroll. The business failed and Lallement returned to France, leaving behind a design which was soon widely copied by American manufacturers. The New York manufacturer Calvin Witty later bought all the rights to Lallement's patent, and demanded royalties for every machine sold as the 'Velocipedomania' craze struck the wealthier residents of the USA.

### The Earliest Races

*The earliest recorded bicycle race was a velocipede race over 2 km (1.24 miles) held at the Parc de St Cloud, Paris on 31 May 1868. It was won by Dr James Moore (UK 1847–1935) who was later made a Chevalier de la Légion d'Honneur. The first American bicycle race was held on 24 May 1878 in Boston's Beacon Park. The winner was C.A. Parker of Boston University who covered the three-mile course in 12 minutes, 27 seconds. The first road race in the USA took place in September 1883 when G.M. Hendrie beat W.G. Rowe. The time trial was devised in 1889–90 by F.T. Bidlake. The object was to avoid the congestion caused by conventional road racing.*

## 1867

Velocipedes made by Pickering and Davis in the USA were imported to Liverpool. They became the standard mount of the first British cycling club, the Liverpool Velocipede Club, which was founded in the same year.

### Meyer and the Suspension Wheel

In Paris an engineer named Meyer invented the wire spoked 'suspension wheel' with individually tightened spokes in 1869. When used with solid rubber tyres, this soon replaced the unforgiving, heavy wooden wheels which were used with the aptly named 'boneshaker' velocipedes. Meyer later also built a chain-driven, all metal early 'bicycle' in collaboration with a watchmaker named Guilmet. It was far ahead of its time, but made little impact.

## 1869

People were starting to ride remarkable distances on machines that must have been extremely difficult to ride. In February 1869 John Mayall Junior rode his velocipede 51.5 miles (83 km) from London to Brighton 'in about 12 hours' accompanied by Charles Spencer and Rowley Turner. *The Times* hailed it as 'an extraordinary velocipede feat'.

■ The first cycle shows in France were held at Carcassonne, Carpentras and at the Pre-Catalan in Paris where four-speed gears, mudguards and a freewheel all made an appearance. Jules Suivray, Superintendant of Prisoners' Workshops, patented and produced ball bearings for use with wheel hubs.

■ Cycling was becoming very popular with the masses. An estimated 10,000 spectators watched the Veloce-Club de Paris meeting of 17 June 1869.

■ In the United States the Scientific American Patent Agency filed 183 velocipede patents. Many inventors concentrated on the monocycle, consisting of a large wheel with the rider or riders sitting inside it. Riding schools were doing excellent business in Boston and New York where as many as 10,000 pupils were estimated to have signed on.

■ The first Paris–Rouen race was organized by *Compagnie Parisienne* and *Velocipede Illustré*. In wet conditions it was won by James Moore who covered the 76 miles (123 km), including stops, at an average speed of 7.5 mph (11.8 kmh). Moore used a 'prototype' which weighed about 55 lb (25 kg) with a 47-inch front wheel and 18-inch rear wheel, heralding the arrival of the 'Ordinary' or 'Penny-farthing' cycle. The 32 other riders who finished inside the 24-hour time limit included one woman, entered as 'Miss America', who finished 29th.

### The First Cycling Magazine

The first French cycle magazine, known as *Le Velocipede*, appeared in Grenoble in 1869 but disappeared after a few issues. It was followed by *Velicopede Illustré*, edited by *Le Grand Jacques* (Richard Lesclide) who announced: 'The Velocipede is rapidly entering our lives and is the only justification we need for starting this new magazine. It is gaining ground at amazing speed, spreading from France to the rest of Europe, from Europe to Asia and Africa. The Velocipede is a step forward along the road traversed by the genius of man. It replaces collective, brutish, unintelligent speed with individual speed, obeying man's will.'

*An early cycle race held in New York c. 1890, by when the ordinary or 'Penny Farthing' had been completely ousted in Europe*

### The Rise and Fall of the 'Ordinary'

The 'Ordinary' with its huge front wheel dominated the 15 or so years after 1870. The Ordinary was later known as the 'Grand Old Ordinary' or the 'Penny-farthing', a reference to the respective size of its front and back wheels. One turn of the pedal corresponded to one turn of the front wheel on an Ordinary, so the higher the wheel the faster it would go. It was also considerably lighter than a Velocipede.

By the end of the decade there was a reaction against the huge front wheels of the Ordinary which unsurprisingly could be somewhat dangerous. The 'Safety Bicycle' began to appear from around 1884, and was designed to use smaller wheels to bring the rider back down nearer the ground. In time it was responsible for the demise of the Ordinary.

### The Oldest Club in Existence

The first meeting of the Pickwick Club was held on 22 June 1870 when six cyclists met at the Downs Hotel, Hackney Downs, East London, and decided to form themselves into a bicycle club. As the formation coincided with the death of Charles Dickens, the name 'Pickwick' was chosen in honour of the novelist. The Pickwick Bicycle Club continues today, and is both the oldest cycling club in the world and the oldest Dickensian Association still in existence.

Its present-day activities, while still maintaining cycling traditions, provide the opportunity for setting aside day-to-day worries and meeting in an atmosphere of conviviality and good fellowship.

*The Pickwick Club goes touring in France in 1888. Note the mixture of safety, tricycle and ordinary machines, and the total absence of cars – though there is a carriage*

### 1870

The Ariel Ordinary bicycle was patented by James Starley and William Hillman of Coventry, West Midlands. It was the first British all-metal bicycle to be produced in quantity, and sold for £8 with lever-tension wheels which allowed the spokes to be adjusted. It was manufactured under licence for almost ten years by Haynes and Jefferis, and became the most popular cycle of its era.

## 1872

Due to the deprivations of the Franco–Prussian War the French cycle trade had come to a halt and allowed Britain to surge ahead as the world's foremost cycle producer. *Le Velocipede Illustré* ceased publication after its 162nd issue when it had foreign correspondents in 34 countries. The concluding editorial by Richard Lesclide stated: '[Cycling] is so deeply rooted that we need have no fear that it will wither away. But it may go through a bad patch and have to lie dormant before we see a revival of its early triumphs.' How right he was.

## 1873

John Keen (UK) was 'World Champion' in 1872, 1873 and 1874. He built his own bicycles, and in 1873 introduced a brake system for the front wheel in an attempt to reduce the number of accidents when riding downhill. This innovation was not widely accepted until the end of the decade.

## 1874

Britain set up permanent cycle-racing cinder tracks. A mile-long race billed as the world championship was run at Wolverhampton. In a field of 75 starters James Moore beat John Keen into second place by 5 ft (1.5m), setting a one mile record of 3 minutes, 2 seconds. The Paris champion Camille Thuillet was soundly beaten in Britain; his front wheel measured 4 ft 1 in (1.25m), while the British had wheels up to 5 ft (1.5m) tall.

■ The first cycling race between Oxford and Cambridge universities took place.

■ James Starley introduced tangential spokes to give a more even distribution of load than the straight spokes of a cart wheel. Tangential spokes are still in common use today.

## 1876

Writing in *The Modern Bicycle* in 1876, Charles Spencer advised novice riders to first learn on 'practisers, or more familiarly boneshakers'. The name 'boneshaker' had come into use to describe early bicycles without the benefit of rubber tyres.

■ F.L. Dodds rode 15.84 miles (25.5 km) in one hour on the racing track at Cambridge University Ground, using a bicycle with a 55-inch front wheel. He was unofficially credited with the first 'Hour' record.

■ In France a man named Tissier won the 137 mile (220 km) Angers–Tours–Angers race by a clear 50-minute margin. His superiority was in part due to

*An 1877 Salvoquadricycle taking part in a veteran cycle run*

Jules Truffault's invention of hollow forks and wheel rims which were made using sabre sheaths. This reduced the weight of racing machines to as little as 22 lb (10 kg). The Coventry Machinists Co bought the rights to his invention.

■ H.J. Lawson patented the term 'Safety Bicycle' which brought the rider back nearer the ground. In France a similar idea was developed by Jules Truffault whose Sphinx cycle had a front wheel of 30 in (0.75m).

■ Open antagonism between the new cyclists and traditional road users was common. In a test case the driver and conductor of the Watford to St Albans coach were fined £2 and £5 respectively, having been found guilty of lashing an overtaking cyclist with a whip and flinging an iron ball attached to a rope through the wheel spokes of his bicycle.

## 1877

In France the Marseilles cyclist Rousseau produced a 'Safety model' with a 35.5 in (0.9m) front wheel and two-speed gears. A Bordeaux mechanic named Georges Juzan rode the 62.25 miles (100 km) from Bordeaux to Libourne in the Dordogne and back in 40 minutes, using a chain-driven bicycle with both wheels the same size.

### Colonel Pope and the USA

Colonel Albert A. Pope was the greatest 19th-century proponent of the bicycle for use by Americans. In 1877 he began to import Singer bicycles from Coventry to the USA. A year later he began to manufacture the Columbia bicycle, and eventually built up 4000 agencies selling the Columbia at a fixed price which beat off imported competition. He also founded the Boston Bicycle Club, said to be the first cycle club in America. As a keen promoter of the bicycle he paid for the distribution of *The American Bicycler*, written by his lawyer Charles Pratt, and in 1882 founded *The Wheelman Magazine* with S.S. McClure as editor, distributing half the issues for free. He helped found the National League of American Wheelmen in 1880, and in the 1890s subsidized a course on road construction at the Massachusetts Institute of Technology.

## 1878

At the Athenaeum Club in London the Stanley Bicycle Club organized a cycle show. It later became known as 'The Stanley', and by 1890 had over 1400 machines on display.

■ The standard target weight for a cycle was judged in 'pounds for inches'. For instance a 50 in (1.27m) touring cycle should weigh no more than 50 lb (23 kg), though a racing cycle of the same size might be half the weight.

■ The Coventry Machinists Co produced the Ordinary Club model which became the classic touring bicycle of its age.

■ Joseph Lucas introduced the 'simple-style' oil lamp, a refined version of the original hub lamp invented by the firm of Salsbury, which was mounted on the front hub of an Ordinary but stayed still while the wheel revolved. A larger 'divided-style' oil lamp which dropped over the hub followed later.

■ The Facile front-wheel-lever-driven bicycle was invented by Beale and Straw. The object was to produce a cycle with a smaller front wheel which was easier to ride, and manufactured by Ellis and Co it remained popular for a decade. It was also noted for its ability to cover long distances. Faciles broke the 24-hour record five times in 1883 when J.H. Adams eventually rode to a record distance of 242 miles (389.5 km), later raising the record to 297 miles (478 km) in 1888. In 1995 a Facile was sold for £8850 at a bicycle auction in Edinburgh.

### The Bicycle Touring Club
Sidney Cottrell founded the Bicycle Touring Club in 1878, and published the first issue of the *Bicycle Touring Club Monthly Circular*. This journal became the *Bicycle Touring Club Monthly Circular and Official Gazette* in 1880; the *BTC Monthly Gazette and Official Record* in 1882; the *Cyclists' Touring Club Monthly Gazette* in 1883; the *CTC Gazette* in 1898; *Cycletouring* in 1963; and *Cycle Touring & Campaigning* in 1988. Sidney Cottrell also introduced a system of hotel grading and

discounts to satisfy the higher expectations and spending power of the more leisured classes who had been drawn to cycling by the introduction of the Safety Bicycle. Many years before the AA came into existence with its well-known Star ratings, he enlisted the help of members and appointed regional officials, known as Consuls, to oversee a list of approved establishments. By 1881 the CTC had 785 hotels and inns under contract which all offered fixed rates, reserved rooms and exclusive lounges for the use of cyclists.

Hoteliers also paid for inclusion in the newly introduced *CTC Handbook*, with great importance placed on the inclusion of temperance hotels (a burning issue of the time); appointments were also made for approved 'Repairers'. By 1895 the tariffs were becoming difficult to maintain and by 1908, after a period of steady decline, the discount system had disappeared as the car began to take over the roads.

## 1879

The Falcon Bicycle Club, founded in 1879 with headquarters at the Frampton Arms in Hackney and a 25 pence membership fee, was one of many cycling clubs established in this period. Most cycling club members wore a uniform; for the Falcon Bicycle Club it was dark blue with a gold monogram badge.

■ The Otto dicycle was patented by E.C.T. Otto. It had two equal-sized wheels mounted on either side of the rider rather than in front and behind, and was steered by braking one of the wheels. It was claimed to be particularly suitable for ladies. Almost 1000 of these strange machines were sold over the next ten years.

■ The Singer Xtraordinary, a lever-driven Ordinary similar to the Facile, was put into production by Singer & Co of Coventry to appeal to those would-be cyclists who were intimidated by the Ordinary. Singer & Co claimed that the Xtraordinary was 'Safe for night riding . . . even a stray dog will be got over successfully.' It was a commercial success as a 'safe' alternative to the bigger-wheeled Ordinary cycles.

■ The police banned riding in Moscow, despite the fact that only five bicycles were known to be in use there. The order was rescinded two years later.

## 1880

A Gloucester shoemaker named Thomas Shergold rode the earliest known chain-driven safety bicycle to Birmingham to offer his design to Starley Brothers, Britain's largest cycle manufacturer. They refused to take up the idea, and without finance Shergold could not develop it.

## 1881

As a publicity stunt, the American Star Bicycle was ridden down the steps of the Capitol in Washington DC. The Star was a most unusual design, with a tiny front wheel and an enormous back wheel which made it look like an Ordinary turned the wrong way round.

## 1882

By 1882 there were 528 known cycling clubs in Britain, of which 199 were in the London area. Regular events such as the 'Liverpool Meet' would attract as many as 500 riders.

■ The authorities were often not sympathetic to cyclists. On 1 November 1882 *The Cyclist* reported that a gentleman 'of most respectable address' whom the police had charged with 'furious driving' at an alleged speed of 10 mph in London, was fined the maximum amount of 40 shillings by the court magistrate.

■ H.L. Cortis became the first man to ride 20 miles (32 km) in one hour, using a 60 in (1.52m) front wheel.

## 1883

The *Bicycle Touring Club* changed its name to the *Cyclists' Touring Club* to accommodate touring tricyclists.

■ J.H Adams set a new 24-hour record of 242 miles (389.5 km) riding a lever-driven Facile.

■ William Terry rode a purpose-built tricycle from London to Dover. Having converted it to a rowing boat supported by two 20-litre air bags, he crossed the Channel to France where he was held on suspicion of smuggling. On his release he demonstrated his unique machine on a nearby canal, and then cycled on to Paris.

### The Tricycle Years

At the Stanley Show between 1883 and 1886 there were more tricycles than bicycles. James Starley was the leading tricycle designer of the time, though he was also well known for bicycles which included the Spider of 1877, renamed the Gentleman's and manufactured by the Coventry Machinists Co, and the Ariel manufactured by Haynes and Jefferis.

James Starley's Coventry Lever Tricycle first appeared in 1877, and was later replaced by the chain-driven Coventry Rotary Tricycle and Rudge Rotary. Customers for his Salvo-Quadricycle – a tricycle with a safety wheel that touched the ground in an emergency – included Queen Victoria who ordered two for her royal household. When she took delivery in 1881 this model was renamed the Royal Salvo. Starley died in the same year. He was hailed as 'the father of the cycle trade', and a monument was erected in his honour by the City of Coventry.

### The First 'Safety Bicycle'

In 1884 John Kemp Starley of Starley and Sutton of Coventry – a nephew of James Starley – produced the Rover 'Safety bicycle' using a chain-driven rear wheel. The chainwheel and rear sprocket could be changed for different gearing, and the handlebar and seat positions could be altered. With extra stays to support the saddle and chainwheel, it also introduced the diamond-shape frame which was to become the norm in bicycle design.

The Rover was exhibited at the Stanley Bicycle Club Show in February 1885. In September 1885, ridden by George Smith, it established a new 100-mile (161 km) record of 7 hours, 5 minutes, 16 seconds. However, its principal defect was that it gave a harder ride over bumps and potholes than the larger-wheeled Ordinary which had a greater suspension effect. By 1890 this was overcome by the addition of pneumatic tyres, and the development of the basic modern bicycle was complete.

## 1884

George Smith won a 100-mile race organized by the firm of Hillman, Herbert and Cooper for their Kangaroo cycle. He rode the distance in a sensational 7 hours, 11 minutes, 10 seconds, breaking the 100-mile record of 7 hours, 18 minutes, 55 seconds set in 1878 on an Ordinary. The Kangaroo was the first of a new generation of 'dwarf' front-wheel cycles, using a chain drive to the hub and changeable sprockets for different gears. By 1888 it had gone out of vogue due

*Can you imagine riding 100 miles on the Kangaroo? With its dwarf front wheel, it was the sensation of 1884*

to the success of the rear-wheel drive Safety bicycle. In 1995 a Kangaroo was sold for £8000 at a bicycle auction in Edinburgh.

## 1885

The riding was hard in the early days of cycling. Not only did the bicycles of the day give their occupants a very unforgiving ride, but they could seldom find a smooth surface to ride on and often had to contend with the 'rough stuff'. In a CTC *Gazette* of 1885, A.W. Rumney described how his front rim 'sank out of sight in the gravel' while riding on the Great North Road in England, now better known as the A1.

## 1886

The Bicyclette made by Rudge became established as the foremost model of the day. Its success was helped by H.O. Duncan who settled in France to race against top French riders such as Charles Terront, de Civry and Medinger. By this stage of development, the better bicycles were extremely light. A private advertisement for a Rudge racing bicycle in the 'Cycles For Sale' column of the Bordeaux cycling weekly *Le Veloce Sport* of 28 January 1886 listed its height as a very high 55 in (1.4m) and its weight as a very low 33 lb (10.5 kg).

■ The Rational Ordinary made by J.H. Dearlove of London was shown at the Stanley Show. It had thick, solid rubber tyres, a larger back wheel measuring 22 in (56 cm) compared to contemporary wheels which could be as small as 16 in (41 cm), and the front forks raked at more of an angle in an effort to provide a smoother ride than the new Safety bicycles. It was widely copied by other manufacturers and flourished until the advent of the pneumatic tyre for the Safety which made the Ordinary redundant.

■ Between 4 and 9 July 1886 G.P. Mills of Anfield Bicycle Club rode a 53-inch Humber Ordinary from Land's End to John O'Groats, covering a distance of 861 miles in 5 days, 1 hour, 45 minutes. His record for the Ordinary stands today.

## 1887

A Humber was advertised as the fastest racing bicycle in the world, having covered 1 mile (1.6 km) in 2 minutes, 30 seconds.

■ Joseph Lucas introduced the Number 42 bicycle bell, the first to be activated by a striking lever. Previously, bicycle bells had been like cow bells, hanging from the handlebars to produce a continuous clanging to warn of their owner's approach.

*J.B. Dunlop shows off his beard with the first pneumatic tyred bicycle, a breakthrough which put his name among the immortals – and made him a very rich man*

■ The Overman Wheel Company introduced the Victor, the first small-wheel Safety bicycle to be manufactured in the USA – a year ahead of the rival Pope Manufacturing Company.

■ Thomas Stevens's book *Around the World on a Bicycle* was published. It told the story of how he completed the first recorded world circumnavigation by bicycle. He rode an Ordinary west to east from San Francisco via Yokohama, carrying a revolver for personal protection all the way.

### Dunlop and the Pneumatic Tyre

The Scottish veterinary surgeon John Boyd Dunlop of Belfast invented the 'hollow rubber tube inflated with air' better known as the pneumatic tyre. The first pneumatic tyres were fitted to the rear wheels of his son Johnnie's Edlin Quadrant on 28 February 1888. Unknown to him, the principle had been discovered by R.W. Thomson in 1845, but was never developed. Backed by the wealth of the du Cros family, production expanded rapidly with the factory moving from Dublin to Belfast and then to Coventry.

Not everyone welcomed the new type of tyre which was given names such as 'bladder-wheel' and 'pudding tyre'. In the House of Commons in 1894, Lord Randolph Churchill warned of the dangers of a tyre that comes 'silently and stealthily upon one'.

## 1888

Frank Bowden founded Raleigh Bicycles in Raleigh Street, Nottingham. Four years later it was estimated that 2300 prizes were won by riders on Raleigh racing machines.

■ Lighting laws came into force for cycles used at night.

■ The Roads Records Association was founded to administer place-to-place records in the UK.

■ Racing cycles continued to get lighter. The James racer weighed an incredible 11 lb (5 kg).

**Winged Wheels**
From 1888 the Cyclists' Touring Club Winged Wheel sign first appeared on buildings as evidence of 'CTC appointments'. They were made of cast iron, measured 24 inches in diameter, and originally had small tabs showing whether the establishment rated as 'A' tariff or the inferior 'B' tariff. These signs remained the property of the CTC (and still do) and hotel owners were required to pay a deposit for them.

Over a century since they first appeared, around 130 CTC wheels remain in their original locations. Well-preserved examples can be seen at the Winged Wheel Cafe at Matlock Bath (Derbyshire); the Dolphin Hotel at Beer (Devon); the White Hart at Christchurch (Dorset); the Berkeley Arms at Berkeley (Gloucestershire); Market Rasen Mail Office (Lincolnshire); News Klip Newsagents at Fakenham (Norfolk); Sykes House at Askrigg (North Yorkshire); the Unicorn at Somerton and the Dolphin Hotel at Ilchester (Somerset); the Red Lion Hotel at Burtwood (Staffordshire); CTC headquarters at Godalming (Surrey); the Smugglers Inn at Alfriston (Sussex); the Castle Hotel at Devizes (Wiltshire); the New Inn at Rhuddlan (Wales); the Alexandra Hotel in Ballater, the Planning Office in Edinburgh and Lothians District Association Hut at Polmood (Scotland).

## 1889

The first race for the Dunlop pneumatic tyre was in May 1889. It took another five years to completely oust the use of solid rubber tyres, but by 1895 they were gone.

## 1890

The Dunlop Company bought the Welch patent for 'wired-on' tyres which fitted into the rims in 1890. Previously they had glued the tyres to the rims, a system that is still used with modern lightweight tubular tyres as used by racing cyclists today.

■ Richard Lesclide relaunched *Le Velocipede Illustré*, still selling at its 1869 price of ten centimes.

*La Petite Reine*
*The 1890s were known as the golden age of the bicycle or in France, La Petite Reine. It was the decade in which the pneumatic-tyred Safety bicycle became the norm for cycling, as it has remained for more than 100 years.*

■ *Histoire Generale de la Velocipedie* by Baudry de Saunier, with a preface by the poet Jean Richepin, was published in France. It became the standard French work on cycling.

■ Even if there were roads, some cyclists went off-road. Amos Sugden provided the first documented evidence of such a ride when he rode and pushed his 50lb bike over Sty Head Pass in the Lake District in 1890.

## 1891

A removable, tubeless tyre was developed by Edouard Michelin in France. Despite suffering five punctures, Charles Terront used these tyres on his Humber to win the first Paris–Brest–Paris race, devised by Pierre Giffard and billed as the greatest race ever. It is still held every four years as a competitive touring event. The following year the Michelin Company organized a race from Paris to Clermont Ferrand to demonstrate the superiority of their tyres over Dunlop.

■ The first Bordeaux–Paris race was won by George

*Edouard Michelin became Dunlop's greatest French rival*

Pilkington Mills, the Humber works manager. As the longest continuous cycle race in the world (around 375 miles/600 km) it became known as the *Derby de la Route*.

■ The Belgian Minister of War banned officers from riding bicycles in uniform while off duty.

## 1892

The International Cyclist Association (ICA) was founded to promote its first World Championships the following year.

■ Arthur Augustus Zimmerman, known as 'The Flying Yankee', visited Europe for the first time. In Britain he won the 1-mile, 5-mile and 50-mile championships.

■ Mr W.F. Collier of the Belsize Bicycle Club cycled 10,073 miles during 1892. The previous 'best' – 20 miles less – was recorded by a Mr Tegetmier of the same club.

■ In France Alfred and Maurice Cherie published a *General Illustrated Directory of Cyclists* for the Universal Cycling Bookshop. It contained 468 pages listing clubs and riders throughout France and ten other countries. It also listed 34 specialist cycling papers and magazines in France, nine in Britain, eight in Austria, seven in Germany, four in Italy, three each in Belgium and Spain, and two each in Holland and the United States.

■ Albert Pope's weldless-steel tubing plant was completed in the USA. He also set up advanced metallurgical laboratories and introduced stress-measuring gauges.

■ A disc wheel first appeared in Britain at the annual Stanley Show. The *CTC Monthly Gazette* reported 'Whether the avoidance of the resistance of the air to the moving spokes is an appreciable advantage can only be proved on extended trial, but on the subject of cross windage the rider can testify to the fact that it is unsafe . . .'

■ Writing in the *English Mechanic*, a correspondent noted: 'Inventors of reputation are manufacturing bicycles principally from an alloy of aluminium or titanium. However titanium is little in demand, and in consequence is extracted in only small quantities.'

■ The pioneering journalist and magazine editor Richard Lesclide died in Paris on 15 May 1892 at the age of 67.

■ Henry Dacre wrote the song 'Daisy Bell' with its immortal words 'a bicycle made for two'.

## 1893

Tessie Reynolds caused a sensation by riding from London to Brighton and back again at the age of 16, covering around 110 miles in eight and a half hours wearing 'a trousered costume'. She offended propriety by her 'immodest and degrading dress', presuming to use a cross-barred bicycle, allowing herself to be paced by male friends, and riding strenuously.

■ The American tandem riders Joseph and Elizabeth Robbins Pennell based themselves in London to undertake a number of marathon cycle trips. They started with an out-and-back ride to Canterbury, followed that with a ride to Rome, and then turned north for the Hebrides. At about the same time William and Fanny Hunter set out from London to cycle south, crossing the Atlas mountains through Algeria and on into the Sahara desert. Their book on the trip was titled *Algerian Memories*.

■ The Prince de Sagan was Chairman of the Supporters' Committee of the first cycle show held in the Salle Wagram in Paris in January 1893. Nearly 300 different firms took part. The show was such a success that it was held again in December. In France the Ordinary had been completely superseded by the Safety bicycle by this time, and many cycle-builders at the show advertised very lightweight machines in the 21–22 lb (9.5–10 kg) range.

■ F. Freeman was one of many long distance tourers of the 1890s. In 1893 he rode a 54-inch Regent Rational Ordinary through the Pyrenees – 'or rather Auverge via Nimes to the Pyrenees and back by the east of France'. He carried a 10 lb roll of luggage on his handlebars, which met every requirement including maps and handbooks. His route included riding up and over the 4920 ft Col d'Aspin on one day, and over the Col du Tourmalet the next. In three years he claimed to have covered 14,000 miles on his Ordinary, including a 'large amount of rough country'.

■ A CTC correspondent gives his views on cycling in darkest Russia in 1893: 'Those who are conversant with conditions under which cycling is practised in the land of the Czar will be aware that for many a long day riding in St Petersburg has been absolutely forbidden. Owing to the instrumentality of General Vladimirovitch Struchoff – a sportsman of the first order – the prohibition has now been withdrawn, and the prospects of the pastime have been materially improved.'

■ In the USA the National Cycling Association Cash Prize League was set up in Philadelphia. Plans to build cycle tracks round baseball grounds belonging to the National Baseball League came to naught.

*Henri Desgrange in later years, flanked by his two sons at the start of the Grenoble-Briancon race in 1937*

### Desgrange and 'The Hour'
In 1893 Henri Desgrange set a one-hour record of 21.9 miles (35.325 km) at the concrete Buffalo velodrome in Paris and was hailed in France as the first 'unpaced hour record-holder'. He later founded and edited the sporting daily paper *L'Auto* and also founded the Tour de France in 1903.

### Zimmerman's World Championship
In 1893 Arthur Zimmerman (USA) beat two other American riders to become the first official amateur track-racing world champion in Chicago, riding in the 10 km sprint. A 100 km motor-paced race was also held at the World Championships, won by L.S. Meintjies of South Africa. Zimmerman raced in Europe, and was sketched in Paris by Henri Toulouse-Lautrec while racing at the Buffalo velodrome. The World Championships continued to be held annually from there on.

### The Ladies' Page
The Ladies' Page began to appear in the *CTC Gazette* during the early 1890s as cycling became established as a popular pastime for both sexes. Observations included the following on the cycling mores of the times:

'On the whole the dress that satisfies all rational requirements is the one with a skirt to the knee. The Irish ladies, who acknowledge that reform of cycling dress is inevitable, are satisfied that it is only a shortened skirt that is called for, and have declared their intention of reforming gradually – a shortening by two inches every year until they reach the knee.'

'There were some photographs of French national dress on the Raleigh stand at the National Show. The full, baggy Turkish trousers were universally voted not half so pretty and so graceful as the short knickerbockers; but almost everybody registered his or her vote in favour of gaiters or long leggings.'

'A small flask of brandy should always be carried with one, and I have found it a great comfort to supplement this with a tiny bottle of Eau-de-Cologne. There is nothing that refreshes one on a hot day like a little of this invaluable toilet necessity, applied to the face with a pocket handkerchief; and a few drops behind the ears will be found as grateful and comforting as Epp's Cocoa.'

'The bicycle stoop is so common a feature among men that one can only suppose they see nothing to object to in it . . . No woman who had experimented in the difference between an upright position and a bent-over one in riding, would give a verdict in favour of the latter.'

## 1894

Chippenham County Court awarded a Bristol cyclist a total of £30 in damages and costs against a farmer who allowed his pigs to stray onto the highway, bringing down the rider and his machine.

■ The Cyclists' Touring Club consented to a group from Northumberland and Durham setting up the first CTC District Association (DA). Minutes of their inaugural meeting included discussions on watering the roads to lay the dust and bind the surface, the cost of taking bikes on trains, the state of road gratings, and the need for erection of warning signs on steep hills.

■ Jules Dubois of France set a new hour record of 38.220 km (23.7 miles) at the Paris Buffalo velodrome.

■ American railways carried an estimated 430,000 cyclists together with their machines.

> ### Leo Tolstoy
> On the occasion of his 67th birthday on 28 March 1895, Count Leo Tolstoy, author of War and Peace, was presented with a bicycle by the Moscow Society of Velocipede Lovers. He promptly learnt to ride the machine, and responding to those who were critical of his new interest wrote: 'I feel that I am entitled to my share of light heartedness, and there is nothing wrong with enjoying oneself simply like a boy.'

■ In France Helene Dutrieu rode 39.190 km (24.5 miles) in an hour, and became the first women's hour record-holder. She later became the first female aviator in France, and was awarded the Legion d'Honneur.

■ New York's 400 social elite formed the Michaux Cycle Club with headquarters on Upper Broadway.

■ The first Liège–Bastogne–Liège race was won by Leon Houa of Belgium.

■ The Scot Hugh Callna set out from Glasgow en route to Jerusalem. His account of the 2800-mile trip, *From the Clyde to the Jordan*, was published during the following year.

## 1895

Robert Jefferson cycled 4281 miles from London to Moscow and back. Having written *Awheel to Moscow and Back – the Record of a Record Cycle Ride* he set out to traverse Siberia the following year, covering 6574 miles. His other cycle marathons included an out-and-back to Constantinople (Istanbul). Jefferson rode an Imperial Rover frame fitted with Dunlop tyres and a Woods' wire saddle. His body was fuelled by Bovril, while his mileages were recorded by a Signal Fork Cyclometer.

■ At much the same time, John Foster Frazer and two companions were riding 19,237 miles round the world in 774 days. Frazer's book on the trip was called *Around the World on a Wheel*.

## 1896

A total of 250 bicycle factories in the USA were estimated to produce 1,200,000 cycles, while 600 accessory manufacturers gave work to 60,000 people. It was estimated that there were between two and four million active cyclists in the USA, while Britain and France had around one million each.

■ The first Paris–Roubaix race, later known as 'The Hell of the North', was won by Josef Fischer of Germany.

■ At the first modern Olympic Games, held in Athens, Léon Flameng of France won the first ever cycling gold medal in the 100 km race held on 8 April. Paul Masson (1874–1945) of France won gold medals in the 1000 metres time-trial, 1000 metres sprint and 10,000 metres track events. To date only three other riders have equalled his record of three cycling gold medals won at a single Olympic Games.

## 1897

Oscar Ven Den Eyne of Belgium claimed a world

*Boom in the USA*
*In 1897 some 400 manufacturers built and sold approximately two million bicycles during America's first boom. This meant that an average of 27.7 bicycles were sold for every 1000 people in the country, a figure not surpassed until the second great bike boom of 1972. Among the entrepreneurs taking advantage of America's obsession with the bicycle were car-builder Henry Ford, aviators Wilbur and Orville Wright, and Glen Curtiss.*

hour record of 39.240 km (24.4 miles) at the Paris Cipale velodrome.

The aristocracy was keen to embrace the bicycle. The *Annuaire des Sportsmen* listed the following royal heads of state among honorary members of the Touring Club de France: 'Their Majesties Leopold II, King of the Belgians; Don Carlos I of Portugal; Alexander I of Serbia; Their Royal Highnesses the Prince of Wales and Prince Nicholas of Greece; Their Imperial Highnesses Grand Duke Sergei Michailovich and Grand Duke Boris Uladimirovich.'

■ The Automobile Association was formed in Britain to help the new breed of motorist. The first patrol was a team of eight cyclists who were required to warn members before they drove through police speed traps.

## 1898

During the Easter week it was estimated that approximately 50,000 cyclists travelled by train to and from Waterloo station.

■ The coloured cyclist Willie Hamilton (USA) claimed a world hour record of 40.781 km (25.3 miles) at Denver, the first attempt on the record at high altitude (over 600 metres above sea level).

■ Alfred Reynolds invented double-butted tubing for bicycles, with thicker walls at the ends than the middle giving a better strength-to-weight ratio than conventional tubing.

### Six-Day Events

In 1899 six-day non-stop team events were introduced in the USA as an antidote to the dangerous excesses of individual cyclists chasing records by riding with no sleep. In previous years they had been expected to ride for 20 hours a day, and complete at least 1350 miles. The team of Charlie Miller and Frank Waller were the first stars of six-day racing, having covered over 2750 miles (4425.5 km) in a six-day period at the Madison Square Garden indoor track in New York in 1899.

**A Fanatical Following**

*In his book* Velocipedie et Automibilisme *(Cycling and Motoring) published in 1898, Frederic Regamey declared: 'Men, women and children are all passionate, even fanatical enthusiasts and their battalions are growing in strength every day. All the various social classes are represented in their army – the idle rich contemplating the possibility of setting up some sensational record rub shoulders with the workers, with the clerk riding to work every day on an engine contemptuously referred to as a "boneshaker" by the lucky owners of thoroughbred models.'*

Charlie Miller was also married in the centre of the Madison Square track.

In Britain six-day style racing using indoor tracks became known as 'Madison racing', though it did not necessarily last a full six days; on the Continent it was known as *racing à l'Americain*.

## 1900

The Union Cycliste International (UCI) was formed.

■ James and Gretchen Hetzel set off on their tandem from St Louis, USA, to cycle round the world.

■ First introduced in 1887, the Marston Sunbeam was built by John Marston & Co of Wolverhampton. It became the Golden Sunbeam with a reputation for high quality as the 'Rolls-Royce of bicycles'. Having been bought out by Nobel Industries in 1919 and then by ICI in 1927, the Sunbeam stayed in production for 70 years until 1957 when Raleigh took over BSA who were its final builders.

## 1903

The first Tour de France was organized by Henri Desgrange. It started at 3.16 pm on 1 July from Villeneuve-Saint-Georges in the south-eastern suburbs of Paris and was won by chimney sweep Maurice Garin of France who averaged 15.8 mph and won 6000 francs. The race covered 2428 km (1510 miles) in six stages, with riders racing through the night. Of the 60 starters, only 21 finished.

## 1904

The first four riders to finish the second Tour de France were disqualified four months after the event

finished. It had been marred by extensive sabotage, crowd violence and conspiracies between competitors and their teams. Henri Desgrange believed his Tour was finished, but it was held once again the following year.

## 1905

The first Giro di Lombardia (Tour of Lombardy) was won by Giovanni Gerbi of Italy.

■ René Pottier (France) won the Tour de France stages over the Ballon d'Alsace in 1905 and 1906, and was hailed as the first 'King of the Mountains'.

## 1907

The first Milan–San Remo race was won by Lucien Petit-Breton of France.

## 1909

The first Giro d'Italia (Tour of Italy) was won by Luigi Ganna of Italy. The race covered 2448 km (3939.5 miles) in eight stages. Of the 127 starters, 49 finished.

■ Paul Guignard (France) became the first motor-paced rider to break the 100 km barrier in an hour, by covering 101.63 km (63.15 miles) at Munich-Milbertshofen on 15 September. In doing so he won back the motor-paced hour record from A.E. Wills (UK) who had become the first cyclist to ride 60 miles in less than 60 minutes the previous year.

## 1911

Octave Lapize (France) won the first of three French professional championships and Paris–Brussels races in succession (1911–1913). He won the Paris–Roubaix in 1909, 1910 and 1911 to give three great hat-tricks. He also won the Paris–Tours in 1911, having won the Tour de France in 1910.

## 1913

The first Tour of Flanders was won by Paul Deman of Belgium.

■ Joe Fogler (USA) won the first *Six Jours de Paris* held from 13–19 February partnered by Alf Goullet of Australia. In the final sprint they beat five other teams who had all covered 1735 km (2792 miles), a distance never beaten in the Paris race. Fogler had won a total of nine six-day races in an age when riders were on the track for the full 144 hours. His victories included taking the New York Six five times with various partners.

## 1914—18

The European war severely curtailed cycle racing. Frenchmen Octave Lapize and Lucien Petit-Breton were amongst the professional racing cyclists who were killed in action.

■ The British army had 14 cycle battalions with a strength of 7000 men. They saw service on the Western Front, where they were used to rush reinforcements to parts of the line.

## 1921

The first World Championship time-trial road race was held in Copenhagen. It was won by Gunnar Skold of Sweden.

■ In Britain the Road Racing Council was set up to supervise the sport of time-trialling which involved individual performance against the clock. The RRC was a loosely-knit body with a code and regulations which were differently applied and interpreted in different areas. It later became the Road Time Trials Council which regularized the regulations and unified the sport throughout the country.

## 1926

There were estimated to be seven million cyclists in France.

## 1930

The Tour de France switched from a trade team event to a national team event, in an effort to make it a fairer competition. The idea did not work, and it later reverted to trade teams which is the format in use today.

## 1932

The first Grand Prix des Nations time-trial road race was won by Maurice Archambaud of France.

## 1933

Cycling could be used to promote all kinds of causes. The National Socialist (Nazi) party organized a mass cycle rally known as 'The Day of the German Cyclist'.

■ The Velocar was introduced in France as the first commercially available recumbent bicycle with the rider in a horizontal position. Having won several unofficial world speed records it was followed by machines such as the Velocino from Belgium, and the Cyclo-Ratio which was first built by the Cycle Gear Company of Birmingham in 1935 and featured four-speed gears and a chain 138 links long.

*Army cyclists in the West End of London at the outset of the First World War where 14 British cycle battalions saw service*

## 1935

The first Vuelta a España (Tour of Spain) was won by Gustave Deloor of Belgium. The race covered 3431 km (2132 miles) in 14 stages.

■ The Triumph Recumbent featured a seat and steering wheel similar to that used on a car. Owing to difficulties with balance, only six were ever built.

■ Reynolds 531 tubing was introduced, made of a manganese molybendum steel alloy with the numbers 531 referring to the approximate ratios of the main alloying constituents – manganese, molybendum and silica. It had more than double the fatigue life (the number of bends needed to break it) of Reynolds High Manganese tubing for high performance cycles. Reynolds supplied the tubing for 27 out of 31 Tour de France winners between 1958 and 1989. Their 531 still remains a popular choice for better quality cycles after 60 years in production.

## 1936

The first Flèche Wallonne was won by Philippe Demeersman of Belgium.

■ As road traffic built up a total of 1496 cyclists were killed and 71,193 injured on British roads, accounting for 31 per cent of all road casualties in that one year.

## 1939—45

War once again severely curtailed Europe's leading events.

## 1940

The Paratroop folding bicycle was introduced by BSA.

*A splendid art-deco style cycle using a monocoque design is shown at the pre-war 'Britain Can Make It' exhibition*

Using small-diameter twin parallel tubes for lightness it folded in half using wing nuts, and was fitted with a twin-cell battery lamp for night work. It was designed to be carried in gliders and landing craft.

## 1942

Percy Stallard founded the British League of Racing Cyclists. He had been banned for life from the National Cycling Union for daring to organize a mass-start cycle race from Llangollen to Wolverhampton, the first to take place on public roads since the UCI and RTTC had decreed that all racing should take place on private roads and tracks. Road racing thrived from there on, and the British League of Racing Cyclists went on to organize the first Tour of Britain.

## 1945

The use of a red rear light became a requirement by law for riding on British roads.

## 1946

The first pursuit World Championship titles were awarded.

## First Cycleways

Britain's first network of segregated cycleways was designed by Eric Claxton, architect of Stevenage New Town. When he was given the job in 1946, the Ministry of Transport were reluctant to grant funds for his planned exclusive provision for cyclists; at the time the Cyclists' Touring Club also refused to support his ideas, believing that separate cycleways were an attempt to get cycles off the roads and out of the way of the growing motoring classes. However, on the eventual completion of the network, the CTC were so impressed they made Eric Claxton an honorary member.

Despite the initial setbacks, Eric Claxton persevered with his ideas for Stevenage New Town's cycleways. They were based on the following principles:

1.    There should be a completely integrated network of cycleways enabling users to reach every area of the New Town without leaving the system.

2.  There should be no petering out of cycleways at awkward or dangerous junctions. At every roundabout cyclists and pedestrians should be provided with underpasses. These should be short in length, wide, airy and not sinister. (Due to Claxton's work, Stevenage claims to be the only town in Europe with just one set of traffic lights.)

3.  The most direct routes for cyclists should be used. If any road user has to detour it should be the motorist.

4.  Gradients should not be so steep as to prohibit their use by wheelchairs, and not so long as to be laborious for cyclists – 1:20 maximum was Claxton's rule of thumb.

5.  Subterranean services should be buried in the grass verges and not under tarmac, so there should be no delays to cycleway users when work was being done and no bodged repairs to the cycleway surface.

6.  Cycleways should mainly be kept separate from pedestrian paths. Where they merged, cyclists must give way.

## 1948

The Japanese introduced keirin, a track race paced by a single motorcycle with a final all-out sprint. The Association of Keirin was founded in 1957 to train riders and regulate the sport which was by then attracting huge amounts in betting receipts with an estimated 40 million spectators attending racing at 50 keirin velodromes each year.

■ Gino Bartali (Italy) won the Tour de France, ten years after his pre-war victory. He was variously known as 'the old one', 'Gino the devout', and 'the iron man'.

## 1950

The first cyclo-cross World Championships were won by Jean Robic of France.

## 1952

The first Tour of Britain for amateur riders was held.

## 1956

Charly Gaul of Luxembourg won the Giro d'Italia for the first time. He won it again in 1959, and the Tour de France in 1958. He was known as the 'Angel of the Mountain' due to his brilliant climbing which won him these events, with a technique that involved sitting very still on his bike and spinning the pedals in a lower gear than any of his rivals.

■ Tom Simpson won a bronze medal with the British pursuit team at the Olympics. He went to Brittany to learn road racing, turning professional in 1959.

## 1957

Teams of three riders rather than the customary two contested the Paris Six-days at the Vélodrome d'Hiver in 1957 and 1958. Both times the winning team were Terruzzi, Darrigade and Jacques Anquetil.

■ Jacques Anquetil of France won his first Tour de France. He went on to win it every year between 1961 and 1964 to give a record five victories. He also won the Tour of Italy twice, and the Tour of Spain once.

## 1958

Separate women's World Championship events were first introduced. The women's Sprint held in Paris was won by Galina Yermolaeva of the USSR; the 59 km women's Road Race was won by E. Jacobs of Luxembourg.

■ The International Cycling Union attempted to revive motor-paced racing by introducing 60-minute amateur World Championships.

■ The Elswick Scoo-Ped made by Elswick-Hopper featured a fully-enclosed frame and wheels with a fibreglass body and leg shields. It was not a success due to its weight and poor access for repairs.

## 1959

The British League of Racing Cyclists and the National Cyclists' Union amalgamated to form the British Cycling Federation which now controls British cycle sport.

## 1960

Tube Investments and Raleigh Industries merged to become TI-Raleigh.

■ Fausto Coppi of Italy died from malaria at the age of 40 after returning from a hunting expedition in Africa. Until the advent of Eddy Merckx he was considered the greatest-ever racing cyclist. His feats ranged from two world 5000m pursuit championships on the track to five victories in the 21-day Tour of Italy. He also held the world one-hour track record for 14 years, was world professional road champion in 1953, and won the Tour de France twice, the Milan–San Remo three times and the Tour of Lombardy five times.

## 1962

The Tour de France reverted back to a trade team event, and has stayed that way with the exceptions of 1967 and 1968.

■ Tom Simpson became the first British rider to wear the *maillot jaune*, eventually finishing sixth overall.

## 1965

The *Fédération de Cyclisme Amateur* (FIAC) and the *Fédération de Cyclisme Professional* (FICP) was formed within the UCI.

■ Tom Simpson (UK) won the professional road race World Championship.

■ The League of American Wheelmen, which had ceased to operate in 1942, was reformed.

## 1966

Daniel Morelon (France) won the first of seven amateur sprint World Championships between 1966 and 1975. He also went on to win three Olympic gold medals, including one for tandem in Mexico City, partnered by Pierre Trentin.

## 1967

Britain's greatest racing cyclist, Tom Simpson, died during the Tour de France while climbing Mont Ventoux. His death was partly caused by illegal stimulants.

*The Chopper came in at the end of the 1960s – the period unmistakably illustrated by this lady's choice of clothing*

■ The London Six-Day Race was revived, but lapsed in 1981.

## 1968

Hugh Porter (UK) won the first of four pursuit World Championships between 1968 and 1973.

## 1970

Raleigh introduced the Chopper Mk1, based on their RSW 16 (Raleigh Small Wheels) which had been designed as their rival to the Moulton. Targeted at 8–14 year olds with outlandish handlebars, saddle and knobbly rear tyre it was a great commercial success.

## 1976

Dr Chester Kyle founded the International Human-Powered Vehicle (HPV) Association in California. HPVs, which are also often known as 'recumbents' due to the rider pedalling while lying flat on his back, have very slowly grown in popularity over the last 20 years. Due to better aerodynamics they have the potential to be faster than conventional bicycles on level ground and downhill, but are usually slower uphill.

## 1980

Russia and East Germany dominated the Olympics, held in Estonia, which had been boycotted by much of the West due to the Russian invasion of Afghanistan. Between them they won all but two of the nine gold medals being contested.

## 1982

The Swedish-made Itera was the first all-plastic bike featuring injection-moulded frame, forks, wheels, and handlebars. Despite being rust-proof, it was a commercial failure.

## 1983

Raleigh introduced the BMX (Bicycle Moto Cross) with injection-moulded plastic wheels.

## 1984

The Department of Transport spent £1 million on a poster campaign designed to make cyclists and motorists more aware of one another. It appeared to make no impact on reducing the number of casualties recorded.

■ The Paris Six-Day Race was revived after a gap of 25 years.

*Top class Bicycle Moto Cross still has a dedicated following*

*Moulton and the Small-Wheel Bicycle*
*In 1961 Alex Moulton introduced his first unisex, mini-wheeled Moulton Stowaway bicycle with front and rear rubber suspension. He had offered the design to Raleigh in 1959, and when they turned it down he decided to manufacture his patented design himself. Having introduced the lightweight Moulton Speed Six racing machine in 1965, Moulton eventually sold out to Raleigh in 1967. Their first new design was the $^7/_8$ scale Moulton Mini of 1968, and by the time they ceased to manufacture Moultons in 1974 some 250,000 different models had been sold worldwide. Alex Moulton continued to manufacture a small line of highly specialized, high-priced Moultons. The low-cost Moulton APB built by Pashley was introduced in 1992, still to the same recognizable original design.*

■ The Americans used a NASA cycle development programme to compete in the Los Angeles Olympics. They took gold in the men's 1000m sprint, 4000m individual pursuit and road race, and in the women's road race.

## 1985

A survey showed that 75 million Americans rode bicycles. Half that number were estimated to be over 16 years old; 26 million were occasional cyclists; and 11 million cycled once a week on average.

## 1987

In 1987 Jeannie Longo (b. France, 31 October 1958) won every major race that she entered – an unprecedented accomplishment in cycling. She won the women's Tour of Norway, Tour of Colombia, Tour de France, Coors Classic (Tour of America) and the World Road Race Championship. She also improved her one-hour, high-altitude record by more than a mile, but a new record was not ratified owing to the presence of ephedrine, a drug prohibited under UCI and IOC rules, in her urine in a post-attempt test. Eight years later she was still winning, taking her World Championship tally to ten after two wins at the 1995 Road Championships in Colombia.

## 1992

Chris Boardman (UK) won gold in the 4000m pursuit by the greatest margin ever in Olympic competition. In the final his time at 3000m was 3 minutes, 21.649 seconds with Jens Lehmann of Germany trailing at 3 minutes, 27.351 seconds.

## 1993

Graeme Obree (UK) and Chris Boardman set new one-hour records in Norway and France. It was a good year for Obree who also won the 4000m pursuit World Championship with a bike of his own design which used parts taken from an old washing machine. His radical hunched riding position was shortly afterwards banned by the UCI. It was also a good year for American cycling, when Lance Armstrong (USA) staged a surprise win in the world professional road race.

### CTC Challenge Rides

In 1993 the Cyclists' Touring Club introduced a series of challenge rides which are now held annually and based on the historic cathedral towns of Canterbury, Gloucester and Chelmsford. At each venue riders have the choice of waymarked routes of 100 miles, 100 km, and 25 miles for those who are less energetic.

## 1994

Miguel Indurain of Spain won the Tour de France for the fourth year in succession. Indurain also set a new one-hour record, but was later surpassed by Tony Rominger (Switzerland). Both riders used the same

*The Spanish rider Miguel Indurain waves to the crowds as he makes history on the final stage of the 1995 Tour de France*

indoor track at Bordeaux. Chris Boardman won both the professional pursuit and time-trial titles at the World Championships in Sicily.

## 1995

Miguel Indurain became the first rider to win the Tour de France five years in succession, humbling Tony Rominger who had led the 1995 Giro d'Italia from start to finish. Later in the year Indurain won the Time-Trial World Championship in Colombia but abandoned an attempt to set a new one-hour record.

■ Yvonne McGregor (UK) set a new women's one-hour record.

■ Graeme Obree won the Pursuit World Championship in Colombia.

■ The 24-year-old German rider Axel Fuhlau set new records for 12 hours, 24 hours and 1,000 km on a carbon frame Low Racer recumbent fitted with a fairing in August 1995. Riding on an indoor track he covered 607.62 km (377.55 miles) in 12 hours at an average of 50.64 kmh (31.46 mph). He went on to reach 1000 km in 23 hours, 21 minutes, 34 seconds, which he increased to 1021.36 km (634.64 miles) in 24 hours.

■ The British bicycle path charity Sustrans applied

*Helmet Legislation*
*In 1990 compulsory helmet legislation was introduced by the State of Victoria in Australia. In 1991 an overall 41 per cent reduction in injuries was recorded among recreational cyclists throughout the state. This included a 37 per cent decline amongst Melbourne cycle commuters, and a 44 per cent decline in the 12–17 age group cyclists around Victoria.*

for funding from the Millenium Commission for a proposed 6500 mile National Cycle Network including the Inverness to Dover, Plymouth to Holyhead and Northern Ireland to Dublin routes. It was awarded £42.5 million, comprising 23 per cent of the total cost – estimated at £183 million. It was hoped that the NCN would be complete by 2005.

## 1996

From 1 January 1996 international cycle sport administered by the UCI became fully 'open' with no distinction between amateur and professional.

# The Record Breakers

## LONG DISTANCE CYCLING

### Round the World Cycling

The greatest mileage amassed on a cycle tour was more than 402,220 miles (646,960 km) by the itinerant lecturer Walter Stolle (b. Sudetenland, 1926) between 24 January 1959 and 12 December 1976. Starting from Romford in Essex he visited 159 countries, filled 18 notebooks, wore out six bicycles, had five bicycles stolen and suffered a total of 236 robberies, was attacked six times by men and once by a wild animal, presented over 2700 colour slide shows in seven languages, was involved in four accidents, and had a period of six months without a puncture balanced by one day's riding when he had a record 18 punctures.

■ Mishreelal Jaiswal (b. 1924) of India cycled through 107 countries between 1950 and 1964, ending in San Francisco, having worn out five bicycles over an estimated 135,000 miles.

■ Visiting every continent, John W. Hathaway (b. England, 13 January 1925) of Vancouver, Canada covered 50,600 miles (81,430 km) in just over 99 weeks between 10 November 1974 and 6 October 1976 when he was aged 50. His ride was a calculated effort to ride 50,000 miles in 100 weeks, travelling a distance equal to two trips round the world and visiting more countries (47) than any other round-the-world cyclist on a planned trip.

■ Veronica and Colin Scargill, of Bedford, cycled 18,120 miles (29,000 km) round the world on a tandem between 25 February 1974 and 27 August 1975. They visited the USA, Canada, Australia, Malaysia, Thailand, India, Nepal, Pakistan, Afghanistan, Iran, Turkey, Greece, Yugoslavia, Italy and France. Ronald and Sandra Slaughter (USA) travelled 18,077.5 miles round the world between 30 December 1989 and 28 July 1991 to claim the US record for tandem cycling round the world. They visited 26 countries and five continents.

■ In June 1982 Adam and Brenda Pleasance left Britain for a round-the-world cycling trip with their sons Duffy, aged 8, and Xavier, aged 5. Using two purpose-built tandems they visted 23 countries, and

*Franco Nicotera of Italy en route to completing a 59-country, 46,000 km world tour. The umbrella was for use in Asia.*

travelled over 20,000 miles of which 15,194 were pedalled, the additional mileage being made up by side trips using public transport to see places of interest. The family arrived back in the UK in September 1985, by which time their sons were three years older and wiser.

■ Ken and Jacques Proctor (USA) claimed to be the oldest couple to bicycle round the world when they completed a nine-year-long circumnavigation on 15 December 1985 at the ages of 70 and 62 respectively. During their cycling odyssey they visited every country in western and eastern Europe, rode from Capetown to Nairobi, toured India and Sri Lanka, followed the Malaysian coastline to Singapore, and rode across the USA to Washington DC.

■ In 1935–36 Fred Birchmore, an American university student, rode his single speed, 43 lb bicycle on a world tour of 40 countries, covering approximately 25,000 miles (40,232.5 km) by bike and 40,000 miles (64,372 km) by boat.

■ In 1947–48 J. Hart Rosdail, another American, rode round the world visiting 46 countries and covering 11,626 miles (18,710 km) by bike.

■ Tal Burt (Israel), a 32-year-old medical doctor, set a new record by riding round the world from Place

*June Siple became the first woman to cycle the length of the western hemisphere. Starting at Anchorage, Alaska in June 1972, she and her husband Greg Siple rode 18,272 miles to Ushuaia, Argentina, which they reached in February 1975.*

du Trocadero, Paris, France, covering 13,253 road miles (21,329 km) in 77 days and 14 hours between 1 June and 17 August 1992 at an average of 171 miles (275 km) a day. He rode through Luxembourg, Germany, Poland, Belorussia, Russia, Siberia, Alaska, Canada, the USA, Portugal, Spain and finally France. His attempt was sponsored by Raleigh and the Israeli newspaper *Maariv*.

■ Jay Aldous and Matt DeWaal cycled 14,290 miles (22,997 km) on a round-the-world tour from *This Is The Place Monument*, Salt Lake City, Utah in 106 days, from 2 April to 16 July 1984 at an average 135 miles (217 km) a day. They cycled east across the USA, riding the 2319 miles (3732 km) to New York City in 17 days. From there they flew to Madrid, riding east through Europe via Spain, France, Switzerland, Germany, Austria, Italy, Yugoslavia and Greece, covering 2769 miles (4456 km) in 21 days. They then flew to Cairo, riding to the Suez Canal and across the Sinai Desert to Tel Aviv, from where they flew to Bombay, riding the width of India to Calcutta and covering 1258 miles (2024 km) in ten days. Their fourth flight took them to Bangkok, from where they rode through Thailand, Malaysia and Singapore, covering 1223 miles (1968 km) in ten days. They then flew to Perth, Australia, riding across 1700 miles (2736 km) of desert to Adelaide, covering a total of 3002 miles (4831 km) across the width of Australia. For their final leg they flew to Alaska via Hawaii, riding down through the Yukon, British Columbia and Alberta before crossing the US border bound for Salt Lake City.

■ Nick Sanders (UK, b.1957 Glossop, Derbyshire) cycled 13,609 miles (21,900 km) round the world in 138 days between 17 February and 4 July 1981 to claim a new round-the-world speed record. He wore out four pairs of shorts, two pairs of cycling shoes and had 43 punctures in the process. In 1985 he cycled round the world once again, starting and finishing at Manchester and riding 13,035 road miles (20,977 km) in 78 days, 3 hours, 30 minutes between 5 July and 21 September 1985, working to a daily schedule of 170 miles (273.6 km) and 16 hours in the saddle. After this achievement he decided to retire from endurance cycling, having ridden an estimated 150,000 miles (241,395 km) through 50 countries before his 28th birthday.

## The Length of America

Ian Hibbell (UK) left Cape Horn in November 1970, and from there cycled the full length of America to become the first man to ride from one end of the western hemisphere to the other. He arrived at Circle City, Alaska in September 1973, after adventures that included a 250-mile, three-month trek through the Darien Gap jungle and a climb over a 17,000 ft pass in Peru. While negotiating the Mexican border, he met Greg Siple (founder of *Bike Centennial* and the *Adventure Cycling Association*) and his wife who bicycled from Alaska to Argentina between 1972 and 1975. She became the first woman to ride the length of the western hemisphere.

■ Dan Buettner, Bret Anderson, Martin Engle and Anne Knabe cycled the length of North, Central and South America from Alaska, USA to Ushuaia, Argentina. They started on 8 August 1986 with their back wheels in the water of Prudhoe Bay, and finished on 13 June 1987 with their back wheels in the water of the Beagle Channel. They cycled a total distance of 15,266 miles (24,568 km).

## Across Russia

Mark Jenkins (USA) led the first supported Soviet/American 'Siberian Passage' team to bicycle across the Soviet Union, covering 7000 miles in 128 days between 20 June and 25 October 1989. They claimed to be first to cross the world's largest country by bicycle, starting at Nakhodka on the Sea of Japan near Vladivostock in the east and finishing at Leningrad in the west. They followed the Trans-Siberian railway for much of the distance, riding on the track where roads and usable paths were not available. Mark Jenkins, Victoria Scott and Tom Freisem (USA) were part of the seven-strong team of cyclists, together with two Russian men and women – Paval and Fyodor Konyokhov, and Natasha Travayanskaya and Tanya Kirova. The back-up team included a cook and film crew, plus as many as four vehicles.

■ On 3 October 1990 the US/Soviet TransCycle expedition – Howard Cooper (USA), Gilles Mingasson (France), Simon Vickers (UK) and Maxim Sokolenko (USSR) – arrived in Vladivostock, Siberia on the Pacific Ocean, having completed the longest (7500 miles/12,070 km) unsupported crossing of the Soviet Union from Leningrad on the Atlantic Ocean with no motorized back-up.

■ On 1 April 1990 the US/Sovietrek round-the-world expedition set off from St Paul, Minnesota, USA on a 12,888 miles (20,741 km), 240-day unsupported circumnavigation following the 45th parallel north. After flying across the Atlantic to France, the route from Arcachon, where the team's rear wheels were placed in the Atlantic, included riding through Italy, Yugoslavia and Romania in order to cross the Soviet Union. During their 124-day crossing of Russia the team spent 106 nights with villagers, had 10 showers, flew 18,000 miles across the USSR and back to get new visas due to a bureaucratic mix-up, and spent three days riding down the Shilka River on a home-made raft to avoid riding through a militarily sensitive area near the Chinese border. After placing their front wheels in the Pacific at Vladivostock, the final part of the trip and a three-week delay took the team by air to Los Angeles, and finally to Minneapolis. Team members were Americans Dan and Steve Buettner and Soviets Alexander Razumenko and Volodya Kovalenko.

## London to Moscow

In 1993 riders on the 'London to Moscow Cycle Adventure' covered a total distance of 3500 km (2175 miles) over six weeks. Thirty riders took part, each of whom had to pay £1000 to cover costs and raise a minimum amount of £500 for the charity Intermediate Technology which works with rural communities in the Third World.

■ The ride started at Greenwich and was routed in stages via Dover, Dunkirk, Brussels, Maastricht and Cologne where the riders stopped for the first rest day. The route then headed through East Germany to Berlin and on to Frankfurt, where a collision between riders resulted in one of the participants being hospitalized and flown home. From Frankfurt the surviving 29 rode on to Warsaw, and then to Brest on the Polish/Byelorussian border. The final haul was a distance of 1128 km (701 miles) along the Russian M1 to Moscow, which happily sometimes had barely a car in sight and no traffic exceeding 50 mph. The 'London to Moscow Cycle Adventure' came to a successful finish at Red Square, five and a half weeks after leaving Greenwich.

## Trans Africa

The Africatrek expedition – Dan and Steve Buettner together with Chip Thomas – completed an 11,855 mile (19,078 km), 272-day bike trek across Africa in 1993. They started with their rear wheels in the Mediterranean sea at Africa's northern extreme, Bizerte in Tunisia on 29 November 1992, finishing with their front wheels in the Indian Ocean at Cape Agulhas, on the continent's southern tip, on 17 August 1993. For parts of the trip they were joined by Nigerian Mobilaje Oduyoye and Ugandan Michael Mpyangu. A total of 27 days were lost trying to cross the closed borders of Niger and Mali and the team were eventually forced to fly across the war zone in the southern Sahara. A further two weeks were lost waiting for spare bike parts to arrive in Uganda.

■ Between 10 July and 6 August 1989 Peter Ramon and Andy Ground of the Cambridge Agromet Saharan Tandem Expedition cycled across the Sahara desert from El Golea in Algeria to Agadès in Niger. They took 27 days, 14 hours, 35 minutes and were accompanied by a five-strong back-up team.

# Audax

*The term Audax was first used in a cycling context in 1897 in Italy. Audax is a Latin word meaning 'daring', and is the root of the words audacious and audacity. A series of athletic assignments included riding 200 km (124.28 miles) in 14 hours – participants rode the distance at a steady pace in groups with a 'Captain'. In 1904 French cyclists who had gained the Brevet d'Audax award formed the Audax Club Parisien (ACP), holding events throughout France which were ridden in groups at a steady, regulated speed. In 1920 new regulations allowed participants to ride individually, and to receive a Brevet de Randonneur award for long distance cycling. Randonée is the French word for a ramble and is widely used in a cycling context. It implies that riders are independent and may travel at their own pace – or in French, 'à allure libre'.*

# A History of the Paris–Brest–Paris

## 1891

In the first long distance cycle race, the 600 km Bordeaux–Paris, the British unexpectedly took the first three places by riding without a rest, G.P. Mills winning in under 27 hours. This event made a great impression on the French public.

Later the same year, Pierre Gifford promoted the 1200 km Paris–Brest–Paris to demonstrate the practicality of the bicycle. Cycles were sealed at the start to ensure riders used the same machine throughout and entries from foreign riders and women were refused. A total of 207 cyclists started on 6 September, including ten tricycles, two tandems and a single ordinary – it is believed to be the only one to have completed the PBP to date, and was ridden by M Duval. Both amateurs and professionals took part, the pros employing crews to carry their gear and ten pacers each. Charles Terront won, riding without sleep for 71 hours 22 minutes, and 99 riders finished with some taking several days having stopped at inns overnight.

In the following years the BP was held annually and the inaugural Vienna–Berlin, Liège–Bastogne–Liège, Rennes–Brest, Spa–Bastogne–Spa, Geneva–Berne, Milan–Turin, Paris–Besancon, Lyon–Paris–Lyon and Paris–Roubaix races also took place.

## 1901

Henri Desgrange divided the entry into coureurs de vitesse who were professional road racers, and touristes routiers who were hard riding tourists, with prizes of 10,000 FF for the former and 2000 FF for the latter. At 0443 hrs on 16 August the 41 pros started, followed 17 minutes later by the touristes routiers. Maurice Garin won in 52 hours 11 minutes and Rosiere was the first tourist back in 62 hours 26 minutes. A total of 72 tourists finished, including the 65-year-old Rousset who took 202 hours.

The PBP was then held every ten years, since the distance was so great that the pros could not adequately train for it as well as conventional road races. However in 1903 Henri Desgrange organized the first Tour de France using stages which allowed the riders to rest. This event was to supplant the PBP as the premier road race as it could be fitted into the conventional racing calendar.

## 1911

The PBP rules were changed to ban pacers and assistance to riders between controls. The pros changed their tactics and stayed together in a pack to Brest with 13 coureurs de vitesse and 120 touristes routiers taking part. The winner was Georget in a time of 50 hours 13 minutes. The first tourist was Heusghen, but he was then disqualified for receiving help en route leaving Ringeval and Garin (the 1901 pro) the winners in that category.

## 1921

On 2 September 43 pros and 63 touristes routiers started the event. The number of secret controls to ensure riders rode the full course had been increased. Mottiat won in 55 hours 7 minutes, and eighth place went to the tourist Ernest Paul who had ridden as a pro in 1911 with a time of 62 hours.

## 1931

Twenty-eight pros and over 100 tourists entered. The touristes routiers were for the first time given a 90-hour limit and called randonneurs. They were divided into the allure libre administered by Audax Club Parisien and audax riders administered by the Union des Audax Cyclistes Parisiens. The Australian Hubert Opperman (later Sir Hubert) won in 49 hours 23 minutes and the first randonneurs were Tranchant, Cottard and Ruard with a time of 68 hours 30 minutes. Four women finished on mixed tandems (Danis, Pitard, Gorgeon and Du Bois) and Mlle Vassard became the first solo woman to complete the PBP. The Pitards were also to ride in 1948 and 1951.

## 1948–1966

In 1948 52 pros, all team members, started but only 11 finished. Hendrickx won in a time of 41 hours 36 minutes and 42 seconds. In 1951 only 41 pros, in ten teams, entered and Diot won in 38 hours 55 minutes, an all-time record. The first randonneurs were Coutelier and Chetiveau. The event was calendared as a professional race in 1956 and 1961, but cancelled due to lack of interest. The randonneurs rode as usual, with Baumann finishing first in 1956 in 52 hours 19 minutes and Fouace in 1961 in 49 hours 15 minutes. The British rider Barry Parslow became the first to complete the PBP on a tricycle in 1966. The winning time that year was 44 hours 21 minutes.

## 1971

This was the last year shared by audax and allure libre randonneurs. A total of 330 audax riders split into 17 groups started four days before the main PBP at 4 a.m. and all finished inside 90 hours. The 328 randonneurs set off with a massed start at 4 p.m. on Monday 6 September. Seven riders who had finished the audax PBP started again the next afternoon as randonneurs, Plaine completing his second PBP trip in 55 hours 42 minutes. There was a record to Brest of 20 hours 26 minutes by Bonny, and first back was the Belgian Herman de Munck in 45 hours 39 minutes. The first woman was Simone Astie in 79 hours 38 minutes.

## 1975

The randonneur event was now held every four years, with the audax riders retaining a five-year interval. This was the first time that qualifications were required (a 600 km event ridden that year), and the last PBP to be run mainly on main roads as tragically two riders were killed. There were 714 starters. First back were De Munck and two French riders, Cohen and Truchi, in 43 hours 27 minutes. The first women were Chantal de la Cruz and Nicole Chabriand with a time of 57 hours.

## 1979

The entry qualification became a full Super Randonneur series requiring at least a 200, 300, 400 and 600 km event to be completed in the same year. A record 1766 riders started, and the start time was split with the prospective 90-hour riders off at 4.00 a.m. A total of 1573 riders finished – with 54 riders AUK won the George Navet Trophy for the club

with the largest number of brevets de randonneur (starters) and the Coupe de la Ville de Paris for the club with the most finishers. First back were Piguet and Baleydier in under 45 hours.

## 1983

A new record of 2106 riders started and 1903 finished. AUK won the Challenge ACP for the club registering the greatest number of brevets de randonneur, and the Coupe de Madame le Ministre du Temps Libre Jeunesse et Sports for the club with the greatest number of finishers under 25 years of age and over 55. First in were the Belgian De Munck and France's Bernard Piguet in under 44 hours which is the randonneur record. The first woman was American Sue Notorangelo, setting the women's record at 54 hours 40 minutes. In all 15 countries took part.

## 1987

A record total of 2597 started and 2117 finished. AUK won the Coupe de Monsieur le Secrétaire d'Etat a la Jeunesse et aux Sports for the greatest numbers of finishers under 25 and over 55 years of age (15); AUK's Debbie Llewellyn won a watch for being the youngest rider; AUK's Barry Parslow and Mark Brooking became the first riders to complete the PBP on tandem trike, and Fliss Beard the first woman to complete the PBP on solo trike. First back was American Scott Dickson in under 45 hours.

## 1991

For the Centenary PBP 3281 started and about 2500 finished. The new start from St Quentin-en-Yvelines to the south-west of Paris proved popular, but a high abandonment was blamed on late start times during the night following the compulsory afternoon Prologue in Paris. Nicole Chabirand of France was the first woman back in 59 hours 42 minutes, and Scott Dickson again first overall in 43 hours 42 minutes, just outside the event record.

## 1995

Scott Dickson was first to finish for the third time, but this time he was in a leading group of nine riders – two from the USA, six French, one Spanish – who were all given a new record time of 43 hours 20 minutes. Brigitte Kerlouet of France also broke the women's record by nine hours to finish in 44 hours 14 minutes.

# RANDONNEUR CLASSICS OF EUROPE

■ Randonneur versions of classic professional cycle road races include the Paris–Roubaix, Ghent–Wevelgem, Liège–Bastogne–Liège, Flèche Wallonne, Paris–Brussels, Milan–San Remo, Zurich Meisterschaft and Flèche Brabant.

■ The great 'raids' are long distance rides from place to place which can be ridden in either direction, usually including at least one mountain range. The best known are:
Calais–Brindisi known as 'The Indian Mail' – 2250 km in 200 hours.
Paris-Gibraltar known as 'La Route des Capitales du Sud – 2600 km in 300 hours.
Randonée Alpine-Cote d'Azur–Lake Geneva – 740 km, 43 mountain cols.
Lake Geneva–Trieste – 1180 km, 40 mountain cols.
Raid Pyreneen – 713 km with 11,000 metres of climbing in 100 hours.

■ Diagonales de France were created in 1930. Nine rides join the extreme corners of the hexagon shape of France using Brest, Strasbourg, Perpignan, Dunkirk, Menton and Henday as start and finish points. The shortest is Strasbourg–Perpignan at 920 km; the longest is Brest–Menton at 1400 km. Time limits are based on an average overall speed of 12 kmh.

■ Brevet Cyclo-Montagnard Francais are mountain events held on fixed dates with distances of 200–250 km including 4000–4500 metres of climbing. There are separate categories for touristes, randonneurs and grand randonneurs with an average minimum of 12 kmh for the slowest category. One event is held each year in each of the principal mountain ranges of France – the Alps, Jura, Massif Central, Pyrenees and Vosges.

## WORLD OF UNICYCLES

*TALLEST: The tallest unicycle ever mastered is one 31.01m (101 ft 9 in) tall. It was ridden by Steve McPeak for a distance of 114.6m (376 ft) in Las Vegas, Nevada, USA in October 1980, using a safety wire suspended from an overhead crane. The freestyle riding of even taller unicycles without any safety harness must inevitably lead to serious injury or fatality.*

*SMALLEST: Peter Rosendahl (Sweden) rode a 20 cm (8 in) high unicycle with a wheel diameter of 2.5 cm (1 in), with no attachments or extensions fitted, a distance of 3.6m (12 ft) at Las Vegas on 25 March 1994.*

*LARGEST: A unicycle nicknamed 'Large Marge' was constructed by Dave Moore, Michael Leebolt and Steve Gordon of Moorpark, California, USA. The largest unicycle made, it featured a 66-inch diameter wheel, and Gordon first rode it on 17 October 1986.*

*FASTEST: Floyd Grandall (USA) set a sprint record for 100 metres (328.1 feet) from a standing start, of 14.89 seconds on 24 March 1980 in Tokyo, Japan. This was first beaten by John Foss (USA) with a time of 13.71 seconds, set in Tokyo on 1 August 1987, and then by Peter Rosendahl who set a new record of 12.74 seconds on 1 July 1990 and then 12.11 seconds at 29.72 kmh*

*BACKWARDS: Peter Rosendahl rode his 24-inch wheel unicycle backwards for a distance of 74.75 km (46.7 miles) in 9 hours, 25 minutes on 19 May 1990 in Las Vegas.*

*ACROSS BRITAIN: Brian Davis, aged 33, of Tillicoultry, Scotland rode 1450 km (901 miles) from Land's End to John O'Groats in 19 days, 1 hour, 45 minutes between 16 May and 4 June 1980. Mike Day (b. 13 March 1965) of Southgate, London and Michel Arets (b. 9 September 1959) of Brussels, Belgium rode 1450 km (901 miles) from Land's End to John O'Groats in 14 days, 12 hours, 41 minutes between 27 August and 10 September 1986.*

# ENDURANCE CYCLING

In the 365 days of 1939 Thomas Edward Godwin (UK, 1912–75) cycled a total distance of 75,065 miles (120,805 km) at an average of 205.65 miles (330.96 km) a day with sponsorship from the Raleigh Cycle Company. A Frenchman who was trying for the same record was about 5000 miles behind. Godwin then rode on to 14 May 1940 to complete 100,000 miles (160,934 km) in 500 days at an average 200 miles (321 km) a day. Sadly he was killed while riding his bike in 1975.

## Japan — End to End

On 7 August 1990 21-year-old Tomio Uranyu set a cycle record from Cape Soya in the far north of Japan to Cape Sata in the far south. He covered the 2681.5 kilometres (1666 miles) in 5 days, 49 minutes including 4 hours, 20 minutes for the ferry crossing between the islands.

## Land's End to John O'Groats

On the evening of 24 July 1880 C.A. Harman and H. Blackwell of Canonbury Bicycle Club wrote to *The Times* from 'John o' Groats House Hotel, Caithness, North Britain':

'The undersigned left Land's End on the 12th of July with the intention of riding to the other corner per bicycle. We arrived here safely this evening, thus completing the journey of 900 miles in under 13 days, and making an average per day of 70 miles. This being the first time the journey has been accomplished, you may think it worth a note in your columns.'

■ The record for riding an Ordinary bicycle (penny-farthing) from Land's End to John O'Groats is 5 days, 1 hour, 45 minutes, set by G.P. Mills of Anfield Bicycle Club. He rode a 53-inch front wheel Humber a distance of 861 miles (1386 km) on 4–9 July 1886. Clive Flint, a 31-year-old police officer from Manchester, rode an Ordinary from Land's End to John O'Groats in 9 days, 6 hours, 52 minutes between 1 and 10 June 1984, averaging 100 miles (160.93 km) each day.

■ The current record for a modern bicycle is held by Andy Wilkinson (b. 22 August 1963) who rode from Land's End to John O'Groats in 1 day, 21 hours, 2 minutes, 18 seconds between 29 September and 1 October 1990. The women's bicycle record is held by Pauline Strong at 2 days, 6 hours, 49 minutes, 45 seconds set between 28 and 30 July 1990. The tricycle record is held by Ralph Dadswell at 2 days, 5 hours, 29 minutes, 1 second between 10 and 12 August 1992.

■ Nine-year-old Alexander Robert Gadd became the youngest person to cycle from Land's End to John O'Groats on 28 August 1993. He set out on 15 August 1993, and averaged 62 miles a day.

■ On 22 June 1991, a 15-strong team from Lincolnshire claimed a new Land's End to John O'Groats relay record of 41 hours, 28 minutes, 26 seconds. The eight riders rode in relays of approximately 90 minutes, with support from accompanying drivers.

■ In August 1985 a relay team of six servicemen took part in *Exercise Saddlesore* to claim a 60-hour record for cycling from Land's End to John O'Groats on standard issue Army bicycles without gears.

*The 'end-to-end' from Land's End to John O'Groats ends by the entrance of the John O'Groats hotel where Paul Carbutt set a record of 1 day, 23 hours, 23 minutes and 1 second in 1979*

## Round Britain

On 5 July 1979 Tony Michetschlager left Hampstead, London to cycle round the coastline of England, Wales and Scotland, taking the nearest possible road to the sea at all times. He crossed the Thames at Tower Bridge, reaching the sea at Seasalter near Herne Bay, and from there following the coast in a clockwise direction. He arrived back at Tower Bridge 165 days later on 16 December, having cycled a total distance of 8339 miles (13,420 km).

■ On 20 June 1987 eight members of the Nottinghamshire Fire Brigade 1987 Appeal left Tower Bridge, London on a non-stop, 24 hours-a-day attempt to cycle round mainland Britain. Taking the best negotiable route for cyclists and support vehicles, they returned to Tower Bridge on 20 June after 10 days, 5 hours of pedalling, having covered 3751 miles (5747 km).

■ Nick Sanders cycled 4802 miles (7728 km) round Britain in 22 days between 11 June and 1 July 1984 at an average 218 miles (351 km) a day. He wrote a book, *22 Days Around the Coast of Britain*, based on his experiences. In between this trip and his record world circumnavigation he also found time to cycle to the source of the Nile.

## The Pennine Way

Between 9 and 11 June 1978 John North of Bronte Wheelers used a cyclo-cross bike to ride and run the 271 miles (436 km) of the Pennine Way from Edale in Derbyshire to Kirk Yetholm in the Borders in 2 days, 8 hours, 45 minutes.

## Trans America

The annual Race Across America (RAM) event follows an approximate 3000-mile (4828 km) course from the Pacific to the Atlantic, using different start and finish cities and passing over mountains, deserts and plains. The US transcontinental men's unpaced record (West Coast to East Coast) was halved between 1972 and 1986 when 43-year-old Pete Penseyres of Fallbrook, California took 8 days, 9 hours 47 minutes to complete the 3107-mile (5000 km) Race Across America from Huntington Beach, California to Atlantic City, New Jersey. A new US Transcontinental women's record of 10 days, 2 hours, 4 minutes, set by Elaine Mariolle of Berkeley, California was also set during the 1986 RAM.

■ The current Trans-America solo records recognized by the Ultra-Marathon Cycling Association of the USA are:
*Men*   Paul Selon in 8 days, 8 hours, 45 minutes.
*Women*   Susan Notorangelo in 9 days, 9 hours, 9 mins.

■ Both records were set in the 5000 km (3107 miles) *Race Across America* from Costa Mesa, California to New York in August 1989, when both riders were 35 years old. Susan Notorangelo had clipped 16 hours, 55 minutes from the previous women's record.

■ The Race Across America has been won twice by five cyclists: Lon Haldeman (1982–83), Pete Penseyres (1984, 1986), and Bob Fourney (1990–91) in the men's division; Susan Notorangelo (1985, 1989), and Seana Hogan (1992–93) in the women's division.

*The American rider Seana Hogan is one of the exclusive group of two-times winners of the Race Across America*

■ Cheryl Marek and Estelle Gray (USA) left Santa Monica, California on 21 June 1984, riding their tandem west to east to City Hall, New York where they arrived on 2 July 1984, setting a new solo, unpaced tandem transcontinental record of 10 days, 22 hours, 48 minutes. This was beaten by Pete Penseyres and Lon Haldeman of Harvard who set a transcontinental tandem record of 7 days, 14 hours, 55 minutes in May 1987 between Huntington Beach and Atlantic City, the fastest ever crossing of the USA by bicycle.

■ Between 15 August and 10 September 1984, 11-year-old Sean Dennis O'Keefe rode 3250 miles (5230 km) from Santa Monica, California to New York City in 21 cycling days, with the entire trip taking 26 days due to time for the news media and repairs. Sean became the youngest person to cycle across America, a record verified by the Ultra-Marathon Cycling Association of the USA. Earlier in his career Sean rode 360 miles (579 km), from Anchorage to Fairbanks, Alaska in two days at the age of nine.

■ In 1992 Stephen Carter set the record for crossing the United States on an Ordinary, penny-farthing bicycle. His journey took 33 days, 7 hours.

*In an event organised by Bike Centennial, a party of riders reach the end of the Trans America Bicycle Trail in 1976*

■ Bob Davenport (USA) claims the frequency record for having cycled across America following the TransAmerica Bicycle Trail 30 times between 1966 and 1992. Acting as leader of Taylor University's Wandering Wheels, he has accompanied more than 2000 riders.

### Adventure Cycling Association (USA)

The Adventure Cycling Association is a non profit-making organization which promotes the bicycle as a means of exploration, discovery and adventure. It was founded as *Bike Centennial* in 1973, and in 1976 opened the TransAmerica Bicycle Trail from Astoria, Oregon to Yorktown, Virginia. In the summer of that *Bike Centennial* year some 4000 cyclists rode the trail with approximately 2000 setting out to ride the full 4250-mile (6839.5 km) distance from coast to coast, making it one of the largest mass participation cycling events of its kind. Since then, the Adventure Cycling Association has added more trails to create a network of more than 20,000 miles (32,186 km) of mapped touring routes. These range from small weekend routes such as the 210-mile (338 km) Tour of the Scioto River Valley (TOSRV) which started as a father-and-son outing in 1962 and now draws more than 6000 riders annually. Others span the USA, and include plans for a 3000-mile long Great Divide route for mountain bikes which will follow as close as possible to the Continental Divide from Canada to Mexico.

## Trans Canada

In 1946 Fred Anderson set the first Trans-Canada record by riding 4000 miles (6437 km) from Vancouver, British Columbia to Sydney, Nova Scotia. In those days 3000 miles (4828 km) of the route was on gravel. Anderson's best day's run was 240 miles (386 km); his worst was 80 miles (129 km). During the attempt he broke his frame, was stuck in mud, had to carry his bike and spent one and a half days flat on his back due to food poisoning.

■ In 1957 John Hathaway rode from Halifax, Nova Scotia to Vancouver in 24 days, 13 hours, 5 minutes. The Trans-Canada Highway was still not complete, the total distance was 3950 miles (6357 km), of which 1000 miles (1609.3 km) were on gravel. Like Anderson, Hathaway's attempt was completely self-supported.

■ The regulations for the Trans-Canada cycling record were formalized in 1967 (and updated in 1980), requiring the attempt to be run between the City Halls of Vancouver and Halifax, following any roads within Canadian territory.

■ In 1967 Reg Davenport abandoned the first Trans-Canada attempt with full motorized back-up due to saddle sores.

■ Ten years later in 1977 Wayne Phillips set a new record by riding from Vancouver to Halifax in 19 days, 22 hours, 57 minutes at an average 187 miles a day for the 3750 miles (6000 km). Phillips' attempt was completely self-supported with no back-up. He carried 6.5 kg (14 lb) of essential gear in two small panniers and had all his other supplies mailed ahead. He bought his own food, and carried five typewritten sheets listing the towns along the Trans-Canada Highway, finding local people to verify his presence twice a day by mailing postcards to the Canadian Cycling Association.

■ In 1981 Gerry and Ted Milner set the Trans-Canada tandem record at 15 days, 15 hours, 4 minutes.

■ Wayne Phillips returned at the age of 32 in 1982 to break both his solo record and the tandem record on a single bike, crossing Canada in 14 days, 22 hours, 47 minutes. For this attempt he was fully supported with an accompanying motorhome, two helpers and two bikes. He increased his average daily pace from 300 to 400 km over the two successful attempts.

■ Ronald Dossenbach set a new Trans-Canada cycling record of 13 days, 15 hours, 4 minutes on 13 August 1988, covering a distance of 5966 km (3728 miles).

■ The current Trans-Canada record is 13 days, 9 hours and 6 minutes set by Bill Narasnek of Lively, Ontario who rode 6037 km (3751 miles) from Vancouver, British Columbia to Halifax, Nova Scotia between 5 and 8 July 1991.

■ Having started at Mile 0, the most westerly point on the Trans-Canada Highway at Victoria, British Columbia on 31 May 1986, 69-year-old Monty Maundrell joined a Cross-Canada Cycle Tour Society group to cycle from Vancouver to Halifax. He arrived there on 23 August to be met by his six-year-old great grandson, becoming the first great grandfather to cycle coast-to-coast across Canada. He then cycled on to Newfoundland and Cape Spears, dipping his front wheel in the Atlantic Ocean at the most easterly point of North America.

## One-Legged Cycling

Hugh Culverhouse lost the use of his left leg at the age of 18 due to an unusual stress fracture at the neck of the femur while training for a cross-country race. Undeterred, he went on to set some extraordinary one-legged cycling records which started when he achieved a distance of 394.705 miles (635.199 km) during the North Road Cycling Club's 24-hour unpaced scratch road ride held on 27–28 August 1983 and was awarded the 'Unplaced Ride of Outstanding Merit' award. The winner cycled 453.561 miles (729.916 km) with the advantage of two working legs.

■ Hugh Culverhouse next turned his attention to Land's End to John O'Groats, riding a 1363-kilometre (847 mile) route in 77 hours, 53 minutes, 17 seconds between 21 and 24 August 1985 at the age of 33. In September 1987 he set a new one-legged Land's End to John O'Groats record of 69 hours, 5 minutes, 4 seconds, averaging 12.35 mph (19.87 kmh) for the 853.2 miles (1373 km) of the course. His time included just over three hours off the bike, with one hour's sleep during the entire ride.

■ In 1986 Hugh Culverhouse also set a new one-legged Trans-America cycle record by completing the Trans-America race, covering the 3000 miles from Los Angeles to New York in a time of 13 days, 11 hours, 1 minute between 20 September and 4 October. This beat the existing record of 17 days, 5 hours, 7 minutes set by the one-legged American Dave Kiefer in 1984. The most exasperating point in the journey came when Hugh lost two hours due to 'about 150 sets of red traffic lights' on the final approach to New York City Hall.

## 24 hours in the Saddle

On 10 September 1974 the Finnish rider Teuvo Louhivuori, aged 44, cycled 830.1 km (515.8 miles) from Tampere to Kolari in 24 hours at an average speed of 21.491 mph (34.585 kmh) to claim a 24-hour endurance place-to-place world road record.

■ On 14 October 1990 Anna Schwartz (USA) completed 24 hours in the saddle to ride 413.6 miles

*John Hathaway made a 28,000 mile tour of the USA in 1993*

and claim the women's 24-hour endurance world record on a 15-mile loop track at Homestead, Florida, breaking the 401.6 mile (665.6 km) 24-hour record set by Susan Notorangelo in 1982. Schwartz took eight breaks during the 24 hours totalling 23 minutes of rest. Her record was soon broken by Nancy Raposo (USA) who used a 17.13-mile (27.57 km) triangular course at Cambridge, Massachusetts to complete 439.65 miles (707.53 km) in 24 hours, finishing at 7.57 a.m. on 22 September 1992.

■ The 24-hour paced world record is 1958.196 km (1216 miles), set by Michael Secrest (b. USA, 20 January 1953) at Phoenix International Raceway, Arizona on 26–27th April 1990, beating Sir Hubert Opperman's motor-paced record of 860 miles (1384 km) set on 23 May 1932 at Melbourne, Australia. Secrest also holds the unpaced 24-hour record, having cycled 516 miles, 427 yards at the Montreal Olympic Velodrome (indoors) on 13–14 March 1985.

■ The 24-hour unpaced tandem road record was set by Rich Fedrigon, aged 38, and stoker Byron Gremley, aged 32 (both USA), who covered 505.25 miles (813.1 km) at an average of just over 21 mph (33.8 kmh) on an 18.399-mile (29.61 km) surveyed course in Kane County, Illinois. They used a standard Santana tandem, starting the attempt at 9 a.m. on 28 July 1990 and having to contend with heavy rain and lightning during the night.

■ In 1987 the one-legged rider Hugh Culverhouse attempted to break 400 miles (643.72 km) in 24 hours. Having covered 209 miles in the first 12 hours, he achieved 385 miles (619.58 km) in the full 24-hour period.

## Track-stand

David Steed (b.1959) of Tucson, Arizona, USA, stayed stationary without support in the track-stand position with both feet on the pedals for 9 hours, 15 minutes on 25 November 1977 during the Wheelerama Vehicle Show. After a five-minute break, he spent another 3 hours, 3 minutes on the bike. He used a standard fixed-gear track bike for the attempt. Between 10 and 11 March 1986 he balanced on his bicycle for 24 hours, 6 minutes non-stop at the NYC Coliseum, without either foot touching the floor and without either of his bike wheels making a full revolution forwards or backwards.

## Non-stop on a Bike

Vivekananda Selva Kumar Anandan (Sri Lanka) cycled for 187 hours, 28 minutes non-stop around Vihara Maha Devi Park, Colombo, on 2–10 May 1979, beating the 168-hour record set by Syed

*World of Cycling: The Most*

*The most participants in an organized bicycle ride are the 31,678 in the 90 km (56 miles) annual event, the London to Brighton Bike Ride, recorded on 19 June 1988. It is estimated that approximately 45,000 cyclists took part in the 75 km (46 miles) Tour de l'Isle de Montréal in Canada on 7 June 1992.*

*The Great Tasmanian Bike Ride is held over nine days every February, and attracts over 1500 cyclists from all over the world. The ride begins in Evandale in Northern Tasmania to coincide with the national penny farthing championships, and riders are accompanied throughout by 'nightly entertainment, back-up transport, a shower wagon and tons of food'.*

*The Australian Bicentennial Caltex Bike Ride covering 1100 km from Melbourne to Sydney (26 November to 10 December 1988) attracted an entry of 2157 starters of whom 2037 finished. The oldest rider was 78 years old and the youngest was five-year-old Sara Clark (who was towed by her mother Donna Clark). They were just two of the 550 Americans taking part in the event. The longest leg was 126 km from Cooma to Canberra.*

*It is estimated than more than ten million people each year turn out to watch part of the three-week long Tour de France, making it the biggest live sporting event in the world.*

*The greatest bicycle participation event involved 2.75 per cent of the entire population of San Juan, Puerto Rico (1,816,300) on 17 April 1988. It was organized by TV personality Joaquin Monserrat, otherwise known as 'Pacheco'.*

*The greatest distance ever covered in one hour is 76 miles, 604 yards by Leon Vanderstuyft (Belgium) on the Montlhéry motor racing circuit on 30 September 1928. This was achieved from a standing start paced by a motorcycle ahead.*

Muhammed Nawab of India in Ethiopia in 1964. He covered a distance of 1476.78 miles (2376.6 km), spending a total time of 42 minutes, 41 seconds off the bicycle for toilet and medical necessities with 99.6% of the total time cycled.

■ Shashi Kumar Bhonsle of India completed 241 hours, 30 minutes of non-stop cycling at the Paljor Stadium, Gangtok, between 5 p.m. on 12 October 1982 and 6.30 p.m. on 22 October 1982, but without a record of the distance recorded.

■ Between 8 and 16 June 1983 Carlos Vieira (Portugal) cycled for 191 hours non-stop round a 650m circuit at Leira in Portugal, covering a total of 2407.65 km (1496.04 miles) and moving for 98.7% of the time.

## Great Wall of China

Kevin Foster (USA), a part-time actor from California aged 30, set out on 11 May 1990 to become the first person to bicycle along the top of the Great Wall of China from one end to the other. He started at the westernmost end at Jiayuguan in Gansu Province, and eventually rode 1879.6 km (1167.9 miles) of the wall's total 6000 km (3728.3 miles) length as far as Shanhaiguan, the First Gate Under Heaven, where he arrived on 29 June 1990. He walked his bike along ruined sections, and was forced to exclude a large stretch of the wall which traversed a closed military area.

■ Kevin Foster's other claims to fame include riding through every line in the New York subway system in a single trip, taking 26 hours, 21 minutes, 8 seconds on 25–26 October 1989. His future projects at the time of writing include becoming the first man to place a bicycle on top of the highest summit in every American state.

## Cycling Blindfold

Niladri Ghosh (India), aged 22, took 12 days to cycle blindfold over a distance of 1034 km (1664 miles) through 15 districts of West Bengal on 20–31 March 1985. His other claimed achievements – without a blindfold – include riding 10,000 km (16,093 miles) through India in 1982–83.

## Ireland End to End

Three Wharfedale rugby players claimed a new record for cycling Ireland end to end. J. Michael Harrison, John McGuinn and Richard Slater set out from Mizzen Head on 23 May 1986, arriving at Malin Head on 26 May, having covered 396.6 km (246.4 miles) in a cycling time of 25 hours, 55 minutes.

## 12 hours Non-Stop Cycling

On 8 October 1987 Stanislaw Grochowski (Poland) rode for 12 hours non-stop on the winding, rolling road between Bielsko-Biala and Mlawa. He dismounted once for 'physiological needs', and covered 465 kilometres (748.3 miles).

## Journey to the Centre of the Earth

On 1 May 1986 Dr Richard Crane from Cumbria and his cousin Nicholas Crane from Norwich, both aged 32, rode off to find 'the centre of the earth'. Their calculations showed the point on the globe furthest from the sea was an unnamed spot in Xinjiang Province, North-West China, at latitude 46 degrees 16.8 minutes north, longitude 86 degrees 40.2 minutes east. Having started from Bangladesh, they rode 3294 miles to their goal on the edge of the Dzungarina Desert where they arrived on 27 June 1986.

## Riding Down Under

On 25 October 1986 Graham Woodrup set off on a seven-day (168-hour) endurance ride, covering a record distance of 2750 miles (4425.6 km) around Port Fairy, Victoria. Two years later Graham Woodrup set a new Perth to Sydney record of 10 days, 17 hours, 56 minutes, 35 seconds between 20 and 30 August 1988. His longest sleep period was just over six hours, with two rests of five hours, one of four hours, and five of three hours. He also set a Perth to Adelaide record of 6 days, 10 hours, 44 minutes; Perth to Melbourne in 8 days, 6 hours, 30 minutes; and Perth to Canberra in 10 days, 26 minutes.

■ Tomio Uranyu (Japan), aged 23, cycled from 62 Newcastle Street, Perth to the Sydney Opera House in 9 days, 23 hours, 25 minutes between 28 March and 7 February 1992, covering 4230 miles (6807.3 km) and setting a new record for cycling across Australia.

■ Willy Bechmann, aged 54, led a four man Danish team – Bechmann plus Jorgen Emil Hansen, Jens Sorensen and Soren Jensen – on the first 80-day cycle tour of Australia in 1985. The team covered 14,284 miles (22,987.2 km), leaving Sydney on 14 July 1985, and arriving back there on a route via Brisbane, Darwin, Perth, Adelaide and Melbourne on 1 October after 79 overnight stops.

■ Rodney Evans set a new record for cycling round Australia of 49 days, 22 hours, 31 minutes between 14 May and 3 July 1989. He covered a distance of 13,965 miles (22,473.9 km), beating the 80-day solo record held by Ian Hay.

■ Barbara Tripp (Canada) claimed to become the first woman to cycle right round Australia when she took part in the 'Bike for Bibles' ride of 1988. She covered 15,687 miles (25,245 km) in 112 days, averaging 140 miles (225.3 km) a day with an actual riding time of 604 hours, 58 minutes. Jill Coore Hale (UK) set out from Melbourne to cycle solo around Australia on 7 April 1984, her 49th birthday. She returned to Melbourne on 17 December 1984 having recorded 12,712 miles (20,457 km), but missed riding to Cairns and Darwin.

■ *Exercise Wallaby Wanderer* cycled 5612 km (3508 miles) non-stop from Perth, Western Australia to Townsville, Queensland in 12 days, 21 hours, 22 minutes, between 7 and 20 April 1994. The 17-strong relay team were drawn from the 6th Queen Elizabeth's Own Gurkha Rifles based in Brunei. With a back-up crew of six, seven Gurkha and four British cyclists took half hourly turns riding four cycles, averaging 500 miles (804.7 km) a day.

## 1000 km/1000 mile Record

Herman de Munck (Belgium) claimed unpaced road records for 1000 km – 32 hours, 4 minutes – and 1000 miles – 51 hours, 12 minutes, 32 seconds - between 23 and 25 September 1983 in the Keerbergen area of Belgium.

## Longest Single-Day Race

The longest single-day 'massed start' road race is the 551–620 km (342–385 miles) Bordeaux–Paris event. Paced over all or part of the route, the highest average speed was set by Herman van Springel (Belgium) in 1981 at 47.186 kmh ( 29.32 mph) for 584.5 km (363.1 miles) in 13 hours, 35 minutes, 18 seconds.

The longest UK race is the 265-mile (426 km) London to Holyhead race. Last held in 1977, when it was known as the Empire Stores Cycle Marathon starting at London's Marble Arch and following the A5 trunk road to Holyhead, it claimed to be the longest, unpaced, single-day 'massed start' cycle race in the world. Tommy Simpson (UK) is the only British rider to win both races, winning the Paris–Bordeaux in 1963 and the London–Holyhead in 1965 when he also became world road race champion.

## The 300,000 Mile Club

The 300,000 Mile Club was set up by Frank Fischer of the Kentish Wheelers Club in 1962. The six founder members had all cycled in excess of 300,000 miles. No entry fee or annual subscription is required for membership, only the careful maintenance of a true record of more than 300,000 miles cycled.

■ By 1993 membership of the Club had swelled to 53, including three women. A total of 14 members had exceeded 500,000 miles. Frank Fischer died in

1993, having cycled 512,209 miles in 67 years.

■ By 1994 the largest total mileage recorded by a member was 799,405 miles (1,286,517 km) by Tommy Chambers (1903–84) of Glasgow over a period of 51 years. This gave him an annual average mileage of 15,675 miles (25,226 km). During this time he kept a precise record of the amount he spent on cycling equipment. This totalled £582 which worked out at a penny spent for every 14 miles cycled. He wore out 10 bicycles, 254 tyres, 64 cyclometers, 39 chainwheels, 76 chains, 126 fixed cogs, 3 freewheels, 33 pedals, 5 saddles and 38 lamps. Sadly, he was knocked off his bike by a younger rider on Christmas Day in 1973 at the age of 72 and never cycled again.

■ Ron Cook of Salisbury died in 1978, having covered 675,575 miles in 47 years. Chris Davies of Havant had recorded 687,371 miles over 44 years by the end of 1993, closely pursued by Les Lowe of Burton-on-Trent who had recorded 668,265 miles in 45 years. Bernard Blow of Altrincham had recorded 624,368 miles in 56 years, while Frank Clark of Southampton had recorded 603,017 miles in 72 years and at the age of 88 was still recording an average of 50 miles a week.

■ The highest annual mileage by a member was recorded by Ron Powney of Kingston Phoenix CC. He rode every day in 1993 to celebrate his 50th year of cycling, amassing 37,753 miles (60,756 km) at a daily average of 98 miles. This eclipsed the previous annual record of 31,615 miles (50,878 km) set by Harty Keates in 1932.

■ The tricycle record among members was claimed by Pat Kenny of Lichfield who recorded 24,216 miles (38,970 km) in 1993, including over 1000 miles on a tandem tricycle.

■ During 1993 members of the 300,000 Miles Club listed time trials, road racing, record-breaking attempts, touring to destinations as far afield as Cuba and Nepal, commuting to work, or just riding round and round their local lanes as methods of clocking up the miles.

# ALTITUDE CYCLING

## The Highest

The cousins Nick and Richard Crane cycled their mountain bikes to the summit of Mount Kilimanjaro in Tanzania at 19,340 ft on 31 December 1984, claiming the record for the highest cyclists in the world.

■ Adrian Crane, brother of Richard Crane, used a Shwinn Sierra mountain bike to descend from the lower summit of Mount Chimborazo in Ecuador, starting at 9.15 a.m. on 11 May 1986 from an altitude of 6267 metres (20,561 ft). He descended to the town of Riobamba at approximately 9000 ft, pushing and carrying the bike on the steep ice and snow slopes and riding when possible. He then rode on down to the sea at Guayquil, reaching there at 2.10 p.m. on 13 May 1986 to claim a greatest man-powered descent record of over 20,000 ft in under 2 days, 5 hours.

■ Mark Merrony (UK) cycled at an altitude of 6410 metres (21,000 ft) on the south summit of the Himalayan mountain Mera Peak in Nepal on 7 May 1989. He was accompanied for the attempt by Carl Evans and Sirder Zhangbu Sherpa.

■ Canadians Bruce Bell, Philip Whelan and Suzanne MacFadyen cycled at an altitude of 6960m (22,834 ft) on the peak of Mount Aconcagua, Argentina on 25 January 1991, having set out from Puenta del Inca on a 15-day expedition. This achievement was equalled by Mozart Hastenreiter Catao (Brazil) on 11 March 1993, and by Tim Sumner and Jonathon Green (UK) who cycled, pushed and carried their bikes to the top on 6 January 1994. Mount Aconcagua is the highest mountain in the western hemisphere.

## British Peaks

Stephen Poulton (UK) cycled and ran from sea level at Caernarvon, Gwynedd, via the three highest peaks of Wales, England and Scotland – Snowdon (3560 ft), Scafell Pike (3210 ft) and Ben Nevis (4406 ft) – and back down to sea level at Fort William in the Scottish Highlands in a time of 41 hours and 51 minutes between 1 and 2 July 1980. His time from the summit of Snowdon to the summit of Ben Nevis via Scafell was 38 hours, 17 minutes. He cycled all the road sections in accordance with the regulations of the Road Time Trials Council, and completed the mountain sections on foot.

■ Between 30 April and 3 May 1988 four members of *Team Rabbit* from Derby – Stuart and Neil Shipley, Adrian Scholes, Richard Dunn – started from sea level at Fort William and cycled over the three peaks of Britain, reaching Caernarvon at sea level in 74 hours, 47 minutes. They used road bikes for the 480 miles of road, and mountain bikes to ride up Snowdon, Scafell Pike and Ben Nevis.

■ Between 23 and 25 July 1989 Martyn Peters and Phil Smart, both firemen from Stourbridge Fire Station, set a new time for cycling the three peaks of 63 hours, 34 minutes.

■ On 1 August 1984 Richard and Nick Crane used Muddy Fox Pathfinders to cycle the 14 Welsh 3000 ft peaks: Foel-fras, Foel-grach, Carnedd Llywellyn, Yr Elen, Carnedd Dafydd, Penyrole-wen, Tryfan,

*World of Cycling: The Fastest*
On 30 June 1899 Charles Minthorpe Murphy (USA) rode one mile in 57.8 seconds behind a pacing locomotive on the Long Island Railroad at an average speed of 100.23 kmh (62.28 mph). This prompted Henry Ford, the car manufacturer, to nickname him 'Charlie-Mile-A-Minute-Murphy'. Charlie also claimed a record for pedalling his indoor home trainer bike for one mile in 38 seconds.

The highest speed ever achieved on a bicycle is 268.831 kmh (167.043 mph). This was set by Dutchman Fred Rompelberg at Bonneville Salt Flats in October 1995 using a dragster-style racing car with a huge fairing that completely enveloped his small wheel, highly geared cycle. It was the culmination of eight years of trying to beat the previous record of 245.077 kmh (152.284 mph) set by 37-year-old John Howard (USA) behind a speed car with a specially modified windshield tail section at the same location on 20 July 1985. Howard was towed until the speed reached 60 mph, when he was able to start pedalling and break the tow, using a double-reduction gear system to stay in the pocket of the relatively thin, smooth air that the speed car created behind it. He broke the 138 mph record set by Dr Alan Abbott in 1973 at his seventh attempt. His speed, electronically timed on the one-mile section used by the Utah Salt Flat Racers' Association, was at an average of 138.674 mph, and at 140.5 mph over three quarters of a mile. John Howard was also a three-times member of the US Olympic cycling team, seven-times national cycling champion, and in 1982 set a record for cycling 514 miles round New York's Central Park in 24 hours.

The British speed record for paced riding is 158.05 kmh (98.21 mph) over 200 metres by track sprint professional David LeGrys (b. 10 August 1955) on a closed section of the M42 at Alvechurch, Warwickshire on 28 August 1985 using a Rover Vitesse with a specially made rear fairing.

### World of Cycling: Eating Bicycles

*Michel Lolito (b. 1950) of Grenoble, France started eating metal and glass in 1959 and became known as Monsieur Mangetout. His diet since 1966 included ten bicycles, as well as a supermarket cart, seven TV sets, six chandeliers and a Cessna light aircraft. Gastroenterologists have described his ability to consume two pounds of metal a day as 'unique'.*

### World of Cycling: Underwater

*Thirty-two certified scuba divers rode a submarine tricycle for 60 hours underwater on the bottom of the Amphi High School pool, Tucson, Arizona, USA on 27–29 November 1981. They covered 64.96 miles.*

*A relay team of 32 bicycled underwater for 72 hours between 28 and 31 March 1984 at Norvik, Norway covering 87.81 miles. Another relay team of 32 scuba divers at Santa Barbara, California, USA spent 75 hours, 20 minutes on a tricycle circling the bottom of the Divers' Den pool for 116.659 miles, 16–19 June 1988.*

### World of Cycling: Water Cycles

*The men's 2000m record for a single rider is 20.66 kmh (12.84 mph) by Steve Hegg on Flying Fish, set at Long Beach, California, USA on 20 July 1987.*

*Distance records were set on water cycles by Yvon Le Caer, a bike racer from Fort Lauderdale, USA, who 'rode' 60 miles from Dania Beach on the Florida coast to Cat Cay in the Bahamas on 9 July 1985. He surpassed that record on 10 September 1985 when he 'rode' his Aquacycle 75 miles from Poole, Dorset across the English Channel to Cherbourg.*

### World of Cycling: Wheelie

*The duration record for a bicycle wheelie is 5 hours, 12 minutes, 33 seconds set by David Robilliard at the Beau Sejour Leisure Centre, St Peter Port, Guernsey, Channel Islands on 28 May 1990.*

Glydr fach, Glydr fawr, Y garn, Elidir Fawr, Crib-Goch, Crib-Y-Ddysgl and Snowdon. From the summit of Foel-fras to the summit of Snowdon took 12 hours 26 minutes; they covered a distance of approximately 28 miles of which 25 were off-road, with a total height gain of 8900 ft.

## Riding the Himalayas

In August 1985 the *King Edward Medical College Karakorum Cycling Expedition* traversed the 800 km long Karakorum Highway in India. With the exception of 4WD tracks it was the world's highest road (before the Leh-Manali road opened to motor vehicles in 1988) with a maximum height of 5682m (18,640 ft). Starting at Islamabad at a height of 1590 feet above sea level, the King Edward team crossed the Babusar Pass (13,600 ft) en route to the Khunjerab Pass (16,188 ft) at the Chinese-Pakistani border. The five members of the expedition were Dr Parvez Ahmed Malik, Dr Aamir Ali, Dr Aamir Rauf, Dr Iqbal Ahmed and Mr Ali Abbas. They claimed records for cycling the Karokarum Highway in nine days; making the greatest ascent achieved on bicycles with an absolute climb of more than 14,000 feet from Islamabad to Khunjerab; and setting a cycling altitude record of 16,188 feet.

■ Between July and September 1985 five Indian Air Force officers of the Trans-Himalayan Cycling Expedition cycled 5740 kilometres from Leh to Pangsu Pass on the Indo-Burma border. They crossed the 18,380 ft Khardungla Pass, taking one and a half days to cover 47 km; they also crossed four other passes above 15,000 ft, and five above 10,000 ft. The members of the expedition were Squadron Leader Anil D'Sousa, Flight Lieutenant Balraj Singh Viridi, and Corporals Morseshwar Gomase, Bhaskar Bhattacharya and Kuldeep Sharma. They used standard Indian-made Hero cycles fitted with three gears, and carried all their own equipment for the trip on racks and panniers with no back-up.

## Ordre des Cols Durs

*Ordre des Cols Durs* is the French pass-climbing club based on the great Alpine passes of the Tour de France – Col d'Izoard, Col du Telegraphe, Galibier and Col de Bonette – with a UK branch known as *OCD Cycloclimbing* founded by Noel Henderson. Each season members total up the heights of the cols they have ridden over, with UK members averaging 20,000 metres per two-week holiday period. The UK total record is held by Emery Woodall at 2,034,000 metres; Emery also holds the record for the biggest claim in one year at 620,000 metres, and for the second and third highest claims in one year at

495,000 and 410,000 metres respectively. Two other members have a total over 1,000,000 metres.

During 1994 *OCD Cycloclimbing* members claimed the highest pass in the Alps (Col de Bonette at 2880m); the highest in Europe (the Veleta in Spain at 3300m); the highest in America (the Trail Ridge Road in Colorado at 3270m); and the highest in the world: the Khardung La, also known as the Beacon Highway, near Leh which reaches 5606m and was closed to foreigners until 1994 when Julie Rattray became the first member to claim it.

■ The most extraordinary feats by any member of *OCD Cycloclimbing* belong to David Pindar. In a whole series of rides he has cycled from Alaska in North America to Tierra del Fuego at the southernmost tip of South America; from Dakar in Senegal across Africa to Nairobi, then south to the Cape of Good Hope; from the UK across Europe, the Middle East and China, through South-East Asia and Indonesia, crossing to Darwin in Australia then down Australia to cycle round Tasmania and then down the length of New Zealand.

David Pindar has also ridden from China north to Seymchan on the Kolyma River in Siberia, claiming Chacaltaya in the Andes at 5200m, Tangula Pass in the Himalayas at 5231m and Kilimanjaro (on foot as cycles past the roadhead at Maranga Gate have been banned since the Crane brothers pushed their bikes to the top), plus the Dead Sea at 400m below sea level.

> ### World of Cycling: Human-Powered Vehicles/Recumbents
>
> *The single rider world speed record for human-powered vehicles or recumbents, set over 200m with a flying start, is 105.36 kmh (65.48 mph) by Fred Markham (b. USA, 9 May 1957). Fred Markham was also the first rider to exceed 50 mph without pacing when he achieved 50.84 mph over 200 metres on 6 May 1979 during the international human-powered speed championships at Ontario, California. He went on to become the first person to pedal a bicycle at 65 mph (104.60 kmh) on a level course unpaced and unaided by wind. Riding on Big Sand Flat, California on 12 May 1986, Markham pedalled his 31 lb recumbent to a record 65.484 mph (105.38 kmh) over 200 metres, having taken approximately two miles to build up to top speed. He used a machine designed by Gardner Martin with a DuPont Kevlar streamlined body. They shared the $18,000 first prize awarded by DuPont for the first cyclist to break 65 mph using their materials.*

*Dave Grylls of California competing in the 1980 Brighton Speed Challenge with the Vector HPV*

# The Racing Disciplines

## ROAD RACING

Road racing is a mass-start sport, held on roads which are closed to all traffic excluding the cars and motorcycles which carry team managers, medical staff, mechanics, journalists and photographers at the top professional levels of the sport. The roads may have to be shared with other traffic at lower levels, but this can lead to problems – for instance, in the 1994 professional Tour of Britain several riders were hit by an errant car driver who attempted to force a way through them.

### One-Day Races

The standard format is a *one-day road race* such as the famous 'Classics' which span the European road race season. These start in early spring with the Milan–San Remo and end in autumn with the Giro di Lombardia, are generally held over distances of around 150 kilometres and take the winner between six and eight hours to complete. The average speed is generally close to 40 kmh.

### Stage Races

A *stage race* links together two or more one-day road races, with first place going to the rider with the lowest combined times – in fact it is possible, though unusual, for the winner of a stage race to be a rider who has been consistently well placed without winning any of the individual stages. This is slightly unsatisfactory from the media point of view, and to increase interest the organizers may run several associated competitions within the race, the best known of which are the 'Points' and 'King of the Mountains' prizes. The points prize rewards the riders who consistently finish close to the front throughout the race, and in the Tour de France is divided between flat, mountain, medium-mountain and time-trial stages. The most points are awarded on the flat stages, which has favoured sprinters such as the Russian rider Djamolidin Abduzhaparov, winner of the Tour de France *maillot vert* for the points prize in 1993–94. The King of the Mountains prize is also awarded on points, based on the riders who are first to the top of each climb. The climbs are graded and weighted for severity ranging from the biggest *hors category* climbs, of which there were five in the 1995 Tour de France, through first,

second, third and fourth category climbs, of which there were 37 in the same race.

■ Professional stage races extend in length from the three-stage/three-day Criterium International which follows the week-long Paris–Nice 'race to the sun' in the early part of the season. However the mightiest stage races are the three great tours – the Giro d'Italia, Tour de France and Vuelta a España – held in June, July and September, which each take approximately three weeks as the riders race over a 3500–4000 km distance, divided into 20 or more stages, with extensive hill-climbing stages in the Alps and Pyrenees that sort out the strongest riders. These races also include individual time-trial stages, which help to open up the field by allowing top riders the chance to gain time on their own merits without the pressures of escaping from the bunch. Many other stages often finish in a large mass with all the riders tightly grouped together, led by a small group who fight it out in the final 200m sprint to be first across the line.

### Road Bikes

Steel remains the favoured material for road race bikes due to its mixture of reliability, riding comfort, rigidity and light weight, although a few teams experiment with materials such as carbon fibre or titanium. The equipment used is also chosen for reliability, and is mainly drawn from top of the range commercially available groupsets by Campagnolo (Italy) or Shimano (Japan). Gears generally feature a 12–21 range on the rear sprockets combined with 53/39 T or 52/42 T chainrings, with modern Campagnolo Ergopower or Shimano STI combination brake/gear shift levers favoured. For mountain stages the rear gear-sprockets may be changed to a 12–23 range for easier climbing.

Brakes are generally dual-pivot Campagnolo Record or Shimano Dura-Ace, used with top-class rims featuring machined braking surfaces; deep section aero rim wheels such as Campagnolo Shamals are also popular. Classic tubulars which are glued to the rims are chosen in preference to high pressure wired-on tyres. All pedals are clipless – Look, Time and Simano Dura-Ace SPD being the favoured models – allowing the rider to lock into the pedals. Saddles are chosen primarily for riding comfort if the distance is long, with two water bottles and their cages and a computer being standard extra fittings.

*An Eddy Merckx bike is one of the top names in road racing competition. Others are made by Carrera, Colnago, Pinarello and Coppi. Design has stayed remarkably consistent*

# TIME TRIALS

The time trial is known as 'the race of truth'. Riders are sent off at intervals, one at a time, for a solitary race against the clock. The rider who goes fastest or furthest over the course is the winner, but not until all the riders have finished is the winner known. Any time lost cannot be regained which makes a time trial more pressurized than a conventional road race, with the rider forced to ride near his performance threshold for the whole of the distance or time, concentrating on maintaining optimum cadence while selecting the shortest, most efficient line. The tactical problems associated with racing in a bunch do not exist, leaving time triallists to pace themselves over the course in what is perceived as the ultimate test of cycle training. However, one disadvantage of this kind of racing is that conditions on the course may change during the competition. For instance in the prologue to the 1995 Tour de France the early starters were able to ride the course when it was fairly dry, while those who started later had to ride through heavy rain which flooded the course.

### Professional Time-Trials

On the professional racing scene the most prestigious time-trial events are the road time-trial world championship, first held at Palermo in Sicily in 1994 when it was won by Chris Boardman (UK) over a 42 km course, and the annual Grand Prix Des Nations, dating from 1932, which rates as one of the great Classics. Time trials also feature as major elements in the big tours, with the consistent winners of modern times such as Miguel Indurain and Tony Rominger usually choosing the time trials to open out a lead on their rivals – Rominger won all three time trials in the 1995 Giro d'Italia and had an easy win overall – while holding their time in the mountains. Events such as the Tour de France may also feature a team time-trial, in which each team rides the course on their own – like a breakaway group in a road race – sharing the pace with the most able riders helping the least able to keep the bunch moving at maximum speed.

### Time Trials in Britain

Time trials have always been particularly popular in the UK. When motor cars began their steady growth in the 1920s, the time trial was perceived as being much safer than mass-start road racing and for much the same reasons it still retains its popularity today. The standard time-trial distances in the UK are over 10, 15, 25, 30, 50 and 100 miles where the riders who take least time win, and also over 12 and 24 hours where it is the distances covered that count.

### Time-Trial Bikes

The types of bikes used by specialist time-trial riders pay particular attention to aerodynamics and light weight. In the UK many time trials are held on flat roads with very smooth surfaces where riders can hold close to their maximum speed for much of the distance. The flatter the course the more dedicated the time-trial bike will be, with features such as a short wheelbase and steep seat and head tube angles plus a smaller 26-inch front wheel designed to give the rider a 'low-pro' crouched, head-down position, aerodynamically-shaped front forks, tri-bars or specially designed handlebars to flatten the rider and aid penetration, and a closely spaced rear gear-sprocket fitted with high gears in the 12–29 range if the course is not hilly, using a single '52' chainwheel with longer cranks than normal on a road bike to keep turning a high gear. A solid aero wheel at the rear with a deep rim on the front can prove aerodynamically superior, but aero wheels are prone to being knocked off line if there is too much wind on the course. The racers themselves will pay close attention to wearing skintight clothing, with the use of aerodynamic teardrop-shaped helmets particularly important to improve penetration.

*A time-trial bike is designed to be as aerodynamically efficient as possible*

# TRACK RACING

Track racing takes place on indoor or outdoor banked velodromes with circuits up to 500 metres (546 yards) long and is among the oldest forms of cycle sport. Indoor circuits are generally constructed from dense hardwood, and with controlled conditions are where most modern speed records such as the 'one hour' are set. Outdoor circuits require a weather-resistant surface provided by smooth concrete or asphalt, with the high-altitude outdoor circuits of Mexico favoured for record breaking by riders such as one-hour record-holders Eddy Merckx (1972) and Francesco Moser (1984).

The tighter the bends, the steeper the banking needs to be in order to allow the riders to race at high speed, with the height of the banking used to launch attacks by accelerating down the slope. From the inside the track itself is divided by a safety line within which no rider is allowed to overtake another rider, a sprinters' line within which a rider can only be overtaken on the outside, and a stayers' line for riding steadily round the track on the outside high up on the banking while waiting to make a move.

## Track Bikes
Track bikes are stripped to the bare essentials with steep frame angles and straight forks for lightning response, as well as high bottom brackets and shorter crank lengths than on a road bike to ensure the pedals stay well clear when riding round the steepest banks. Sprinting, in particular, puts a great deal of stress onto the bike, not least because sprinters tend to be powerfully-built heavyweights known for their formidable thighs. They require a frame, forks, saddle and wheels which are strong enough to withstand the sprinting action without distorting, using a steeply sloping stem with the saddles at full height to give an extreme head-down, backside-up posture for the sprint to the line.

Track bikes also have no brakes with a fixed single-gear rear sprocket driven by a single chainwheel, the size of which is matched to suit the track. The fixed wheel-drive and short wheelbase makes control much more precise than on a road bike, with the track-stand position in which the rider holds the bike absolutely still with both feet locked onto the pedals a standard track-racing technique.

## WORLD CHAMPIONSHIP TRACK DISCIPLINES

### Sprint
Most of the action in a sprint race takes place beyond a line marked 200 metres from the finish. Races are usually contested over three laps by two, three or four riders, with the opening laps sometimes so slow that the riders come to a dead halt and go into the track-stand position. The problem is that the rider who wins will usually come from behind, getting a tow from the slipstream of the front rider until launching an explosive effort to be first across the line, and no one wants to take the lead until he hits the finish line. Tactics play a major role in deciding what happens in the final 200 metres, with riders using the banking to accelerate into the lead or block challengers from behind. The world championships also feature a tandem sprint.

*Track bikes are reduced to the bare essentials with fixed-wheel drive and no brakes. Note the head-down position*

## Points

In a 'points' competition, the riders sprint to accumulate points at the end of each lap. At the end of the race the rider with the highest number of points is the winner.

## Keirin

*Keirin* is a track discipline which originated in Japan and has become popular worldwide. A motorbike called a *Derny* paces a field of about eight, leading them faster and faster round the track for three laps until it peels away and leaves the riders to a sprint at maximum speed. A great deal of aggression is required to get into pole position for the sprint.

## 4000m Pursuit

For pursuit racing the start lines are marked midway along each straight on opposite sides of the track. The two riders start at the same time half a lap apart, chasing one another until the set 4000m distance has been passed. The rider who has made ground wins and moves on to the next round with the competition culminating in semi-finals and finals. Winning technique requires the ability to set a fast pace for the full distance, with risky tactical possibilites such as taking off at such high speed that the other rider gives up the chase. Winning times are now below four and a half minutes, with Chris Boardman taking the 1994 world title in 4 minutes, 27.742 seconds.

## 4000m Team Pursuit

Team pursuit features two four-man teams racing from either side of the track, changing the lead and pacing one another to maximum effect which makes it a marginally faster race than the solo pursuit. To keep the teams together, the third man across the line is counted on each lap until the finish at the end of 4000 metres.

## 1000m Time Trial

This is a solo discipline which lasts little more than a minute – 1994 world champion Florian Rousseau (France) finished in a winning time of 1:03.163. It combines sprinting ability with a time trial on a track. The winning technique is to maintain full power for the whole kilometre, without blowing up on the final 200 metres.

## 100 km Team Time-Trial

This is the longest world championship event, requiring endurance and commitment. The winning Italian team at the 1994 championship finished in a time of 1 hour, 57:54.1.

## Motor-Paced Race

Hour-long events in which each rider is paced by a motorcycle at speeds of around 80 kmh. Overtaking is complicated by the fact that the rider must use a great deal of effort to get past another motorcycle's slipstream. The race is decided on points.

# THE MANCHESTER VELODROME

*Manchester's velodrome is the UK's first purpose-built indoor cycling stadium. It was built at a cost of £9 million on the site of the Stuart Street Power Station, opening in late 1993 with an international Superdrome meeting in which the star turn was provided by a 4000m pursuit race between hour record-holders Chris Boardman and Tony Rominger – it was won by Boardman. The 10,000 sq ft building is covered by an aluminium roof supported by a 122m-span main arch. The main feature is the 250m Baltic pine-board track, designed and constructed by Ron Webb which is banked at 12.5 degrees on the straight and a maximum 42 degrees on the curves in order to catapult riders down the straight with gravity forces up to 4 G. There is seating capacity for 3500 spectators on the straights, and the building also includes suites of changing rooms, workshops, a sports injury clinic, drug testing and physiological suites, weight-training and rest rooms, meeting areas and the offices of the British Cycling Federation. A bronze statue of Reg Harris – Britain's greatest ever track cyclist – sculpted by James Butler RA, overlooks the finishing straight.*

*A young Patrick Sercu (left) waits to go on the track during the six-day cycle race at Wembley in 1966*

## SIX-DAY RACING

Modern six-day racing is a highly specialized competition. It consists of two-man teams racing during late afternoon and night-time sessions at indoor banked velodromes. The main six-day events on the prestigious European winter circuit starting in late October are held at cities including Grenoble, Dortmund, Munich, Bordeaux, Ghent, Vienna, Zurich, Bremen, Stuttgart and Copenhagen.

■ A maximum number of 30 riders compete in four main six-day disciplines:

■ *The madison*: The foundation of the modern six-day event. It was originally introduced to enable one rider to rest while his partner pedalled, and takes its name from Madison Square Gardens in New York, where non-stop team racing was first held at the turn of the century. Madison is a distance race, usually over 30 minutes or one hour, where the two-man teams operate a relay system. The aim of each team is to gain a lap over the rest of the field. One team member races at full speed on the inside of the track, while his partner circles round the outside high up on the banking until it is time to take over – approximately after every one and a half laps. As in a relay race the riders have to touch, using a technique to throw the new rider into the race by slinging him forward hand to hand or giving him a powerful shove from behind. The team covering the greatest number of laps is the winner of each madison session. At the end of the six days, the team which has covered the greatest number of laps wins overall. If two teams are on the same lap, points gained in the other disciplines are used to split them.

■ *The points race:* Held over a set number of laps, with points awarded every five or ten laps, and double points for the sprint finish.

■ *The derny-paced race:* Also held over a set number of laps, the first man across the line is the winner.

■ *The devil take the hindmost:* A competition in which the last rider across the line is pulled out of the race at the end of each lap or double lap, until two riders are left to contest the final sprint to the finish. This guarantees a succession of sprints as riders battle to avoid being last, and is a track-racing discipline which is also popular outside six-day racing.

## TRACK RIDERS

Track riders can be divided into various ability groups. Sprinters are powerfully-built men who use their thighs to drive the pedals and their upper body to drive the bike. Their main aim is to play a cat-and-mouse game before suddenly accelerating for the finish. Pursuit racers are less heavily-built racers who require high speed endurance for up to four minutes' duration. All-round points-race specialists combine both sets of skills, needing endurance and sprinting ability. Six-day specialists combine these skills with very high levels of tactical ability.

## Top of the Track

**Marty Nothstein** from Allentown, Pennsylvania, USA became the first American to win the world sprint title since 1912 when he triumphed in the world championships at Palermo, Sicily in August 1994 at the age of 23. He then took the 1994 world keirin title, having finished second in 1993. At 6 feet 2 inches tall and weighing 200 pounds (90.72 kg) Nothstein's powerful physique is typical of a top sprinter, though he was introduced to cycle competition via BMX racing in times when he was presumably rather smaller.

■ **Florian Rousseau**, rated as the world's fastest man over the one-kilometre time trial, retained his kilometre title at the 1994 world championships in Sicily when he clocked a flying 1 minute, 3.153 seconds. He was also world junior champion in 1992.

■ **Patrick Sercu** (Belgium) stands alone as the greatest ever six-day rider. He won 88 of the 228 six-day races he took part in, in a career lasting from 1965 to 1983. During that time he won his home six-day event at Ghent 11 times, and he also won eight London six-day events between 1969 and 1979. Patrick Sercu's six-day partners included Rik Van Looy, Merckx, Moser, Saronni, Maertens, De Vlaeminck and Dietrich Thurau. His most successful partnership was with Peter Post (Belgium), whom he eventually overtook as the most successful six-day rider of all time.

■ **Tony Doyle MBE** was twice world professional pursuit champion in 1980 and 1986 and became the most successful British rider in modern six-day competition, forming a winning partnership with Danny Clark (Australia) which won 18 victories. Doyle also won six-day events teamed with Francesco Moser and Etienne De Wilde (Belgium), and despite a near-fatal accident at the Munich Six in 1989 came back to win the same event a year later. Other British six-day riders have included Tom Simpson, Barry Hoban, Tony Gowland, and most recently the team of Spencer Wingrave and Shaun Wallace.

■ **Bruno Risi** and **Kurt Betschart** (both Switzerland) dominated the 1994–95 six-day circuit, with wins that included the three most prized events in Germany at Munich, Cologne and Bremen; they also won at Bordeaux and Manchester, and finished second in the remaining events at Dortmund, Zurich and Stuttgart.

■ **Urs Frueler** (Switzerland) is a legend of track racing, having won ten world championships – the points race eight times and the keirin twice. In 1994 he won the Zurich six-day race at the age of 36, teamed with Carsten Wolf (Germany).

■ **Chris Boardman** won the 4000m pursuit at the 1992 Olympics, and two years later won the 4000m pursuit title at the 1994 world championships in Sicily, having been beaten by Graeme Obree at the world championships in Norway in 1993.

■ **Ingrid Haringa** (Holland), a policewoman by profession, won the women's points race three years in succession between 1992 and 1994, completing her hat trick at the age of 30 at the 1994 world championships in Sicily.

■ **Reg Harris** (UK) stands alone as Britain's greatest track racer. He was world amateur champion in 1947, and world professional sprint champion in 1949–51 and 1954. He also broke the world kilometre record on five occasions, with a best time of 1 minute, 0.08 seconds.

■ **Hugh Porter** (UK) is considered Britain's most successful pursuit racer. He won four 5000m professional world championships (1968, 1970, 1972–73), and has scored more world championship wins than anyone else in this discipline.

■ The greatest track-race sprinter ever is the Japanese rider **Koichi Nakano** who won the world professional sprint title for ten years in succession between 1977–86.

---

*A Racer at the White House*

*Freddie Spencer (USA) competed during the golden years of American track racing. Between 1925 and 1938 he took part in 102 six-day races, completing 99 and winning six in New York and Chicago. President Calvin Coolidge was so impressed with Spencer's 1925 Madison Square Garden win that he invited Freddie and his team mate, Bobby Walthour Jr, to the White House. Between 1925 and 1929 Spencer won 65 straight match sprints, defeating two incumbent world champions and capturing the US national sprint title in 1925 and 1928–29. During his career he also set world records in the 1/10 mile, half-mile, 10-mile, 20-mile and 25-mile categories. His 25-mile record of 49 minutes, 28 seconds set in August 1929 lasted as the US record for nearly 60 years. Retiring from track racing in 1938, Spencer worked in maintenance and as an athletic trainer for New Jersey public schools. He died in 1992 at the age of 88.*

# Mountain Bike Competitions

## Cross-Country

Cross-country is the principal discipline in mountain-bike racing, and usually the hardest. After a massed start, competitors race round a clearly marked course and the first rider to cross the finish line is the winner. The course can be up to ten miles in length or even longer, with the number of laps determining the eventual length of the race – a professional Grundig Series event is likely to be around 30 miles long, taking the winner over two hours to complete, while local amateur events will be considerably shorter.

■ Cross-country racing is a mass-participation sport which requires intense individual effort. There is little opportunity for the kind of team tactics that are used in a road race, and no slipstreaming or cruising while waiting for someone to make a break. The fastest riders usually hit the front of the field as soon as they can and stay there, not least because overtaking can be difficult and dangerous on single-track or technical descents. The course should be designed to provide a testing mixture of terrain including plenty of hard climbing and fast downhills. In wet weather lack of traction may force riders to dismount and run with their bikes in cyclo-cross fashion which can make a race particularly gruelling. Crashes are not unusual, although few serious injuries result; punctures which can suddenly stop a rider are an ever-present hazard. No outside help is permitted, and top professional riders are so skilled that they have been known to change a flat tyre in no more than a minute.

■ The bikes used for cross-country are little different from high performance stock bikes marketed for general off-road use. Those used by top professionals may be a little lighter and made to measure for the rider's height and reach, and will almost certainly feature top groupsets and other equipment. Clipless pedals are standard issue, and virtually all riders now use front-suspension units which are generally much faster on downhills due to their ability to absorb bumps without loss of speed. Acceptance of full suspension has been slow amongst top riders, though three-times world champion Hendrik Djernis opted to change to the all-suspension Pro-Flex team at the start of the 1995 season.

## Downhill

Racing downhill at high speeds is potentially the most dangerous form of mountain-bike competition, and is primarily staged as an off-road time-trial discipline. Riders start at intervals, and whoever records the quickest time from top to bottom of the course is the winner. Despite its simple nature it is a discipline which requires a very positive mental approach. Riders must know their limits, possess a high level of physical fitness allied to superb bike-handling skills, and be able to read the course at high speeds and set the bike up for each bend. Maintaining control is the vital ingredient for winning.

■ The downhill course used at Vail for the 1994 mountain bike world championship was typical of the type of highly demanding course set for top professionals. Starting at an altitude of 10,250 ft it dropped 2000 ft over 4.5 km, combining high-speed open sections with technical single-track through winding woodland and very tight turns. Winner François Gachet took 6 minutes, 22.52 seconds to cover the course in the finals. Gachet was also world downhill champion in 1993, and won the Grundig/UCI Downhill World Cup series both in 1993 and 1994.

■ With slight modifications a conventional bike can be successfully used for downhill events at amateur level. A more upright position is favoured than for cross-country to give good forward vision and precise control, with the saddle lowered to keep the centre of gravity down for fast cornering and the handlebars widened with bar ends removed. Brake systems can be uprated to more powerful hydraulics; wide tyres with maximum traction are preferred; and a chain-retaining device is necessary to prevent the chain bouncing off the outer chainring at speed.

■ At the professional end of the sport a bike for downhill is likely to be heavily modified or specially built for the purpose of going very fast while staying in control. François Gachet's custom-built 1994 world championship-winning bike had a relatively long wheelbase at 43 inches to maximize control, and weighed over 34 pounds which illustrates the point that a strong bike which will withstand a downhill hammering is much more important than

*Above: In 1994 the French rider François Gachet won both the World Championships and the World Cup series*

the light weight which is needed to help propel a cross-country bike uphill. Full suspension is mandatory to cope with the lumps and bumps on most downhill courses, with Gachet's bike featuring three inches of suspension travel provided by air/oil shocks at the front and four inches of travel provided by a single-spring coil mounted on a pivoting swing-arm at the rear. Gachet used a single, oversize 48-tooth chainring combined with an 8-speed 12-tooth 30 rear-sprocket cluster activated by a twist-grip shifter to ensure he could sprint through the sections where his speed eased off. His chain was held firmly on the chainring by being fed through a jockey wheel cage just below and behind the chainring. His stopping power was provided by a hydraulic disc brake at the rear with a conventional cantilever brake at the front, though many downhillers also opt for front wheel disc hydraulics.

## Downhill Variations

One problem with downhill is that there is no direct man-on-man element to interest spectators since the solitary rider is racing against the clock. To compensate for this, some race organizers run downhill events in which two racers set off together, with the first to the finish being the winner and heats held on a knock-out basis leading through to the finals.

■ The most popular variation is downhill dual slalom, a discipline based on snow-skiing dual slalom. Two riders set off together to head down parallel courses marked by gates, weaving their way down around the left- and right-turn flags to the finish at the bottom. This requires a short, steep hill which is sufficiently wide to give two competitors virtually identical terrain all the way down the course.

■ A downhill refinement which seems set to grow in popularity is the head-to-head downhill, a discipline which was pioneered by the 1993 Reebok Eliminator at Mammoth in California. This event was designed specifically for TV coverage, with competitors racing man on man down a course based on the world-famous Kamikaze, starting at 11,000 ft and dropping to 2150 ft in three and a half miles. The paired riders were allowed two races down the course with the winner decided on combined times, and a maximum five-second time penalty in each race to ensure that crashing in one run would not mean automatic elimination. To ensure that riders raced all the way down the course, the first to the halfway stage got a cash prize.

## Racing Categories

**Fun/Novice**
'Have a go' for anyone over 10 years old with no competition experience.

**Youth** From 12 years old to 31 December of year of 16th birthday.

**Junior** From 1 January of year of 17th birthday to 31 December of year of 18th birthday.

**Senior** From 1 January of year of 19th birthday to 31 December of year of 34th birthday. This category is sub-divided into four ability ranges:

*Pro/Elite* The top international category for full time professional riders.

*Expert* Experienced riders who have progressed from Sport or Junior.

*Sport 1* From 1 January of year of 19th birthday to 31 December of year of 26th birthday.

*Sport 2* From 1 January of year of 27th birthday to 31 December of year of 34th birthday.

**Veteran** From 1 January of year of 35th birthday to 31 December of year of 44th birthday.

**Master** From 1 January of year of 45th birthday to 31 December of year of 54th birthday.

**Super Master**
From 1 January of year of 55th birthday.

## Professional Series and Venues

The mountain-bike professional season is dominated by the Grundig World Cup series and the annual world championship, with the first cross-country Olympics to be staged in 1996. The modern World Cup came into being in 1991 when the European Grundig series combined with the American NORBA series, in collaboration with the UCI. It is targeted worldwide with as many as ten events held each year in Australia, the USA and western and eastern Europe. At every event cross-country is the major discipline, with a shorter series of Grundig/UCI World Downhill Cup events held at the same time when the venues are suitable.

■ The World Cup series winner is decided on points amassed throughout the season, but the single big event that all professionals want to win is the world championship. This has been held at venues in Europe and the USA since 1990. The disciplines are cross-country and downhill with most interest in the senior men's and women's classes. However, it can be a big event – at the 1994 world championship at Vail there were also classes for juniors and veterans plus an unofficial dual slalom world championship, which produced a 900-strong entry drawn from 44 countries and also as many as 30,000 spectators. This was followed by the 1995 world championship at Kirchzarten in the Black Forest area of Germany, staged on a 4.7 km downhill course and the 8.6 km Bickenreut cross-country circuit which climbed 285 metres per lap.

■ The most famous international venue of all time is Mammoth in California. Located 300 miles to the north of Los Angeles, this was the site of the American-organized world championships from 1987 to 1989. It features the legendary Kamikaze downhill course, starting from an altitude of 11,000 feet at the top of Mammoth Mountain. During the 1994 Grundig World Cup series the Mammoth event was a festival of cycle racing, attracting over 3000 starters in 18 different events over a five-day period. This included 500 beginners entered in their own cross-country event, while a total of 180 Dual Slalom and Reebok Eliminator rounds took place.

## World Championships

*1990 Durango, Colorado USA*

| | |
|---|---|
| Senior Cross-Country Men: | 1. Ned Overend (USA); 2. Thomas Frischknecht (SWI); 3. Tim Gould (UK). |
| Senior Cross-Country Women: | 1. Julie Furtado (USA); 2. Sara Ballantyne (USA); 3. Ruthie Matthes (USA). |
| Senior Downhill Men: | 1. Greg Herbold (USA); 2. Mike Kloser (USA); 3. Paul Thomasberg |
| Senior Downhill Women: | 1. Cindy Devine (USA); 2. Elladee Brown (CDN); 3. Penny Davidson (USA). |

*1991 Lucca, Italy*

| | |
|---|---|
| Senior Cross-Country (Men): | 1. John Tomac (USA); 2. Thomas Frischknecht (SWI); 3. Ned Overend (USA). |
| Senior Cross-Country (Women): | 1. Ruthie Matthes (USA); 2. Eva Orvosova (Slovakia); 3.Silvia Furst (SWI). |
| Senior Downhill (Men): | 1. Albert Iten (SWI); 2. John Tomac (USA); 3. Glen Adams (USA). |
| Senior Downhill (Women): | 1. Giovanna Bonazzi (I); 2. Nathalie Fiat (F); 3. Cindy Devine (CDN). |

*1992 Bromont, Quebec, Canada*

| | |
|---|---|
| Senior Cross-Country Men: | 1. Henrik Djernis (DNK); 2. Thomas Frischknecht (SWI); 3. Dave Baker (UK). |
| Senior Cross-Country (Women): | 1. Silvia Furst (SWI); 2. Alison Sydor (CDN); 3. Ruthie Matthes (USA). |

Senior Downhill (Men):     1. Dave Cullinan (USA); 2. Jimmy Deaton (USA); 3. Christian Taillefer (F).
Senior Downhill (Women):   1. Julie Furtado (USA); 2. Kim Sonier (USA); 3. Cindy Devine (CDN).

*1993 Métabief, France*
Senior Cross-Country (Men):     1. Henrik Djernis (DNK); 2. Marcel Gerritsen (NL); 3. Jan Ostergaard (DNK).
Senior Cross-Country (Women):   1. Paola Pezzo (I); 2. Jeannie Longo (F); 3. Ruthie Matthes (USA).
Senior Downhill (Men):          1. Mike King (USA); 2. Paolo Caramellino (I); 3. Myles Rockwell (USA).
Senior Downhill (Women):        1. Giovanna Bonazzi (I); 2. Kim Sonier (USA); 3. Missy Giove (USA).

*1994 Vail, Colorado, USA*
Senior Cross-Country (Men):     1. Henrik Djernis (DNK); 2. Tinker Juarez (USA); 3. Bart Brentjens (NL).
Senior Cross-Country (Women):   1. Alison Sydor (CDN); 2. Susan DeMattei(USA); 3. Sara Ballantyne (USA).
Senior Downhill (Men):          1. François Gachet (F); 2. Tommy Johansson (SWE); 3. Corado Herin (I).
Senior Downhill (Women):        1. Missy Giove (USA); 2. Sophie Kempf (F); 3. Giovanna Bonazzi (I).

*1995 Kirchzarten, Germany*
Senior Cross-Country (Men):     1. Bart Brentjens (NL); 2. Miguel Martinez (F);
                                3. Jan-Eric Ostergaard (DNK).
Senior Cross-Country (Women):   1. Alison Sydor (CDN); 2. Silvia Fürst (SWI); 3 Chantal Daucourt (SWI).
Senior Downhill (Men):          1. Nicolas Vouilloz (F); 2. François Gachet (F); 3. Mike King (USA).
Senior Downhill (Women):        1. Leigh Donovan (USA); 2. Mercedes Gonzalez (ESP); 3. Giovanna Bonazzi (I)

# Grundig/UCI World Cup Series

*1991*
Men's Cross-Country:     1. John Tomac (USA); 2. Gerhard Zarobilek (A); 3. David Wiens (USA).
Women's Cross-Country:   1. Sara Ballantyne (USA); 2. Juli Furtado (USA); 3. Regina Stiefl (D).
Men's Downhill:          1. Albert Iten (SWI); 2. John Tomac (USA); 3. Glen Adams (USA).
Women's Downhill:        1. Giovanna Bonazzi (I); 2. Nathalie Fiat (F); 3. Cindy Devine (CDN).

*1992*
Men's Cross-Country:     1. Thomas Frischknecht (SWI); 2. John Tomac (USA);
                         3. Ned Overend (USA).
Women's Cross-Country:   1. Ruthie Matthes (USA); 2. Juli Furtado (USA); 3. Chantal Daucourt (SWI).
Men's Downhill:          1. Dave Cullinan (USA); 2. Jimmy Deaton (USA); 3. Christian Taillefer (F).
Women's Downhill:        1. Juli Furtado; 2. Kim Sonier (USA); 3. Cindy Devine (CDN).

*1993*
Men's Cross-Country:     1. Thomas Frischknecht (SWI); 2. John Tomac (USA); 3. Peter Hric (SLK)
Women's Cross-Country:   1. Juli Furtado (USA); 2. Ruthie Matthes (USA); Alison Sydor (CDN).
Men's Downhill:          1. Jürgen Beneke (D); 2. John Tomac (USA); 3. Stefano Migliorini (I).
Women's Downhill:        1. Regina Steifl (D); 2. Giovanna Bonazzi (I); Missy Giove (USA).

*1994*
Men's Cross-Country:     1. Bart Brentjens (NL); 2. Ned Overend (USA); 3. Tinker Juarez (USA).
Women's Cross-Country:   1. Juli Furtado (USA); 2. Caroline Alexander (UK); 3. Alison Sydor (CDN).
Men's Downhill:          1. François Gachet (F); 2. Jürgen Beneke (D). 3. Nicolas Vouilloz (F).
Women's Downhill:        1. Kim Sonier (USA); 2. Anne-Caroline Chausson (F); 3. Missy Giove (USA).

*1995*
Men's Cross-Country:     1. Thomas Frischknecht (SWI); 2. Rune Hoydahl (NOR);
                         3. Jan-Eric Ostergaard (NL).
Women's Cross-Country:   1. Juli Furtado (USA); 2. Alison Sydor (CDN); 3. Silvia Fürst (SWI).
Men's Downhill:          1. Nicolas Vouilloz (F); 2. Mike King (USA); 3. Myles Rockwell (USA).
Women's Downhill:        1. Regina Stiefl (D); 2. Giovanna Bonazzi; 3. Kim Sonier (USA).

# European Championships

### 1993 Klosters, Switzerland
Senior Cross-Country (Men): 1. Thomas Frischknecht (SWI); 2. Danile Bruschi (I); 3. Peter Hric (SLK).
Senior Cross-Country (Women): 1. Chantal Daucourt (SWI); 2. Caroline Alexander (UK); 3. Cornelia Suizer (A).

### 1994 Métabief, France
Senior Cross-Country (Men): 1. Albert Iten (SWI); 2. Gary Foord (UK); 3. Benny Heylen (B).
Senior Cross-Country (Women): 1. Paola Pezzo (I); 2. Sophie Eglin (F); 3. Maria Paola Turcutto (I).
Senior Downhill (Men): 1. Nicolas Vouilloz (F); 2. Tommy Johansson (SWE); 3. Corado Herin (I).
Senior Downhill (Women): 1. Anne-Caroline Chausson (F); 2. Giovanna Bonazzi (I); 3.Brigitta Kasper (SWI).

### 1995 Spindleruv Mlyn, Czechoslovakia
Senior Cross-Country (Men): 1. Jean-Christophe Savignoni (F); 2. Luca Bramati (I); 3. Christophe Dupouey (F).
Senior Cross-Country (Women): 1. Caroline Alexander (UK); 2. Silvia Rossa (ESP); 3.Katerina Neuannova (CZ).
Senior Downhill (Men): 1. François Gachet (F); 2. Nicolas Vouilloz (F); 3. Alexander Balaud (F).
Senior Downhill (Women): 1. Caroline Chausson (F); 2. Giovanna Bonazzi (I); 3. Carole Grange (F).

## STAGE RACING

Long distance cross-country stage racing is growing in interest and may be of major importance in years to come. In 1995 the world-famous Tour de France road-race organizers launched the first mountain-bike Tour de France known as the Tour VTT (Velo Tour Terrain – the French term for a mountain bike). The nine-day event was contested by 20 teams, each comprising five senior men and one woman. It was held on the same daily-stage principles as the Tour de France, with the racers and support teams housed in a huge tented village which moved with the event. After an opening off-road prologue, each day was divided into timed stages and untimed linking stages. This gave a total ride distance of 540 km over a mountainous landscape between the start at Métabief – site of the 1993 world championships and 1994 European championships – and the finish at La Bourboule in south-eastern France with a one million franc prize fund.

■ The inaugural mountain bike Vuelta a España was held in Spain 1995. It was an eight-day stage race starting from Madrid, featuring a prologue and seven short stages ranging in length from 4.5 – 13.5 km, with Briton Barrie Clarke the overall winner for the Raleigh Team in a time of 4 hours, 33 minutes, 20 seconds. Another European seven-stage race held in 1995 was the Tour de Suisse VTT in Switzerland, won by Norwegian Rune Hoydahl in 7 hours, 51 minutes, 31 seconds with Britain's Tim Gould third overall.

■ In Australia the 1995 Crocodile Trophy was billed as 'the longest and most difficult mountain-bike stage race in the world', held over 2556 km between Darwin and Cairns with average daily stages of 150 km. It started in the Kakadu National Park, with most of the route over dusty bush tracks, across mountains, through tropical rainforests and over unbridged rivers which came complete with crocodiles – hence the name of the race. It was held as an open event for both professionals and amateurs, with a tented camp following the race to provide full back-up. After 17 stages Austria's Harold Maier finished as overall winner seven minutes ahead of second placed Rudy De Bie of Belgium.

*Left, facing page: Andy Grayson, winner of the trials section of the 1994 World Championships, in action*

## TRIALS and ENDURO

Observed trials are based on a popular discipline in off-road motorcycle sport. An event is decided on a series of technical sections which are designed to be extremely difficult to ride. Speed is not a winning element, though there may be a time limit. The competition is likely to be decided on how many times each competitor puts a foot down or grasps something to stay balanced. Points are added on for every incident, and the rider with the lowest total wins overall. Due to their technical difficulty and lack of any high-speed excitement, trials tend to be a minority interest.

■ Enduro is a long-distance event which combines trials with a cross-country course. Riders win on a combination of technical riding skills on the special stages, speed over the ground between the stages, and map-reading skills to find their way round the course. Trailquest combines orienteering with mountain biking, and places high emphasis on navigation. A refinement is the two-day Polaris Challenge held in Britain. Teams sleep out overnight while finding their way between checkpoints in wilderness country, carrying all the necessary survival equipment on their bodies and bikes.

## Mountain Bike Speed Record

The ultimate downhill competition must be the annual Diesel Speed Challenge for the unofficial mountain bike world speed record. In 1995 this was set at 178.66 kmh (111.66 mph) by the Frenchman Christian Taileffer, during the second Diesel Speed Challenge at Vars in the French Alps. The course used a high-speed ski run, dropping at 45 degrees from a height of 2720m, entering the measured kilometre which dropped to 2285m at the finish where average speeds were recorded, with a one-kilometre run-out ending in a slight uphill. Of the four professional downhill racers who had been invited, the only woman entrant – Giovanna Bonazzi of Italy – was slowest with a speed of 142.63 kmh (88.23 mph). All the competitors wore speed-skiers' suits with aerodynamic helmets, had 70-tooth chainrings to accelerate away from the start, and used spiked tyres to grip the hard-packed snow.

■ Later in 1995 the French rider Eric Braone took just two runs on the speed course at the French ski resort of Les Arcs 2000 to push the record to a new high of 193.548 kmh, moving mountain biking close to breaking the 200 kmh barrier which seems likely to fall before long. In the same year the Swiss rider Iris Jordan  set a new women's world record of 157.205 kmh.

# Cyclo-Cross Championships

Cyclo-cross is a cross-country event which combines cycle racing and running. Despite its obvious similarities, it is a competition which evolved long before the advent of the mountain bike. In the earliest days it was conceived as a winter sport for roadmen, using virtually standard road-bikes, but in recent years it has become much more closely allied to mountain biking where the popularity of a highly-paid professional circuit seems likely to continue to drain any outstanding talent that cyclo-cross produces. Two of the greatest riders who made the transition to become mountain-bike champions are Thomas Frischknecht of Switzerland, winner of the cyclo-cross amateur title in 1991, and Henrik Djernis of Denmark who won the amateur title in 1993.

## World Championships

The first cyclo-cross world championships were held in Paris in 1950. The 1947 Tour de France winner Jean Robic took the title, and remains the only man to have won both events. The world championships continued as an open event until 1967, when the amateur and professional titles were split. The junior event, first held in 1976, was held at a different venue from the senior titles until 1980. The traditional weekend programme of junior and senior amateur races on the Saturday, followed by the professional race on Sunday, then came to a temporary end in 1994 when the professional and amateur events were once again combined into one open championship. The other most important cyclo-cross events in the annual calendar are the World Cup and Super Prestige series.

## Top Riders

The most successful cyclo-cross rider of all time is Eric de Vlaeminck of Belgium who won seven world championships in eight years. His first professional title came in 1966, his debut year, at the age of 20. A year later he slipped to fifth and was lapped by the winner Renato Longo of Italy. His run of six straight world championship wins then started in 1968, the year in which his brother Roger de Vlaeminck took the amateur world championship. Eric de Vlaeminck's last world championship win was at the 1973 event held in London. Roger de Vlaeminck won the professional world championship two years

*Running uphill with the bike makes cyclo-cross an intense sport which is favoured as winter training*

later, and proved an equally successful rider on the road with four Paris–Roubaix wins in six years.

■ The two other most successful cyclo-cross riders are André Dufraisse of France who won the world championship five times between 1954 and 1958, and Albert Zweifel of Switzerland who won four times between 1976 and 1979.

■ Britain's best results in cyclo-cross world championships have been in the junior class. Robert Dane's junior silver in 1984 was Britain's first ever cyclo-cross world championship medal, and was followed by gold medal wins for Stuart Marshall at Lambeek, Belgium in 1986 and for Roger Hammond at Leeds in 1992. British national titles (instituted in 1955) have been won most often by John Atkins (b. 7 April 1942) with five amateur (1961–62, 1966–68), seven professional (1969–75) and one open title (1977).

## Cyclo-Cross Bikes

Early modifications to make standard road-bikes suitable for cyclo-cross included fitting lower gears, increasing frame clearance to prevent mud building up, fitting cantilever brakes for better stopping power in slippery conditions, and using fatter tyres to give better grip. More recent trends have been towards using purpose-built aluminium frames since the lightest possible weight makes it easier to shoulder the bike and run. The use of SPD clipless pedals rather than toeclips has also come into favour; toeclips are prone to breaking due to hitting objects such as rocks and tree roots, and are usually doubled up. Modern cyclo-cross bikes also have high-pressure knobbled or even studded tyres, while the riders fit spikes to the toes of their shoes for better traction while running. Handlebar gear-changers or combined Ergopower/STI style gear and brake levers are used for superior control.

## Cyclo-Cross Courses

Cyclo-cross races are extremely demanding and usually last little more than an hour, using a short circuit in the region of two miles (three kilometres) long. This helps to make it an excellent spectator sport with the field usually limited to around 50 riders who start on a wide section of level ground before entering the main circuit. Then the top riders attempt to sprint ahead and stay there, as overtaking on narrow, difficult terrain can be difficult and time wasting.

■ The circuit should ideally include some fast riding on hard surfaces, which may range from grass to a short stretch of gravel or even tarmac. In between, there will be obstacles to negotiate such as ditches, hurdles and steep banks, together with some very steep, short climbs and descents, and the possibility of muddy, waterlogged sections on any part of the course if there has been a lot of rain. To succeed, a rider must be able to handle a bike confidently on a wide range of different surfaces while racing in a group. One of the great skills is to take an instant decision on when it is time to dismount, shoulder the bike and run – for instance on a steep uphill or when an obstruction has to be negotiated. The rider will then jump on again once the course permits fast enough riding. Another unique feature of a cyclo-cross event is that riders can change their bikes during a race, and may choose to use as many as three machines. Bikes can soon become clogged with mud, and a major event such as the world championship will feature pit areas with high-pressure bike-washing facilities to enable riders to change their bikes on each lap if required.

## Open and Professional World Champions

| Year | Location | Champion |
|---|---|---|
| 1950 | Paris | Jean Robic (F) |
| 1951 | Luxembourg | Roger Rondeaux (F) |
| 1952 | Geneva | Roger Rondeaux (F) |
| 1953 | Onate | Roger Rondeaux (F) |
| 1954 | Crenna | André Dufraisse (F) |
| 1955 | Saarbrücken | André Dufraisse (F) |
| 1956 | Luxembourg | André Dufraisse (F) |
| 1957 | Edelare | André Dufraisse (F) |
| 1958 | Limoges | André Dufraisse (F) |
| 1959 | Geneva | Renato Longo (I) |
| 1960 | Tolosa | Rolf Wolfshohl (FRG) |
| 1961 | Hannover | Rolf Wolfshohl (FRG) |
| 1962 | Esch-sur-Alzette | Renato Longo (I) |
| 1963 | Calais | Rolf Wolfshohl (FRG) |
| 1964 | Overboelare | Renato Longo (I) |
| 1965 | Cavaria | Renato Longo (I) |
| 1966 | Beasain | Eric de Vlaeminck (B) |
| 1967 | Zurich | Renato Longo (I) |
| 1968 | Luxembourg | Eric de Vlaeminck (B) |
| 1969 | Magstadt | Eric de Vlaeminck (B) |
| 1970 | Zolder | Eric de Vlaeminck (B) |
| 1971 | Apeldoorn | Eric de Vlaeminck (B) |
| 1972 | Prague | Eric de Vlaeminck (B) |
| 1973 | London | Eric de Vlaeminck (B) |
| 1974 | Vera de Bidasoa | Albert van Damme (B) |
| 1975 | Melchnau | Roger de Vlaeminck (B) |
| 1976 | Chazay d'Azergues | Albert Zweifel (SWI) |
| 1977 | Hannover | Albert Zweifel (SWI) |
| 1978 | Amorebieta | Albert Zweifel (SWI) |
| 1979 | Saccolongo | Albert Zweifel (SWI) |
| 1980 | Wetzikon | Roland Liboton (B) |
| 1981 | Tolosa | Johannes Stamsnijder (NL) |
| 1982 | Lanarvilly | Roland Liboton (B) |
| 1983 | Birmingham | Roland Liboton (B) |
| 1984 | Oss | Roland Liboton (B) |
| 1985 | Munich | Klaus-Peter Thaler (FRG) |
| 1986 | Lembeek | Albert Zweifel (SWI) |
| 1987 | Mlada Boleslav | Klaus-Peter Thaler (FRG) |
| 1988 | Hägendorf | Pascal Richard (SWI) |
| 1989 | Pontchâteau | Danny de Bie (B) |
| 1990 | Getxo | Henk Baars (NL) |
| 1991 | Gieten | Radomir Simunek (CZ) |
| 1992 | Leeds | Mike Kluge (D) |
| 1993 | Corva | Dominique Arnould (F) |
| 1994 | Koksijde | Paul Herisgers (B) |
| 1995 | Eshenbach | Dieter Runkel (SWI) |

**Most Professional World Championship Wins**

| | |
|---|---|
| 7 | Eric de Vlaeminck |
| 5 | André Dufraisse, Renato Longo |

*Roger de Vlaeminck followed his brother Eric as a cyclo-cross world champion and went on to become a top road racer*

## Amateur World Champions

*Held at same venues as professionals; combined as an Open event since 1993.*

1967   Michel Pelchat (F)
1968   Roger de Vlaeminck (B)
1969   René Declercq (B)
1970   Robert Vermeire (B)
1971   Robert Vermeire (B)
1972   Norbert de Deckere (B)
1973   Klaus-Peter Thaler (FRG)
1974   Robert Vermeire (B)
1975   Robert Vermeire (B)
1976   Klaus-Peter Thaler (FRG)
1977   Robert Vermeire (B)
1978   Roland Liboton (B)
1979   Vito di Tano (I)
1980   Fritz Saladin (SWI)
1981   Milos Fisera (CZ)
1982   Milos Fisera (CZ)
1983   Radomir Simunek (CZ)
1984   Radomir Simunek (CZ)
1985   Mike Kluge (FRG)
1986   Vito di Tano (I)
1987   Mike Kluge (FRG)
1988   Karel Camrda (CZ)
1989   Ondrej Glajza (CZ)
1990   Andreas Brüsser (SWI)
1991   Thomas Frischknecht (SWI)
1992   Daniele Pontoni (I)
1993   Henrik Djernis (DNK)

**Most Amateur World Championship Wins**
5         Robert Vermeire

## Junior World Champions

*Held at Jelina Gora in 1976, Volkegem-Ouden in 1977, Stuttgart-Valhingen in 1978, Villafranca in 1979; afterwards held at same venues as professional and amateur events.*

1976   Ralf Wincke (FRG)
1977   Ralf Wincke (FRG)
1978   Pavel Velek (CZ)
1979   José Vijande (CZ)
1980   Radomir Simunek (CZ)
1981   Rigobert Matt (FRG)
1982   Beat Schumacher (FRG)
1983   Roman Kreuziger (CZ)
1984   Ondrej Glajza (CZ)
1985   Beat Wabel (SWI)
1986   Stuart Marshall (UK)
1987   Marc Janssens (B)
1988   Thomas Frischknecht (SWI)
1989   R. Groenendaal (NL)
1990   Erik Boezewinkel (NL)
1991   Ondrej Lukes (CZ)
1992   Roger Hammond (UK)
1993   Kamil Ausbuher (CZ)
1994   Gretienus Gommers (NL)
1995   Zdenek Mlynar (CZ)

## Team Champions

*An unofficial championship listing based on top-three Amateur results from each country to 1993, after which it was based on Open results.*

1979   Poland
1980   Switzerland
1981   Italy
1982   Czechoslovakia
1983   Czechoslovakia
1984   Czechoslovakia
1985   Switzerland
1986   Belgium
1987   Czechoslovakia
1988   Switzerland
1989   Czechoslovakia
1990   Switzerland
1991   Switzerland
1992   Switzerland
1993   Czechoslovakia
1994   Belgium
1995   Switzerland

# The Great Track Events

Cycling world championships were first held in 1893 in Chicago when there were two amateur events, a sprint and a motor-paced race over 100 kilometres. The first professional world championships were held in 1895. A road race was first held in 1921, and women's events were introduced in 1959. Separate world championships were not contested in Olympic years for events on the Olympic programme. From 1993 most track events were combined into an Open class for both amateurs and professionals.

■ The most wins at a particular event is ten by Koichi Nakano (b. Japan, 14 November 1955) in professional sprint from 1977 to 1986.

■ The most wins at a men's amateur event is seven by Daniel Morelon (France) in sprint (1966–67, 1969–71, 1973 and 1975); and by Leon Meredith (GB) in 10 km motor-paced in 1904–5, 1907–9, 1911 and 1913.

■ The most world championship women's titles is ten by Jeannie Longo (France). On the track she won them in pursuit in 1986 and 1988–89, and in the points race in 1989. She also won the road race in 1985–87, 1989 and 1995, and the road time-trial in 1995.

■ The most world titles won by an American cyclist is six, at women's 3 km pursuit, by Rebecca Twigg in 1982, 1984–85, 1987, 1993 and 1995 when she set a new world record of 3 minutes, 36.081 seconds. She rode the 1995 event with seven steel pins in her right shoulder, having broken her collar bone in a crash while training just 13 days earlier.

*The indoor velodrome used for the 1990 track World Championships held at Maebashi, Japan*

# WORLD TRACK CHAMPIONS

## MEN (AMATEUR)

### Amateur Sprint
*First held 1893. Open to both amateurs and professionals from 1993.*

| | |
|---|---|
| 1893 | A. Zimmermann (USA) |
| 1894 | Augustus Lehr (D) |
| 1895 | J. Eden (NL) |
| 1896 | H. Reynolds (IRL) |
| 1897 | E. Schraeder (DNK) |
| 1898 | Paul Albert (D) |
| 1899 | Summersgill (UK) |
| 1900 | A. Didier-Nauts (B) |
| 1901 | E. Maitrot (F) |
| 1902 | C. Piard (F) |
| 1903 | A.L. Reed (UK) |
| 1904 | M. Hurley (USA) |
| 1905 | J.S. Benyon (UK) |
| 1906 | F. Verri (I) |
| 1907 | J. Devoissoux (F) |
| 1908 | V. L. Johnson (UK) |
| 1909 | W. J. Bailey (UK) |
| 1910 | W. J. Bailey (UK) |
| 1911 | W. J. Bailey (UK) |
| 1912 | D. McDougall (USA) |
| 1913 | W. J. Bailey (UK) |
| 1920 | M. Peeters (NL) |
| 1921 | H.B. Andersen (DNK) |
| 1922 | H. T. Johnson (UK) |
| 1923 | L. Michard (F) |
| 1924 | L. Michard (F) |
| 1925 | Jaap Meijer (NL) |
| 1926 | A. Martinetti (I) |
| 1927 | M. Engel (D) |

| | |
|---|---|
| 1928 | W. F. Hansen (DNK) |
| 1929 | A. Mazairac (NL) |
| 1930 | L. Gerardin (F) |
| 1931 | H. Harder (DNK) |
| 1932 | A. Richter (D) |
| 1933 | J. van Egmond (NL) |
| 1934 | Ben Pola (I) |
| 1935 | T. Merkens (D) |
| 1936 | Arie Van Vliet (NL) |
| 1937 | Van De Vijver (NL) |
| 1938 | Van De Vijver (NL) |
| 1939 | J. Derksen (NL) |
| 1946 | O. Plattner (SWI) |
| 1947 | Reg Harris (UK) |
| 1948 | M. Chella (I) |
| 1949 | S. Patterson (AUS) |
| 1950 | M. Verdeun (F) |
| 1951 | E. Sacchi (I) |
| 1952 | E. Sacchi (I) |
| 1953 | M. Morretini (I) |
| 1954 | G. Peacock (UK) |
| 1955 | Giuseppe Ogna (I) |
| 1956 | M. Rousseau (F) |
| 1957 | M. Rousseau (F) |
| 1958 | V. Gasparella (I) |
| 1959 | V. Gasparella (I) |
| 1960 | S. Gaiardoni (I) |
| 1961 | S. Bianchetto (I) |
| 1962 | S. Bianchetto (I) |
| 1963 | Patrick Sercu (B) |
| 1964 | Pierre Trentin (F) |
| 1965 | Omar Phakadze (USSR) |
| 1966 | Daniel Morelon (F) |
| 1967 | Daniel Morelon (F) |
| 1968 | Luigi Borghetti (I) |
| 1969 | Daniel Morelon (F) |
| 1970 | Daniel Morelon (F) |
| 1971 | Daniel Morelon (F) |
| 1973 | Daniel Morelon (F) |
| 1974 | Anton Tkac (CZ) |
| 1975 | Daniel Morelon (F) |
| 1977 | Hans-Jürgen Geschke (GDR) |
| 1978 | Anton Tkac (CZ) |
| 1979 | Lutz Hesslich (GDR) |
| 1981 | Sergey Kopylov (USSR) |
| 1982 | Sergey Kopylov (USSR) |
| 1983 | Lutz Hesslich (GDR) |
| 1985 | Lutz Hesslich (GDR) |
| 1986 | Michael Hubner (GDR) |
| 1987 | Lutz Hesslich (GDR) |
| 1989 | Bill Huck (GDR) |
| 1990 | Bill Huck (GDR) |
| 1991 | Jens Fiedler (D) |

Most wins: 7, Daniel Morelon (F) 1966–7, 1969–71, 1973, 1975; 4, William Bailey (UK) 1909–11, 1913: 4, Lutz Hesslich (GDR) 1979, 1983, 1985, 1987.

*Daniel Morelon after winning the Amateur Sprint in 1970*

**Amateur 1 km Time-Trial**
*First held 1966. Open to both amateurs and professionals from 1993.*

| | |
|---|---|
| 1966 | Pierre Trentin (F) |
| 1967 | Niels Fredborg (DNK) |
| 1968 | Niels Fredborg (DNK) |
| 1969 | Gianni Sartori (I) |
| 1970 | Niels Fredborg (DNK) |
| 1971 | Eduard Rapp (USSR) |
| 1973 | Janusz Kierzkowski (POL) |
| 1974 | Eduard Rapp (USSR) |
| 1975 | Klaus Grunke (GDR) |
| 1977 | Lothar Thomas (GDR) |
| 1978 | Lothar Thomas (GDR) |
| 1979 | Lothar Thomas (GDR) |
| 1981 | Lothar Thomas (GDR) |
| 1982 | Fredy Schmidtke (FRG) |
| 1983 | Sergey Kopylov (USSR) |
| 1985 | Jens Glucklich (GDR) |
| 1986 | Maik Malchow (GDR) |
| 1987 | Martin Vinnicombe (AUS) |
| 1989 | Jens Glucklich (GDR) |
| 1990 | Aleksandr Kirichenko (CIS) |
| 1991 | José Manuel Moreno (ESP) |

Most wins: 4, Lothar Thomas (GDR) 1977–79, 1981; 3, Niels Fredborg (DNK) 1967–8, 1970.

## Amateur 4 km Pursuit

*First held 1946. Open to both amateurs and professionals from 1993.*

| | |
|---|---|
| 1946 | R. Rioland (F) |
| 1947 | A. Benfenati (I) |
| 1948 | G. Messina (I) |
| 1949 | K. E. Andersen (DNK) |
| 1950 | Sidney Patterson (AUS) |
| 1951 | M. De Rossi (I) |
| 1952 | M. Van Heusden (NL) |
| 1953 | G. Messina (I) |
| 1954 | Leandro Faggin (I) |
| 1955 | Norman Sheil (UK) |
| 1956 | Ercole Baldini (I) |
| 1957 | Carlo Simonigh (I) |
| 1958 | Norman Sheil (UK) |
| 1959 | Rudi Altig (FDR) |
| 1960 | M. Delattre (F) |
| 1961 | Henk Nijdam (NL) |
| 1962 | K. E. Jensen (DNK) |
| 1963 | Jan Walschaerts (B) |
| 1964 | Tiemen Groen (NL) |
| 1965 | Tiemen Groen (NL) |
| 1966 | Tiemen Groen (NL) |
| 1967 | Gert Bongers (NL) |
| 1968 | Mogens Frey (DNK) |
| 1969 | Xavier Kurmann (SWI) |
| 1970 | Xavier Kurmann (SWI) |
| 1971 | Martin-Emilio Rodriguez (COL) |
| 1973 | Knut Knudsen (Norway) |
| 1974 | Hans Lutz (FRG) |
| 1975 | Thomas Huschke (GDR) |
| 1977 | Norbert Durpisch (GDR) |
| 1978 | Detlef Macha (GDR) |
| 1979 | Nikolay Makarov (USSR) |
| 1981 | Detlef Macha (GDR) |
| 1982 | Detlef Macha (GDR) |
| 1983 | Viktor Kupovets (USSR) |
| 1985 | Vyacheslav Yekimov (USSR) |
| 1986 | Vyacheslav Yekimov (USSR) |
| 1987 | Gintautas Umaras (USSR) |
| 1989 | Vyacheslav Yekimov (USSR) |
| 1990 | Yevgeniy Berzhin (USSR) |
| 1991 | Jens Lehmann (D) |

Most wins: 3, Tiemen Groen (NL) 1964–6; 3, Vyacheslav Yekimov (USSR) 1985–86, 1989; 3, Detlef Macha (GDR) 1978, 1981–82.

## Amateur Team Pursuit

*First held 1962. Open to both amateurs and professionals from 1993.*

Most Wins:

| | |
|---|---|
| 8 | Germany: FRG 1962, 1964, 1970 1973–5, |

1983; Germany 1991.

| | |
|---|---|
| 7 | USSR: 1963, 1965, 1967, 1969, 1982, 1987, 1990 |
| 5 | GDR: 1977–9, 1981, 1989 |
| 4 | Italy: 1966, 1968, 1971, 1985 |
| 1 | Czechoslovakia: 1986 |
| 1 | Australia: 1993 |

## Amateur Tandem Sprint

*First held 1966. Open to both amateurs and professionals from 1993.*

| | |
|---|---|
| 1966 | Daniel Morelon & Pierre Trentin (F) |
| 1967 | Verzini & Gonzato (I) |
| 1968 | Gorini & Turrini (I) |
| 1969 | Otto & Geschke (GDR) |
| 1970 | Jürgen Barth & Rainer Müller (FRG) |
| 1971 | Jürgen Geschke & Werner Otto (GDR) |
| 1973 | Vladimir Vackar & Miroslav Vymazal (CZ) |
| 1974 | Vladimir Vackar & Miroslav Vymazal (CZ) |
| 1976 | Benedykt Kocot & Janusz Kotlinski (POL) |
| 1977 | Vladimir Vackar & Miroslav Vymazal (CZ) |
| 1978 | Vladimir Vackar & Miroslav Vymazal (CZ) |
| 1979 | Yave Cahard & Frank Depine (F) |
| 1980 | Vvan Kucirek & Pavel Martinek (CZ) |
| 1981 | Vvan Kucirek & Pavel Martinek (CZ) |
| 1982 | Vvan Kucirek & Pavel Martinek (CZ) |
| 1983 | Philippe Vernet & Frank Depine (F) |
| 1984 | Jürgen Greil & Frank Weber (FRG) |
| 1985 | Vitezlav Voboril & Roman Rehousek (CZ) |
| 1986 | Vitezlav Voboril & Roman Rehousek (CZ) |
| 1987 | Fabrice Colas & Frederic Magne (F) |
| 1988 | Fabrice Colas & Frederic Magne (F) |
| 1989 | Fabrice Colas & Frederic Magne (F) |
| 1990 | Gianluca Capitano & Federico Paris (I) |
| 1991 | Eyk Pokorny & Emanuel Raasch (D) |
| 1992 | Gianluca Capitano & Federico Paris (I) |

Most Wins: 4, Vladimir Vackar & Miroslav Vymazal (CZ) 1973–74, 1977–78.

## Amateur Points Race

*First held 1976. Open to both amateurs and professionals from 1993.*

| | |
|---|---|
| 1976 | Walter Baumgartner (SWI) |
| 1977 | Stan Tourne (B) |
| 1978 | Noel de Jonckheere (B) |
| 1979 | Jiri Slama (CZ) |
| 1980 | Gary Sutton (AUS) |
| 1981 | Lutz Haueisen (GDR) |
| 1982 | Hans-Joachim Pohl (GDR) |
| 1983 | Michael Marcussen (DNK) |
| 1985 | Martin Penc (CZ) |
| 1986 | Dan Frost (DNK) |

| | |
|---|---|
| 1987 | Marat Ganeeyev (USSR) |
| 1989 | Dan Frost (DNK) |
| 1990 | Stephen McGlede (AUS) |
| 1991 | Bruno Risi (SWI) |

**Amateur Motor-Paced**
*Held at 100 km 1893–1914; for one hour 1958–1971; at 50 km from 1972. Open to both amateurs and professionals from 1993.*

| | |
|---|---|
| 1893 | L. S. Meintjies (SA) |
| 1894 | W. Hente (NOR) |
| 1895 | M. Cordang (NL) |
| 1896 | F. Ponscarme (F) |
| 1897 | E. Gould (UK) |
| 1898 | A. J. Cherry (UK) |
| 1899 | J. A. Nelson (USA) |
| 1900 | L. Bastien (F) |
| 1901 | Heinrich Sievers (D) |
| 1902 | A. Goernemann (D) |
| 1903 | E. Audemars (SWI) |
| 1904 | Leon Meredith (UK) |
| 1905 | Leon Meredith (UK) |
| 1906 | M. Bardonneau (F) |
| 1907 | Leon Meredith (UK) |
| 1908 | Leon Meredith (UK) |
| 1909 | Leon Meredith (UK) |
| 1910 | H. Hens (B) |
| 1911 | Leon Meredith (UK) |
| 1913 | Leon Meredith (UK) |
| 1914 | C. Blekemolen (NL) |
| 1958 | Lothar Meister (GDR) |
| 1959 | A. V. Houwelingen (NL) |
| 1960 | Georg Stotze (GDR) |
| 1961 | L. Vandermeulen (NL) |
| 1962 | R. De Loof (B) |
| 1963 | R. De Loof (B) |
| 1964 | J. Oudkerk (NL) |
| 1965 | Miguel Mas (ESP) |
| 1966 | Piet De Wit (NL) |
| 1967 | Piet De Wit (NL) |
| 1968 | Giuseppe Grassi (I) |
| 1969 | Bert Boom (NL) |
| 1970 | Cees Stam (NL) |
| 1971 | Horst Gnas (FRG) |
| 1972 | Horst Gnas (FRG) |
| 1973 | Horst Gnas (FRG) |
| 1974 | Jean Breuer (FRG) |
| 1975 | Gaby Minneboo (NL) |
| 1976 | Gaby Minneboo (NL) |
| 1977 | Gaby Minneboo (NL) |
| 1978 | Rainer Podlesch (GDR) |
| 1979 | Matthe Pronk (NL) |
| 1980 | Gaby Minneboo (NL) |
| 1981 | Matthe Pronk (NL) |
| 1982 | Gaby Minneboo (NL) |
| 1983 | Rainer Podlesch (GDR) |

| | |
|---|---|
| 1984 | Jan de Nijs (NL) |
| 1985 | Roberto Dotti (I) |
| 1986 | Mario Gentili (I) |
| 1987 | Mario Gentili (I) |
| 1988 | Vincenzo Colmartino (I) |
| 1989 | Roland Konigshofer (A) |
| 1990 | Roland Konigshofer (A) |
| 1991 | Roland Konigshofer (A) |
| 1992 | Carsten Podlesch (D) |

Most wins: 7, Leon Meredith (UK) 1904–5, 1907–9, 1911, 1913; 5, Gaby Minneboo (NL) 1975–77, 1980, 1982; 3 Horst Gnas (FRG) 1971–73; 3, Roland Konigshofer (A) 1989–91.

## MEN (OPEN)

*From 1993 most of the track events in the men's Amateur and Professional Class were replaced by men's Open Class events.*

**Sprint**

| | |
|---|---|
| 1993 | Gary Neiwand (AUS) |
| 1994 | Marty Nothstein (USA) |
| 1995 | Darryn Hill (AUS) |

**Individual Pursuit**

| | |
|---|---|
| 1993 | Graeme Obree (UK) |
| 1994 | Chris Boardman (UK) |
| 1995 | Graeme Obree (UK) |

**Points**

| | |
|---|---|
| 1993 | Etienne de Wilde (B) |
| 1994 | Bruno Risi (SWI) |
| 1995 | Silvio Martinelli (I) |

**Keirin**

| | |
|---|---|
| 1993 | Gary Neiwand (AUS) |
| 1994 | Marty Nothstein (USA) |
| 1995 | Frédéric Magne (F) |

**1 km Time-Trial**

| | |
|---|---|
| 1993 | Florian Rousseau (F) |
| 1994 | Florian Rousseau (F) |

**Motor Paced**

| | |
|---|---|
| 1993 | J. Veggerby (DNK) |
| 1994 | Carsten Podlesch (D) |

**Tandem Sprint**

| | |
|---|---|
| 1993 | F. Paris and R. Chiappa (I) |
| 1994 | F. Colas and Frédéric Magne (F) |
| 1995 | *Not held* |

**Madison**
*Held as a 150-lap team race in Colombia in 1995.*

| | |
|---|---|
| 1995 | Silvio Martinello and Marco Villa (I) |

## 4000m Team Pursuit

1993    Australia
1994    Germany
1995    Australia

## Olympic Sprint

*First held as a team event in 1995 in Colombia.*

1995    Denmark

# MEN (PROFESSIONAL)

## Professional Sprint

*Open to both amateurs and professionals from 1993.*

1895    R. Protin (B)
1896    Paul Bourillon (F)
1897    W. Arend (DNK)
1898    G. A. Banker (USA)
1899    Major Taylor (USA)
1900    E. Jacquelin (F)
1901    Thorvald Ellegaard (DNK)
1902    Thorvald Ellegaard (DNK)
1903    Thorvald Ellegaard (DNK)
1904    Y. Lawson (USA)
1905    G. Poulain (F)
1906    Thorvald Ellegaard (DNK)
1907    E. Friol (F)
1908    Thorvald Ellegaard (DNK)
1909    V. Dupre (F)
1910    E. Friol (F)
1911    Thorvald Ellegaard (DNK)
1912    Frank Kramer (USA)
1913    W. Rutt (DNK)
1920    R. Spears (AUS)
1921    Piet Moeskops (NL)
1922    Piet Moeskops (NL)
1923    Piet Moeskops (NL)
1924    Piet Moeskops (NL)
1925    E. Kaufmann (SWI)
1926    Piet Moeskops (NL)
1927    Lucien Michard (F)
1928    Lucien Michard (F)
1929    Lucien Michard (F)
1930    Lucien Michard (F)
1931    W. F. Hansen (DNK)
1932    Jef Scherens (B)
1933    Jef Scherens (B)
1934    Jef Scherens (B)
1935    Jef Scherens (B)
1936    Jef Scherens (B)
1937    Jef Scherens (B)
1938    Arie Van Vliet (NL)
1946    J. Derksen (NL)
1947    Jef Scherens (B)
1948    Arie Van Vliet (NL)
1949    Reg Harris (UK)

1950    Reg Harris (UK)
1951    Reg Harris (UK)
1952    Oscar Plattner (SWI)
1953    Arie Van Vliet (NL)
1954    Reg Harris (UK)
1955    Antonio Maspes (I)
1956    Antonio Maspes (I)
1957    Jan Derksen (NL)
1958    M. Rousseau (F)
1959    Antonio Maspes (I)
1960    Antonio Maspes (I)
1961    Antonio Maspes (I)
1962    Antonio Maspes (I)
1963    Sante Gaiardoni (I)
1964    Antonio Maspes (I)
1965    Giuseppe Beghetto (I)
1966    Giuseppe Beghetto (I)
1967    Patrick Sercu (B)
1968    Giuseppe Beghetto (I)
1969    Patrick Sercu (B)
1970    Gordon Johnson (AUS)
1971    Leijin Loevesijn (NL)
1972    Robert van Lancker (B)
1973    Robert van Lancker (B)
1974    Peder Pedersen (DNK)
1975    John Nicholson (AUS)
1976    John Nicholson (AUS)
1977    Koichi Nakano (JPN)
1978    Koichi Nakano (JPN)
1979    Koichi Nakano (JPN)
1980    Koichi Nakano (JPN)
1981    Koichi Nakano (JPN)

*Koichi Nakano of Japan, seen here in action in 1986*

1982    Koichi Nakano (JPN)
1983    Koichi Nakano (JPN)
1984    Koichi Nakano (JPN)
1985    Koichi Nakano (JPN)
1986    Koichi Nakano (JPN)
1987    Noboyuki Tawara (JPN)
1988    Stephen Pate (AUS)
1989    Claudio Golinelli (I)
1990    Michael Hubner (GDR)
1991    *Left vacant after winner Cary Hall (AUS) failed a drug test*
1992    Michael Hubner (D)

Most wins: 10, Koichi Nakano (JPN) 1977–86; 7, Jef Scherens (B) 1932–7, 1947; 7, Antonio Maspes (I) 1955–6, 1959–62, 1964; 6, Thorvald Ellegaard (DNK) 1901–3, 1906, 1908, 1911; 5, Piet Moeskops (NL) 1921–4, 1926; 4, Lucien Michard (F) 1927–30; Reg Harris (UK) 1949–51, 1954.

## Professional 5 km Pursuit
*First held in 1939 when it was left unfinished due to the outbreak of war, then from 1946. Open to both amateurs and professionals from 1993 over 4000 metres.*

1946    G. Peters (NL)
1947    Fausto Coppi (I)
1948    G. Schulte (NL)
1949    Fausto Coppi (I)
1950    A. Bevilacqua (I)
1951    A. Bevilacqua (I)
1952    S. Patterson (AUS)
1953    S. Patterson (AUS)
1954    Guido Massina (I)
1955    Guido Massina (I)
1956    Guido Massina (I)
1957    Roger Rivière (F)
1958    Roger Rivière (F)
1959    Roger Rivière (F)
1960    Rudi Altig (FDR)
1961    Rudi Altig (FDR)
1962    Henk Nijdam (NL)
1963    Leandro Faggin (I)
1964    Ferdinand Bracke (B)
1965    Leandro Faggin (I)
1966    Leandro Faggin (I)
1967    Tiemen Groen (NL)
1968    Hugh Porter (UK)
1969    Ferdinand Bracke (B)
1970    Hugh Porter (UK)
1971    Dirk Baert (B)
1972    Hugh Porter (UK)
1973    Hugh Porter (UK)
1974    Roy Schuiten (NL)
1975    Roy Schuiten (NL)
1976    Francesco Moser (I)
1977    Gregor Braun (FRG)

*At the age of 28 Hugh Porter became the first British rider to win the professional pursuit when he beat Ole Ritter in the final of the 1968 World Championships in Rome*

1978    Gregor Braun (FRG)
1979    Bert Osterbosch (NL)
1980    Tony Doyle (UK)
1981    Alain Bondue (F)
1982    Alain Bondue (F)
1983    Steele Bishop (AUS)
1984    Hans-Henrik Oersted (DNK)
1985    Hans-Henrik Oersted (DNK)
1986    Tony Doyle (UK)
1987    Hans-Henrik Oersted (DNK)
1988    Lech Piasecki (POL)
1989    Colin Sturgess (UK)
1990    Vyacheslav Yekimov (CIS)
1991    Francis Moreau (F)
1992    Mike McCarthy (USA)

Most wins: 4, Hugh Porter (UK) 1968, 1970, 1972–3; 3, Guido Massina (I) 1954–6; Roger Rivière (F) 1957–9; Leando Faggin (I) 1963, 1965–6; Hans-Henrik Oersted (DNK) 1984–85, 1987.

## Professional Keirin
*First held 1980. Open to both amateurs and professionals from 1993.*

1980    Danny Clark (AUS)
1981    Danny Clark (AUS)
1982    Gordon Singleton (CDN)
1983    Urs Freuler (SWI)
1984    Robert Dill-Bundi (SWI)
1985    Urs Freuler (SWI)
1986    Michel Vaarten (B)

| | |
|---|---|
| 1987 | Harumi Honda (JPN) |
| 1988 | *Left vacant after winner Claudio Golinelli (I) failed drugs test* |
| 1989 | Claudio Golinelli (I) |
| 1990 | Michael Hubner (D) |
| 1991 | Michael Hubner (D) |
| 1992 | Michael Hubner (D) |

**Most wins:** 3, Michael Hubner (D) 1990–92.

## Professional Points Race
*First held 1980. Open to both amateurs and professionals from 1993.*

| | |
|---|---|
| 1980 | Stan Tourne (B) |
| 1981 | Urs Freuler (SWI) |
| 1982 | Urs Freuler (SWI) |
| 1983 | Urs Freuler (SWI) |
| 1984 | Urs Freuler (SWI) |
| 1985 | Urs Freuler (SWI) |
| 1986 | Urs Freuler (SWI) |
| 1987 | Urs Freuler (SWI) |
| 1988 | Daniel Wyder (SWI) |
| 1989 | Urs Freuler (SWI) |
| 1990 | Laurent Biondi (F) |
| 1991 | Vyacheslav Yekimov (USSR) |
| 1992 | Bruno Risi (SWI) |

**Most wins:** 8, Urs Freuler (SWI) 1981–87, 1989.

## Professional Motor-Paced
*First held 1895. At 100 km 1895–1971; over one hour from 1972. Open to both amateurs and professionals from 1993.*

| | |
|---|---|
| 1895 | J. Michael (UK) |
| 1896 | Arthur Chase (UK) |
| 1897 | J. W. Stocks (UK) |
| 1898 | R. Palmer (UK) |
| 1899 | H. Gibson (UK) |
| 1900 | C. Huret (F) |
| 1901 | T. Robel (D) |
| 1902 | T. Robel (D) |
| 1903 | P. Dickentman (NL) |
| 1904 | R. A. Walthour (USA) |
| 1905 | R. A. Walthour (USA) |
| 1906 | L. Darragon (F) |
| 1907 | L. Darragon (F) |
| 1908 | F. Ryser (SWI) |
| 1909 | G. Parent (F) |
| 1910 | G. Parent (F) |
| 1911 | G. Parent (F) |
| 1912 | G. Wiley (USA) |
| 1913 | P. Guignard (F) |
| 1920 | G. Seres (F) |
| 1921 | Victor Linart (B) |
| 1922 | L. Vanderstuyft (B) |
| 1923 | P. Suter (SWI) |
| 1924 | Victor Linart (B) |
| 1925 | R. Grassin (F) |

| | |
|---|---|
| 1926 | Victor Linart (B) |
| 1927 | Victor Linart (B) |
| 1928 | W. Sawall (D) |
| 1929 | G. Paillard (F) |
| 1930 | E. Moeller (D) |
| 1931 | W. Sawall (D) |
| 1932 | G. Paillard (F) |
| 1933 | C. Lazquehay (F) |
| 1934 | E. Metze (D) |
| 1935 | C. Lazquehay (F) |
| 1936 | A. Raynaud (F) |
| 1937 | W. Lohmann (D) |
| 1938 | E. Metze (D) |
| 1946 | E. Frosto (I) |
| 1947 | R. Lesueur (F) |
| 1948 | J. J. Lamboley (F) |
| 1949 | E. Frosio (I) |
| 1950 | R. Lesueur (F) |
| 1951 | Jan Pronk (NL) |
| 1952 | A. Verschueren (B) |
| 1953 | A. Verschueren (B) |
| 1954 | A. Verschueren (B) |
| 1955 | Guillermo Timoner (ESP) |
| 1956 | Graham French (AUS) |
| 1957 | Paul Depaepe (B) |
| 1958 | Walther Bucher (SWI) |
| 1959 | Guillermo Timoner (ESP) |
| 1960 | Guillermo Timoner (ESP) |
| 1961 | K. H. Marsell (D) |
| 1962 | Guillermo Timoner (ESP) |
| 1963 | Leo Proost (B) |
| 1964 | Guillermo Timoner (ESP) |
| 1965 | Guillermo Timoner (ESP) |
| 1966 | Roman De Loof (B) |
| 1967 | Leo Proost (B) |
| 1968 | Leo Proost (B) |
| 1969 | Jaap Oudkerk (NL) |
| 1970 | Ehrenfried Rudolph (FRG) |
| 1971 | Theo Verschueren (B) |
| 1972 | Theo Verschueren (B) |
| 1973 | Cees Stam (NL) |
| 1974 | Cees Stam (NL) |
| 1975 | Dieter Kemper (FRG) |
| 1976 | Wilfried Peffgen (FRG) |
| 1977 | Cees Stam (NL) |
| 1978 | Wilfried Peffgen (FRG) |
| 1979 | Martin Venix (NL) |
| 1980 | Wilfried Peffgen (FRG) |
| 1981 | René Kos (NL) |
| 1982 | Martin Venix (NL) |
| 1983 | Bruno Vicini (I) |
| 1984 | Horst Schutz (FRG) |
| 1985 | Bruno Vicini (I) |
| 1986 | Bruno Vicini (I) |
| 1987 | Max Hurtzler (SWI) |
| 1988 | Danny Clark (AUS) |

| | | |
|---|---|---|
| 1989 | Giovanni Renosto (I) | |
| 1990 | Walter Brugna (I) | |
| 1991 | Danny Clark (AUS) | |
| 1992 | Peter Steiger (SWI) | |

Most wins: 6, Guillermo Timoner (ESP) 1955, 1959–60, 1962, 1964–5; 4, Victor Linart (B) 1921, 1924, 1926–7.

## WOMEN (OPEN)

**Women's Sprint**
*First held 1958.*

| | |
|---|---|
| 1958 | Galina Yermoleyeva (USSR) |
| 1959 | Galina Yermoleyeva (USSR) |
| 1960 | Galina Yermoleyeva (USSR) |
| 1961 | Galina Yermoleyeva (USSR) |
| 1962 | V. Savina (USSR) |
| 1963 | Galina Yermoleyeva (USSR) |
| 1964 | Irina Kiritchenko (USSR) |
| 1965 | V. Savina (USSR) |
| 1966 | Irina Kiritchenko (USSR) |
| 1967 | V. Savina (USSR) |
| 1968 | Baguinlantz (USSR) |
| 1969 | Galina Tsareva (USSR) |
| 1970 | Galina Tsareva (USSR) |
| 1971 | Galina Tsareva (USSR) |
| 1972 | Galina Yermoleyeva (USSR) |
| 1973 | Sheila Young (USA) |
| 1974 | Tamara Piltsikova (USSR) |
| 1975 | Sue Novarra (USA) |
| 1976 | Sheila Young (USA) |
| 1977 | Galina Tsareva (USSR) |
| 1978 | Galina Tsareva (USSR) |
| 1979 | Galina Tsareva (USSR) |
| 1980 | Sue Reber *née Novarra* (USA) |
| 1981 | Sheila Ochowitz *née Young* (USA) |
| 1982 | Connee Paraskevin (USA) |
| 1983 | Connee Paraskevin (USA) |
| 1984 | Connee Paraskevin (USA) |
| 1985 | Isabelle Nicoloso (F) |
| 1986 | Christa Rothenburger (GDR) |
| 1987 | Erika Salumyae (USSR) |
| 1989 | Erika Salumyae (USSR) |
| 1990 | Connie Young-Paraskevin (USA) |
| 1991 | Ingrid Haringa (NL) |

*Uniquely, Jeannie Longo (France) won three world championship events in one year in 1989, when she won the women's road race, women's 30 km points and women's 3 km pursuit.*

*Three women's cycling world champions – Beth Heiden (USA), Sheila Young (USA) and Christa Rothenburger (GDR) – have also been world champions at speed skating.*

| | |
|---|---|
| 1992 | *Not held* |
| 1993 | Tanya Dubnifoff (CDN) |
| 1994 | Galina Eniovkhina (RUS) |
| 1995 | Felicia Ballanger (F) |

Most wins: 6, Galina Yermoleyeva (USSR) 1958–61, 1963, 1972; Galina Tsareva (USSR) 1969–71, 1977–79.

**Women's 3 km Pursuit**

| | |
|---|---|
| 1958 | L. Kotchetova (USSR) |
| 1959 | Beryl Burton (UK) |
| 1960 | Beryl Burton (UK) |
| 1961 | Yvon Reynders (B) |
| 1962 | Beryl Burton (UK) |
| 1963 | Beryl Burton (UK) |
| 1964 | Yvon Reynders (B) |
| 1965 | Yvon Reynders (B) |
| 1966 | Beryl Burton (UK) |
| 1967 | T. Garkuskina (USSR) |
| 1968 | R. Obodovskaya (USSR) |
| 1969 | R. Obodovskaya (USSR) |
| 1970 | Tamara Garkushina (USSR) |
| 1971 | Tamara Garkushina (USSR) |
| 1972 | Tamara Garkushina (USSR) |
| 1973 | Tamara Garkushina (USSR) |
| 1974 | Tamara Garkushina (USSR) |
| 1975 | Keetie van Oosten-Hage (NL) |
| 1976 | Keetie van Oosten-Hage (NL) |
| 1977 | Vera Kuznetsova (USSR) |
| 1978 | Keetie van Oosten-Hage (NL) |
| 1979 | Keetie van Oosten-Hage (NL) |
| 1980 | Nadezhda Kibardina (USSR) |
| 1981 | Nadezhda Kibardina (USSR) |
| 1982 | Rebecca Twigg (USA) |
| 1983 | Connie Carpenter (USA) |
| 1984 | Rebecca Twigg (USA) |
| 1985 | Rebecca Twigg (USA) |
| 1986 | Jeannie Longo (F) |
| 1987 | Rebecca Twigg (USA) |
| 1988 | Jeannie Longo (F) |
| 1989 | Jeannie Longo (F) |
| 1990 | Leontien van Moorsel (NL) |
| 1991 | Petra Rossner (D) |
| 1992 | *Not held* |
| 1993 | Rebecca Twigg (USA) |
| 1994 | Marion Clignet (F) |
| 1995 | Rebecca Twigg (USA) |

Most wins: 6, Tamara Garkushina (USSR) 1967, 1970–4; 6, Rebecca Twigg (USA) 1982, 1984–85, 1987, 1993, 1995; 5, Beryl Burton (UK) 1959–60, 1962–3, 1966; 4, Keetie van Oosten-Hage (NL) 1975–76, 1978–79.

**Women's 30 km Points**

| | |
|---|---|
| 1988 | Sally Hodge (UK) *Demonstration event* |
| 1989 | Jeannie Longo (F) |

*American rider Rebecca Twigg won the women's pursuit six times between 1982 and 1995*

| | |
|---|---|
| 1990 | Karen Holliday (NZ) |
| 1991 | Ingrid Haringa (NL) |
| 1992 | Ingrid Haringa (NL) |
| 1993 | Ingrid Haringa (NL) |
| 1994 | Ingrid Haringa (NL) |
| 1995 | Svetlana Samokhvalova (RUS) |

Most wins: 4, Ingrid Haringa (NL) 1991–94.

### Women's 50 km Team-Trial
*Last held in 1994.*

| | |
|---|---|
| 1987 | USSR |
| 1988 | Italy |
| 1989 | USSR |
| 1990 | Holland |
| 1991 | France |
| 1992 | USA |
| 1993 | Russia |
| 1994 | Russia |

### Women's 500m
*First held in 1995 in Colombia.*

| | |
|---|---|
| 1995 | Felicia Ballanger (F) |

## JUNIOR

### Sprint

| | |
|---|---|
| 1975 | Oattavio Dazzan (ARG) |
| 1976 | Lutz Hesslich (GDR) |
| 1977 | Lutz Hesslich (GDR) |
| 1978 | Serge Kopilov (USSR) |
| 1979 | Fred Schmidtke (D) |
| 1980 | Maic Malchow (GDR) |

| | |
|---|---|
| 1981 | Olof Arndt (GDR) |
| 1982 | Nikolai Kovche (USSR) |
| 1983 | Takashi Seiko (JPN) |
| 1984 | Michael Schulze (GDR) |
| 1985 | Oleg Borzunov (USSR) |
| 1986 | Denis Lemyre (F) |
| 1987 | Eyk Pokorny (GDR) |
| 1988 | Jens Fiedler (GDR) |
| 1989 | Gianluca Capitano (I) |
| 1990 | Ainars Kikis (RUS) |
| 1991 | Roberto Chiappa (I) |
| 1992 | Ivan Quaranta (I) |
| 1993 | Michael Scheurer (D) |
| 1994 | Julio Herrera (CUBA) |
| 1995 | René Wolff (D) |

### 1000m Time-Trial

| | |
|---|---|
| 1977 | R. Honisch (GDR) |
| 1978 | Frank Micke (GDR) |
| 1979 | Fred Schmidtke (FDR) |
| 1980 | Maic Malchow (GDR) |
| 1981 | Marc Alexandre (ARG) |
| 1982 | Andreas Ganske (FDR) |
| 1983 | Allan Miller (NZ) |
| 1984 | Jens Glucklich (GDR) |
| 1985 | Silvio Boarin (I) |
| 1986 | Vladimir Soultanov (USSR) |
| 1987 | Ronny Kirchhoff (GDR) |
| 1988 | Kai Melcher (GDR) |
| 1989 | Konstantin Smurigny (RUS) |
| 1990 | Aleksej Khromykh (RUS) |
| 1991 | Laurent Accart (F) |

| | | | | |
|---|---|---|---|---|
| 1992 | Florian Rousseau (F) | | 1979 | USSR |
| 1993 | Michael Scheurer (D) | | 1980 | USSR |
| 1994 | Jan Van Eijden (NL) | | 1981 | USSR |
| 1995 | Joshua Kersten (AUS) | | 1982 | USSR |
| | | | 1983 | Denmark |

**Individual Pursuit**

| | | | | |
|---|---|---|---|---|
| 1975 | Robert Dill-Bundi (SWI) | | 1984 | USSR |
| 1976 | Robert Dill-Bundi (SWI) | | 1985 | GDR |
| 1977 | Hans J. Pohl (GDR) | | 1986 | USSR |
| 1978 | Axel Grosser (GDR) | | 1987 | USSR |
| 1979 | Gadis Lapinch (USSR) | | 1988 | USSR |
| 1980 | Dainis Lapinch (USSR) | | 1989 | USSR |
| 1981 | Reinhardt Alber (D) | | 1990 | Russia |
| 1982 | Carsten Wolf (GDR) | | 1991 | Russia |
| 1983 | Dean Woods (AUS) | | 1992 | Russia |
| 1984 | Dean Woods (AUS) | | 1993 | Germany |
| 1985 | Arturas Kasputis (USSR) | | 1994 | Australia |
| 1986 | Sergei Vodopianov (USSR) | | 1995 | Australia |
| 1987 | Jevgenij Anashin (USSR) | | | |
| 1988 | Dimitri Neljubin (USSR) | | | |
| 1989 | Dimitri Neljubin (RUS) | | | |

**Team Time-Trial**

| | | | | |
|---|---|---|---|---|
| 1990 | Vassili Jakovlev (RUS) | | 1975 | USSR |
| 1991 | Roman Saprykine (RUS) | | 1976 | Italy |
| 1992 | Roman Saprykine (RUS) | | 1977 | GDR |
| 1993 | Bradley McGee (AUS) | | 1978 | GDR |
| 1994 | Bradley McGee (AUS) | | 1979 | USSR |
| 1995 | Luke Roberts (AUS) | | 1980 | USSR |
| | | | 1981 | GDR |

**Points**

| | | | | |
|---|---|---|---|---|
| 1975 | Henri Rinklin (FDR) | | 1982 | GDR |
| 1976 | Rudiger Leitlof (FDR) | | 1983 | Denmark |
| 1977 | Miroslav Junek (CZ) | | 1984 | USSR |
| 1978 | Ken De Maerteleire (B) | | 1985 | Italy |
| 1979 | Ten Van Vliet (NL) | | 1986 | Italy |
| 1980 | Uwe Messerschmidt (D) | | 1987 | Italy |
| 1981 | Fabio Lana (I) | | 1988 | Italy |
| 1982 | Mauro Ribeiro (BRA) | | 1989 | Italy |
| 1983 | Andreas Kapes (FDR) | | 1990 | Russia |
| 1984 | Vjatcheslav Ekimov (USSR) | | 1991 | Russia |
| 1985 | Robert Waller (AUS) | | 1992 | Italy |
| 1986 | Stefan Steinweg (FDR) | | 1993 | Italy |
| 1987 | Marcel Beumer (NL) | | 1994-95 | *Not held* |
| 1988 | Andreas Beikirch (FDR) | | | |
| 1989 | Dimitri Neljubin (USSR) | | | |

**Women's Individual Pursuit**

| | | | | |
|---|---|---|---|---|
| 1990 | Aleksandr Zaitsev (RUS) | | 1987 | Jane Eickhoff (USA) |
| 1991 | Aleksej Ivankin (RUS) | | 1988 | Catherine Marsal (F) |
| 1992 | Bernard Panton (AUS) | | 1989 | Svetlana Samochvalova (RUS) |
| 1993 | Thorsten Rund (D) | | 1990 | Elena Tchalykhe (RUS) |
| 1994 | Marion Perez (COL) | | 1991 | Jessica Grieco (USA) |
| 1995 | Cristian Leon (ARG) | | 1992 | Hanka Kupfernagel (D) |
| | | | 1993 | Marina Jongeling (NL) |
| | | | 1994 | Sarah Ulmer (NZ) |
| | | | 1995 | Narelle Peterson (AUS) |

**Team Pursuit**

**Women's Sprint**

| | | | | |
|---|---|---|---|---|
| 1975 | USSR | | 1987 | Jane Eickhoff (USA) |
| 1976 | GDR | | 1988 | Felicia Ballanger (F) |
| 1977 | GDR | | 1989 | Magali Humbert (F) |
| 1978 | USSR | | 1990 | Katrin Freitag (GDR) |

| 1991 | Katrin Freitag (D) |
|------|--------------------|
| 1992 | Katrin Freitag (D) |
| 1993 | Ina Heineman (D) |
| 1994 | Ina Heineman (D) |
| 1995 | Roberta Passoni (ITA) |

**Women's Points**

| 1989 | Svetlana Samochvalova (USSR) |
|------|------------------------------|
| 1990 | I. Y. Teutenberg (FRG) |

| 1991 | Hanka Kupfernagel (D) |
|------|-----------------------|
| 1992 | I. Y. Teutenberg (D) |
| 1993 | Maria Jongeling (NL) |
| 1994 | Sarah Ulmer (NZ) |
| 1995 | Jet Jongeling (AUS) |

**Women's 500m Time-Trial**

| 1995 | Roberta Passoni (ITA) |
|------|-----------------------|

# INTERNATIONAL SPEED RECORDS

In 1993 the UCI opted to make a profound simplification of the existing world record system, by radically reducing the number of categories from a previous total of 94 to just 20 Absolute World Records which included Men's, Women's, One hour and Junior categories. All other world records as recorded by the UCI have therefore been frozen in time. In the same year the UCI also removed the distinction between professionals and amateurs by creating an Open class, as well as removing the distinction between open and covered tracks. Absolute world records are given as recognised by the UCI at the end of 1995.

## MEN

### Standing Start Absolute World Records

| Event | min:sec | Cyclist | Location | Date |
|-------|---------|---------|----------|------|
| 1 km | 1:00.613 | Shane Kelly (AUS) | Bogota | 26/09/95 |
| 4 km | 4:20.894 | Graeme Obree (UK) | Hamar | 19/08/93 |
| 4 km | 4:03.840 | Australia | Hamar | 20/08/93 |
| (Team) | | (Brett Aitken | | |
| | | Stuart O'Grady | | |
| | | Tim O'Shanessy | | |
| | | Billy Joe Shearsby) | | |

### Pre-1993 world records

| 5 km | 5:38.08 | Chris Boardman (UK) | Leicester | 22/08/93 |
|------|---------|---------------------|-----------|----------|
| 10 km | 11:31.968 | V. Yekimov (USSR) | Moscow | 07/04/90 |
| 20 km | 23:14.553 | V. Yekimov (USSR) | Moscow | 03/02/89 |
| 100 km | 2 hr 09:11.312 | Kent Bostich (USA) | Colorado Springs | 13/10/89 |

### Flying Start Absolute World Records

| 200m | 9.865 | Curt Harnett (CDN) | Bogota | 28/09/95 |
|------|-------|--------------------|---------|----------|
| 500m | 26.649 | A. Kiritchenko (USSR) | Moscow | 29/10/88 |

### Pre-1993 world records

| 1 km | 57.260 | A. Kiritchenko (USSR) | Moscow | 25/04/89 |
|------|--------|-----------------------|--------|----------|

### 1 Hour Absolute World Record

| 1 hr | 55.291 km | Tony Rominger (SWI) | Bordeaux | 05/11/94 |
|------|-----------|---------------------|----------|----------|

### Motor Paced Pre-1993 world records

| 50 km | 32:56.746 | A. Romanov (USSR) | Moscow | 21/02/87 |
|-------|-----------|-------------------|--------|----------|
| 100 km | 1 hr 05:58.031 | A. Romanov (USSR) | Moscow | 21/02/87 |
| 1 hr | 91.131 km | A. Romanov (USSR) | Moscow | 21/02/87 |

*In 1992 Chris Boardman set a new 5km world record at the British Track Championships in Leicester*

## WOMEN

**Standing Start Absolute world records**

| | | | | |
|---|---|---|---|---|
| 500m | 34.017 | Felica Ballanger (F) | Bogota | 29/09/95 |
| 3 km | 3:36.081 | Rebecca Twigg (USA) | Bogota | 30/09/95 |

**Pre-1993 world records**

| | | | | |
|---|---|---|---|---|
| 1 km | 1:11.708 | Isabelle Nicoloso (F) | Bordeaux | 17/11/91 |
| 5 km | 6:14.135 | Jeannie Longo (F) | Mexico City | 27/09/89 |
| 10 km | 12:54.260 | Jeannie Longo (F) | Paris/Bercy | 19/10/89 |
| 20 km | 26:51.222 | Jeannie Longo (F) | Moscow | 29/10/89 |
| 100 km | 2 hr 24:57.618 | T. Vikstedt-Myman (FIN) | Moscow | 30/10/90 |

**Flying Start Absolute world records**

| | | | | |
|---|---|---|---|---|
| 200m | 0:10.831 | Olga Sliossareva (USSR) | Moscow | 25/04/93 |
| 500m | 0:29.655 | Erika Salumyae (USSR) | Moscow | 06/08/87 |

**Pre-1993 world records**

| | | | | |
|---|---|---|---|---|
| 1 km | 1:05.23 | Erika Salumyae (USSR) | Moscow | 31/05/87 |

**1 Hour Absolute world record**

| | | | | |
|---|---|---|---|---|
| 1 hr | 47.411 km | Yvonne McGregor (UK) | Manchester | 17/06/95 |

## JUNIOR MEN

**Standing Start Absolute world records**

| | | | | |
|---|---|---|---|---|
| 1 km | 1:04.586 | Florian Rousseau (F) | Athens | 14/09/92 |
| 3 km | 3:19.878 | Bradley McGee (AUS) | Adelaide | 07/03/94 |
| 4 km | 4:16.567 | Australia | Adelaide | 10/03/94 |
| (Team) | | (Bradley McGee | | |
| | | Ian Christison | | |
| | | Kris Denham | | |
| | | Scott McGrath) | | |

**Flying Start Absolute world records**

| | | | | |
|---|---|---|---|---|
| 200m | 10.236 | V. Dolguinov (USSR) | Moscow | 01/08/90 |
| 500m | 26.969 | A. Khromikhe (USSR) | Moscow | 01/08/90 |

## JUNIOR WOMEN

**Standing Start Absolute world records**

| | | | | |
|---|---|---|---|---|
| 500m | 36.035 | Nancy Contreras (MEX) | Bogota | 29/09/95 |
| 2 km | 2:25.279 | Hanka Kupfernagel (D) | Athens | 14/09/92 |

**Flying Start Absolute world records**

| | | | | |
|---|---|---|---|---|
| 200m | 11.291 | Ian Heinemann (D) | Quito | 27/07/94 |
| 500m | 30.230 | Svetlana Potemkina (RUS) | Moscow | 29/10/91 |

# THE ONE-HOUR RECORD

*Francesco Moser adopted the Obree tucked position – which was later banned – for his comeback attempt in 1994*

The world hour record is one of the most exclusive titles in the international cycling calendar, and is measured by the distance that can be cycled from a standing start without outside assistance in one hour. Attempts are usually held on an indoor banked track. In recent times, efforts have required minute preparation and the design and construction of specialist bikes. Surprisingly, most of the great names in the world hour record role of honour have been road racers rather than track specialists, whose other achievements have included winning the major Tours and Classics.

## The Record Breakers

The earliest recorded hour-breaker was F.L. Dodds who achieved 25.508 km (15.85 miles) at Cambridge University Ground, Cambridge, England on 25 March 1876. However the first official hour record was 35.525 km, set by Henri Desgrange in Paris on 11 May 1893. He had only learned to ride a bicycle the previous year, and went on to found the Tour de France in 1903. The coloured rider Willie Hamilton was the first to take the record past 40 km when he set a new distance of 40.781 km at Denver on 9 July 1898.

■ In more recent times Eddy Merckx capped his career by taking the hour record on 25 October 1972, after his best-ever season in which he won five classics (Milan–San Remo, followed by Ghent–Wevelgem, Liège–Bastogne–Liège, Flèche Wallonne and Tour of Lombardy) and two major stage races (Tour de France and Giro d'Italia) with 50 road wins to his credit.

■ Francesco Moser took the record past 50 kilometres riding on a high-altitude course in Mexico where he covered 50.808 km on 19 January 1984, increasing the distance to 51.181 km with a second attempt on 23 January 1984. The hour record was next broken almost ten years later, twice by British riders in 1993. The Scottish rider Graeme Obree set a new distance of 51.596 km at a covered track at Hamar in Norway on 17 July. Obree was the first amateur to take the record since Ercole Bandini of Italy in 1933. He rode a bike of his own design and construction, using bearings taken from a washing machine and featuring the hunched 'Obree position' in which the rider's hands are pulled back level with his shoulders. Obree's non-conventional approach angered the riding establishment, and his riding position was later banned by the UCI as 'unsafe'. Less than a week after Obree's success, the British 4000m individual pursuit gold medallist Chris Boardman raised the distance by 674 metres to 52.270 km at Bordeaux Lac on 23 July. At the time he was also an amateur.

## The 1994 Records

In 1994 Francesco Moser emerged from retirement to attempt to win back his record at the age of 43. He went further than Obree, but failed to reach Boardman's record. However, later the same year the hour record fell four times on the Bordeaux Lac track. First Graeme Obree won it back with a new distance of 52.713 km at Bordeaux on 27 April. Then Miguel Indurain raised the distance to 53.040 km on the same track. His record was set on 2 September, just over a month after winning his fourth Tour de France.

■ Two months later, on 3 November, the three times Tour of Spain winner Tony Rominger raised the record to 53.832 km on the same track, and then on 5 November extended the distance to an unprecedented 55.291 km. Unlike Boardman and Indurain who both used monocoque carbon bikes, he used a steel-frame bike which was at least fairly conventional in appearance. Rominger set his record by the greatest margin in modern times, only exceeded by Jules Dubois of France in 1894. He lapped the track at an average 65.11 seconds per kilometre, finishing 3.021 km ahead of Boardman and 2.251 km ahead of Indurain. Had the three riders been on the track at the same time, Rominger would have lapped Boardman every five minutes and Indurain every six. At the end of the hour Boardman would have been 12 laps behind, and Indurain nine laps behind. It was widely predicted that Rominger's new record would stand for many years to come. Indurain attempted to beat it at high altitude on the open-air track used for the 1995 World Championships in Colombia, but abandoned his attempt at the halfway stage due to adverse wind and an early morning chill. At 28 kilometres he was 53 seconds behind Rominger's record.

## World Hour Record-Holders – Men

*Paris – Buffalo*
1893    Henri Desgrange (F) 35.325 km (21.95 miles)
1894    Jules Dubois (F) 38.220 km (23.747 miles) + 2.895 km

*Paris – Cipale*
1897    Oscar van den Eynde (B) 39.240 km (24.383 miles) + 1.020 km

*Denver – Colorado*
1898    Willie Hamilton (USA) 40.781 km (25.340 miles) + 1.541 km

*Graeme Obree's 1993 bike used old washing-machine bearings*

*Paris – Buffalo*
1905    Lucien Petit-Breton (F) 41.110 km (25.545 miles) + 0.329 km
1907    Marcel Berthet (F) 41.520 km (25.799 miles) + 0.410 km
1912    Oscar Egg (SWI) 42.360 km (26.321 miles) + 0.840 km
1913    Marcel Berthet (F) 42.741 km (26.558 miles) + 0.381 km
1913    Oscar Egg (SWI) 43.525 km (27.045 miles) + 0.784 km
1913    Marcel Berthet (F) 43.775 km (27.200 miles) + 0.250 km
1914    Oscar Egg (SWI) 44.247 km (27.494 miles) + 0.472 km

*St Trond – Belgium*
1933    Maurice Richard (F) 44.777 km (27.823 miles) + 0.530 km

*Milan – Vigorelli*
1935    Guiseppe Olmo (I) 45.090 km (28.012 miles) + 0.313 km
1936    Maurice Richard (F) 45.398 km (28.209 miles) + 0.308 km
1937    Frans Slaats (NL) 45.558 km (28.308 miles) + 0.160 km
1937    Maurice Archambaud (F)  45.840 km (28.484 miles) + 0.282 km
1942    Fausto Coppi (I) 45.871 km (28.503 miles) + 0.031 km
1956    Jacques Anquetil (F) 46.159 km (28.282 miles) + 0.288 km

1956    Ercole Baldini (I) 46.393 km (28.827 miles) + 0.234 km

1957    Roger Rivière (F) 46.923 km (29.157 miles) + 0.530 km

1958    Roger Rivière (F) 47.346 km (29.419 miles) + 0.423 km

*Rome – Olympic*
1967    Ferdinand Bracke (B) 48.093 km (29.884 miles) + 0.747 km

*Mexico – Olympic*
1968    Ole Ritter (D) 48.653 km (30.232 miles) + 0.560 km

1972    Eddy Merckx (B) 49.431 km (30.715 miles) + 0.778 km

*Mexico – Municipal*
1984    Francesco Moser (I) 50.808 km (31.571 miles) +1.377 km

1984    Francesco Moser (I) 51.151 km (31.784 miles) +0.343 km

*Hamar – Norway*
1993    Graeme Obree (GB) 51.596 km (32.060 miles) + 0.445 km

*Bordeaux – Lac*
1993    Chris Boardman (GB) 52.270 km (32.479 miles) + 0.674 km

1994    Graeme Obree (GB) 52.713 km (32.754 miles) + 0.443 km

1994    Miguel Indurain (E) 53.040 km (32.957 miles) + 0.770 km

1994    Tony Rominger (SWI) 53.832 km (33.449 miles) + 0.792 km

1994    Tony Rominger (SWI) 55.291 km (34.356 miles) + 1.459 km

# World Hour Record-Holders – Women

Yvonne McGregor (UK) set a new women's one-hour record of 47.411 kilometres at the Manchester velodrome on 17 June 1995. The 34-year-old from Bradford became the fourth British rider to break the toughest record in bike racing, and the first ever to break the record at a British velodrome. She improved on the previous record by 299 metres, despite being 25 seconds down at the 25-kilometre mark. She used a Level 4 frame built with Reynolds 853 oval tubing by Terry Dolan, and Corima disc wheels. The bike was fitted with an SRM Powercrank computer which recorded her power output, heart rate, pedal revs and speed throughout the attempt.

*The Swiss rider Tony Rominger smashed the hour record on 5 November 1994*

## Women's Records
*Irkustsk*
1955    Tamara Novikova (USSR)   38.473 km (23.907 miles)

*Milan – Vigorelli*
1958    Renée Vissac (F) 38.569 km (23.966 miles) + 0.096 km

1958    Millie Robinson (UK) 39.718 km (24.680 miles) + 1.149 km

1958    Elsie Jacobs (LUX) 41.347 km (25.693 miles) + 1.629 km

*Munich*
1979    Keetie van Oosten (NL)   43.082km (26.771 miles) + 1.735 km

*Milan – Vigorelli*
1986    Jeannie Longo (F) 43.587 km (27.084 miles) + 0.505 km

*Mexico City*
1989    Jeannie Longo (F) 46.352 km (28.803 miles) + 2.765 km
        (Jeannie Longo also achieved 44.770 km and 44.9 km at the high-level Mexico City track before sea-level and altitude records were unified in 1993.)

*Bordeaux*
1995    Catherine Marsal (F) 47.112 km (29.275 miles) + 0.76 km
*Manchester*
1995    Yvonne McGregor (UK) 47.411 km (29.461 miles) + 0.299 km

# The Great Road Events

## THE WORLD ROAD RACE CHAMPIONSHIPS

The world professional road race championships are held in a different location every year, and are equal in status to the great Classic one-day races with the winning rider wearing the coveted rainbow jersey for the following season. The race format is usually 15–20 laps of a circuit in the region of 15 km long, and tactics can be complicated by the fact that normal professional team loyalties are supplemented by loyalties to national squads.

■ The first world professional road race championship was held in 1927 on the Nürburgring in Germany. The 182 km race was won by Alfredo Binda, the first of his three world championship wins – he also won in 1930 and 1932. Rik Van Steenbergen (Belgium) also won the world championship three times in 1949, 1956 and 1957, as did Eddy Merckx in 1967, 1971 and 1974. Greg LeMond won twice in 1983 and 1989, and Gianni Bugno twice in 1991 and 1992.

■ The only Briton to ever win the World Professional Road Race rainbow jersey was Tommy Simpson, who outsprinted Rudi Altig in an exciting finish in 1965. The next best result belongs to the Scottish rider Robert Millar who was sixth in 1984. The most successful man has been Greg LeMond, winner of the professional road race in 1983 and 1989, a title won by Lance Armstrong in 1993. Apart from Greg LeMond, two other world champions from English-speaking countries are Stephen Roche of Ireland who won in 1987 and American Lance Armstrong who scored a surprise win in 1993.

## World Professional Road Race Results

1927 Nürburgring (Germany): 1. Alfredo Binda (I). 2. Costante Girardengo (I) @ 7.15. 3. D. Piemontesi (I) @ 10.51. 4. Gaetano Belloni (I) @ 11.11. 5. Jean Aerts (B) @ 11.51. *Distance: 182.480 km. Winning speed: 27.544 kmh.*

1928 Budapest (Hungary): 1. Georges Ronsse (B). 2. Costante Giradengo (I) @ 7.15. 3. D. Piemontesi (I) @ 10.51. 4. Jef Dervaes (B) @ 36.13. 5. Walter Cap (A).

*Distance: 192 km. Winning speed: 30.302 kmh.*

1929 Zurich (Switzerland): 1. Georges Ronsse (B). 2. Nicolas Frantz (LUX) 3. Alfredo Binda (I) 4. Jef Dervaes (B) @ 1.00. 5. L. Frascarelli (I).
*Distance: 200 km. Winning speed: 29.405 kmh.*

1930 Liège (Belgium): 1. Alfredo Binda (I). 2. Learco Guerra (I). 3. Georges Ronsse (B). 4. Kurt Stoepel (D). @ 1.00 5. Allegro Grandi (I) @ 5.00.
*Distance: 210 km. Winning speed: 27.953 kmh.*

1931 Copenhagen (Denmark): 1. Learco Guerra (I). 2. F. Le Drogo (F) @ 4.37. 3. Albert Büchi (SWI) @ 4.48. 4. Fabio Battensini (I) @ 5.57. 5. Max Bulla (A) @ 6.23.
*Distance: 172 km. Winning speed: 35.135 kmh.*

1932 Rome (Italy): 1. Alfredo Binda (I). 2. Remo Bertoni (I) @ 15 secs. 3. Nicolas Frantz (LUX) @ 4.52. 4. Ricardo Montero (E) @ 5.15. 5. Learco Guerra (I) @ 5.39.
*Distance: 206.100 km. Winning speed: 29.340 kmh.*

1933 Montlhéry (France): 1. Georges Speicher (F). 2. Antonin Magne (F) @ 5.03. 3. Marin Valentijn (NL) @ 5.04. 4. A. Haemerlinck (B) @ 11.03. 5. A. Schepers (B).
*Distance: 250 km. Winning speed: 34.967 kmh.*

1934 Leipzig (Germany): 1. Karel Kaers (B) 2. Learco Guerra (I) 3. Gustaaf Danneels (B) 4. Gerhard Huschke (D) 5. Gerrit Van der Ruit (NL).
*Distance: 225.600 km. Winning speed: 37.994 kmh.*

1935 Floreffe (Belgium): 1. Jean Aerts (B). 2. Luciano Montero (E) @ 2.57. 3. Gustaaf Danneels (B) @ 9.08. 4. Alfredo Bini (I) @ 11.03. 5. Leo Amberg (SWI) @ 11.08.
*Distance: 216 km. Winning speed: 35.476 kmh.*

1936 Bern (Switzerland): 1. Antonin Magne (F). 2. Aldo Bini (I) @ 9.27. 3. T. Middelkamp (NL). 4. Paul Egli (SWI). 5. W. Hansen (DK).
*Distance: 218.400 km. Winning speed:*

37.065 kmh.

1937 Copenhagen (Denmark): 1. Eloi Meulenberg (B). 2. Emil Kijewski (D). 3. Paul Egli (SWI). 4. Jean Majerus (LUX). 5. Georges Speicher (F).
*Distance: 297.500 km. Winning speed: 37.203 kmh.*

1938 Valkenburg (Holland): 1. Marcel Kint (B). 2. Paul Egli (SWI). 3. Leo Amberg (SWI). 4. Piet Van Nek (NL) @ 11 secs. 5. Edward Vissers (B) @ 1.18.
*Distance: 273 km. Winning speed: 34.599 kmh.*

1946 Zürich (Switzerland): 1. Hans Knecht (SWI). 2. Marcel Kint (B) @ 10 secs. 3. Rik Van Steenbergen (B) @ 59 secs. 4. Mario Ricci (I) @ 1.46. 5. Gerrit Schulte (NL) @ 2.42. *Distance: 270 km. Winning speed: 36.488 kmh.*

1947 Reims (France): 1. T Middelkamp (NL). 2. Albert Sercu (B) @ 10 secs. 3. Jef Jansen (NL). 4. Fiorenzo Magni (I). 5. E. Fachleitner (F) @ 44 secs.
*Distance: 274.035 km. Winning speed: 36.677 kmh.*

1948 Valkenburg (Holland): 1. Briek Schotte (B). 2. Apo Lazaridès (F) @ 1 second. 3. Luc Teisseire (F) @ 3.41. 4. Luciano Maggini (I) @ 6.33. 5. Marcel Dupont (B) @ 6.59.
*Distance: 266.800 km. Winning speed: 35.517 kmh.*

1949 Copenhagen (Denmark): 1. Rik Van Steenbergen (B). 2. Ferdi Kübler (SWI). 3. Fausto Coppi (I). 4. Briek Schotte (B). 5. Gerrit Schulte (NL).
*Distance: 290 km. Winning speed: 38.013 kmh.*

1950 Moorslede (Belgium): 1. Briek Schotte (B). 2. T. Middelkamp (NL) @ 1.01. 3. Ferdi Kübler (SWI) @ 1.48. 4. Gerrit Schulte (NL). 5. Louison Bobet (F).
*Distance: 284 km. Winning speed: 36.263 kmh.*

1951 Varèse (Italy): 1. Ferdi Kübler (SWI). 2. Fiorenzo Magni (I). 3. A. Bevilacqua (I). 4. Jos De Feyter (B). 5. Gerrit Voorting (NL).
*Distance: 295.200 km. Winning speed: 34.834 kmh.*

1952 Luxembourg: 1. Heinz Müller (D). 2. G Weilenmann (SWI). 3. Ludwig Hörmann (D). 4. Fiorenzo Magni (I) 5. Robert Varnajo (F).
*Distance: 280 km. Winning speed: 39.449 kmh*

1953 Lugano (Switzerland): 1. Fausto Coppi (I). 2. Germain Derijke (B) @ 6.22. 3. Stan

*The great Belgian rider Rik Van Steenbergen was world champion two years running, in 1956 and 1957*

Ockers (B) @ 7.29. 4. M Gismondi (I) @ 7.40. 5. Nino Defilippis (I) @ 9.17.
*Distance: 270 km. Winning speed: 35.921 kmh.*

1954 Solingen (Denmark): 1. Louison Bobet (F). 2. Fritz Schär (SWI) @ 12 secs. 3. Charly Gaul (LUX) 2.12. 4. M Gismondi (I) 3.03. 5. Jacques Anquetil (F).
*Distance: 240 km. Winning speed: 32.388 kmh.*

1955 Frascati (Italy): 1. Stan Ockers (B). 2. J-P Schmitz (LUX) @ 1.03. 3. Germain Derijcke (B) @ 1.15. 4. Gastone Nencini (I) 5. Marcel Janssens (B) @ 1.40.293.
*Distance: 132 km. Winning speed: 33.593 kmh.*

1956 Ballerup (Denmark): 1. Rik Van Steenbergen (B) 2. Rik van Looy (B) 3. Gerrit Schulte (NL) 4. Stan Ockers (B) 5. Fred De Bruyne (B).
*Distance: 285.120 km. Winning speed: 38.335 kmh.*

1957 Waregem (Belgium): 1. Rik Van Steenbergen (B) 2. Louison Bobet (F) 3. André Darrigade (F) 4. Rik van Looy (B) 5. Fred De Bruyne (B).
*Distance: 285.600 km. Winning speed: 36.997 kmh.*

1958    Reims (France): 1. Ercole Baldini (I). 2. Louison Bobet (F) @ 2.09. 3. André Darrigade (F) @ 3.47. 4. Vito Favero (I). 5. Jean Forestier (F).
*Distance: 276.794 km. Winning speed: 36.944 kmh.*

1959    Zandvoort (Holland): 1. André Darrigade (F). 2. M Gismondi (I). 3. Noël Foré (B). 4. Tom Simpson (GB). 5. Diego Ronchini (I).
*Distance: 292.033 km. Winning speed: 38.875 kmh.*

1960    Sachsenring (GDR): 1. Rik van Looy (B). 2. André Darrigade (F). 3. Pino Cerami (B). 4. Imerio Massignan (I). 5. Raymond Poulidor (F).
*Distance: 279.392 km. Winning speed: 35.861 kmh.*

1961    Bern (Switzerland): 1. Rik van Looy (B) 2. Nino Defilippis (I) 3. Raymond Poulidor (F) 4. José Bernardez (E) 5. Jo De Roo (NL).
*Distance: 285.252 km. Winning speed: 36.681 kmh.*

1962    Salo (Italy): 1. Jean Stablinski (F) 2. Seamus Elliott (IRL) @ 1.22. 3. Jos Hoevenaars (B) 1.44. 4. Rolf Wolfshohl (D) @ 1.54. 5. Arnaldo Pambianco (I) @ 2.04.
*Distance: 296.240 km. Winning speed: 38.374 kmh.*

1963    Ronse (Belgium): 1. Benoni Beheyt (B) 2. Rik van Looy (B) 3. Jo De Haan (NL) 4. André Darrigade (F) 5. Raymond Poulidor (F).
*Distance: 278.800 km. Winning speed: 37.554 kmh.*

1964    Sallanches (France): 1. Jan Janssen (NL) 2. Vittorio Adorni (I) 3. Raymond Poulidor (F) 4. Tom Simpson (GB) @ 6 secs. 5. Italo Zilioli (I).
*Distance: 290 km. Winning speed: 38.169 kmh.*

1965    Lasarte (Spain) 1. Tom Simpson (GB) 2. Rudi Altig (D) 3. Roger Swerts (B) @ 3.40. 4. Peter Post (NL) 5. Karl-Heinz Kunde (D).
*Distance: 267.400 km. Winning speed: 40.178 kmh.*

1966    Nürburgring (Germany): 1. Rudi Altig (D) 2. Jacques Anquetil (F) 3. Raymond Poulidor (F) 4. Gianni Motta (I) @ 8 secs. 5. Jean Stablinski (F) @ 10 secs.
*Distance: 273.720 km. Winning speed: 36.401 kmh.*

1967    Heerlen (Holland): 1. Eddy Merckx (B) 2. Jan Janssen (NL) 3. Ramon Saez (E) 4. Gianni Motta (I).
*Distance: 265.180 km. Winning speed: 39.315 kmh.*

1968    Imola (Italy): 1. Vittorio Adorni (I). 2. Hermann Vanspringel (B) @ 9.50. 3. M Dancelli (I) @ 10.18. 4. Franco Bitossi (I). 5. Vito Tacone (I).
*Distance: 277.308 km. Winning speed: 37.168 kmh.*

1969    Zolder (Belgium): 1. Harm Ottenbros (NL). 2. Julien Stevens (B). 3. M Dancelli (I) @ 2.18. 4. Guido Reybrouck (B) @ 2.21. 5. Roger Swerts (B).
*Distance: 262.860 km. Winning speed: 41.100 kmh.*

1970    Leicester (UK): 1. J-P Monsere (B). 2. Leif Mortensen (DNK) @ 2 secs. 3. Felice Gimondi (I). 4. Leslie West (GB) @ 3 secs. 5. Charles Rouxel (F) @ 5 secs.
*Distance: 271.960 km. Winning speed: 41.418 kmh.*

1971    Medrisio (Switzerland): 1. Eddy Merckx (B) 2. Felice Gimondi (I) 3. Cyrille Guimard (F) @ 1.13. 4. Giancarlo Polidori (I) 5. Georges Printens (B).
*Distance: 268.800 km. Winning speed: 40.410 kmh.*

1972    Gap (France): 1. Marino Basso (I) 2. Franco Bitossi (I) 3. Cyrille Guimard (F) 4. Eddy Merckx (B) 5. Joop Zoetemelk (NL).
*Distance: 272.574 km. Winning speed: 38.392 kmh.*

1973    Montjuich (Spain): 1. Felice Gimondi (I). 2. Freddy Maertens (B). 3. Luis Ocana (E). 4. Eddy Merckx (B). 5. Joop Zoetemelk (NL) @ 1.46.
*Distance: 248.659 km. Winning speed: 38.115 kmh.*

1974    Montreal (Canada): 1. Eddy Merckx (B). 2. Raymond Poulidor (F) @ 2 secs. 3. Mariano Martinez (F) @ 37 secs. 4. G Santambrogio (I) @ 39 secs. 5. Bernard Thévenet (F) @ 2.10.
*Distance: 262.500 km. Winning speed: 38.194 kmh.*

1975    Yvoir (Belgium): 1. Hennie Kuiper (NL). 2. Roger De Vlaeminck (B) @ 17 secs. 3. J-P Danguillaume (F). 4. Pedro Torrès (E). 5. Joop Zoetemelk (NL).
*Distance: 266 km. Winning speed: 39.968 kmh.*

1976    Ostuni (Italy): 1. Freddy Maertens (B). 2. Francesco Moser (I). 3. Tino Conti (I) @ 11 secs. 4. Joop Zoetemelk (NL). 5. Eddy Merckx (B) @ 26 secs.
*Distance: 288 km. Winning speed: 40.547 kmh.*

1977    San Cristobal (Venezuela): 1. Francesco Moser (I) 2. Dietrich Thurau (D) 3. Franco Bitossi (I) @ 1.19. 4. Hennie Kuiper (NL) 5. Domingo Perurena (E) @ 1.35.

*Distance: 255 km. Winning speed: 38.597 kmh.*

1978    Nürburgring (Germany): 1. G Knetemann (NL) 2. Francesco Moser (I) 3. Jörgen Marcussen (DNK) @ 20 secs. 4. Giuseppe Saronni (I) @ 28 secs. 5. Bernard Hinault (F). *Distance: 273.720 km. Winning speed: 36.329 kmh.*

1979    Valkenburg (Holland): 1. Jan Raas (NL). 2. Dietrich Thurau (D). 3. Jean-René Bernaudeau (F). 4. André Chalmel (F) @ 5 secs. 5. Henk Lubberding (NL) @ 12 secs. *Distance: 274.800 km. Winning speed: 38.965 kmh.*

1980    Sallanches (France): 1. Bernard Hinault (F). 2. G Baronchelli (I) @ 1.01. 3. Juan Fernandez (E) @ 4.25. 4. Wladimiro Panizza (I). 5. Jonathan Boyer (USA). *Distance: 268 km. Winning speed: 35.554 kmh.*

1981    Prague (Czechoslovakia): 1. Freddy Maertens (B) 2. Giuseppe Saronni (I) 3. Bernard Hinault (F) 4. G Duclos-Lassalle (F) 5. Guido Van Calster (B). *Distance: 281.400 km. Winning speed: 38.200 kmh.*

1982    Goodwood (UK): 1. Giuseppe Saronni (I) 2. Greg LeMond (USA) @ 5 secs. 3. Sean Kelly (IRL) @ 10 secs. 4. Joop Zoetemelk (NL) 5. Marino Lejarreta (E). *Distance: 275.130 km. Winning speed: 41.026 kmh.*

1983    Altenrhein (Switzerland): 1. Greg LeMond (USA). 2. Adri Van der Poel (NL) @ 1.11. 3. Stephen Roche (IRL). 4. Faustino Ruperez (E). 5. Claude Criquielion (B). *Distance: 269.892 km. Winning speed: 38.432 kmh.*

1984    Barcelona (Spain): 1. C Criquielion (B). 2. Claudio Corti (I) @ 14 secs. 3. Steve Bauer (CDN) @ 1.01. 4. Hubert Seiz (SWI) 5. Bernard Bourreau (F). *Distance: 255.550 km. Winning speed: 37.694 kmh.*

1985    Giavera Montello (Italy): 1. Joop Zoetemelk (NL). 2. Greg LeMond (USA) @ 3 secs. 3. Moreno Argentin (I). 4. Marc Madiot (F). 5. Harald Maier (A). *Distance: 265.500 km. Winning speed: 41.501 kmh.*

1986    Colorado Springs (USA): 1. Moreno Argentin (I). 2. Charly Mottet (F) @ 1 second. 3. Giuseppe Saronni (I) @ 9 secs. 4. Juan Fernandez (E). 5. Sean Kelly (IRL). *Distance: 261 km. Winning speed: 40.007 kmh.*

1987    Villach (Austria): 1. Stephen Roche (IRL). 2.

*Stephen Roche of Ireland took a great double when he was world champion and winner of the Tour de France in 1987*

Moreno Argentin (I) @ 1 second. 3. Juan Fernandez (E) 4. Rolf Gölz. 5. Sean Kelly (IRL). *Distance: 276 km. Winning speed: 40.386 kmh.*

1988    Ronse (Belgium): 1. Maurizio Fondriest (I). 2. Martial Gayant (F) @ 27 secs. 3. Juan Fernandez (E) @ 41 secs. 4. Hartmut Bölts (D). 5. Mauro Gianetti (SWI). *Distance: 274 km. Winning speed: 38.940 kmh.*

1989    Chambéry (France): 1. Greg LeMond (USA) 2. Dimitri Konyshev (SU) 3. Sean Kelly (IRL) 4. Steven Rooks (NL) 5. Thierry Claveyrolat (F). *Distance: 259.350 km. Winning speed: 38.329 kmh.*

1990    Utsunomiya (Japan): 1. Rudy Dhaenens (B). 2. Dirk De Wolf (B). 3. Gianni Bugno (I) @ 8 secs. 4. Greg LeMond (USA). 5. Sean Kelly (IRL). *Distance: 261 km. Winning speed: 38.011 kmh.*

1991    Stuttgart (Germany): 1. Gianni Bugno (I). 2. Steven Rooks (NL). 3. Miguel Indurain (E). 4. Alvaro Mejia (COL). 5. Kai Hundertmarck (D) @ 11 secs. *Distance: 252.8 km. Winning speed: 39.875 kmh.*

1992    Benidorm (Spain): 1. Gianni Bugno (I). 2. Laurent Jalabert (F). 3. Dimitri Konyshev (RUS). 4. Tony Rominger (SWI). 5. Steven Rooks (NL). *Distance: 261.6 km. Winning speed: 39.790 kmh.*

*Italian Gianni Bugno became the second rider to win the world championships two years running in 1991 and 1992*

1993 Oslo (Norway): 1. Lance Armstrong (USA). 2. Miguel Indurain (E). 3. Olaf Ludwig (D) 4. Johan Museeuw (B) 5. Maurizio Fondriest (I).
*Distance: 257.6 km. Winning speed: 40.979 kmh.*

1994 Sicily (Italy): 1. Luc Leblanc (F). 2. Claudio Chiappucci (I) @ 27 secs. 3. Richard Virenque (F). 4. M. Ghirotto (I). 5. Dimitri Konyshev (R).
*Distance: 251.8 km. Winning speed: 38.35 kmh*

1995 Duitama (Colombia): 1. Abraham Olano (E). 2. Migule Indurain (E) @ 35 seconds. 3. Mario Pantani (I). 4. Mauro Gianetti (SWI). 5. Pascal Richard (SWI).
*Distance 265 km. Winning speed: 37.011 kmh.*

Most World Championship wins: 3, Alfredo Binda (Italy) 1927, 1930, 1932; Rik Van Steenbergen (Belgium) 1949, 1956–7; Eddy Merckx (Belgium) 1967, 1971, 1974; 2, Greg LeMond (USA) 1983, 1989; Gianni Bugno (Italy) 1991–92.

**World Amateur Road Race Winners**

| | |
|---|---|
| 1921 | Gunnar Skold (SWE) |
| 1922 | Dave Marsh (UK) |
| 1923 | L. Ferrario (I) |
| 1924 | André Leducq (F) |
| 1925 | H. Hoevenaers (B) |
| 1926 | O. Dayen (F) |
| 1927 | Jean Aerts (B) |
| 1928 | Allegor Grandi (I) |
| 1929 | P. Bertolazzo (I) |
| 1930 | Giuseppe Martano (I) |
| 1931 | Hanry Hansen (DNK) |
| 1932 | Giuseppe Martano (I) |
| 1933 | Paul Egli (SWI) |
| 1934 | K. Pellenaars (NL) |
| 1935 | Ivo Mancini (I) |
| 1936 | E. Buchwalder (SWI) |
| 1937 | A. Leoni (B) |
| 1938 | Hans Knecht (SWI) |
| 1946 | Henry Aubry (F) |
| 1947 | Alfio Ferrari (I) |
| 1948 | Harry Snell (SWE) |
| 1949 | Henk Faanhof (NL) |
| 1950 | Jack Hoobin (AUS) |
| 1951 | Gianni Ghidini (I) |
| 1952 | Luciano Ciancola (I) |
| 1953 | Ricardo Filippi (I) |
| 1954 | Emiel Van Cauter (B) |
| 1955 | Sante Ranucci (I) |
| 1956 | Frans Mahn (NL) |
| 1957 | Louis Proost (B) |
| 1958 | Gustav Adolf Schur (GDR) |
| 1959 | Gustav Adolf Schur (GDR) |
| 1960 | Bernhardt Eckstein (GDR) |
| 1961 | Jean Jourden (F) |
| 1962 | Renato Boncioni (I) |
| 1963 | Flaviano Vincentini (I) |
| 1964 | Eddy Merckx (B) |
| 1965 | Jacques Botherel (F) |
| 1966 | Evert Dolman (NL) |
| 1967 | Graham Webb (UK) |
| 1968 | Vittorio Marcelli (I) |
| 1969 | Leif Mortensen (DNK) |
| 1970 | Jorgen Schmidt (DNK) |
| 1971 | Regis Ovion (F) |
| 1973 | Ryszard Szurkowski (POL) |
| 1974 | Janusz Kowalski (POL) |
| 1975 | Andre Gevers (NL) |
| 1977 | Claudio Corti (I) |
| 1978 | Gilbert Glaus (SWI) |

| | |
|---|---|
| 1979 | Gianni Giacomini (I) |
| 1981 | Andrey Vedernikov (USSR) |
| 1982 | Bernd Drogan (GDR) |
| 1983 | Uwe Raab (GDR) |
| 1985 | Lech Piasecki (POL) |
| 1986 | Uwe Ampler (GDR) |
| 1987 | Richard Vivien (F) |
| 1989 | Joachim Halupczok (POL) |
| 1990 | Mirko Gualdi (I) |
| 1991 | Viktor Ryaksinskiy (USSR) |
| 1992 | *Not held* |
| 1993 | J. Ullrich (D) |
| 1994 | Alex Pedersen (DNK) |
| 1995 | Danny Neilssen (NL) |

Most wins: 2, Giuseppe Martano (I) 1930, 1932; 2, Gustav Adolf Schur (GDR) 1958–9.

## Professional Time-Trial
*First held 1994*

| | |
|---|---|
| 1994 | Chris Boardman (UK) |
| 1995 | Miguel Indurain (ESP) |

## Amateur Team Time-Trial
*First held 1962. Contested on the roads at approx 100 km. Not held in 1992.*

| | |
|---|---|
| 6 wins | Italy 1962, 1964–5, 1987, 1991, 1993. |
| 5 | USSR 1970, 1977, 1983, 1985, 1990 |
| 3 | Sweden 1967–9, 1974 |
| 3 | Netherlands 1978, 1982, 1986 |
| 3 | GDR 1979, 1981, 1989 |
| 2 | Poland 1973, 1975 |
| 1 | France 1963, Denmark 1966 |
| 1 | Belgium 1971 |

## Women's Road Race
*First held 1958*

| | |
|---|---|
| 1958 | E. Jacobs (LUX) |
| 1959 | Yvon Reynders (B) |
| 1960 | Beryl Burton (UK) |
| 1961 | Yvon Reynders (B) |
| 1962 | M. R. Gaillard (B) |
| 1963 | Yvon Reynders (B) |
| 1964 | E. Sonka (USSR) |
| 1965 | E. Eicholz (DDR) |
| 1966 | Yvon Reynders (B) |
| 1967 | Beryl Burton (UK) |
| 1968 | C. Hage (NL) |
| 1969 | A. McElmury (USA) |
| 1970 | Anna Konkina (USSR) |
| 1971 | Anna Konkina (USSR) |
| 1972 | Genevieve Gambillon (F) |
| 1973 | Nicole Vandenbroeck (B) |
| 1974 | Genevieve Gambillon (F) |
| 1975 | Trijntje Fopma (NL) |
| 1976 | Keetie van Oosten-Hage (NL) |

| | |
|---|---|
| 1977 | Josiane Bost (F) |
| 1978 | Beate Habetz (FRG) |
| 1979 | Petra de Bruin (NL) |
| 1980 | Beth Heiden (USA) |
| 1981 | Ute Enzenauer (FRG) |
| 1982 | Mandy Jones (UK) |
| 1983 | Marianne Berglund (SWE) |
| 1985 | Jeannie Longo (F) |
| 1986 | Jeannie Longo (F) |
| 1987 | Jeannie Longo (F) |
| 1989 | Jeannie Longo (F) |
| 1990 | Catherine Marsal (F) |
| 1991 | Leontien van Moorseel (NL) |
| 1992 | *Not held* |
| 1993 | Leontien van Moorseel (NL) |
| 1994 | Monica Valvik (NOR) |
| 1995 | Jeannie Longo (F) |

Most wins: 5, Jeannie Longo (F) 1985–89, 1995; 4, Yvonne Reynders (B) 1959, 1961, 1963, 1966.

## Women's Time-Trial
*First held 1994*

| | |
|---|---|
| 1994 | Karen Kurreck (USA) |
| 1995 | Jeannie Longo (F) |

## Junior Road Race

| | |
|---|---|
| 1975 | Robert Visentini (I) |
| 1976 | Ronald Bessens (NL) |
| 1977 | Ronny Van Holen (B) |
| 1978 | Vladimir Makarin (USSR) |
| 1979 | Greg LeMond (USA) |
| 1980 | Roberto Ciampi (I) |
| 1981 | Beat Schumacher (SWI) |
| 1982 | Roger Six (B) |
| 1983 | Soren Lilholt (DNK) |
| 1984 | Tom Cordes (NL) |
| 1985 | Raymond Meijs (NL) |
| 1986 | Michel Zanoli (NL) |
| 1987 | Pavel Tonkov (USSR) |
| 1988 | Gianluca Tarocco (I) |
| 1989 | Patrick Vetsch (SWI) |
| 1990 | Marco Serpelli (I) |
| 1991 | Jeff Evanshire (USA) |
| 1992 | Giuseppe Palumbo (I) |
| 1993 | Giuseppe Palumbo (I) |
| 1994 | *Not held* |

## Women's Junior Road Race

| | |
|---|---|
| 1987 | Catherine Marsal (F) |
| 1988 | Gitte Hjortflod (DNK) |
| 1989 | Deirdre Demet (USA) |
| 1990 | I. Y. Teutenberg (FRG) |
| 1991 | Elisabeth Vink (NL) |
| 1992 | Hanka Kupfernagel (D) |
| 1993 | E. Chevanne-Brunel (F) |
| 1994 | Diane Ziliute (LUX) |

# ONE-DAY CLASSIC ROAD RACES

A 'Classic' is a one-day event with top class status in the professional road-race calendar. Most of the leading Classics are now part of the World Cup, although the events chosen for this series are subject to change each year and exclude some Category 1.1 events such as the Flèche Wallonne and Ghent–Wevelgem which have important historical status and continue to be ridden by leading stars.

## MILAN–SAN REMO

The Milan–San Remo in Italy, also called the *Primavera*, is always held on the weekend closest to the first day of spring. It was first staged by the newspaper *Gazzetta dello Sport* in 1907, when 33 riders were led home by Lucien Petit-Breton who won 300 lire in gold as his prize. In 1908 there were 80 riders, and since then the Milan–San Remo has been an established Classic which missed just three years in the calendar owing to two world wars – 1916, 1944 and 1945.

### The Route

The modern Milan–San Remo starts from Piazza Del Duomo by Milan Cathedral. The route heads through the suburbs, and then for 100 km or so across the Lombardy Plain to the major climb of the race which leads to the top of the 1745 ft (532m) Turchino Pass where the road is usually banked high with snow. The descent from Turchino is one of the fastest of the Classic year, bringing the riders down to Savona by the Mediterranean where they follow the winding coast road. A number of short hillclimbs were added in 1960 to increase interest in the race within the final 50 km to San Remo. These culminate with the famous 4 km long Poggio, where the final attack is usually made as the leaders speed down to the finish at San Remo.

■ The distance of the Milan–San Remo has crept up over the years from 281 km for the first event to 297 km in 1989, and it usually takes around eight hours to complete. Eddy Merckx holds the average speed race record of 44.805 kmh set in 1967. The slowest race-winning average was 23.33 kmh, recorded by Eugene Cristophe in 1910. In that year only four out of 71 riders finished, owing to appalling weather conditions including riding through eight-inch deep snow at the top of the Turchino Pass. Cristophe eventually won by an hour, despite having stopped to warm himself at an inn for over 30 minutes.

### The Riders

French, Belgian and Italian riders shared the laurels in the first few years. From 1914 it became an Italian-dominated event, and the mould was only broken after 50 years when Rik van Steenburgen won in 1954. After that it became a truly international race once again, won by famous names including national hero Fausto Coppi in 1946, Raymond Poulidor in 1961, Tom Simpson in 1964 who remains the only Briton to win the event, Eddy Merckx who is the all-time record holder with seven wins, Sean Kelly of Ireland in 1986 and 1992, and Laurent Fignon in 1988 and 1989.

■ The first Italian rider to be awarded the title of *Campionissimo* (Champion of Champions) was Costante Girardengo who won the Milan–San Remo six times (1918, 1921, 1923, 1925, 1926 and 1928). He was also first to finish in 1915, but was disqualified for failing to respect the route, a loss which put Merckx ahead of him in the table of wins. Eddy Merckx won the Milan–San Remo in 1966, 1967, 1969, 1971, 1972, 1975 and 1976. His biggest race-winning margin was 30 seconds; three of his wins were in sprints; his only other top-ten finish was in 1970 when he finished eighth behind eventual winner Michele Dancelli.

■ Giuseppe Saronni won the Tour of Lombardy, the Milan–San Remo and the Tour of Italy in 1983, a record unsurpassed in Italian cycling history. He also won the world championship and the Tour of Lombardy in 1982. Irish hero Sean Kelly scored his first win in the Milan–San Remo in 1986 when he left Italian Mario Beccia and American Greg LeMond on the ride up the Poggia. He scored his second win in 1992, when as a 35-year-old father of two he stormed down the other side of the Poggia to overtake pre-race favourite Moreno Argentin who had been first to the summit. He later said 'I took every risk. It was a kamikaze descent. I had nothing to lose had I fallen.' It was Kelly's last Classic win before his retirement in 1994.

### Milan–San Remo Winners

|  |  | Av speed (kmh) |
|------|-------------------------|------|
| 1907 | Lucien Petit-Breton (F) | 26.606 |
| 1908 | Cyrille van Hauwaert (B) | 25.108 |
| 1909 | Luigi Ganna (I) | 30.240 |
| 1910 | Eugene Christophe (F) | 23.330 |
| 1911 | Gustave Garrigou (F) | 29.570 |
| 1912 | Henri Pelissier (F) | 29.722 |
| 1913 | Odiel Defraye (B) | 31.143 |
| 1914 | Ugo Agostoni (I) | 27.200 |
| 1915 | Ezio Corlaita (I) | 27.263 |
| 1917 | Gaetano Belloni (I) | 22.500 |
| 1918 | Costante Girardengo (I) | 24.279 |

| 1919 | Angelo Gremo (I) | 24.800 |
| 1920 | Gaetano Bellonhi (I) | 30.317 |
| 1921 | Costante Girardengo (I) | 30.105 |
| 1922 | Giovanni Brunero (I) | 27.973 |
| 1923 | Costante Girardengo (I) | 27.996 |
| 1924 | Pietro Linari (I) | 26.400 |
| 1925 | Costante Girardengo (I) | 27.722 |
| 1926 | Costante Girardengo (I) | 29.284 |
| 1927 | Pietro Chesi (I) | 29.485 |
| 1928 | Costante Girardengo (I) | 24.680 |
| 1929 | Alfredo Binda (I) | 31.628 |
| 1930 | Michele Mara (I) | 29.485 |
| 1931 | Alfredo Binda (I) | 29.843 |
| 1932 | Alfredo Bovet (SWI) | 34.432 |
| 1933 | Learco Guerra (I) | 36.138 |
| 1934 | Josef Demuysere (B) | 35.978 |
| 1935 | Giuseppe Olmo (I) | 36.089 |
| 1936 | Angelo Varetto (I) | 36.479 |
| 1937 | Cesarde del Cancia (I) | 37.408 |
| 1938 | Giuseppe Olmo (I) | 38.517 |
| 1939 | Gino Bartali (I) | 37.386 |
| 1940 | Gino Bartali (I) | 36.670 |
| 1941 | Pierino Favalli (I) | 36.155 |
| 1942 | Adolfo Leoni (I) | 34.469 |
| 1943 | Cino Cinelli (I) | 34.753 |
| 1946 | Fausto Coppi (I) | 35.940 |
| 1947 | Gino Bartali (I) | 33.300 |
| 1948 | Fausto Coppi (I) | 37.284 |
| 1949 | Fausto Coppi (I) | 39.397 |
| 1950 | Gino Bartali (I) | 38.538 |
| 1951 | Louison Bobet (F) | 37.578 |
| 1952 | Loretto Petrucci (I) | 38.270 |
| 1953 | Loretto Petrucci (I) | 40.340 |
| 1954 | Rik Van Steenbergen (B) | 39.344 |
| 1955 | Germain Derijcke (B) | 39.927 |
| 1956 | Fred de Bruyne (B) | 40.415 |
| 1957 | Miguel Poblet (E) | 40.687 |
| 1958 | Rik van Looy (B) | 42.178 |
| 1959 | Miguel Poblet (E) | 41.575 |
| 1960 | René Privat (F) | 42.640 |
| 1961 | Raymond Poulidor (F) | 37.474 |
| 1962 | Emile Daems (B) | 42.342 |
| 1963 | Joseph Groussard (F) | 41.178 |
| 1964 | Tom Simpson (GB) | 43.420 |
| 1965 | Arle den Hartog (NL) | 41.641 |
| 1966 | Eddy Merckx (B) | 43.128 |
| 1967 | Eddy Merckx (B) | 44.805 |
| 1968 | Rudi Altig (D) | 41.945 |
| 1969 | Eddy Merckx (B) | 43.425 |
| 1970 | Michele Dancelli (I) | 43.976 |
| 1971 | Eddy Merckx (B) | 39.152 |
| 1972 | Eddy Merckx (B) | 43.909 |
| 1973 | Roger de Vlaeminck (B) | 41.782 |
| 1974 | Felice Gimondi (I) | 42.533 |
| 1975 | Eddy Merckx (B) | 37.530 |
| 1976 | Eddy Merckx (B) | 42.015 |

| 1977 | Jan Raas (NL) | 42.986 |
| 1978 | Roger de Vlaeminck (B) | 42.396 |
| 1979 | Roger de Vlaeminck (B) | 40.588 |
| 1980 | Pierino Gavazzi (I) | 42.972 |
| 1981 | Fons de Wolf (B) | 43.081 |
| 1982 | Marc Gomez (F) | 41.584 |
| 1983 | Giuseppe Saronni (I) | 41.216 |
| 1984 | Francesco Moser (I) | 38.871 |
| 1985 | Hennie Kuiper (NL) | 38.636 |
| 1986 | Sean Kelly (IRL) | 42.120 |
| 1987 | Erich Maechler (SWI) | 41.913 |
| 1988 | Laurent Fignon (F) | 41.376 |
| 1989 | Laurent Fignon (F) | 41.184 |
| 1990 | Gianni Bugno (I) | 45.806 |
| 1991 | Claudio Chiappucci (I) | 42.342 |
| 1992 | Sean Kelly (IRL) | 39.052 |
| 1993 | Maurizio Fondriest (I) | 39.989 |
| 1994 | Giorgio Furlan (I) | 41.445 |
| 1995 | Laurent Jalabert (F) | 43.519 |

*Giuseppe Saronni took the classic Italian triple in 1983: the Milan-San Remo, Tour of Lombardy and Tour of Italy*

# TOUR OF FLANDERS/RONDE VAN VLAANDEREN

The Tour of Flanders, or *Ronde van Vlaanderen* as it is known by the Flemish, follows a fortnight after the Milan–San Remo, and is the first of the northern European Spring Classics. It covers the area of Flanders in western Belgium and north-west France, with a distance that usually ranges upwards from 260 km from the start at St Niklaas to the finish at Meerbeke with Ghent roughly in the centre.

### The Flemish 'Bergs'

The Tour of Flanders is known for its cobbled climbs or *bergs* which are reached at around the 130 km mark after a fairly flat first half of the race. The route is changed each year to vary the 12 or so bergs, but the best known include the Molenberg, Kwaremont, Pattersberg, Kortekeer, Taaenberg, Ten Houte, Eikenberg, Varent, Leberg, Berendries, Geraardsbergen and, last of all, the Bosberg. After 12 years the infamous 600m long Koppenberg was excluded from the race, when in 1987 Jesper Skibby of Denmark fell on the slippery, 25 per cent steep slope and was run over by the race director's car.

### Race History

The Tour of Flanders was first held in 1913 when it was organized by Karel Steyaert, who worked for the newspaper *Het Nieuwsblad-Sportswereld* which is still very much involved in cycle racing. A statue of Karel Steyaert now stands at the top of the Kwaremont. The race was not held between 1915 and 1918, but has been held every year since 1919 to give it the longest non-stop run of any Classic event in the calendar.

### The Riders

The Belgian rider Paul Deman won the first Tour of Flanders in 1913. During World War One he was sentenced to death when he was caught on a secret mission in Holland. The Armistice came just in time to save him, and his war exploits were rewarded by French, British and Belgian medals for bravery.

■ Between 1913 and 1948 the only non-Belgian to win the Tour of Flanders was the Swiss rider Henri Suter who sprinted clear to win in 1923. Then Fiorenzo Magni of Italy once again broke the mould to win the sprint to the finish in 1949, having travelled to take part in the Tour which was a part of the new Desgranges-Colombo Challenge points championship. He went on to win the Tour of

*The bump-bump-bump of the cobbles is what makes the Tour of Flanders such a challenge, and difficult to ride in the wet*

Flanders by 2 minutes, 6 seconds in 1950, and by 5 minutes, 35 seconds in 1951, equalling the triple victory of Achiel Buysse in 1940, 1941 and 1943. Eric Leman later became the third rider to score three Tour of Flanders' victories (1970, 1972 and 1973).

■ The 1934 world road race champion Karel Kaers won the Tour of Flanders in 1939 without intending to do so. As a change from his normal track racing, he decided to use the Tour of Flanders as a training run for the Paris–Roubaix. He gave instructions for his car to be left at the top of the Kwaremont 140 km from the start of the race, so that he could pull out at the halfway mark without finishing. Kaers and his training partner led the way to the top of the Kwaremont by over a minute, only to discover that his manager had removed the car. After a fruitless search he was forced to ride on, and eventually won the sprint to the finish.

■ Eddie Merckx, one of the very few non-Flemish Belgians to win the Tour of Flanders, first won the race in 1969 when conditions included a blizzard and rain, having failed in the previous two years. He next won in 1975, narrowly beating the Flemish rider Frans Verbeek who finished second two years running. Evert Dolman holds the speed record for the Tour of Flanders, at an average 43.225 kmh over the 268 km race in 1971. Tom Simpson scored the one and only British victory in the Tour of Flanders in 1961. He beat Nino Defillipis of Italy who had misread the finish line as he sprinted ahead of Simpson with his arm raised in victory, leaving Simpson to sprint for the true line which still lay ahead.

## Tour of Flanders/Ronde Van Vlaanderen Winners

| Year | Winner | Av speed (kmh) |
|------|--------|----------------|
| 1913 | Paul Denman (B) | 26.800 |
| 1914 | Marcel Buysse (B) | 27.097 |
| 1919 | H. van Lerberghe (B) | 26.421 |
| 1920 | Jules van Hevel (B) | 26.105 |
| 1921 | René Vermandel (B) | 25.168 |
| 1922 | Leon de Vos (B) | 27.956 |
| 1923 | Henri Suter (SWI) | 26.211 |
| 1924 | Gerard Debaets (B) | 27.528 |
| 1925 | Julien Delbecque (B) | 25.860 |
| 1926 | Denis Verschueren (B) | 30.104 |
| 1927 | Gerard Debaets (B) | 30.827 |
| 1928 | Jan Mertens (B) | 32.530 |
| 1929 | Jozet Dervaes (B) | 30.713 |
| 1930 | Frans Bonduel (B) | 32.199 |
| 1931 | Romain Gijssels (B) | 33.058 |
| 1932 | Romain Gijssels (B) | 32.506 |
| 1933 | Alfons Schepers (B) | 33.139 |
| 1934 | Gaston Rebry (B) | 33.172 |
| 1935 | Louis Duerloo (B) | 34.899 |
| 1936 | Louis Hardiquest (B) | 33.333 |
| 1937 | Michel D'Hooghe (B) | 35.679 |
| 1938 | Edgard de Caluwe (B) | 33.766 |
| 1939 | Karel Kaers (B) | 35.204 |
| 1940 | Achiel Buysse (B) | 34.972 |
| 1941 | Achiel Buysse (B) | 35.148 |
| 1942 | Briek Schotte (B) | 34.242 |
| 1943 | Achiel Buysse (B) | 33.424 |
| 1944 | Rik Van Steenbergen (B) | 35.091 |
| 1945 | Sylvain Grysolle (B) | 34.961 |
| 1946 | Rik Van Steenbergen (B) | 36.282 |
| 1947 | Emiel Faignaert (B) | 38.823 |
| 1948 | Briek Schotte (B) | 38.263 |
| 1949 | Fiorenzo Magni (I) | 36.462 |
| 1950 | Fiorenzo Magni (I) | 33.090 |
| 1951 | Fiorenzo Magni (I) | 35.503 |
| 1952 | Roger Decock (B) | 34.630 |
| 1953 | Wim van Est (NL) | 34.578 |
| 1954 | Raymond Impanis (B) | 33.774 |
| 1955 | Louison Bobet (F) | 35.302 |
| 1956 | Jean Forestier (F) | 38.690 |
| 1957 | Fred de Bruyne (B) | 40.223 |
| 1958 | Germain Derijcke (B) | 37.602 |
| 1959 | Rik van Looy (B) | 38.823 |
| 1960 | Arthur Decabooter (B) | 38.693 |
| 1961 | Tom Simpson (GB) | 40.052 |
| 1962 | Rik van Looy (B) | 38.438 |
| 1963 | Noël Fore (B) | 40.683 |
| 1964 | Rudi Altig (D) | 40.990 |
| 1965 | Jo de Roo (NL) | 40.577 |
| 1966 | Edward Sels (B) | 41.303 |
| 1967 | Dino Zandegu (I) | 39.050 |
| 1968 | Walter Godefroot (B) | 42.443 |
| 1969 | Eddy Merckx (B) | 40.894 |
| 1970 | Eric Leman (B) | 41.406 |
| 1971 | Evert Dolman (NL) | 43.225 |
| 1972 | Eric Leman (B) | 41.152 |
| 1973 | Eric Leman (B) | 41.379 |
| 1974 | Cees Bal (NL) | 41.513 |
| 1975 | Eddy Merckx (B) | 40.690 |
| 1976 | Walter Planckaert (B) | 42.324 |
| 1977 | Roger de Vlaeminck (B) | 39.207 |
| 1978 | Walter Godefroot (B) | 41.935 |
| 1979 | Jan Raas (NL) | 40.971 |
| 1980 | Michel Pollentier (B) | 38.459 |
| 1981 | Hennie Kuiper (NL) | 40.650 |
| 1982 | René Martens (B) | 40.492 |
| 1983 | Jan Raas (NL) | 41.061 |
| 1984 | Johan Lammerts (NL) | 39.692 |
| 1985 | Eric Vanderaerden (B) | 39.658 |
| 1986 | Adri van der Poel (NL) | 38.297 |
| 1987 | Claude Criquielion (B) | 37.350 |
| 1988 | Eddy Planckaert (B) | 37.810 |
| 1989 | Edwig van Hooydonck (B) | 37.466 |
| 1990 | Moreno Argentin (I) | 39.026 |
| 1991 | Edwig van Hooydonck (B) | 37.109 |
| 1992 | Jacky Durand (F) | 39.263 |
| 1993 | Johan Museeuw (B) | 40.305 |
| 1994 | Gianni Bugno (I) | 39.671 |
| 1995 | Johan Museeuw (B) | 39.506 |

# GHENT–WEVELGEM

First run as a race for juniors in 1934, and opened to semi-professionals in 1936, the Ghent–Wevelgem entered the fully professional calendar in 1945. It is now sandwiched between the Tour of Flanders and the Paris–Roubaix, and while it is not part of the World Cup series it is contested by most leading one-day Classic riders.

■ Since 1990 the 210 km route has started at Ghent in north-west Belgium, crossing into France and then turning back at Cassel before the finish at Wevelgem, just over the border on Belgian soil. In previous years a longer route followed the Belgian coastline and French border in a loop from Ghent to Wevelgem; the longest and hilliest ever Ghent–Wevelgem was held over 277 km in 1977 and was won by the young Bernard Hinault by a decisive 1 minute, 24 seconds after the final time trial. Apart from the climb over the Kemmelberg, the modern route is totally flat and very exposed to the elements. If the wind is strong riders will be helped or hindered by the tailwind or headwind, and if the wind is side-on they will resort to riding in small bunches spread diagonally across the road.

## The Riders

In 1974 Barry Hoban scored one of the very few Classic victories by a British rider when he pushed the great Eddy Merckx into second place. After the Swiss rider Rolf Graf in 1954, Hoban became the second ever non-Belgian to win the race. The only other English-speaking rider to win is Irishman Sean Kelly in 1988. In 1991 Djamolidin Abduzhaparov, known as 'the Tashkent Terror', became the first rider from the Soviet Union to win. He was also first over the line in 1992, but was disqualified for dangerous riding. This gave the Italian Mario Cipollini the first of two wins in succession, with Abduzhaparov losing the sprint to finish third in 1993. In 1995 Lars Michaelsen became the first Dane to win. The Ghent–Wevelgem speed record is held by Guido Bontempi, set at 44.776 kmh in 1986. The most victories have been scored by the Belgians Rik van Looy (1956, 1957 and 1962) and Eddy Merckx (1967, 1970 and 1973) in the days when Belgium dominated the race.

## Ghent–Wevelgem Winners

| | | Av speed (kmh) |
|---|---|---|
| 1934 | Gust van Belle (B) | - |
| 1935 | Albert Depreitere (B) | - |
| 1936 | Robert van Eenaeme (B) | - |
| 1937 | Robert van Eenaeme (B) | - |
| 1938 | Hubert Godart (B) | - |
| 1939 | André Declerk (B) | - |
| 1945 | Robert van Eenaeme (B) | 35.820 |
| 1946 | Ernest Sterckx (B) | 35.088 |
| 1947 | Maurice Desimpelaere (B) | 34.074 |
| 1948 | Valère Ollivier (B) | 36.720 |
| 1949 | Marcel Kint (B) | 33.708 |
| 1950 | Briek Schotte (B) | 37.872 |
| 1951 | André Rosseel (B) | 38.363 |
| 1952 | Raymond Impanis (B) | 37.210 |
| 1953 | Raymond Impanis (B) | 30.784 |
| 1954 | Rolf Graf (SWI) | 35.968 |
| 1955 | Briek Schotte (B) | 37.120 |
| 1956 | Rik van Looy (B) | 35.905 |
| 1957 | Rik van Looy (B) | 40.142 |
| 1958 | Noël Fore (B) | 41.597 |
| 1959 | Leon van Daele (B) | 42.776 |
| 1960 | Frans Aerenhouts (B) | 38.430 |
| 1961 | Frans Aerenhouts (B) | 41.202 |
| 1962 | Rik van Looy (B) | 39.449 |
| 1963 | Benoni Beheyt (B) | 39.449 |
| 1964 | Jacques Anquetil (F) | 41.572 |
| 1965 | Noël de Pauw (B) | 41.964 |
| 1966 | Herman Vanspringel (B) | 38.324 |
| 1967 | Eddy Merckx (B) | 39.349 |
| 1968 | Walter Godefroot (B) | 42.171 |
| 1969 | Willy Vekemans (B) | 43.346 |
| 1970 | Eddy Merckx (B) | 40.195 |
| 1971 | Georges Pintens (B) | 44.576 |
| 1972 | Roger Swerts (B) | 42.000 |
| 1973 | Eddy Merckx (B) | 39.682 |

*Barry Hoban is one of the few British riders to win a Classic and the only one to win the Ghent-Wevelgem. He is pictured winning the Bordeaux stage of the 1969 Tour de France*

| 1974 | Barry Hoban (GB) | 44.383 |
| 1975 | Freddy Maertens (B) | 40.106 |
| 1976 | Freddy Maertens (B) | 41.892 |
| 1977 | Bernard Hinault (F) | 41.191 |
| 1978 | Ferdi van den Haute (B) | 38.281 |
| 1979 | Francesco Moser (I) | 43.448 |
| 1980 | Henk Lubberding (NL) | 42.127 |
| 1981 | Jan Raas (NL) | 43.988 |
| 1982 | Frank Hoste (B) | 39.200 |
| 1983 | Leo van Vliet (NL) | 39.331 |
| 1984 | Guido Bontempi (I) | 41.463 |
| 1985 | E. Vanderaerden (B) | 41.957 |
| 1986 | Guido Bontempi (I) | 44.776 |
| 1987 | Teun van Vliet (NL) | 42.384 |
| 1988 | Sean Kelly (IRL) | 38.364 |
| 1989 | Gerrit Solleveld (NL) | 39.750 |
| 1990 | Herman Frison (B) | 35.139 |
| 1991 | Djam Abduzhaparov (SU) | 39.036 |
| 1992 | Mario Cipollini (I) | 43.599 |
| 1993 | Mario Cipollini (I) | 38.989 |
| 1994 | Wilfried Peeters (B) | 40.909 |
| 1995 | Lars Michaelsen (DNK) | 41.959 |

# PARIS–ROUBAIX

The Paris–Roubaix was first held in 1896, following the success of the Bordeaux–Paris and Paris–Brest–Paris races. A total of 188 riders took part in the first paced race, with the favourite Josef Fischer leading the way across the finish line at the Roubaix Velodrome. Pacing, both by bicycle and car, continued until 1910 when Octave Lapize sprinted to his second victory in succession. He also won the following year when no pacing was allowed, finishing more than three minutes clear. The Paris–Roubaix was interrupted for three years by World War One in 1915, 1916 and 1918, and once again by World War Two in 1940, 1941 and 1942. Octave Lapize was killed in 1917, while flying a plane in action.

## 'Hell of the North'

Due to its very difficult riding conditions the Paris–Roubaix is known as the 'Hell of the North', although it is also commemorated as *La Pascale* due to its Easter date. On its route through the north of France the riders have to contend with cobbles (*pave*), narrow roads, farm tracks and, depending on the weather, mud or dust. In a total distance of just under 270 kilometres, 60 kilometres of the route may be over cobbles which are at their worst in areas such as the Wallers-Arenberg Forest and Camphin-en-Pevele where falls and crashes are frequent.

## The Riders

Roger de Vlaeminck of Belgium holds the record for the most number of wins in the Paris–Roubaix, having won in 1972, 1974, 1975 and 1977. Octave Lapize was the only man to win the race three years running (1909, 1910 and 1911) until Francesco Moser equalled his feat by winning in 1978, 1979 and 1980. The race record is held by Dutchman Peter Post at an average speed of 45.129 kmh over 265 kilometres in 1965.

■ In 1921 French brothers Henri and Francis Pelissier finished first and second. This was a double victory for the riders, since they had refused to sign a contract with the manufacturers which fixed pay and prize money over a two-year period. They led home approximately 130 contracted riders who had been instructed by their bosses that the Pelissier brothers must not be allowed to win at any cost.

■ In 1923 it was estimated that 156 riders took part in the final sprint to the finish of the race, making it the biggest sprint finish of any Classic in history. The Swiss sprinter Henri Suter won. In 1934 Frenchman Roger Lapébie punctured close to the finish while leading the race with Gaston Rebry. Lapébie borrowed a bike from a spectator and went on to cross the finish line ahead of Rebry, but was later disqualified for an illegal change of bicycle. Having also won the race in 1931, Gaston Rebry went on to claim his third Paris–Roubaix victory in 1935.

■ In 1949 Serge Coppi and André Mahe were awarded equal first place after an unusual mix-up. Mahe was in a leading group of three who were directed the wrong way to the entrance of the Roubaix Velodrome near the finish. They were eventually forced to carry their bikes in through a turnstile, having lost so much time that they finished behind the peloton which had Serge Coppi at its head. The following year Fausto Coppi, the famous brother of Serge, scored his only win in the Paris–Roubaix.

■ The Belgian Rik van Looy won three and lost two in the Paris–Roubaix. He won in 1961, 1962 and 1965. He should have won in 1963, but came second when his team-mate Armand Desmet was boxed in and unable to let him through at the finish. In 1967 Rik van Looy was second again, having been held back at the finish in questionable circumstances. His countryman Eddy Merckx restored Belgian pride in 1968, and won the race again in 1979 and 1973. Between 1968 and 1977 every winner of the Paris–Roubaix was Belgian. Former world cyclo-cross champion Roger de Vlaeminck took part in the Paris–Roubaix a total of 14 times. He won four times, in 1972, 1974, 1975 and 1977, before the

*The field streams past in the 1989 Paris-Roubaix. Many riders now use bikes with suspension for the 'Hell of The North'*

Italian Francesco Moser broke the mould with three straight wins in 1978, 1979 and 1980.

**Paris–Roubaix Winners**

| Year | Winner | Av speed (kmh) |
|------|--------|------|
| 1896 | Josef Fischer (D) | 30.162 |
| 1887 | Maurice Garin (F) | 28.124 |
| 1888 | Maurice Garin (F) | 32.599 |
| 1889 | Albert Champion (F) | 31.976 |
| 1900 | Emile Gouhours (F) | 37.352 |
| 1901 | Luc Lesna (F) | 25.861 |
| 1902 | Luc Lesna (F) | 28.088 |
| 1903 | H. Aucouturier (F) | 29.104 |
| 1904 | H. Aucouturier (F) | 32.518 |
| 1905 | Louis Trousselier (F) | 33.206 |
| 1906 | Henri Cornet (F) | 27.034 |
| 1907 | Georges Passerieu (F) | 30.971 |
| 1908 | C. van Hauwaert (B) | 25.630 |
| 1909 | Octave Lapize (F) | 30.469 |
| 1910 | Octave Lapize (F) | 29.274 |
| 1911 | Octave Lapize (F) | 31.345 |
| 1912 | Charles Crupelandt (F) | 31.294 |
| 1913 | François Faber (LUX) | 35.333 |
| 1914 | Charles Crupelandt (F) | 30.332 |
| 1919 | Henri Pelissier (F) | 22.857 |
| 1920 | Paul Deman (B) | 24.377 |
| 1921 | Henri Pelissier (F) | 29.068 |
| 1922 | Albert Dejohghe (B) | 34.690 |
| 1923 | Henri Suter (SWI) | 30.098 |
| 1924 | Jules van Hevel (B) | 25.962 |
| 1925 | Felix Sellier (B) | 28.031 |
| 1926 | Julien Delbecque (B) | 31.962 |
| 1927 | Georges Ronsee (B) | 30.449 |
| 1928 | André Leducq (F) | 33.597 |
| 1929 | Charles Meunier (B) | 29.168 |
| 1930 | Julien Vervaecke (B) | 31.146 |
| 1931 | Gaston Rebry (B) | 36.342 |
| 1932 | Romain Gijssels (B) | 37.320 |
| 1933 | Sylveer Maes (B) | 36.523 |
| 1934 | Gaston Rebry (B) | 32.415 |
| 1935 | Gaston Rebry (B) | 37.363 |
| 1936 | Georges Speicher (F) | 36.137 |
| 1937 | Jules Rossi (I) | 34.935 |
| 1938 | Lucien Storme (B) | 30.936 |
| 1939 | Emile Mason Jr (B) | 35.934 |
| 1943 | Marcel Kint (B) | 41.822 |
| 1944 | M. Desimpelaere (B) | 39.897 |
| 1945 | Paul Maye (F) | 31.212 |
| 1946 | Georges Claes (B) | 34.055 |
| 1947 | Georges Claes (B) | 39.831 |
| 1948 | Rik Van Steenbergen (B) | 43.612 |
| 1949 | André Mahe (F) and | |
| | Serge Coppi (I) | 39.356 |
| 1950 | Fausto Coppi (I) | 39.123 |

| | | |
|---|---|---|
| 1951 | A. Bevilacqua (I) | 40.355 |
| 1952 | Rik Van Steenbergen (B) | 41.938 |
| 1953 | Germain Derijcke (B) | 43.523 |
| 1954 | Raymond Impanis (B) | 35.590 |
| 1955 | Jean Forestier (F) | 40.741 |
| 1956 | Louison Bobet (F) | 41.831 |
| 1957 | Alfred de Bruyne (B) | 34.738 |
| 1958 | Leon van Daele (B) | 33.300 |
| 1959 | Noël Fore (B) | 42.760 |
| 1960 | Pino Cerami (B) | 43.538 |
| 1961 | Rik van Looy (B) | 41.700 |
| 1962 | Rik van Looy (B) | 38.321 |
| 1963 | Emile Daems (B) | 37.681 |
| 1964 | Peter Post (NL) | 45.129 |
| 1965 | Rik van Looy (B) | 41.847 |
| 1966 | Felice Gimondi (I) | 37.546 |
| 1967 | Jan Janssen (NL) | 36.464 |
| 1968 | Eddy Merckx (B) | 36.606 |
| 1969 | Walter Goodefroot (B) | 38.939 |
| 1970 | Eddy Merckx (B) | 41.644 |
| 1971 | Roger Rosiers (B) | 42.108 |
| 1972 | Roger de Vlaeminck (B) | 36.709 |
| 1973 | Eddy Merckx (B) | 36.370 |
| 1974 | Roger de Vlaeminck (B) | 37.582 |
| 1975 | Roger de Vlaeminck (B) | 40.406 |
| 1976 | Marc de Meyer (B) | 40.811 |
| 1977 | Roger de Vlaeminck (B) | 40.464 |
| 1978 | Francesco Moser (I) | 36.494 |
| 1979 | Francesco Moser (I) | 41.010 |
| 1980 | Francesco Moser (I) | 43.105 |
| 1981 | Bernard Hinault (F) | 40.868 |
| 1982 | Jan Raas (NL) | 36.733 |
| 1983 | Hennie Kuiper (NL) | 40.308 |
| 1984 | Sean Kelly (IRL) | 36.074 |
| 1985 | Marc Madiot (F) | 36.109 |
| 1986 | Sean Kelly (IRL) | 39.374 |
| 1987 | Eric Vanderaerden (B) | 36.982 |
| 1988 | Dirk Demol (B) | 40.324 |
| 1989 | Jean-Marie Wampers (B) | 39.164 |
| 1990 | Eddy Planckaert (B) | 34.855 |
| 1991 | Marc Madiot (F) | 37.332 |
| 1992 | Gilbert Duclos-Lassalle (F) | 41.480 |
| 1993 | Gilbert Duclos-Lassalle (F) | 41.650 |
| 1994 | Andrei Tchmile (MOL) | 41.305 |
| 1995 | Franco Ballerini (I) | 41.303 |

# FLÈCHE WALLONNE

The mid-week, 200 km long Belgian Flèche Wallonne or 'Walloon Arrow' which was created by the newspaper Les Sports in 1936 is the junior partner to the Liège–Bastogne–Liège, held a few days later. It is centred in the Ardennes region of Belgium with long, winding climbs on the route from Spa to Huy, and while the Flèche does not have World Cup status it can be viewed as an important prologue to its Belgian partner. To date only the Swiss rider Ferdi Kubler (1951, 1952), the Belgians Stan Ockers (1955) and Eddy Merckx (1972), and the Italian Moreno Argentin (1991) have been able to win both races in the same year.

The Belgians Marcel Kint and Eddy Merckx have most Flèche victories, having both won three times in 1943, 1944 and 1945 and 1967, 1970 and 1972 respectively. The 1995 Flèche Wallonne was Laurent Jalabert's tenth win of the spring season which included major victories in the Paris–Nice, Milan–San Remo and Criterium International. He also set a new race record of 41.958 km/h.

### Ardennais Classics
Together, the Flèche Wallonne and Liège–Bastogne–Liège are known as the 'Ardennes Classics'. Between 1950 and 1964 they were held back to back over a two-day 'Weekend Ardennais', and due to this demanding régime riders began to drop out of the Flèche in order to concentrate on the Liège–Bastogne–Liège. This prompted the organizers to move the two races four days apart to restore the status of the Flèche, and the possibility of riders scoring a double victory with the 'Weekend Ardennais' title reintroduced by the Tour de France organization in 1993.

### Flèche Wallonne Winners

| | | Av speed (kmh) |
|---|---|---|
| 1936 | Philip Demeersman (B) | 33.376 |
| 1937 | Adolf Braeckeveldt (B) | 31.285 |
| 1938 | Emile Mason Jr (B) | 35.785 |
| 1939 | E Delathouwer (B) | 35.668 |
| 1941 | Sylv Grysolle (B) | 38.198 |
| 1942 | Karel Thijs (B) | 35.657 |
| 1943 | Marcel Kint (B) | 36.705 |
| 1944 | Marcel Kint (B) | 33.638 |
| 1945 | Marcel Kint (B) | 34.344 |
| 1946 | Désiré Keteleer (B) | 36.246 |
| 1947 | Ernest Sterckx (B) | 31.663 |
| 1948 | Fermo Camellini (I) | 34.400 |
| 1949 | Rik Van Steenbergen (B) | 36.419 |
| 1950 | Fausto Coppi (I) | 36.654 |
| 1951 | Ferdi Kubler (SWI) | 34.556 |
| 1952 | Ferdi Kubler (SWI) | 36.668 |

*The Italian Moreno Argentin takes his position as a three-times winner of the Flèche Wallonne. He was equally successful in the Liège-Bastogne-Liège, with four wins putting him one down on the great Eddy Merckx*

| 1953 | Stan Ockers (B) | 34.337 | 1975 | André Dierickx (B) | 38.711 |
|---|---|---|---|---|---|
| 1954 | Germain Derijcke (B) | 33.350 | 1976 | Joop Zoetemelk (NL) | 39.569 |
| 1955 | Stan Ockers (B) | 35.453 | 1977 | Francesco Moser (I) | 37.630 |
| 1956 | Rich van Genechten (B) | 36.520 | 1978 | Michel Laurent (F) | 37.545 |
| 1957 | Raymond Impanis (B) | 37.477 | 1979 | Bernard Hinault (F) | 39.786 |
| 1958 | Rik Van Steenbergen (B) | 36.061 | 1980 | Giuseppe Saronni (I) | 38.313 |
| 1959 | Jos Hoevanaars (B) | 36.524 | 1981 | Daniël Willems (B) | 41.260 |
| 1960 | Pino Cerami (B) | 36.535 | 1982 | Mario Beccia (I) | 37.450 |
| 1961 | Willy Vannitsen (B) | 39.569 | 1983 | Bernard Hinault (F) | 36.650 |
| 1962 | Henri Dewolf (B) | 35.321 | 1984 | Kim Andersen (DNK) | 39.538 |
| 1963 | Raymond Poulidor (F) | 34.667 | 1985 | Claude Criquielion (B) | 38.701 |
| 1964 | Gilbert Desmet (B) | 34.246 | 1986 | Laurent Fignon (F) | 38.685 |
| 1965 | Roberto Poggiali (I) | 33.369 | 1987 | Jean Claude Leclercq (F) | 38.747 |
| 1966 | Michele Dancelli (I) | 38.614 | 1988 | Rolf Gölz (D) | 37.084 |
| 1967 | Eddy Merckx (B) | 37.373 | 1989 | Claude Criquielion (B) | 39.190 |
| 1968 | Rik van Looy (B) | 36.575 | 1990 | Moreno Argentin (I) | 38.878 |
| 1969 | Jos Huysmans (B) | 38.034 | 1991 | Moreno Argentin (I) | 38.884 |
| 1970 | Eddy Merckx (B) | 38.682 | 1992 | Giorgio Furlan (I) | 37.253 |
| 1971 | Roger de Vlaeminck (B) | 38.028 | 1993 | Maurizio Fondriest (I) | 38.870 |
| 1972 | Eddy Merckx (B) | 38.880 | 1994 | Moreno Argentin (I) | 41.550 |
| 1973 | André Dierickx (B) | 36.479 | 1995 | Laurent Jalabert (F) | 41.958 |
| 1974 | Frans Verbeeck (B) | 38.028 | | | |

# LIÈGE—BASTOGNE—LIÈGE

Liège–Bastogne–Liège, known as *La Doyenne*, is the most senior of the one-day Classics. It was first held in 1892, although it didn't become a professional event until 1894 when Leon Houa (Belgium) won, having also won the event as an amateur in 1890. The race was run again for amateurs in 1909, 1910 and 1911, with the next professional event in 1912 followed by another long gap to 1919 and six years to 1930 when the race was again run for amateurs. After 1930 it became a fully fledged professional event, but was interrupted for four years by World War Two.

■ Foul weather sometimes afflicts the race. In 1957 hail and snow forced half the field to retire by the halfway mark at Bastogne. The Belgians Frans Schoubben and Germain Derycke were eventually declared equal first overall. Derycke was first across the line, having led in a small group who had all crossed a railway at a closed gate which could have resulted in disqualification. Schoubben, who had crossed when the gate was open and finished some three minutes behind, could have claimed first place. When he refused to contest the result, Derycke asked that the race should be declared a dead heat. Conditions were equally bad in 1980 when 21 riders finished out of 174 starters as snow fell throughout the race. Bernard Hinault rode the last 80 kilometres and eight remaining climbs alone, to win by 9 minutes, 24 seconds.

## Beating the Hills
The principal challenge in the 260 km race lies in endless hills. After a gentle uphill ride through the Ardennes to the first climb at Saint Roch after about 65 km, the real action begins at Côte de Wanne at around 150 km. From there on Côte des Hezalles, Côte des Rosiers and Côte de La Redoute are among the nine or so climbs that decide the race. La Redoute is neither the longest nor the steepest, but is the one that has seen the most action.

## Other Troubles
Due to improper marshalling in the 1988 race, the entire 200-man bunch sped down into Houffalize where they hit roadworks that brought down more than 50 riders. Among those who sustained serious leg injuries was French hero Laurent Fignon who was off racing for two weeks and threatened legal proceedings against the race organizers. Despite the hold-up, race winner Adri van der Poel of Holland set a race record of 38.801 kmh.

■ It is not always the riders who get into trouble. In 1985 a motorbike carrying a TV cameraman fell while filming the leaders on La Redoute, bringing down Australian Phil Anderson and blocking the road. Moreno Argentin got past with a small group and went on to win.

## The Riders
Moreno Argentin won the Liège–Bastogne–Liège in 1985, 1986 and 1987, scoring three straight wins to equal Eddy Merckx who won in 1971, 1972 (when he also won the Flèche Wallonne to take the double) and 1973. However Merckx also won the race in 1969 and 1975 to score an unrivalled five wins which gave him the nickname 'Mr Ardennes'.

■ A British rider has never won the race. Best results have been achieved by Barry Hoban who was third behind Merckx in 1969, and Robert Millar of Scotland who was third behind Adri van der Poel in 1988.

### Liège–Bastogne–Liège Winners

| | | Av speed (kmh) |
|---|---|---|
| 1894 | Leon Houa (B) | 25.150 |
| 1912 | Omer Verschoore (B) | 29.941 |
| 1919 | Leon Devos (B) | 24.101 |
| 1920 | Leon Scleur (B) | 28.710 |
| 1921 | Louis Mottiat (B) | 28.306 |
| 1922 | Louis Mottiat (B) | 29.229 |
| 1923 | René Vermandel (B) | 29.376 |
| 1924 | René Vermandel (B) | 28.053 |
| 1930 | Herman Buse (D) | 27.445 |
| 1931 | Alfons Schepers (B) | 28.435 |
| 1932 | Marcel Houyoux (B) | 32.752 |
| 1933 | François Gardier (B) | 34.975 |
| 1934 | Theo Herckenrath (B) | 34.171 |
| 1935 | Alfons Schepers (B) | 36.219 |
| 1936 | Albert Beckaert (B) | 36.067 |
| 1937 | Eloi Meulenberg (B) | 36.188 |
| 1938 | Alfons Deloor (B) | 37.051 |
| 1939 | Albert Ritserveldt (B) | 37.345 |
| 1943 | Richard Depoorter (B) | 37.679 |
| 1945 | Jean Engels (B) | 32.929 |
| 1946 | P. Depredomme (B) | 33.974 |
| 1947 | Richard Depoorter (B) | 36.286 |
| 1948 | Maurice Mollin (B) | 34.943 |
| 1949 | C. Danguillaume (F) | 36.775 |
| 1950 | P. Depredomme (B) | 35.427 |
| 1951 | Ferdi Kubler (SWI) | 37.124 |
| 1952 | Ferdi Kubler (SWI) | 35.400 |
| 1953 | Alois de Hertog (B) | 34.215 |
| 1954 | Marcel Ernzer (LUX) | 34.016 |
| 1955 | Stan Ockers (B) | 34.747 |
| 1956 | Fred de Bruyne (B) | 34.973 |
| 1957 | Frans Schouben (B) and | |
| | Germain Derycke (B) | 34.386 |
| 1958 | Fred Debruyne (B) | 34.480 |
| 1959 | Fred Debruyne (B) | 35.511 |
| 1960 | Abe Geldermans (NL) | 36.401 |

| 1961 | Rik van Looy (B) | 37.224 |
| 1962 | Jos Planckaert (B) | 36.581 |
| 1963 | Frans Melckenbeeck (B) | 37.179 |
| 1964 | Willy Bocklant (B) | 34.615 |
| 1965 | Carmine Preziosi (I) | 36.051 |
| 1966 | Jacques Anquetil (F) | 36.164 |
| 1967 | Walter Godefroot (B) | 35.971 |
| 1968 | Valeer van Sweefelt (B) | 36.380 |
| 1969 | Eddy Merckx (B) | 37.024 |
| 1970 | Roger de Vlaeminck (B) | 35.971 |
| 1971 | Eddy Merckx (B) | 36.115 |
| 1972 | Eddy Merckx (B) | 36.488 |
| 1973 | Eddy Merckx (B) | 37.869 |
| 1974 | Georges Pintens (B) | 38.537 |
| 1975 | Eddy Merckx (B) | 38.247 |
| 1976 | Jos Bruyere (B) | 37.396 |
| 1977 | Bernard Hinault (F) | 37.654 |
| 1978 | Jos Bruyere (B) | 36.464 |
| 1979 | Dietrich Thurau (D) | 36.713 |
| 1980 | Bernard Hinault (F) | 34.716 |
| 1981 | Josef Fuchs (SWI) | 35.362 |
| 1982 | Silvano Contini (I) | 34.033 |
| 1983 | Steven Rooks (NL) | 35.516 |
| 1984 | Sean Kelly (IRL) | 36.366 |
| 1985 | Moreno Argentin (I) | 37.021 |
| 1986 | Moreno Argentin (I) | 37.673 |
| 1987 | Moreno Argentin (I) | 38.700 |
| 1988 | Adri van der Poel (NL) | 38.801 |
| 1989 | Sean Kelly (IRL) | 36.243 |
| 1990 | Eric van Lancker (B) | 35.560 |
| 1991 | Moreno Argentin (I) | 36.827 |
| 1992 | Dirk de Wolf (B) | 35.882 |
| 1993 | Rolf Sorensen (DNK) | 36.072 |
| 1994 | Evgeni Berzin (RUS) | 36.910 |
| 1995 | Mauro Gianetti (SWI) | 39.307 |

**'Weekend Ardennais' Winners**

| 1950 | Raymond Impanis (B) |
| 1951 | Ferdi Kubler (SWI) |
| 1952 | Ferdi Kubler (SWI) |
| 1953 | Jean Storms (B) |
| 1954 | Marcel Erzner (LUX) |
| 1955 | Stan Ockers (B) |
| 1956 | Rick van Genechten (B) |
| 1957 | Frans Schoubben (B) |
| 1958 | Fred de Bruyne (B) |
| 1959 | Frans Schoubben (B) |
| 1960 | Albert Geldermans (NL) |
| 1961 | Rik van Looy (B) |
| 1962 | Jos Planckaert (B) |
| 1963 | Raymond Poulidor (F) |
| 1964 | Willy Bocklandt (B) |
| 1993 | Maurizio Fondriest (I) |
| 1994 | Evgeni Berzin (RUS) |
| 1995 | Laurent Jalabert (F) |

# AMSTEL GOLD RACE

The Amstel Gold is Holland's only one-day Classic, usually held on the Saturday of the last weekend in April when many professional teams are preparing for the first big national Tour in Spain. Having been first held in 1966, the Amstel Gold is one of the youngest Classics with the race routed through the Limburg province of Holland.

There are surprisingly numerous hills and very narrow roads which restrict access for press cars and motorbikes. Unlike other major road races in Europe, the roads are not completely closed to traffic, but motor vehicles are required to stop and pull over as the race passes them by.

**Amstel Uphills**

Among the 15 or so climbs of the Amstel Gold, most of the action takes place on the Gulpenberg, the Konig van Espanje and the Keutenberg with 500 metres of hill at between 25 and 28 per cent steepness. With the exception of its first year when the course covered 302 km, the race has never been

*Jan Raas won the Amstel Gold every year between 1977 and 1980. He also won the race in 1982 and would have achieved six straight wins had not Bernard Hinault spoiled his score in 1981*

longer than 250 km as it follows an intricate, winding route which never gets further than 45 km from the start at Heerlen or the finish at Meersen.

## The Riders

Jan Raas is the Dutch hero of the Amstel Gold, having won the race four times in succession between 1977 and 1980 when he was also world champion. In 1981 he was prevented by Bernard Hinault from becoming the first rider to win a single Classic race five years running, but was partly compensated by winning the Amstel Gold for his fifth and last time in 1982. The only other rider to win the Amstel Gold more than once has been Eddy Merckx – in 1973 and 1975.

Joop Zoetemelk, another Dutch hero, was world champion at the age of 38 in 1985. Two years later in 1987 he won the Amstel Gold by a clear half minute at the age of 40. The Amstel Gold race record is held by Dutchman Arie den Hertog, set at 43.711 kmh in 1967. In 1983 Phil Anderson became the first and only native English-speaker to win the race.

### Amstel Gold Winners

| | | Av speed (kmh) |
|------|----------------------|----------------|
| 1966 | Jean Stablinski (F) | 38.649 |
| 1967 | Arie den Hartog (NL) | 43.711 |
| 1968 | Harry Steevens (NL) | 41.704 |
| 1969 | Guido Reybrouck (B) | 40.782 |
| 1970 | Georges Pintens (B) | 37.745 |
| 1971 | Frans Verbeeck (B) | 37.622 |
| 1972 | Walter Planckaert (B) | 37.653 |
| 1973 | Eddy Merckx (B) | 35.650 |
| 1974 | Gerrie Knetemann (NL) | 38.963 |
| 1975 | Eddy Merckx (B) | 37.231 |
| 1976 | Freddy Maertens (B) | 39.078 |
| 1977 | Jan Raas (NL) | 39.894 |
| 1978 | Jan Raas (NL) | 37.803 |
| 1979 | Jan Raas (NL) | 39.507 |
| 1980 | Jan Raas (NL) | 41.417 |
| 1981 | Bernard Hinault (F) | 39.741 |
| 1982 | Jan Raas (NL) | 38.354 |
| 1983 | Phil Anderson (AUS) | 41.434 |
| 1984 | Jacques Hanegraaf (NL) | 40.584 |
| 1985 | Gerrie Knetemann (NL) | 37.446 |
| 1986 | Steven Rooks (NL) | 39.665 |
| 1987 | Joop Zoetemelk (NL) | 38.943 |
| 1988 | Jelle Nijdam (NL) | 37.386 |
| 1989 | Eric van Lancker (B) | 40.187 |
| 1990 | Adri van der Poel (NL) | 41.507 |
| 1991 | Frans Maassen (NL) | 40.135 |
| 1992 | Olaf Ludwig (D) | 38.219 |
| 1993 | Rolf Jaermann (SWI) | 37.343 |
| 1994 | Johan Museeuw (B) | 37.260 |
| 1995 | Mauro Gianetti (SWI) | 38.513 |

# SAN SEBASTIAN–SAN SEBASTIAN

The *Classica Ciclista San Sebastian–San Sebastian* follows a route of around 240 km from the northern Spanish seaside resort of San Sebastian, up into the Basque mountains, and back down to San Sebastian again with a number of demanding first and second category climbs. First held in 1981, Spain's only World Cup event is very much a newcomer to the scene and lacks the status of the old Classics; its entry also suffers due to being held soon after the Tour de France in early August.

■ San Sebastian has been won three times by Spaniard Marino Lejarreta in 1981, 1982 and 1987. The highest-placed British finisher is Graham Jones who was second in 1981; the only other English-language rider to be placed in the first three was Sean Kelly who was third in 1990, until Lance Armstrong won the race in 1995.

### San Sebastian Winners

| | | Av. speed |
|------|--------------------------|-----------|
| 1981 | Marino Lejarreta (E) | - |
| 1982 | Marino Lejarreta (E) | - |
| 1983 | Claude Criquielion (B) | - |
| 1984 | Niki Ruttimann (SWI) | - |
| 1985 | Adri van der Poel (NL) | - |
| 1986 | Inaki Gaston (E) | - |
| 1987 | Marino Lejarreta (E) | 38.618* |
| 1988 | Gert-Jan Theunisse (NL) | 39.610 |
| 1989 | Gerhard Zadrobilek (A) | 38.108 |
| 1990 | Miguel Indurain (E) | 39.159 |
| 1991 | Gianni Bugno (I) | 39.180 |
| 1992 | Raul Alcala (MEX) | 39.187 |
| 1993 | Claudio Chiappucci (I) | 41.052 |
| 1994 | Armand de las Cuevas (F) | 43.975 |
| 1995 | Lance Armstrong (USA) | 41.659 |

* San Sebastian was first held as a premier event in 1987.

# WINCANTON/LEEDS CLASSIC

Britain's only major one-day event is the newest race on the World Cup circuit, which also suffers from an early August date close to the end of the Tour de France. The race was first held at Newcastle-upon-Tyne in 1989, at Brighton in 1990 and 1991, and has been staged at Leeds since 1992. The highest-placed rider with English as his first language was Sean Kelly, third in 1989 and second in 1990, until Max Sciandri won the race in 1995. Sciandri was born in Britain of Italian parentage, first raced as an Italian professional, and then changed his nationality to become a British professional in 1995.

**Wincanton/Leeds Classic Winners**

|      |                        | Av speed (kmh) |
|------|------------------------|---------------|
| 1989 | Frans Maassen (NL)     | 39.487        |
| 1990 | Gianni Bugno (I)       | 38.772        |
| 1991 | Eric van Lancker (B)   | 37.411        |
| 1992 | Massimo Ghirotto (I)   | 37.222        |
| 1993 | Alberto Volpi (I)      | 40.636        |
| 1994 | Gianluca Bortolami (I) | 38.131        |
| 1995 | Max Sciandri (UK)      | 38.850        |

*Right: Max Sciandri scored a well timed win in the Leeds Classic in 1995*

# MEISTERSCHAFT VON ZURICH

Swiss riders dominated the *Meisterschaft von Zurich* or 'Zurich Championship' between 1914 and 1956, winning 34 out of 41 years (the race was not held in 1915 and 1916). Henri Suter holds the record for the highest number of victories, having won six times (1919–20, 1922, 1924, 1928 and 1929).

■ Since 1957 international riders have taken over, and Swiss riders have only won three times. The Meisterschaft is one of the few Classics that Eddy Merckx never won; the closest he came was second in 1975 behind fellow countryman Roger de Vlaeminck. Phil Anderson is the only English-language rider to have won the Meisterschaft in 1984. He also set the third highest speed for the race at 40.738 kmh, 0.510 kmh slower than the speed record of 42.228 kmh set by Gino Bartali 38 years earlier in 1946 when he beat Fausto Coppi into second place on a 280 km course in 1946.

■ Among other English-speaking riders, Eric Mackenzie of New Zealand was first to finish in 1982, but was disqualified when he failed a dope test. Canadian Steve Bauer was second in 1986; Greg LeMond second in 1990; and Lance Armstrong second in 1992.

■ Since 1988 the Meisterschaft von Zurich has followed five laps of a 50 km route round Zurich, with the decider being the tough Regensburg climb.

**Meisterschaft Von Zurich Winners**

|      |                          | Av speed (kmh) |
|------|--------------------------|---------------|
| 1914 | Henri Rheinwald (SWI)    | -             |
| 1917 | Charles Martinet (I)     | -             |
| 1918 | Anton Sieger (SWI)       | -             |
| 1919 | Henri Suter (SWI)        | -             |
| 1920 | Henri Suter (SWI)        | -             |
| 1921 | Ricardo Maffeo (I)       | 30.238        |
| 1922 | Henri Suter (SWI)        | 30.534        |
| 1923 | Adolf Huschke (D)        | 27.818        |
| 1924 | Henri Suter (SWI)        | 32.914        |
| 1925 | Hans Kaspar (SWI)        | 30.738        |
| 1926 | Albert Blattmann (SWI)   | 31.260        |
| 1927 | Kastor Notter (SWI)      | 29.702        |
| 1928 | Henri Suter (SWI)        | 29.608        |
| 1929 | Henri Suter (SWI)        | 33.149        |
| 1930 | Omer Taverne (B)         | 31.070        |
| 1931 | Max Bulla (A)            | 31.491        |
| 1932 | August Erne (SWI)        | 31.715        |
| 1933 | Walter Blattmann (SWI)   | 27.438        |
| 1934 | Paul Egli (SWI)          | 32.539        |
| 1935 | Paul Egli (SWI)          | 33.602        |
| 1936 | Werner Buchwalder (SWI)  | 35.292        |
| 1937 | Leo Amberg (SWI)         | 37.300        |
| 1938 | Hans Martin (SWI)        | 35.110        |
| 1939 | Karl Litschi (SWI)       | 33.268        |
| 1940 | Robert Zimmermann (SWI)  | 35.909        |
| 1941 | Walter Diggelman (SWI)   | 36.479        |
| 1942 | Paul Egli (SWI)          | 36.270        |
| 1943 | Ferdi Kubler (SWI)       | 38.347        |
| 1944 | Ernst Naef (SWI)         | 35.286        |

| | | |
|---|---|---|
| 1945 | Leo Weilemann (SWI) | 38.388 |
| 1946 | Gino Bartali (I) | 42.228 |
| 1947 | Charles Guyot (SWI) | 37.567 |
| 1948 | Gino Bartali (I) | 36.477 |
| 1949 | Fritz Schaer (SWI) | 37.796 |
| 1950 | Fritz Schaer (SWI) | 36.170 |
| 1951 | Jean Brun (SWI) | 32.188 |
| 1952 | Hugo Koblet (SWI) | 32.368 |
| 1953 | Eugen Kamber (SWI) | 39.377 |
| 1954 | Hugo Koblet (SWI) | 38.432 |
| 1955 | Max Schellenberg (SWI) | 37.105 |
| 1956 | Carlo Clerici (SWI) | 39.516 |
| 1957 | Hans Junkermann (D) | 38.875 |
| 1958 | Giuseppe Cainero (I) | 38.443 |
| 1959 | Angelo Conterno (I) | 38.163 |
| 1960 | Freddy Ruegg (SWI) | 37.936 |
| 1961 | Rolf Maurer (SWI) | 38.034 |
| 1962 | Jan Janssen (NL) | 36.443 |
| 1963 | Franco Balmanion (I) | 38.464 |
| 1964 | Guido Reybrouck (B) | 38.608 |
| 1965 | Franco Bitossi (I) | 38.229 |
| 1966 | Italo Zilioli (I) | 39.782 |
| 1967 | Robert Hagmann (SWI) | 39.797 |
| 1968 | Franco Bitossi (I) | 38.472 |
| 1969 | Roger Swerts (B) | 38.193 |
| 1970 | Walter Godefroot (B) | 38.767 |
| 1971 | Herman Vanspringel (B) | 38.650 |
| 1972 | Willy Vanneste (B) | 38.603 |
| 1973 | André Dierickx (B) | 37.414 |
| 1974 | Walter Godefroot (B) | 36.734 |
| 1975 | Roger de Vlaeminck (B) | 36.605 |
| 1976 | Freddy Maertens (B) | 39.857 |
| 1977 | Francesco Moser (I) | 37.804 |
| 1978 | Dietrich Thurau (D) | 39.594 |
| 1979 | Giuseppe Saronni (I) | 40.546 |
| 1980 | Gery Verlinden (B) | 37.298 |
| 1981 | Beat Breu (SWI) | 38.595 |
| 1982 | Adri van der Poel (NL) | 40.059 |
| 1983 | Johan van de Velde (NL) | 38.417 |
| 1984 | Phil Anderson (AUS) | 40.738 |
| 1985 | Ludo Peeters (B) | 38.573 |
| 1986 | Acacio da Silva (POR) | 40.084 |
| 1987 | Rolf Gölz (D) | 33.733 |
| 1988 | Steven Rooks (NL) | 39.531 |
| 1989 | Steve Bauer (CDN) | 37.834 |
| 1990 | Charly Mottet (F) | 39.222 |
| 1991 | Johan Museeuw (B) | 38.074 |
| 1992 | Viatcheslav Ekimov (RUS) | 39.998 |
| 1993 | Maurizio Fondriest (I) | 37.410 |
| 1994 | Ginaluca Bortolami (I) | 39.061 |
| 1995 | Johan Museeuw (B) | 42.190 |

*Phil Anderson has been Australia's most successful road racer.
Having worn the Tour de France maillot jaune in 1982, he
won the Meisterschaft von Zurich two years later*

# PARIS–TOURS

The Paris–Tours is known as the 'Sprinters Classic',
or sometimes as the *Grand Prix de l'Automne*. It was
first run as an amateur event in 1896, following a
route from the centre of Paris to Tours in the Loire
Valley. The newspaper *Paris Velo* gave prizes and
certificates for all those who finished the course
within 18 hours. The race was held for the second
time in 1901 when it was open to professionals, and
for the third time in 1906 with backing from *L'Auto*.

■ As the road surfaces improved and the riders
grew fitter and faster, the Paris–Tours began to
degenerate into a mass promenade for most of the
distance over easy terrain with a final bunch
sprint to the finish. In an effort to make the race

more interesting, *derailleurs* were banned in 1965 and riders had to use a single freewheel with a hand change for the two chainrings. The idea was not a success, but it enabled Belgian Gerben Karstens to set a race record of 45.029 kmh which he held until 1992, when his fellow countryman Hendrik Redant set a new record of 46.337 kmh.

### Blois–Chaville

Between 1974 and 1987 the Paris–Tours was run south to north as the Blois–Chaville, a race originally held in 1917 and 1918. Since 1988 the race has started at Chaville in the Paris suburbs and finished at Tours, with a slightly tougher route to link the two cities.

### The Riders

In 1921 Frenchman Francis Pelissier won in atrocious conditions. Due to heavy snow almost half the riders retired at Chartres; at Chateaudun his brother Henri was one of those who retired, handing his cape to Francis while reviving himself with a glass of rum in a roadside café. Francis wore two capes for the rest of the race, leading until he punctured near the finish. With his hands frozen it is said he tore the tyre off with his teeth, riding on the bare rim and retaking the lead on the climb out of Azay-le-Rideau. Henri Pelissier won the race the next year.

■ Eddy Merckx never won the event. In 1968 he was placed to win, but pulled over to let team-mate Guido Reybrouck through as a reward for his help earlier in the season. Gustaaf Danneels, Paul Maye and Guido Reybrouck all won the race three times. Gustaaf Daneels and Guido Reybrouck were uncle and nephew to one another. When he retired Guido Reybrouck celebrated by calling his car-wash business the Paris–Tours, the same name Gustaaf Daneels had given to his garage.

■ The best British results in the race have been by Tommy Simpson who was second in 1963, and Barry Hoban who was second in 1967. Sean Kelly won in 1984 and was third in 1985; Phil Anderson won in 1986 and was second in 1990.

### Paris–Tours Winners

|      |                           | Av speed (kmh) |
|------|---------------------------|----------------|
| 1901 | Jean Fischer (F)          | 26.982         |
| 1906 | Lucien Petit-Breton (F)   | 29.557         |
| 1907 | Geo Passerieu (F)         | 32.186         |
| 1908 | Omer Beaugendre (F)       | 30.690         |
| 1909 | François Faber (LUX)      | 30.680         |
| 1910 | François Faber (LUX)      | 32.105         |
| 1911 | Octave Lapize (F)         | 27.054         |
| 1912 | Louis Heuschem (B)        | 26.348         |
| 1913 | C Crupelandt (F)          | 33.931         |
| 1914 | Oscar Egg (SWI)           | 32.147         |
| 1917 | Philippe Thijs (B)        | 34.009         |
| 1918 | C Mantelet (F)            | 30.182         |
| 1919 | H Thiberghien (B)         | 27.178         |
| 1920 | E Christophe (F)          | 25.570         |
| 1921 | Francis Pelissier (F)     | 22.893         |
| 1922 | Henri Pelissier (F)       | 29.653         |
| 1923 | Paul Deman (B)            | 25.014         |
| 1924 | Louis Mottiat (B)         | 28.423         |
| 1925 | D Verschueren (B)         | 27.469         |
| 1926 | Henri Suter (SWI)         | 28.230         |
| 1927 | Henri Suter (SWI)         | 35.324         |
| 1928 | D Verschueren (B)         | 34.746         |
| 1929 | Nicolas Frantz (LUX)      | 27.355         |
| 1930 | Jean Marechal (F)         | 34.112         |
| 1931 | André Leducq (F)          | 31.276         |
| 1932 | Julien Moineau (F)        | 37.251         |
| 1933 | Jules Merviel (F)         | 37.528         |
| 1934 | Gustaaf Danneels (B)      | 38.358         |
| 1935 | René le Greves (F)        | 37.886         |
| 1936 | Gustaaf Danneels (B)      | 41.455         |
| 1937 | Gustaaf Danneels (B)      | 41.092         |
| 1938 | Jules Rossi (I)           | 42.097         |
| 1939 | Frans Bonduel (B)         | 39.655         |
| 1941 | Paul Maye (F)             | 36.096         |
| 1942 | Paul Maye (F)             | 36.024         |
| 1943 | Gaby Gaudin (F)           | 37.422         |
| 1944 | Lucien Teisseire (F)      | 41.452         |
| 1945 | Paul Maye (F)             | 37.161         |

*Tommy Simpson finished second in the 1963 Paris–Tours, the same year in which he won the Bordeaux–Paris Classic. Here he celebrates his win at the Parc des Princes in the capital*

| 1946 | Briek Schotte (B) | 37.714 |
|------|-------------------|--------|
| 1947 | Briek Schotte (B) | 35.678 |
| 1948 | Louis Caput (F) | 43.096 |
| 1949 | Albert Ramon (B) | 41.377 |
| 1950 | André Mahe (F) | 39.536 |
| 1951 | Jacques Dupont (F) | 41.691 |
| 1952 | Raymond Guegan (F) | 40.861 |
| 1953 | Jozef Schils (B) | 43.529 |
| 1954 | Gilbert Scodeller (F) | 40.881 |
| 1955 | Jacques Dupont (F) | 43.766 |
| 1956 | Albert Bouvet (F) | 40.844 |
| 1957 | Alfred de Bruyne (B) | 42.842 |
| 1958 | Gilbert de Smet (B) | 37.148 |
| 1959 | Rik van Looy (B) | 37.791 |
| 1960 | Jo de Haan (NL) | 40.001 |
| 1961 | Jos Wouters (B) | 38.407 |
| 1962 | Jo de Roo (NL) | 44.903 |
| 1963 | Jo de Roo (NL) | 39.162 |
| 1964 | Guido Reybrouck (B) | 36.466 |
| 1965 | Gerben Karstens (NL) | 45.029 |
| 1966 | Guido Reybrouck (B) | 43.355 |
| 1967 | Rik van Looy (B) | 41.720 |
| 1968 | Guido Reybrouck (B) | 44.584 |
| 1969 | Herman Vanspringel (B) | 43.038 |
| 1970 | Jurgen Tschan (D) | 41.011 |
| 1971 | Rik van Linden (B) | 40.766 |
| 1972 | Noel Vantyghem (B) | 40.697 |
| 1973 | Rik van Linden (B) | 42.076 |
| 1988 | Peter Pieters (B) | 34.202 |
| 1989 | Jelle Nijdam (NL) | 39.402 |
| 1990 | Rolf Sorensen (DNK) | 39.601 |
| 1991 | Johan Capiot (B) | 38.406 |
| 1992 | Hendrik Redant (B) | 46.337 |
| 1993 | Johan Museeuw (B) | 38.140 |
| 1994 | Eric Zabel (D) | 39.934 |
| 1995 | Daniele Nardello (I) | 36.000 |

## Blois–Chaville Winners

| | Av speed (kmh) | |
|------|-------------------|--------|
| 1917 | Charles Deruyter (B) | 30.318 |
| 1918 | Phillippe Thijs (B) | 27.918 |
| 1974 | Francesco Moser (I) | 43.268 |
| 1975 | Freddy Maertens (B) | 41.241 |
| 1976 | Ronald Dewitte (B) | 43.519 |
| 1977 | Joop Zoetemelk (NL) | 44.531 |
| 1978 | Jan Raas (NL) | 38.896 |
| 1979 | Joop Zoetemelk (NL) | 41.638 |
| 1980 | Daniel Willems (B) | 39.498 |
| 1981 | Jan Raas (NL) | 40.113 |
| 1982 | J L Vandenbroucke (B) | 40.777 |
| 1983 | Ludo Peeters (B) | 43.431 |
| 1984 | Sean Kelly (IRL) | 41.411 |
| 1985 | Ludo Peeters (B) | 38.622 |
| 1986 | Phil Anderson (AUS) | 43.500 |
| 1987 | Adri van der Poel (NL) | 38.734 |

# GIRO DI LOMBARDIA

The Giro Di Lombardia is the one-day Classic that closes the Italian season, and is known as the 'Race of the Falling Leaves'. It is also the oldest of the Italian Classics, dating back to 1905 when Giovanni Gerbi won by more than 40 minutes on a course that followed rough roads and mule tracks. In that first Giro the Italian supporters were not at all sporting – a bicycle was thrown into the path of two Frenchmen chasing Gerbi, and while friendly enthusiasts helped to pace or push him to victory, tacks were thrown into the path of his rivals.

In 1985 the start was switched to Como at the southern end of Lake Como, and the finish to Milan. Since 1990 the Giro Di Lombardia has started at Monza to the north of Milan, and finished at Como.

## The Riders

Fausto Coppi holds the record number of victories in the Giro Di Lombardia with five, having won four years running between 1946 and 1949, and once in 1954. Henri Pelissier, Costante Girardengo, Alfredo Binda and Sean Kelly have all won the race three times. For Sean Kelly, his 1983 win was his first Classic victory. Eddy Merckx won the race in 1971 and 1972. In 1973 he finished four minutes clear of second-placed Felice Gimondi but was disqualified for failing a urine test. The only British winner of the Giro di Lombardia is Tom Simpson in 1965, the same year in which he won the world championship.

## Giro di Lombardia Winners

| | | Av speed (kmh) |
|------|-------------------|--------|
| 1905 | Giovanni Gerbi (I) | 24.950 |
| 1906 | Giuseppe Brambilla (I) | 26.452 |
| 1907 | Gustave Garrigou (F) | 27.668 |
| 1908 | François Faber (LUX) | 28.750 |
| 1909 | Giovanni Cuniolo (I) | 30.850 |
| 1910 | Giovanni Micheletto (I) | 27.030 |
| 1911 | Henri Pelissier (F) | 30.660 |
| 1912 | Carlo Oriani (I) | 31.298 |
| 1913 | Henri Pelissier (F) | 30.400 |
| 1914 | Lauro Bordin (I) | 32.290 |
| 1915 | Gaetano Belloni (I) | 28.330 |
| 1916 | Leopoldo Torricelli (I) | 25.330 |
| 1917 | Philippe Thijs (B) | 29.280 |
| 1918 | Gaetano Belloni (I) | 26.500 |
| 1919 | Costante Girardengo (I) | 26.391 |
| 1920 | Henri Pelissier (F) | 28.819 |
| 1921 | Costante Girardengo (I) | 27.449 |
| 1922 | Costante Girardengo (I) | 27.349 |
| 1923 | Giovanni Brunero (I) | 26.497 |
| 1924 | Giovanni Brunero (I) | 28.935 |
| 1925 | Alfredo Binda (I) | 28.804 |

| | | | | | | |
|------|----------------------------|--------|------|------------------------------|--------|
| 1926 | Alfredo Binda (I) | 26.120 | 1962 | Jo de Roo (NL) | 35.633 |
| 1927 | Alfredo Binda (I) | 28.182 | 1963 | Jo de Roo (NL) | 37.085 |
| 1928 | Gaetano Belloni (I) | 27.606 | 1964 | Gianni Motta (I) | 38.550 |
| 1929 | Piero Fossati (I) | 28.958 | 1965 | Tom Simpson (GB) | 39.213 |
| 1930 | Michele Mara (I) | 30.913 | 1966 | Felice Gimondi (I) | 38.272 |
| 1931 | Alfredo Binda (I) | 27.385 | 1967 | Franco Bitossi (I) | 38.092 |
| 1932 | Antonio Negrini (I) | 30.576 | 1968 | Herman Vanspringel (B) | 38.092 |
| 1933 | Domenico Piemontesi (I) | 32.502 | 1969 | Jean-Pierre Monsere (B) | 40.009 |
| 1934 | Learco Guerra (I) | 32.368 | 1970 | Franco Bitossi (I) | 38.241 |
| 1935 | Enrico Mollo (I) | 32.268 | 1971 | Eddy Merckx (B) | 39.365 |
| 1936 | Gino Bartali (I) | 35.616 | 1972 | Eddy Merckx (B) | 39.127 |
| 1937 | Aldo Bini (I) | 33.297 | 1973 | Felice Gimondi (I) | 37.315 |
| 1938 | Cino Cinelli (I) | 34.974 | 1974 | Roger de Vlaeminck (B) | 37.290 |
| 1939 | Gino Bartali (I) | 33.715 | 1975 | Francesco Moser (I) | 35.945 |
| 1940 | Gino Bartali (I) | 34.405 | 1976 | Roger de Vlaeminck (B) | 39.326 |
| 1941 | Mario Ricci (I) | 33.670 | 1977 | Gibi Baronchelli (I) | 36.453 |
| 1942 | Aldo Bini (I) | 36.073 | 1978 | Francesco Moser (I) | 39.213 |
| 1945 | Mario Ricci (I) | 36.177 | 1979 | Bernard Hinault (F) | 40.008 |
| 1946 | Fausto Coppi (I) | 36.046 | 1980 | Alfons de Wolf (B) | 35.747 |
| 1947 | Fausto Coppi (I) | 32.876 | 1981 | Hennie Kuiper (NL) | 39.642 |
| 1948 | Fausto Coppi (I) | 37.849 | 1982 | Giuseppe Saronni (I) | 40.754 |
| 1949 | Fausto Coppi (I) | 38.002 | 1983 | Sean Kelly (IRL) | 39.164 |
| 1950 | Renzo Soldani (I) | 38.093 | 1984 | Bernard Hinault (F) | 40.831 |
| 1951 | Louison Bobet (F) | 38.626 | 1985 | Sean Kelly (IRL) | 41.208 |
| 1952 | Giuseppe Minardi (I) | 37.293 | 1986 | Gibi Baronchelli (I) | 37.329 |
| 1953 | Bruno Landi (I) | 36.812 | 1987 | Moreno Argentin (I) | 38.576 |
| 1954 | Fausto Coppi (I) | 37.415 | 1988 | Charly Mottet (F) | 38.134 |
| 1955 | Cieto Maule (I) | 38.670 | 1989 | Tony Rominger (SWI) | 38.368 |
| 1956 | André Darrigade (F) | 38.468 | 1990 | Gilles Delion (F) | 39.704 |
| 1957 | Diego Ronchini (I) | 38.945 | 1991 | Sean Kelly (IRL) | 39.176 |
| 1958 | Nino Defilippis (I) | 39.705 | 1992 | Tony Rominger (SWI) | 39.311 |
| 1959 | Rik van Looy (B) | 40.899 | 1993 | Pascal Richard (SWI) | 39.821 |
| 1960 | Emile Daems (B) | 40.627 | 1994 | Vladislav Bobrik (RUS) | 40.291 |
| 1961 | Vito Taccone (I) | 35.604 | 1995 | Gianni Faresin (I) | 43.321 |

*Jacques Anquetil dominated the Grand Prix des Nations. Here, in 1953 at the age of 19, he is cheered on to his first of nine wins*

# Grand Prix Des Nations

The Grand Prix des Nations is the sole one-day, road-race time trial in the World Cup series. Because the racers ride alone, it is sometimes known as the 'Truth Race'. For many years it was regarded as the unofficial world time trial championship, but that role was superseded when a time trial was installed as a major part of the official world road race championships.

## Changing Venues

The Grand Prix Des Nations was first held in 1932 in the Chevreuse Valley to the west of Paris, and during World War Two was twice held at occupied and non-occupied locations – the latter at Toulouse in 1941 where Jules Rossi won and at Avignon-Marseilles in 1942 where J-M Goasmat won. The Grand Prix continued to be held near Paris where the course was reduced from 140 km to 100 km and then to 73 km. In 1973 the Grand Prix was held at St Jean de Monts. In 1974, 1975 and 1976 it was held at Angers, before moving to a double circuit above Cannes between 1977 and 1989 when it was part of the Pernod points competition.

■ In 1990 the Grand Prix des Nations was relocated as the final event in the annual World Cup, moving to a new course around Lac de Madine in Lorraine in eastern France, where two circuits total 84.5 kilometres and climbs are long rather than steep with nothing much higher than 150 metres.

## The Riders

No Briton has ever won the Grand Prix des Nations. The best result has been fourth place by Chris Boardman in 1993. English-speaking riders have fared better – Sean Kelly won in 1986; Stephen Roche took second in 1981; Greg LeMond was second in 1983; and Stephen Hodge also finished second in 1993.

■ The record number of wins in the Grand Prix des Nations is held by Jacques Anquetil with nine victories between 1953 and 1966, including winning every year between 1953 and 1958. The only rider to approach this is Bernard Hinault who won the Grand Prix five times. Anquetil also holds the race records at Chevreuse for the 140.3 km course (40.226 kmh in 1955) and the 100 km course (43.591 kmh in 1961). Felice Gimondi holds the record for the Chevreuse 73.5 km course (47.518 kmh in 1968). Roy Schuiten holds the record for the Angers 90 km course (44.980 kmh in 1975). Laurent Fignon holds the record for the Cannes 89 km course (45.660 kmh in 1989). Fignon used tri-bars for the first time on this occasion, and partly made up for his disappointment at being beaten by Greg LeMond in the Tour de France earlier the same year.

■ Among the smallest victory margins in the Grand Prix des Nations are two five second wins – Sean Kelly over Laurent Fignon in 1986 and Johan Bruyneel over Tony Rominger in 1992. An even smaller margin was the four second win for Aldo Moser over Roger Rivière of France in 1959.

## Grand Prix des Nations Winners

| | | |
|---|---|---|
| 1932 M Archambaud (F) | 1954 Jacques Anquetil (F) | 1976 Freddy Maertens (B) |
| 1933 Ray Louviot (F) | 1955 Jacques Anquetil (F) | 1977 Bernard Hinault (F) |
| 1934 Antonin Magne (F) | 1956 Jacques Anquetil (F) | 1978 Bernard Hinault (F) |
| 1935 Antonin Magne (F) | 1957 Jacques Anquetil (F) | 1979 Bernard Hinault (F) |
| 1936 Antonin Magne (F) | 1958 Jacques Anquetil (F) | 1980 J L Vandenbroucke (B) |
| 1937 Pierre Cogan (F) | 1959 Aldo Moser (I) | 1981 Daniel Gisiger (SWI) |
| 1938 Louis Aimar (F) | 1960 Ercole Baldini (I) | 1982 Bernard Hinault (F) |
| 1941 Jules Rossi (I) | 1961 Jacques Anquetil (F) | 1983 Daniel Gisiger (SWI) |
| 1941 Louis Aimar (F) | 1962 Ferdinand Bracke (B) | 1984 Bernard Hinault (F) |
| 1942 J-M Goasmat (F) | 1963 Raymond Poulidor (B) | 1985 Charly Mottet (F) |
| 1942 Emile Idee (F) | 1964 Walter Boucquet (B) | 1986 Sean Kelly (IRL) |
| 1943 Jozef Somers (B) | 1965 Jacques Anquetil (F) | 1987 Charly Mottet (F) |
| 1944 Emile Carrara (F) | 1966 Jacques Anquetil (F) | 1988 Charly Mottet (F) |
| 1945 Eloi Tassin (F) | 1967 Felice Gimondi (I) | 1989 Laurent Fignon (F) |
| 1946 Fausto Coppi (I) | 1968 Felice Gimondi (I) | 1990 Thomas Wegmuller (SWI) |
| 1947 Fausto Coppi (I) | 1969 Herman Vanspringel (B) | 1991 Tony Rominger (SWI) |
| 1948 René Berton (F) | 1970 Herman Vanspringel (B) | 1992 Johan Bruyneel (B) |
| 1949 Charles Coste (F) | 1971 Luis Ocana (B) | 1993 Armand de las Guevas (F) |
| 1950 Maurice Blomme (B) | 1972 Roger Swerts (B) | 1994 Tony Rominger (SWI) |
| 1951 Hugo Koblet (SWI) | 1973 Eddy Merckx (B) | 1995 *Not held due to clash* |
| 1952 Louison Bobet (F) | 1974 Roy Schuiten (NL) | *with World Time Trial* |
| 1953 Jacques Anquetil (F) | 1975 Roy Schuiten (NL) | *Championship.* |

# The Great Stage Races

## TOUR DE FRANCE

The Tour de France, known as *La Grande Boucle* (the big loop), is the world's premier stage race. It was founded by Henri Desgranges in 1903, and came about as an indirect result of the famous Dreyfus affair in which an innocent Jewish army officer was found guilty of being a spy. When the cycling newspaper *Le Velo* published a pro-Dreyfus article, its main financial backer – the bicycle builder Baron de Dion – pulled out his support and started a rival paper, *L'Auto Velo*, which soon changed its name to *L'Auto*. Its editor was the first world hour-record holder Henri Desgranges, who organized the Tour de France to create interest in the new paper and build its circulation.

### Early Tours and Corruption

The first tour of 1903 was composed of six very long stages which involved riding through the night:
Paris–Lyon 290 miles (467 km)
Lyon–Marseille 230 miles (370 km)
Marseille–Toulouse 270 miles (434 km)
Toulouse–Bordeaux 170 miles (274 km)
Bordeaux–Nantes 265 miles (426 km)
Nantes–Ville d'Avray 290 miles (467 km)

The entry was open to professionally sponsored *coureurs* and *tourist-routiers*. It was won by Maurice Garin of France who was also first to finish the second Tour in 1904 when *tourist-routiers* took second and third overall, but was later disqualified along with the second, third and fourth place riders after the event had suffered all forms of abuse. Nails were thrown onto the road; the leaders were held by a mob during a night-time mountain stage until the favoured rider had gone through; and riders were given bottles of dirty water to make them ill. In addition one rider was given a soporific which caused him to crash, a second had his shirt filled with itching powder, and a third had his frame cut with a file so that it collapsed when it was ridden. The organizers resorted to secret starts, changed routes and police protection, but conspiracies between riders and teams, and tales of cars and motorcycles giving their riders illegal lifts or tows dragged the 1904 Tour down to a level where Desgranges said it was finished forever.

Thankfully he was wrong. In 1905 the Tour continued with more stages held over shorter distances and no night riding. In 1906 the Tour had almost doubled in length, reaching a record distance of 5795 kilometres with 17 stages in 1926.

Sabotage, drug-taking and collusion between teams continued to be rife; attempts to solve these problems included the introduction of random urine samples – in one celebrated case a rider was found to be drug-free but pregnant, having borrowed a sample from a female friend! The organizers also replaced trade teams with national teams after 1930 in an effort to make the Tour less prone to the cheating caused by commercial pressures. The Tour reverted back to trade teams in 1962, but is now a much more stable and rigorously policed event which has stayed as a trade team race every year except 1967 and 1968.

### Winners and Losers

In 1913 Eugene Cristophe broke his front forks while leading the Tour over the Pyrenees on the unpaved Tourmalet. He ran the seven miles down to a village with the bike on his shoulder, and welded the forks back together in the blacksmith's shop. The stage winner, Philippe Thijs, went on to win the Tour, while Cristophe was penalized for accepting outside help as a boy had operated the blacksmith's bellows.

■ The Tour was not held between 1915 and 1918, and in 1919 Henri Desgranges introduced the idea of the race leader wearing a yellow jersey, which was won for the first time by Eugene Cristophe on the Nice–Grenoble stage. History repeated itself on the Metz–Dunkirk stage, when Cristophe, still wearing the yellow jersey, fell and broke his forks, found a blacksmith, repaired them, and rode on. Firmin Lambot won the stage and the Tour, beating the unfortunate Cristophe into third place.

■ In the 1934 Tour René Vietto of France was riding so well in the mountains that he became a favourite to win overall. When his team captain Antonin Magne broke a wheel on the Hopitalet Pass, Vietto gave him one of his own and was left to wait five minutes by the roadside for a replacement. The following day Magne broke a wheel again and called out to Vietto who was ahead. Vietto rode back, gave him his wheel, and waited by the roadside once again. Five years later Vietto was second in the 1939 Tour. When the Tour started up once again in 1947, Vietto led overall from the Alps to the Pyrenees, but lost the Tour for good during a time trial.

■ Frenchman Raymond Poulidor never won the Tour despite coming very close on several occasions. His record was:

| | |
|---|---|
| 1962 | 3rd |
| 1963 | 8th |
| 1964 | 2nd |
| 1965 | 2nd |
| 1966 | 3rd |
| 1967 | 9th |
| 1968 | did not finish |
| 1969 | 3rd |
| 1970 | 7th |
| 1971 | did not start |
| 1972 | 3rd |
| 1973 | did not finish |
| 1974 | 2nd |
| 1975 | 19th |
| 1976 | 3rd |

The closest he came to winning was in 1964 when Jacques Anquetil was off form in the Alps. This allowed Poulidor to change a 30 second deficit to a four minute advantage on the Envalira climb from Andorra. However, he failed to capitalize on this advantage and eventually lost the Tour to Anquetil by 55 seconds.

■ Laurent Fignon won the Tour in 1983 and 1984. In the 1989 Tour, Fignon led Greg LeMond by 50 seconds going into the last-stage time trial in Paris. LeMond pulled back 58 seconds to win the Tour by eight seconds, the closest margin in history. Part of LeMond's success was due to his innovative use of triathlon-style aero bars to give himself a more stretched, aerodynamic riding position.

*So near and yet so far: Laurent Fignon saw a 50-second overall lead evaporate in the final stage of the 1989 Tour*

■ Laurent Jalabert of France, who won the points title in 1992, suffered a serious crash at the start of the 1994 Tour which put him out of racing for the rest of the season. In 1995 he stormed back, winning a series of one day Classics and taking the *maillot jaune* on the second stage of the Tour. From there he went on to take the points title for the second time.

## The British

***Boardman's Ups and Downs***
*Chris Boardman started his first Tour de France in 1994 in sensational style, winning the time-trial Prologue and wearing the race leader's maillot jaune for the first three days of the Tour, a feat unsurpassed by a 'novice' rider. After the first week he pulled out as planned to prepare for the world championships. Having built his next season around a good result in the 1995 Tour, Chris Boardman crashed on a wet patch just 90 seconds after his Tour de France start while attempting to win the time-trial prologue and was run down by his own team car, his first serious crash in his racing career. He fractured his ankle in two places and his wrist, putting him out of racing for much of the season.*

Brian Robinson and Tony Hoar became the first British riders to finish the Tour de France in 1955. In 1958 Brian Robinson became the first British rider to win a tour stage, a feat which he repeated in 1960.

■ Tommy Simpson became the first British rider to wear the race leader's *maillot jaune* on 5 July 1962, though only for one day. In 1965 he fell so badly on the Tour that doctors feared they might have to amputate his arm, but he went on to win the Tour of Lombardy and world road race championship in the same season. Two years later he collapsed while climbing Mont Ventoux on the 1967 Tour. Attempts to revive him failed, and he died partly as a result of the illegal stimulants which he was found to have taken. His death resulted in severe anti-drug restrictions the following year and a much easier route for the Tour.

## Prologue Problems

Apart from Chris Boardman, four other riders crashed in the 1995 time-trial Prologue – Marino Alonso, Wilfried Nelissen, Sergio Barbero and Alex Zülle, although Zülle eventually finished second overall. With the first rider leaving the start at 6.19 p.m. it was the first time the Prologue had been held as a semi-nocturne since 1967, but it was ruined for both riders and spectators when heavy rain started to fall after the first hour making visibility appalling and road conditions treacherous. After Boardman's crash, Miguel Indurain opted to ride a standard road bike without tri-bars.

■ In 1978 the results of the Prologue did not count in the overall classification and the winner was not awarded the yellow jersey as the organizers judged conditions to be too dangerous. In 1989 Tour favourite Pedro Delgado missed his chance of an overall win by arriving late for his start in the Prologue.

## Did You Know?

The earliest Tour de France bikes were fitted with a single gear and a plunger brake which pressed a rubber block down onto the front tyre. Tyres were large-section tubulars mounted on wooden sprint rims.

■ In 1932 the organizers supplied the bikes for all the tour riders in an effort to make the tour fairer.

■ In the 1951 tour the Dutch rider Wim van Est overcooked it and went off the road in the Pyrenees while leading overall. He survived the 50m fall, and was hauled back up by a 'rope' made from tubular tyres. However he was in no condition to continue riding, and retired from the tour.

*The Millar's Tale*
The Scottish rider Robert Millar is Britain's highest finisher in the Tour de France having come fourth overall in 1984. In that year he also won the King of the Mountains, and is the only English-speaking rider to have taken that title. In 1995, after 16 years as a professional, he would have ridden his twelfth Tour de France – a British record. However, just before the start of the tour his French team, Le Groupement, went bust and was forced to pull out. Millar and Sean Yates now jointly hold the UK riders' record of 11 tours.

1983  14th + one stage win
1984   4th + one stage win + King of the
       Mountains
1985  11th
1986  did not finish
1987  19th
1988  did not finish
1989  10th + one stage win
1990  did not finish
1991  72nd
1992  18th
1993  24th
1994  did not start

■ In 1956 Roger Walkowiak of France sprung from obscurity to win the tour as a member of a French regional team. He had no other wins of note in a nine year racing career.

■ In 1971 Spaniard Luis Ocana took the *maillot jaune* from Eddy Merckx after gaining over eight minutes on a mountain stage. Three days later Ocana crashed out of the tour on a downhill in heavy rain. Merckx took back the *maillot jaune*, but did not wear it on the day that followed as a mark of respect to Ocana. Two years later Ocana became the first tour rider to use a titanium bike for the mountain stages when he won overall in 1973, using a Speedwell frame made in Birmingham.

■ In 1975 Eddy Merckx wore his 96th and last yellow jersey as he led over Col d'Allos, but was caught by the eventual tour winner Bernard Thévenet with four kilometres to go.

■ Since the first tour in 1903 the city of Bordeaux has hosted more than 70 stage finishes, more than any other city or town in the tour's history.

*In 1969 Eddy Merckx became the first Belgian to win the Tour for 30 years*

### Sean Yates – A Decade of Racing
*Sean Yates raced in every Tour de France between 1984 and 1995. His first major success came in 1988 when he won a time-trial stage win, but his most rewarding tour came in 1994 when he was allowed to lead the peloton past his home in Ashdown Forest when the tour briefly visited the UK, and then took the yellow jersey for a day when the tour was back on French soil, becoming only the third British rider to wear it after Tom Simpson and Chris Boardman.*

*1984  81st*
*1985  122nd*
*1986  112th*
*1987  did not finish due to illness*
*1988  59th + time-trial stage win*
*1989  45th*
*1990  119th*
*1991  did not finish due to crash*
*1992  83rd*
*1993  88th*
*1994  71st + maillot jaune*
*1995  did not finish due to leg injury*

## The Great Winners

*Two Victories:*
Lucien Petit-Breton (F) 1907, 1908
Firmin Lambot (B) 1919, 1922
Ottavio Bottecchia (I) 1924, 1925
Nicolas Frantz (LUX) 1927, 1928
André Leducq (F) 1930, 1932
Antonin Magne (F) 1931, 1934
Sylvere Maes (B) 1936, 1939
Gino Bartali (I) 1938, 1948
Fausto Coppi (I) 1949, 1952
Bernard Thévenet (F) 1975, 1977
Laurent Fignon (F) 1983, 1984

*Three Victories:*
Phillipe Thijs (B) 1913, 1914, 1920
Louison Bobet (F) 1953, 1954, 1955
Greg LeMond (USA) 1986, 1989, 1990

*Five Victories:*
Jacques Anquetil (F) 1957, 1961, 1962, 1963, 1964
Eddy Merckx (B) 1969, 1970, 1971, 1972, 1974
Bernard Hinault (F) 1978, 1979, 1981, 1982, 1985
Miguel Indurain (E) 1991, 1992, 1993, 1994, 1995

■ Two riders have won the Tour de France four times in succession: Jacques Anquetil and Eddy Merckx. In 1995 the Spaniard Miguel Indurain surpassed them with his fifth consecutive victory.

■ The only riders from English-speaking countries to win the Tour de France are Greg LeMond (USA) in 1986, 1989 and 1990 and Stephen Roche (Ireland) in 1987.

### The Greatest Winning Margins
| | |
|---|---|
| 1903 | 1. Maurice Garin (F); 2. L Pothier (F) at 2 hours, 49 minutes. |
| 1904 | 1. Henri Cornet (F); 2. J B Dortignac (F) at 2 hours, 16 minutes, 14 seconds. |
| 1927 | 1. Nicolas Frantz (LUX); 2. M Dewaele (B) at 1 hour, 48 minutes, 21 seconds. |
| 1919 | 1. Firmin Lambot (B); 2. J Alavoine (F) at 1 hour, 42 minutes, 45 seconds. |
| 1926 | 1. Lucien Buysse (B); 2. Nicolas Frantz (LUX) at 1 hour, 22 minutes, 25 seconds. |

### The Smallest Winning Margins
| | |
|---|---|
| 1989 | 1. Greg LeMond (USA); 2. Laurent Fignon (F) at 8 seconds. |
| 1968 | 1. Jan Janssen (NL); 2. H Vanspringel (B) at 38 seconds. |
| 1987 | 1. Stephen Roche (IRL); 2. Pedro Delgado (E) at 40 seconds. |
| 1977 | 1. Bernard Thevenet (F); 2. H. Kuiper (NL) at 48 seconds. |
| 1964 | 1. Jacques Anquetil (F); 2. Raymond Poulidor (F) at 55 seconds. |

*Laurent Jalabert scored his first points win in 1992 and then won the points title again in 1995*

### Greatest Number of Tour Rides (to 1993)
| Rider | Years | Tour Starts | Tour Finishes | Best Result |
|---|---|---|---|---|
| Joop Zoetemelk (NL) | 1970–1986 | 16 | 16 | 1st 1980 |
| Lucien Van Impe (B) | 1969–1985 | 15 | 15 | 1st 1976 |
| Sean Kelly (IRL) | 1978–1993 | 15 | 12 | 4th 1985 |
| André Darrigade (F) | 1953–1966 | 14 | 13 | 16th 1956/60 |
| Raymond Poulidor (F) | 1962–1976 | 14 | 12 | 2nd 1964/65/74 |

### Nations with Most Wins
| | |
|---|---|
| France | 36 |
| Belgium | 18 |
| Italy | 8 |
| Spain | 8 |
| Luxembourg | 4 |
| USA | 3 |
| Switzerland | 2 |
| Holland | 2 |
| Ireland | 1 |

## Tour De France Points Prize

This title is awarded on a points basis for consistent high placings, and is primarily a prize for sprinters. The Points leader/winner wears the green jersey.

■ Eddy Merckx won the Tour de France overall and on points in 1969, 1971 and 1972. The only other riders to have won both the yellow and green jersey prizes in the same Tour are Bernard Hinault in 1979, Fausto Coppi in 1949 and 1952, Gino Bartali in 1938 and 1948, and Sylvere Maes in 1939.

### Points Winners
| | |
|---|---|
| 1933 | V Trueba (E) |
| 1934 | R Vietto (F) |
| 1935 | F Vervaecke (B) |
| 1936 | J Berrendero (E) |
| 1937 | F Vervaecke (B) |
| 1938 | Gino Bartali (I) |
| 1939 | Sylvere Maes (B) |
| 1947 | P Brambilla (I) |
| 1948 | Gino Bartali (I) |

| | |
|---|---|
| 1949 | Fausto Coppi (I) |
| 1950 | Louison Bobet (F) |
| 1951 | Raphaël Geminiani (F) |
| 1952 | Fausto Coppi (I) |
| 1953 | F Schaer (SWI) |
| 1954 | Ferdi Kübler (SWI) |
| 1955 | S Ocker (B) |
| 1956 | S Ocker (B) |
| 1957 | J Forestier (F) |
| 1958 | J Graczyck (F) |
| 1959 | André Darrigade (F) |
| 1960 | J Graczyck (F) |
| 1961 | André Darrigade (F) |
| 1962 | Rudi Altig (D) |
| 1963 | Rik Van Looy (B) |
| 1964 | J Janssen (NL) |
| 1965 | J Janssen (NL) |
| 1966 | W Plankaert (B) |
| 1967 | J Janssen (NL) |
| 1968 | F Bitossi (I) |
| 1969 | Eddy Merckx (B) |
| 1970 | W Godefroot (B) |
| 1971 | Eddy Merckx (B) |
| 1972 | Eddy Merckx (B) |
| 1973 | Herman Vanspringel (B) |
| 1974 | Patrick Sercu (B) |
| 1975 | Van Linden (B) |
| 1976 | F Maertens (B) |
| 1977 | J Escalssan (F) |
| 1978 | F Maertens (B) |
| 1979 | Benard Hinault (F) |
| 1980 | R Pevenage (B) |
| 1981 | F Maertens (B) |
| 1982 | Sean Kelly (IRL) |
| 1983 | Sean Kelly (IRL) |
| 1984 | F Hoste (B) |
| 1985 | Sean Kelly (IRL) |
| 1986 | E Vanderaerden (B) |
| 1987 | J P Van Poppel (NL) |
| 1988 | E Planckaert (B) |
| 1989 | Sean Kelly (IRL) |
| 1990 | Olaf Ludwig (D) |
| 1991 | Djamolodin Abduzhaparov (URS) |
| 1992 | Laurent Jalabert (F) |
| 1993 | Djamolodin Abduzhaparov (UZB) |
| 1994 | Djamolodin Abduzhaparov (UZB) |
| 1995 | Laurent Jalabert (F) |

## King of the Mountains

The King of the Mountains title is awarded on a points basis to the best climber. Every climb on the Tour counts with the first rider to the top judged the winner. Each climb is graded for severity, with Hors Categorie climbs counting maximum points. The leader/winner wears a red polka dot jersey.

■ Belgian Lucien van Impe holds the record with six King of the Mountains' titles (1971, 1972, 1975, 1977, 1981 and 1983). The only non-European to win the King of the Mountains title is the Colombian rider Luis Herrera in 1985 and 1987. The only native English-speaker to win the title is Robert Millar of Scotland in 1984.

### King of the Mountains Winners

| | |
|---|---|
| 1953 | J. Lorono (E) |
| 1954 | Federico Bahamontes (E) |
| 1955 | Charly Gaul (LUX) |
| 1956 | Charly Gaul (LUX) |
| 1957 | Gastone Nencini (I) |
| 1958 | Federico Bahamontes (E) |
| 1959 | Federico Bahamontes (E) |
| 1960 | I Massignan (I) |
| 1961 | I Massignan (I) |
| 1962 | Federico Bahamontes (E) |
| 1963 | Federico Bahamontes (E) |
| 1964 | Federico Bahamontes (E) |
| 1965 | J Jiminez (E) |
| 1966 | J Jiminez (E) |
| 1967 | J Jiminez (E) |
| 1968 | A Gonzales (E) |
| 1969 | Eddy Merckx (B) |
| 1970 | Eddy Merckx (B) |
| 1971 | Lucien Van Impe (B) |
| 1972 | Lucien Van Impe (B) |
| 1973 | P Torres (E) |
| 1974 | D Perurena (E) |
| 1975 | Lucien Van Impe (B) |
| 1976 | G Bellini (I) |
| 1977 | Lucien Van Impe (B) |
| 1978 | M Martinez (F) |
| 1979 | G Battaglin (I) |
| 1980 | R Martin (F) |
| 1981 | Lucien Van Impe (B) |
| 1982 | B Vallet (F) |
| 1983 | Lucien Van Impe (B) |
| 1984 | Robert Millar (GB) |
| 1985 | Luis Herrera (COL) |
| 1986 | Bernard Hinault (F) |
| 1987 | Luis Herrera (COL) |
| 1988 | S Kooks (NL) |
| 1989 | G-J Theunisse (NL) |
| 1990 | T Claveyrolat (F) |
| 1991 | Claudio Chiappucci (I) |
| 1992 | Claudio Chiappucci (I) |
| 1993 | Tony Rominger (SWI) |
| 1994 | R Virenque (F) |
| 1995 | R Virenque (F) |

## Young Rider Title

The Young Rider title is a points prize for riders aged 23 and under. However, it ceased to count as a Podium prize in 1993. The only Young Rider winner to win the Tour de France in the same year was Laurent Fignon in 1983 at the age of 22; he also won the Tour in 1984. The only other Young Rider winner to go on to win the Tour was Greg LeMond in 1986, 1989 and 1990. The only other native English-speaking rider to win the title was Phil Anderson.

**Young Rider Winners**

1975   Silvio Moser (I)
1976   M Martinez (F)
1977   Thurau (D)
1978   H. Lubberding (NL)
1979   J-R Bernaudeau (F)
1980   J Van De Velde (NL)
1981   P Winnen (NL)
1982   Phil Anderson (AUS)
1983   Laurent Fignon (F)
1984   Greg LeMond (USA)
1985   F Parra (COL)
1986   Andy Hampsten (USA)
1987   R Alcala (MEX)
1988   E Breukink (NL)
1989   *Not awarded*
1990   G Delion (F)
1991   A Meija (COL)
1992   E Bouwmans (NL)
1993   A Martin (E)

## Youngest & Oldest Tour winners

*Age*   *Rider*
20   Henri Cornet (F) 1904.
22   François Faber (LUX) 1909, Octave Lapize (F) 1910, Romain Maes (B) 1935, Felice Gimondi (I) 1965, Laurent Fignon (F) 1983.
23   Philippe Thijs (B) 1913, Jacques Anquetil (F) 1957, Bernard Hinault (F) 1978, Laurent Fignon (F) 1984.
24   Louis Trousellier (F) 1905, Lucien Petit-Breton (F) 1907, Odile Defraeye (B) 1912, Philippe Thijs (B) 1914, Gino Bartali (I) 1938, Eddy Merckx (B) 1969, Bernard Hinault (F) 1979.
25   Lucien Petit-Breton (F) 1908, Lucien Amar (F) 1966, Eddy Merckx (B) 1970, Greg LeMond 1986.
26   André Leducq (F) 1930, Georges Speicher (F) 1933, Roger Lapébie (F) 1937, Jean Robic (F) 1947, Hugo Koblet (SWI) 1951, Charly Gaul (LUX) 1958, Eddy Merckx (B) 1971, Bernard Hinault (F) 1981.

27   René Pottier (F) 1906.
28   Nicolas Frantz (LUX) 1927, André Leducq (F) 1932, Louison Bobet (F) 1953, Jacques Anquetil (F) 1962, Jan Janssen (NL) 1968, Luis Ocana (E) 1973, Pedro Delgado (E) 1988, Greg LeMond (USA) 1989, Miguel Indurain (E) 1992.
29   Nicolas Frantz (LUX) 1928, Fausto Coppi (I) 1949, Louison Bobet (F) 1954, R. Walkowiak (F) 1956, Jacques Anquetil (F) 1963, Eddy Merckx (B) 1974, Lucien Van Impe (B) 1976, Bernard Thévenet (F) 1977, Greg LeMond (USA) 1990, Miguel Indurain (E) 1993.
30   Philippe Thijs (B) 1920, Ottavio Bottechia (I) 1924, Antonin Magne (F) 1934, Sylvere Maes (B) 1939, Louison Bobet (F) 1955, Gastone Nencini (I) 1960, Jacques Anquetil (F) 1965, Bernard Hinault (F) 1985, Miguel Indurain (E) 1994.
31   Ottavio Bottechia (I) 1925, Ferdi Kübler (SWI) 1950, Federico Bahamontes (E) 1959, Miguel Indurain (E).
32   Maurice Garin (F) 1903, Fausto Coppi (I) 1952.
33   Firmin Lambot (B) 1919, Leon Scieur (B) 1921, Lucien Buysse (B) 1926, Maurice Dewaele (B) 1929, Joop Zoetemelk (NL) 1980.
34   Henri Pelissier (F) 1923, Gino Bartali (I) 1948.
35   Firmin Lambot (B) 1922.

*Laurent Fignon is the only Young Rider winner to win the Tour overall in the same year. With victory just before his 23rd birthday he is the youngest Tour winner of modern times*

## Longest and Shortest Tours

### The Ten Longest

| Distance (km) | Stages | Average (km) | Year |
|---|---|---|---|
| 5795 | 17 | 340 | 1926 |
| 5560 | 15 | 370 | 1919 |
| 5503 | 15 | 366 | 1920 |
| 5488 | 15 | 365 | 1924 |
| 5485 | 15 | 365 | 1921 |
| 5476 | 22 | 248 | 1928 |
| 5440 | 18 | 302 | 1925 |
| 5398 | 24 | 224 | 1927 |
| 5386 | 15 | 359 | 1923 |
| 5380 | 15 | 359 | 1914 |

### The Ten Shortest

| Distance (km) | Stages | Average (km) | Year |
|---|---|---|---|
| 2388 | 6 | 398 | 1904 |
| 2428 | 6 | 404 | 1903 |
| 2994 | 11 | 272 | 1905 |
| 3250 | 21 | 154 | 1989 |
| 3284 | 22 | 149 | 1988 |
| 3448 | 21 | 164 | 1990 |
| 3507 | 21 | 167 | 1982 |
| 3689 | 20 | 184 | 1971 |
| 3714 | 20 | 186 | 1993 |
| 3753 | 24 | 156 | 1981 |

## The Most Stage Wins

### In a Single Tour

8   Charles Pelissier (F) 1930, Eddy Merckx (B) 1970 & 1974, F. Maertens (B) 1976.

7   Gino Bartali (I) 1948, Bernard Hinault (F) 1979.

6   E. Georget (F) 1907, François Faber (LUX) 1909, M. Buysse (B) 1913, André Leducq (F) 1932, J. Aerts (B) 1933, R. Le Grevas (F) 1936, Eddy Merckx (B) 1969 & 1972.

5   Louis Trousellier (F) 1905, René Pottier (F) 1906, François Faber (LUX) 1908, Philippe Thijs (B) 1922, Nicolas Frantz (LUX) 1928, André Leducq (F) 1929, Charles Pelissier (F) 1931, R. Di Paco (I) 1931, L. Guerra (I) 1933, Roger Lapébie (F) 1934, Hugo Koblet (SWI) 1951, Fausto Coppi (I) 1952, André Darrigade (F) 1958, Bernard Hinault (F) 1981, F. Maertens (B) 1981, Laurent Fignon (F) 1984.

### Most Stage Wins Overall

| Rider | Stages |
|---|---|
| Eddy Merckx (B) | 35 |
| Bernard Hinault (F) | 28 |
| André Leducq (F) | 25 |
| André Darrigade (F) | 22 |
| Nicolas Frantz (LUX) | 20 |

## The Winning Teams

| Year | Team | Year | Team | Year | Team |
|---|---|---|---|---|---|
| 1903 | La Francaise-Dunlop | 1929 | Alcyon | 1961 | France |
| 1904 | La Francaise | 1930 | France | 1962 | Saint Raphael-Helyett |
| 1905 | Peugeot | 1931 | Belgium | 1963 | Saint Raphael-Gitane |
| 1906 | Peugeot | 1932 | Italy | 1964 | Pelforth-Lejeune-Sauvage |
| 1907 | Peugeot | 1933 | France | | |
| 1908 | Peugeot | 1934 | France | 1965 | Kas |
| 1909 | Alcyon Pneus-Dunlop | 1935 | Belgium | 1966 | Kas |
| 1909 | Alcyon Pneus-Dunlop | 1936 | Belgium | 1967 | France |
| 1910 | Alcyon Pneus-Dunlop | 1937 | France | 1968 | Spain |
| 1911 | Alcyon Pneus-Dunlop | 1938 | Belgium | 1969 | Faema |
| 1912 | Alcyon Pneus-Dunlop | 1939 | Belgium | 1970 | Salvarini |
| 1913 | Peugeot | 1947 | Italy | 1971 | Bic |
| 1914 | Peugeot | 1948 | Belgium | 1972 | Gan-Mercier |
| 1919 | La Sportive | 1949 | Italy | 1973 | Bic |
| 1920 | La Sportive | 1950 | Belgium | 1974 | Kas |
| 1921 | La Sportive | 1951 | France | 1975 | Gan-Mercier |
| 1922 | Peugeot-Pneus Lion | 1952 | Italy | 1976 | Kas |
| 1923 | Automoto-Hutchinson | 1953 | Holland | 1977 | TI-Raleigh |
| 1924 | Automoto-Hutchinson | 1954 | Switzerland | 1978 | Miko-Mercier |
| 1925 | Automoto-Hutchinson | 1955 | France | 1979 | Renault |
| 1926 | Automoto-Hutchinson | 1956 | Belgium | 1980 | Miko-Mercier |
| 1927 | Alcyon | 1957 | France | 1981 | Peugeot |
| 1928 | Alcyon | 1958 | Belgium | 1982 | Coop-Mercier |
| | | 1959 | Belgium | 1983 | Raleigh |
| | | 1960 | France | 1984 | Renault |

| 1985 | La Vie Claire | 1989 | PDM | 1993 | Banesto |
|------|---------------|------|-----|-------|---------|
| 1986 | La Vie Claire | 1990 | Z | 1994 | Banesto |
| 1987 | Systeme U | 1991 | Banesto | 1995 | Banesto |
| 1988 | PDM | 1992 | Banesto | | |

## The Big Climbs

| | Height (m) | First to the top | Year |
|---|---|---|---|
| Col de Restefonds | 2802 | Federico Bahamontes (E) | 1962 |
| Col d'Iseran | 2770 | F Vervaecke (B) | 1938 |
| Col du Galibier | 2645 | E Georget (F) | 1911 |
| Col d'Izoard | 2361 | Philippe Thijs (B) | 1922 |
| Col de Tourmalet | 2115 | Octave Lapize (F) | 1910 |
| Mont Ventoux | 1912 | L Lazarides (F) | 1951 |
| L'Alpe d'Huez | 1860 | Fausto Coppi (I) | 1952 |
| Puy de Dome | 1415 | Fausto Coppi (I) | 1952 |

*Eventual winner Miguel Indurain shadows world champion Gianni Bugno on the hard climb up to Alpe Huez in 1992*

# Tour De France Results

*Times are in Hrs:Min.Sec*

1903  1. Maurice GARIN (F). 2. Lucien Pothier (F) @ 2:49.00. 3. Fernand Augereau (F). 4. Rodolfo Muller (I). 5. Jean Fisher (F).
*No. of stages: 6; Distance: 2428 km; Av. winning speed: 25.283 kmh; No. of starters 60; No. of finishers 21.*

1904  1. Henri CORNET (F). 2. J B Dortignacq (F) @ 2:16.14. 3. Philippe Jousselin (F). 4. Rodolfo Muller (I). 5. Camille Fily (F).
*No. of stages: 6; Distance 2388 km; Av. winning speed: 24.292 kmh; No. of starters: 88; No. of finishers: 23.*

1905  1. Louis TROUSSELIER (F) 35 points. 2. Lucien Pothier (F) 26 points. 3. J B Dortignacq (F). 4. Léon Georget (F). 5. Luc Petit-Breton (F).
*No. of stages: 11; Distance: 2975 km; Av. winning speed: 27.284 kmh; No. of starters: 60; No. of finishers: 24.*

1906  1. René POTTIER (F) 31 points. 2. Geo Passerieu (F) 28 points. 3. Louis Trousselier (F). 4. Luc Petit-Breton (F). 5. Emile Georget (F).
*No. of stages: 13; Distance: 4637 km; Av. winning speed: 24.463 kmh; No. of starters: 75; No. of finishers: 14.*

1907  1. Lucien Petit-Breton (F) 47 points. 2. Gustave Garrigou (F) 19 points. 3. Louis Trousselier (F). 4. Georges Passerieu (F). 5. O. Beaugendre (F).
*No. of stages: 14; Distance: 4488 km; Av. winning speed: 28.470 kmh; No. of starters: 93; (No. of finishers) 33.*

1908  1. Lucien PETIT-BRETON (F) 36 points. 2. François Faber (LUX) 32 points. 3. Georges Passerieu (F). 4. Gustave Garrigou (F). 5. Luigi Ganna (I).
*No. of stages: 14; Distance: 4488 km; Av. winning speed: 28.740 kmh; No. of starters: 114; No. of finishers: 36.*

1909  1. François FABER (LUX) 37 points. 2. Gustave Garrigou (F) 20 points. 3. Jean Alavoine (F). 4. Paul Duboc (F). 5. C Van Hauwaert (B).
*No. of stages: 14; Distance: 4497 km; Av. winning speed: 28.658 kmh; No. of starters: 150; No. of finishers 55.*

1910  1. Octave LAPIZE (F) 63 points 2. François Faber (LUX) 4 points. 3. Gustave Garrigou (F). 4. C Van Hauwaert (B). 5. Charles Cruchon (F).
*No. of stages: 15; Distance: 4700 km; Av. winning speed: 28.680 kmh; No. of starters: 110; No. of finishers: 41.*

1911  1. Gustave GARRIGOU (F) 43 points. 2. Paul Duboc (F) 41 points. 3. Emile Georget (F). 4. Charles Crupelandt (F). 5. Louis Heusghem (B).
*No. of stages: 15; Distance: 5544 km; Av. winning speed: 27.322 kmh; No. of starters: 84; No. of finishers: 28.*

1912  1. Odile DEFRAYE (B) 49 points. 2. E Christophe (F) 59.5 points. 3. Gustave Garrigou (F). 4. Marcel Buysse (B). 5. Jean Alavoine (F).
*No. of stages: 15; Distance: 5229 km; Av. winning speed: 27.894 kmh; No. of starters: 131; No. of finishers: 41.*

1913  1. Philippe THIJS (B). 2. Gustave Garrigou (F) 8.37. 3. Marcel Buysse (B). 4. Firmin Lambot (B). 5. François Faber (LUX).
*No. of stages: 15; Distance: 5387 km; Av. winning speed: 27.625 kmh; No. of starters: 140; No. of finishers: 25.*

1914  1. Philippe THIJS (B). 2. Henri Pelissier (F) @ 1.50. 3. Jean Alavoine (F). 4. Jean Rossius (B). 5. Gustave Garrigou (F).
*No. of stages: 15; Distance: 5414 km; Av. winning speed: 27.028 kmh; No. of starters: 146; No. of finishers 54.*

1919  1. Firmin LAMBOT (B). 2. Jean Alavoine (F) @ 42.45. 3. Eugène Christophe (F). 4. Léon Scieur (B). 5. Honoré Barthélemy (F).
*No. of stages: 15; Distance: 5560 km; Av. winning speed: 24.954 kmh; No. of starters: 69; No. of finishers: 11.*

1920  1. Philippe THIJS (B). 2. Hector Heusghem (B) @ 57.00. 3. Firmin Lambot (B). 4. Léon Scieur (B). 5. E. Massonsen (B).
*No. of stages: 15; Distance: 5503 km; Av. winning speed: 24.131 kmh; No. of starters: 113; No. of finishers: 22.*

1921  1. Léon SCIEUR (B). 2. Hector Heusghem (B) @ 19.02. 3. Honoré Barthélemy (F). 4. Luigi Lucotti (I). 5. Hector Thiberghien (B).
*No. of stages: 15; Distance: 5484 km; Av. winning*

*speed: 27.720 kmh; No. of starters: 123; No. of finishers: 38.*

1922   1. Firmin LAMBOT (B). 2. Jean Alavoine (F)
       @ 41.15. 3. Félix Sellier (B). 4. Hector
       Heusghem (B). 5. Victor Lenaers (B).
*No. of stages: 15; Distance: 5375 km; Av. winning speed: 24.202 kmh; No. of starters: 121; No. of finishers: 38.*

1923   1. Henri PELISSIER (F). 2. Ottavio
       Bottecchia (I) @ 30.41. 3. Romain Bellenger
       (F).
       4. Hector Thiberghien (B). 5. Arséne
       Alancourt (F).
*No. of stages: 15; Distance: 5386 km; Av. winning speed: 24.428 kmh; No. of starters: 139; No. of finishers 48.*

1924   1. Ottavio BOTTECCHIA (I). 2. Nicolas
       Frantz (LUX) @ 35.36. 3. Lucien Buysse
       (B). 4. Bartolomeo Aymo (I). 5. Théo
       Beeckman (B).
*No. of stages: 15; Distance: 5427 km; Av. winning speed: 23.958 kmh; No. of starters: 157; No. of finishers: 60.*

1925   1. Ottavio BOTTECCHIA (I). 2. Lucien
       Buysse (B) @ 54.20. 3. Bartolomeo Aymo
       (I). 4. Nicolas Frantz (LUX). 5. Albert De
       Jonghe (B).
*No. of stages: 18; Distance: 5430 km; Av. winning speed: 24.775 kmh; No. of starters: 130; No. of finishers 49.*

1926   1. Lucien BUYSSE (B). 2. Nicolas Frantz
       (LUX) @ 1:22.25. 3. Bartolomeo
       Aymo (I). 4. Théo Beeckman (B). 5. Felix
       Sellier (B).
*No. of stages: 17; Distance: 5745 km; Av. winning speed: 24.065 kmh; No. of starters: 126; No. of finishers: 41.*

1927   1. Nicolas FRANTZ (LUX). 2. Maurice
       Dewaele (B) @ 1:48.21. 3. Julien Vervaecke
       (B). 4. André Leducq (F). 5. Antonin Magne
       (F).
*No. of stages: 24; Distance: 5321 km; Av. winning speed: 26.839 kmh; No. of starters: 142; No. of finishers: 39.*

1928   1. Nicolas FRANTZ (LUX) 192:48.58. 2.
       André Leducq (F) @ 50.07. 3. Maurice
       Dewaele (B). 4. Jean Mertens (B). 5. Julien
       Vervaecke (B).
*No. of stages: 22; Distance: 5377 km; Av. winning*

*speed: 27.833 kmh; No. of starters: 162; No. of finishers: 41.*

1929   1. Maurice DEWAELE (B). 2. Giuseppe
       Pancera (I) @ 32.07. 3. Jos Demuysere (B).
       4. Salvadore Cardona (E). 5. Nicolas Frantz
       (LUX).
*No. of stages: 22; Distance: 5288 km; Av. winning speed: 28.320 kmh; No. of starters: 155; No. of finishers: 60.*

1930   1. André LEDUCQ (F). 2. Learco Guerra (I)
       @ 14.19. 3. Antonin Magne (F). 4. Jos
       Demuysere (B). 5. Marcel Bidot (F)
*No. of stages: 21; Distance: 4818 km; Av. winning speed: 27.979 kmh; No. of starters: 100; No. of finishers: 59.*

1931   1. Antonin MAGNE (F). 2. J Demuysere (B).
       @ 12.56. 3. Antonio Pesenti (I). 4.
       Gaston Rebry (B). 5. Maurice Dewaele (B)
*No. of stages: 24; Distance: 5095 km; Av. winning speed: 28.758 kmh; No. of starters: 81; No. of finishers: 35.*

1932   1. André LEDUCQ (F). 2. Kurt Stoepel (D) @
       24.03. 3. Francesco Camusso (I) 4. A
       Pesenti (I) 5. Georges Ronsse (B).
*No. of stages: 21; Distance: 4502 km; Av. winning speed: 29.215 kmh; No. of starters: 80; No. of finishers: 57.*

1933   1. Georges SPEICHER (F). 2. Learco Guerra
       (I) @ 4.01. 3. Giuseppe Martano (I). 4.
       G Lemair (B). 5. Maurice Archambaud (F).
*No. of stages: 23; Distance: 4395 km; Av. winning speed: 29.697 kmh; No. of starters: 80; No. of finishers: 40.*

1934   1. Antonin MAGNE (F). 2. G Martano (I) @
       27.31. 3. Roger Lapébie (F). 4. F
       Vervaecke (B) 5. René Vietto (F).
*No. of stages: 23; Distance: 4363 km; Av. winning speed: 29,460; No. of starters: 60; No. of finishers: 39.*

1935   1. Romain MAES (B). 2. Ambrogio Morelli
       (I) @ 17.52. 3. Félicien Vervaecke (B) 4.
       Sylvère Maes (B). 5. Jules Lowie (B).
*No. of stages: 21; Distance: 4302 km; Av. winning speed: 30.559 kmh; No. of starters: 93; No. of finishers: 46*

1936   1. Sylvère MAES (B). 2. Antonin Magne (F) @
       26.55. 3. Félicien Vervaecke (B). 4.
       Pierre Clemens (L). 5. Arsène Mersch (L).

*French rider Cosson leads up the Col de Castillon in 1939*

No. of stages: 21; Distance: 4442 km; Av. winning speed: 31.072 kmh; No. of starters: 90; No. of finishers: 43.

1937  1. Roger LAPÉBIE (F). 2. Mario Vicini (I) @ 7.17. 3. Leo Amberg (SWI). 4. Francisco Camusso (I). 5. Sylvain Marcailou (F).
No. of stages: 20; Distance: 4415 km; Av. winning speed: 31.741 kmh; No. of starters: 98; No. of finishers: 46.

1938  1. Gino BARTALI (I). 2. F. Veraecke (B) @ 18.27. 3. Victor Cosson (F). 4. Edward Vissers (B). 5. Mathias Clemens (L).
No. of stages: 21; Distance: 4694 km; Av. winning speed: 31.560 kmh; No. of starters: 96; No. of finishers: 55.

1939  1. Sylvère MAES (B). 2. René Vietto (F) @ 30.08. 3. Lucien Vlaemynck (B) 4. Mathias Clemens (L) 5. Edward Vissers (B).
No. of stages: 18; Distance: 4224 km; Av. winning speed: 31.886 kmh; No. of starters: 79; No. of finishers: 49.

1947  1. Jean ROBIC (F). 2. E. Fachleitner (F) @ 3.58. 3. Pierre Brambilla (I). 4. Aldo Ronconi (I). 5. René Vietto (F).
No. of stages: 21; Distance: 4640 km; Av. winning speed: 31.497 kmh; No. of starters: 100; No. of finishers: 53.

1948  1. Gino Bartali (I). 2. Briek Schotte (B) @ 26.16. 3. Guy Lapébie (F). 4. Louison Bobet (F). 5. Jean Kirchen (L).
No. of stages: 21; Distance: 4922 km; Av. winning speed: 33.402 kmh; No. of starters: 120; No. of finishers: 44.

1949  1. Fausto COPPI (I). 2. Gino Bartali (I) @ 10.55. 3. Jacques Marinelli (F). 4. Jean Robic (F). 5. Marcel Dupont (B).
No. of stages: 21; Distance: 4813 km; Av. winning speed: 32.122 kmh; No. of starters: 120; No. of finishers: 55

1950  1. Ferdi KÜBLER (SWI). 2. Stan Ockers (B) @ 9.30. 3. Louison Bobet (F). 4. Raphaël Geminiani (F). 5. Jean Kirchen (LUX).
No. of stages: 22; Distance: 4776 km; Av. winning speed: 32.781 kmh; No. of starters: 116; No. of finishers: 51.

1951  1. Hugo KOBLET (SWI). 2. Raphaël Geminiani (F) @ 22.00. 3. Lucien Lazaridés (F). 4. Gino Bartali (I). 5. Stan Ockers (B).
No. of stages: 24; Distance: 4474 km; Av. winning speed: 31.432 kmh; No. of starters: 123; No. of finishers: 66.

1952  1. Fausto COPPI (I). 2. Stan Ockers (B) @ 28.17. 3. Bernardo Ruiz (E) 4. Gino Bartali (I). 5. Jean Robic (F).
No. of stages: 23; Distance: 4807 km; Av. winning speed: 31.602 kmh; No. of starters: 122; No. of finishers: 78.

1953  1. Louison BOBET (F) 2. Jean Malléjac (F) @ 14.18. 3. Giancarlo Astrua (I) 4. Alex Close (B). 5. Wout Wagtmans (NL).
No. of stages: 22; Distance: 4479 km; Av. winning speed: 34.605 kmh; No. of starters: 119; No. of finishers: 76.

1954  1. Louison BOBET (F). 2. Ferdi Kübler (SWI) @ 15.49. 3. Fritz Schaer (SWI). 4. Jean Dotto (F). 5. Jean Malléjac (F).
No. of stages: 23; Distance: 4855 km; Av. winning speed: 34.639 kmh; No. of starters: 110; No. of finishers: 69

1955 1. Louison BOBET (F). 2. Jean Brankart (B)
@ 4.53. 3. Charly Gaul (LUX). 4.
Pasquale Fornara (I). 5. Antonin Rolland (F).
*No. of stages: 22; Distance: 4495 km; Av. winning speed: 34.434 kmh; No. of starters: 130; No. of finishers: 69.*

1956 1. Roger WALKOWIAK (F). 2. Gilbert Bauvin
(F) @ 1.25. 3. Jan Adriaensens (B). 4.
Federico Bahamontes (E). 5. Nino Defilippis (I).
*No. of stages 22; Distance: 4528 km Av. winning speed: 36.512 kmh; No. of starters: 120; No. of finishers: 88.*

1957 1. Jacques ANQUETIL (F). 2. M Janssens (B)
@ 14.56. 3. Adolf Christian (A) 4.
Jean Forestier (F). 5. Jesus Lorono (E).
*No. of stages: 22; Distance: 4555 km; Av. winning speed: 34.507 kmh; No. of starters: 120; No. of finishers: 56.*

1958 1. Charly GAUL (LUX). 2. Vito Favero (I) @
3.10. 3. Raphaël Geminiani (F) 4. Jean
Adriaensens (B). 5. Gastone Nencini (I).
*No. of stages: 24; Distance: 4319.5 km; Av. winning speed: 36.905 kmh; No. of starters: 120; No. of finishers: 78.*

1959 1. Federico BAHAMONTES (E). 2. Henri
Anglade (F) @ 4.01. 3. Jacques Anquetil
(F). 4. Roger Rivière (F). 5. François Mahé
(F).
*No. of stages: 22; Distance: 4363 km; Av. winning speed: 35.241 kmh; No. of starters: 120; No. of finishers: 65.*

1960 1. Gastone NENCINI (I) 2. G. Battistine (I) @
5.02. 3. Jan Adrianensens (B). 4. Hans
Junkermann (D) 5. Jef Planckaert (B).
*No. of stages: 21; Distance: 4272 km; Av. winning speed: 37.210 kmh; No. of starters: 128; No. of finishers: 81.*

1961 1. Jacques ANQUETIL (F). 2. Guido Carlesi
(I) @ 12.14. 3. Charly Gaul (LUX) 4. Imerio
Massignan (I). 5. Hans Junkermann (D).
*No. of stages: 21; Distance: 4394 km; Av. winning speed: 36.284 kmh; No. of starters: 132; No. of finishers: 72.*

1962 1. Jacques ANQUETIL (F). 2. Jef Planckaert
(B) @ 4.59. 3. Raymond Poulidor (F). 4.
Gilbert Desmet I (B). 5. Abe Geldermans (NL).
*No. of stages: 22; Distance: 4272.5 km; Av. winning speed: 37.306 kmh; No. of starters: 149; No. of finishers: 94.*

1963 1. Jacques ANQUETIL (F). 2. Federico
Bahamontes (E) @ 3.35. 3. José Perez-Frances
(E). 4. Jean-Claude Lebaube (F). 5. Armand
Desmet (B).
*No. of stages: 21; Distance: 4140.8 km; Av. winning speed: 36.456 kmh; No. of starters: 130; No. of finishers: 76.*

1964 1. Jacques ANQUETIL (F). 2. Raymond
Poulidor (F) @ 55 secs. 3. Federico
Bahamontes (E). 4. Henry Anglade (F). 5.
Georges Groussard (F).
*No. of stages: 22; Distance: 4505.2 km; Av. winning speed: 35.420 kmh; No. of starters: 132; No. of finishers: 81.*

1965 1. Felice GIMONDI (I). 2. Raymond Poulidor
(F) @ 2.40. 3. Gianni Motta (I). 4. Henry
Anglade (F). 5. Jean-Claude Lebaube (F).
*No. of stages: 22; Distance: 4175.9 kmh; Av. winning speed: 36.086; No. of starters: 130; No. of finishers: 96.*

1966 1. Lucien AIMAR (F); 2. Jan Janssen (NL) @
1.07. 3. Raymond Poulidor (F) 4. J A
Momene (E) 5. Marcello Mugniani (I).
*No. of stages: 22; Distance: 4329 km; Av. winning speed: 36.602 kmh; No. of starters: 130; No. of finishers: 82.*

1967 1. Roger Pingeon (F). 2. Julio Jimenez (E) @
3.40. 3. Franco Balmanion (I). 4. Désiré
Letort (F). 5. Jan Janssen (NL).
*No. of stages: 22; Distance: 4780 km; Av. winning speed: 34.755 kmh; No. of starters: 130; No. of finishers: 88.*

1968 1. Jan Janssen (NL). 2. Herman Vanspringel
(B) @ 38 secs. 3. Ferdinand Bracke (B) 4.
G San Miguel (E). 5. Roger Pingeon (F).
*No. of stages: 22; Distance: 4662.3 km; Av. winning speed: 34.894 kmh; No. of starters: 110; No. of finishers: 63.*

1969 1. Eddy MERCKX (B). 2. Roger Pingeon (F)
@ 17.54. 3. Raymond Poulidor (F). 4.
Felice Gimondi (I). 5. Andres Gandarias (E).
*No. of stages: 22; Distance: 4102 km; Av. winning speed: 35.296 kmh; No. of starters: 129; No. of finishers: 86.*

1970 1. Eddy MERCKX (B). 2. Joop Zoetemelk
(NL) @ 12.41. 3. Gösta Pettersson
(SWE). 4. M Van den Bossche (B) 5. Marinus
Wagtmans (NL).
*No. of stages: 23; Distance: 4366.8 km; Av. winning*

*speed: 35.371 kmh; No. of starters: 132; No. of finishers: 88.*

1971 1. Eddy MERCKX (B). 2. Joop Zoetemelk (NL) @ 9.51. 3. Lucien Van Impe (B). 4. Bernard Thévenet (F). 5. Joaquim Agostinho (POR).
*No. of stages: 20; Distance: 3689.6 km; Av. winning speed: 36.925 kmh; No. of starters: 129; No. of finishers: 94.*

1972 1. Eddy MERCKX (B). 2. Felice Gimondi (I) @ 10.41. 3. Lucien Van Impe (B). 5. Joop Zoetemelk (NL).
*No. of stages: 20; Distance: 3846.6 km; Av. winning speed: 35.371 kmh; No. of starters: 132; No. of finishers: 88.*

1973 1. Luis OCANA (E). 2. Bernard Thévenet (F) @ 15.51. 3. José-Manuel Fuente. 4. Joop Zoetemelk (NL). 5. Lucien Van Impe (B).
*No. of stages: 20; Distance: 4140.4 km; Av. winning speed: 33.918 kmh; No. of starters: 132; No. of finishers: 87.*

1974 1. Eddy MERCKX (B) 2. Raymond Poulidor (F) @ 8.04. 3. Vicente Lopez-Carril (E). 4. Wlad Panizza (I). 5. Gonzalo Aja (E).
*No. of stages: 22; Distance: 4098.2 km; Av. winning speed: 35.243 kmh; No. of starters: 130; No. of finishers: 105.*

1975 1. Bernard THEVENET (F). 2. Eddy Merckx (B) @ 2.47. 3. Lucien Van Impe (B). 4. Joop Zoetemelk (NL). 5. Vicente Lopez-Carril (E).
*No. of stages: 22; Distance: 3999.1 km; Av. winning speed: 34.899 kmh; No. of starters: 140; No. of finishers: 86.*

1976 1. Lucien VAN IMPE (B). 2. Joop Zoetemelk (NL) @ 4.14. 3. Raymond Poulidor (F). 4. Raymond Delisle (F). 5. Walter Riccomi (I).
*No. of stages: 22; Distance: 4016.5 km; Av. winning speed: 34.511 kmh; No. of starters: 130; No. of finishers: 87.*

1977 1. Bernard THEVENET (F) 2. Hennie Kuiper (NL) @ 48 secs. 3. Lucien Van Impe (B) 4. F Galdos (E). 5. Dietrich Thurau (D).
*No. of stages: 22; Distance: 4092.9 km; Av. winning speed: 35.585 kmh; No. of starters: 100; No. of finishers: 53.*

1978 1. Bernard HINAULT (F). 2. Joop Zoetemelk

*Four times second, Joop Zoetemelk led a Dutch 1–2 in 1980*

(NL) @ 3.56. 3. Joaquim Agostinho (POR) 4. Jos Bruyère (B). 5. Christian Seznec (F).
*No. of stages: 22; Distance: 3913.8 km; Av. winning speed: 34.929 kmh; No. of starters: 110; No. of finishers: 1978.*

1979 1. Bernard HINAULT (F). 2. Joop Zoetemelk (NL) @ 13.37. 3. Joaquim Agostinho (POR) 4. Hennie Kuiper (NL). 5. J R Bernaudeau (F).
*No. of stages: 24; Distance: 3720.4 km; Av. winning speed: 36.073 kmh; No. of starters: 150; No. of finishers: 89.*

1980 1. Joop ZOETEMELK (NL). 2. Hennie Kuiper (NL) @ 6.55. 3. Raymond Martin (F). 4. Johan De Muynck (B). 5. Joaquim Agostinho (POR).
*No. of stages: 22; Distance: 3945.5 km; Av. winning speed: 35.317 kmh; No. of starters: 130; No. of finishers: 85.*

1981 1. Bernard Hinault (F). 2. Lucien Van Impe (B) @ 14.34. 3. Robert Alban (F) 4. Joop Zoetemelk (NL) 5. Peter Winnen (NL)
*No. of stages: 22; Distance: 3756.6 km; Av. winning speed: 37.987 kmh; No. of starters: 150; No. of finishers: 121.*

*Stephen Roche won the Tour de France for Ireland in 1987. He is pictured here on the climb to Isola during the 1993 Tour*

1982  1. Bernard HINAULT (F). 2. Joop Zoetemelk
(NL) @ 6.21. 3. J. Van der Velde (NL) 4. Peter
Winnen (NL). 5. Phil Anderson (AUS).
*No. of stages: 21; Distance: 3512 km; Av. winning
speed: 37.470 kmh; No. of starters: 169; No. of
finishers: 125.*

1983  1. Laurent FIGNON (F). 2. Angel Arroyo (E)
@ 4.04. 3. Peter Winnen (NL). 4.
Lucien Van Impe (B). 5. Robert Alban (F).
*No. of stages: 22; Distance: 3962 km; Av. winning
speed: 35.914 kmh; No. of starters: 140; No. of
finishers: 88.*

1984  1. Laurent FIGNON (F). 2. Bernard Hinault
(F) @ 10.32. 3. Greg LeMond (USA).
4. Robert Millar (GB). 5. Sean Kelly (IRL)
*No. of stages: 23; Distance: 4020.9 km; Av. winning
speed: 34.906 kmh; No. of starters: 140; No. of
finishers: 124.*

1985  1. Bernard HINAULT (F) 2. Greg LeMond
(USA) @ 1.42. 3. Stephen Roche (IRL)
4. Sean Kelly (IRL). 5. Phil Anderson (AUS).
*No. of stages: 22; Distance: 4127.3 km; Av. winning
speed: 36.215 kmh; No. of starters: 179; No. of*

*finishers: 144.*

1986  1. Greg LEMOND (USA). 2. Bernard Hinault
(F) @ 3.10. 3. Urs Zimmermann
(SWI) 4. Andrew Hampsten (USA) 5. Claude
Criquielion (B).
*No. of stages: 23; Distance: 4083 km; Av. winning
speed: 36.9183 kmh; No. of starters: 210; No. of
finishers: 132.*

1987  1. Stephen ROCHE (IRL). 2. Pedro Delgado
(E) @ 40 secs. 3. J F Bernard (F). 4.
Charly Mottet (F). 5. Luis Herrera (COL).
*No. of stages: 25; Distance: 4231.1 km; Av. winning
speed: 36645 km; No. of starters: 207; No. of
finishers: 135.*

1988  1. Pedro DELGADO (E) 2. Steven Rooks
(NL) @ 7.13. 3. Fabio Parra (COL) 4.
Steve Bauer (CDN). 5. Eric Boyer (F).
*No. of stages: 22; Distance: 3281.5 km; Av. winning
speed: 39.909 kmh; No. of starters: 198; No. of
finishers: 151.*

1989  1. Greg LEMOND (USA) 2. Laurent Fignon
(F) @ 8 secs. 3. Pedro Delgado (E) 4.

Gert-Jan Theunisse (NL) 5. Marino Lejarreta (E).

*No. of stages: 21; Distance: 3285.3 km Av. winning speed: 37.487 kmh; No. of starters: 198; No. of finishers: 138*

1990 1. Greg LEMOND (USA). 2. Claudio Chiappucci (I) @ 2.16. 3. Erik Breukink (NL) 4. Pedro Delgado (E) 5. Marino Lejarreta (E).

*No. of stages: 21; Distance: 3.448.8 km; Av. winning speed: 38.621; No. of starters: 198; No. of finishers: 156.*

1991 1. Miguel INDURAIN (E). 2. Gianni Bugno (I) @ 3.36. 3. Claudio Chiappucci (I) 4. Charly Mottet (F) 5. Luc Leblanc (F)

*No. of stages: 22; Distance: 3914.4 km; Av. winning speed: 38.747 kmh; No. of starters: 198; No. of finishers: 158.*

1992 1. Miguel INDURAIN (E). 2. Claudio Chiappucci (I) @ 4.35. 3. Gianni Bugno (I). 4. Andy Hampsten (USA). 5. Pascal Lino (F).

*No. of stages: 21; Distance: 3983 km; Av. winning speed: 39.504 kmh; No. of starters: 198; No. of finishers: 130.*

1993 1. Miguel INDURAIN (E). 2. Tony Rominger (SWI) @ 4.59. 3. Zenon Jaskula (POL) 4. Alvaro Mejia (COL). 5. Bjarne Riis (DNK).

*No. of stages: 20; Distance: 3714.3 km; Av. winning speed: 38.709 kmh; No. of starters: 180; No. of finishers: 136.*

1994 1. Miguel INDURAIN (E) 2. Piotr Ugrumov (LAT) @ 5.39. 3. Marco Pantani (I) 4. Luc Leblanc (F) 5. Richard Virenque (F).

*No. of stages: 21; Distance: 3,978 km; Av. winning speed: 38.383 kmh; No. of starters: 180; No. of finishers: 117.*

1995 1. Miguel INDURAIN (E) 2. Alex Zülle (SWI) @ 4.35. 3. Bjarne Riis (DNK). 4. Laurent Jalabert (F). 5. Ivan Gotti (I).

*No. of stages: 20; Distance: 3634.3 km; Av. winning speed 39.184 kmh; No. of starters 189; No. of finishers: 115*

## The Women's Tour de France

The inaugural women's Tour de France was held in 1984. Between 1987 and 1990, Jeannie Longo of France won the event a record four times. In 1993 Marie Purvis from the Isle of Man became the only UK rider to win a race stage, a feat she then repeated in 1995.

*No one has dominated the Tour like Miguel Indurain (below), winner five times in succession in the 1990s*

# GIRO D'ITALIA

The Giro d'Italia was launched by the sports newspaper La Gazzetta dello Sport at the Bologna bike show of 1908. Within 24 hours of discovering that the first stage race round Italy modelled on the Tour de France was being planned by their main rival, the Corriere della Sera, the editor of La Gazzetta announced that the first Giro would take place. It started at 2.53 p.m. on 13 May 1909 from Piazza Loreto in Milan, with Luigi Ganna winning over a total distance of 2448.2 kilometres and just 43 of the 127 starters finishing.

■ The ultimate stage race 'double' is winning the Giro and the Tour de France in the same year. Six riders have succeeded a total of 11 times. Eddy Merckx alone has won both tours three times; Stephen Roche alone has won both Tours and the world road race championship; and Miguel Indurain alone has won both tours two years running. Gino Bartali in 1949 and Claudio Chiappucci in 1992 both took double second places in the Giro and Tour; Greg LeMond was third in the 1985 Giro and second in the 1985 Tour.

**The Double Winners**
Fausto Coppi – 1949, 1952.
Jacques Anquetil – 1964.
Eddy Merckx – 1970, 1972, 1974.
Bernard Hinault – 1982, 1985.
Stephen Roche – 1987.
Miguel Indurain – 1992, 1993.

## The Maglias

The Giro race leader wears the pink jersey, *la maglia rosa*, to match the pink of *La Gazzetta dello Sport* which still sponsors the tour. The pink jersey was introduced in 1931, the 19th time the tour was run, and the first man to wear it was Learco Guerra of Italy. Only four riders have worn the pink jersey from start to finish – Costante Girardengo in 1919, Alfredo Binda in 1927, Eddy Merckx in 1973 and Gianni Bugno in 1990. Eddy Merckx also holds the record for the number of days spent wearing the pink jersey, with a total of 78. He is followed by Alfredo Binda (60), Francesco Moser (57), Gino Bartali (50), Giuseppe Saronni (49) and Jacques Anquetil (42).

■ The Giro King of the Mountains wears the green jersey, *la maglia verde*. The first King of the Mountains was Alfredo Binda in 1933. Gino Bartali holds the King of the Mountains record, having won the title in 1935–37, 1939–40, and 1946–48. José-Manuel Fuente of Spain won four times in succession

*Horrible conditions greet Charly Gaul at the Bormio on top of the Alps during the 1960 Giro.*

in 1971–74; the Italians Fausto Coppi (1948–1950), Franco Bitossi (1964–66), and Claudio Bortolotto (1979–81) each won three times. The only Briton to win the King of the Mountains is the Scottish rider Robert Millar in 1987 when he also finished second overall. In 1988 the American Andy Hampsten won both the King of the Mountains and the overall title.

■ The Giro points leader wears the maroon jersey, *la maglia ciclamina*. The first points winner was Gianni Motta in 1966. Giuseppe Saronni (1979–81, 1983) and Francesco Moser (1976–78, 1982) share the record of four Giro points wins. The only English-speaking riders to be placed in the points competition are Stephen Roche who was third in 1987 when he also won the Giro overall, and Phil Anderson who was second in 1990.

■ The leader of the Intergiro sprint competition at the halfway stage of the Giro wears the blue jersey, *la maglia azzurra*. The best young rider, an award first introduced in 1976, is presented with the white jersey, *la maglia bianca*.

## The Records

Felice Gimondi holds the record for top three Giro placings. He won overall in 1967, 1969 and 1976; was second in 1970 and 1973; and was third in 1965, 1968, 1974 and 1975. The youngest ever winner of the Giro was Fausto Coppi in 1940 at the age of 20 years and eight months. The oldest ever winner was Fiorenzo Magni in 1955 at the age of 35.

■ Alfredo Binda won a record number of 41 stages on the Giro. Eddy Merckx won 25, Giuseppe Saronni won 24, Francesco Moser won 23, and Fausto Coppi and Roger de Vlaeminck both won 22. The record for the number of stage wins in a single Giro is also held by Alfredo Binda who won 12 out of 15 stages in 1927. Roger de Vlaeminck (1975), Freddy Maertens (1977) and Giuseppe Saronni (1980) have each won seven stages in one Giro. Alfredo Binda also holds the record for the number of stage wins in succession, having won eight stages one after the other in 1929. The only rider to come anywhere close to this achievement is Vito Taccone who won four consecutive stages (10–13) in 1964.

■ The shortest ever Giro was the first year in 1909 when it was 2448 km (1530 miles) long. The longest ever Giro was 4337 km (2711 miles) in 1954 at the end of which Fiorenzo Magni beat Fausto Coppi by just 13 seconds. A year later the closest Giro finish happened when Fiorenzo Magni beat Fausto Coppi by just 12 seconds in 1955. The record was equalled in 1974 when Eddy Merckx beat Gianbattista Bartonchelli by the same margin. The longest ever single stage in the Giro was 430 km (269 miles) from Lucca to Rome in 1914.

■ The highest point in the Giro is the Colle del Angelo. The climb to the top is 14.5 km long at an average gradient of 6.25 per cent, gaining 910 metres to reach 2748 metres above sea level. The first rider over the summit wins the 'Cima Coppi' presented in honour of Fausto Coppi.

■ The first time-trial stage was held in the 1933 Giro over a 62 km course from Bologna to Ferrara. It was won by Alfredo Binda. Francesco Moser holds the Giro record with 12 time-trial victories. Jacques Anquetil and Eddy Merckx both won six Giro time-trials, Miguel Indurain four and Gianni Bugno three.

■ The Giro speed record is held by Giuseppe Saronni who averaged 38.9 kmh (24.335 mph) over the 3922 km course in 1983. In 1990 Gianni Bugno led from start to finish at an average 37.609 kmh (23.472 mph) over 3450 kilometres. The slowest winning speed for the Giro is 23.374 kmh over 3162 kilometres by Alfonso Calzolari in 1914. The speed record for a stage of the Giro was set by Armand de la Cuevas who averaged 53.39 kmh (33.36 mph) on the second time-trial stage in Bologna in 1994.

■ Italian riders have won the Giro 54 times; Belgian riders have won seven times including five wins by Eddie Merckx; French riders have won six times; Swiss riders have won three times; riders from Luxembourg and Spain have won twice; and riders from Ireland, Sweden, Switzerland, Russia and the USA have each won once.

■ Wladimior Panizza holds the record for competing in the most Giros, having started 18 and finished 16. Pierino Gavazzi had 17 starts and 14 finishes; Gino Bartali started and finished 14 times; Felice Gimondi started and finished 12 times. The highest number of starters was 298 in 1928.

■ Russian Evgeni Berzin deprived Miguel Indurain of his third successive Giro win when he won in 1993 in his second season as a professional; he also gave Indurain the worst time-trial defeat of his career when he finished 2 minutes, 34 seconds behind Berzin on the eighth time-trial stage. By winning, Berzin became the first Eastern European rider to win a major tour.

■ In 1995 Tony Rominger led the Giro all the way from the second stage, winning all three time trials and a mountain stage to win the points jersey and the InterGiro award as well as winning overall. He became the first Swiss winner of the Giro since Carlo Clerici in 1954 – Clerici was Italian-born but had Swiss nationality.

## Giro D'Italia Results

1909   1. Luigi GANNA (I). 2. Carlo Galetti (I) @ 2 points. 3. Giovanni Rossignoli (I). 4. Clemente Canepari (I) 5. Carlo Oriani (I).
*No. of stages: 8; Distance: 2448.2 km; Av. winning speed: 27.260 kmh; No. of starters: 127; No. of finishers: 49.*

1910   1. Carlo GALETTI (I). 2. Eberardo Pavesi (I) @ 18 points. 3. Luigi Ganna (I). 4. Ezio Carlaita (I). 5. Emilio Chironi (I).
*No. of stages: 10; Distance: 29,874 km; Av. winning speed: 26.113 km; No. of starters: 101; No. of finishers: 20.*

1911   1. Carlo GALETTI (I). 2. Giovanni Rossignoli (I) @ 8 points. 3. Giovanni Gerbi (I). 4. Giuseppe Santhia (I). 5. Ezio Corlaita (I).
*No. of stages: 12; Distance: 3530.2 km; Av. winning speed: 26.216 kmh; No. of starters: 86; No. of finishers: 24.*

1912   1. 'ATALA'. 2. 'Peugeot' @ 10 points. 3. 'Gerbi'. 4. 'Goericke'. 5. 'Globo'.
*No. of stages: 8; Distance: 2439.6 km; Av. winning speed: 27.323 kmh; No. of starters: 54; No. of finishers: 26.*

1913    1. Carlo ORIANI (I). 2. Eberardo Pavesi (I) @ 6 points. 3. Giuseppe Azzini (I). 4. Pierino Albini (I). 5. Luigi Ganna (I).
*No. of stages: 9; Distance: 2932 km; Av. winning speed: 26.379 kmh; No. of starters: 99; No. of finishers: 34.*

1914    1. Alfonso CALZOLARI (I). 2. Pierino Albini (I) @ 1:57.26. 3. Luigi Licotti (I). 4. Clemente Canepari (I). 5. Enrico Sala (I).
*No. of stages: 8; Distance: 3162 km; Av. winning speed: 23.374 kmh; No. of starters: 81; No. of finishers: 8.*

1919    1. Costante GIRARDENGO (I). 2. Gaetano Belloni (I) @ 50.56. 3. Marcel Buysse (B). 4. Clemente Canepari (I). 5. Ugo Agostoni (I).
*No. of stages: 10; Distance: 2984 km; Av. winning speed: 26.440 kmh; No. of starters: 63; No. of finishers: 15.*

1920    1. Gaetano BELLONI (I). 2. Angelo Gremo (I) @ 32.25. 3. Jean Alavoine (F). 4. Emilio Petica (I). 5. Domenico Schierano (I).
*No. of stages: 8; Distance: 2632.8 km; Av. winning speed: 25.639 kmh; No. of starters: 49; No. of finishers: 10.*

1921    1. Giovanni BRUNERO (I) 2. Gaetano Belloni (I) @ 1.00. 3. Bartolomeo Aymo (I) 4. Lucien Buysse (B). 5. Angelo Gremo (I).
*No. of stages: 10; Distance: 3107.5 km; Av. winning speed: 25.592 kmh; No. of starters: 69; No. of finishers: 27.*

1922    1. Giovanni BRUNERO (I). 2. Bartolomeo Aymo (I) @ 12.20. 3. Giuseppe Enrici (I). 4. Alfredo Sivocci (I). 5. Domenico Schierano (I).
*No. of stages: 10; Distance: 3095.5 km; Av. winning speed: 25.856 kmh; No. of starters: 75; No. of finishers: 15.*

1923    1. Costante GIRARDENGO (I). 2. Giovanni Brunero (I) @ 37 secs. 3. Bartolomeo Aymo (I). 4. Federico Gay (I). 5. Ottavio Bottecchia (I).
*No. of stages: 10; Distance: 3202.7 km; Av. winning speed: 25.895 kmh; No. of starters: 96; No. of finishers: 38.*

1924    1. Giuseppe ENRICI (I). 2. Frederico Gay (I) @ 58.21. 3. Angioli Gabrielli (I). 4. S Martinetto (I). 5. Enea Dal Flume (I).
*No. of stages: 12; Distance: 3613 km; Av. winning speed: 25.138 kmh; No. of starters: 90; No. of finishers: 30.*

1925    1. Alfredo BINDA (I). 2. Costante Girardengo (I) @ 4.58. 3. Giovanni Brunero (I). 4. Gaetano Belloni (I). 5. Nello Ciaccheri (I).
*No. of stages: 12; Distance: 3250.5 km; Av. winning speed: 25.600 kmh; No. of starters: 126; No. of finishers: 39.*

1926    1. Giovanni BRUNERO (I). 2. Alfredo Binda (I) @ 15.38. 3. Arturo Bresciani (I). 4. Ermanno Vallazza (I). 5. Giuseppe Enrici (I).
*No. of stages: 2; Distance: 3429.7 km; Av. winning speed: 25.113 kmh; No. of starters: 204; No. of finishers: 40.*

1927    1. Alfredo BINDA (I). 2. Giovanni Brunero (I) @ 27.24. 3. Antonio Negrini (I). 4. Ermanno Vallazza (I) 5. Giuseppe Pancera (I)
*No. of stages: 15; Distance: 3758.3 km; Av. winning speed: 25.847 kmh; No. of starters: 258; No. of finishers: 79.*

1928    1. Alfredo BINDA (I). 2. Giuseppe Pancera (I) @ 18.13. 3. Bartolomeo Aymo (I). 4. Victor Fontan (F). 5. Egido Picchiottino (I).
*No. of stages: 2; Distance: 3044.6 km; Av. winning speed: 26.748 kmh; No. of starters: 298 No. of finishers: 124.*

1929    Alfredo BINDA (I). 2. D Piemontesi (I) @ 3.44. 3. Leonida Frascarelli (I). 4. Antonio Negrini (I). 5. Luigi Giacobbe (I).
*No. of stages: 14; Distance: 2920.3 km; Av. winning speed: 27.292 kmh; No. of starters: 166; No. of finishers: 99.*

1930    1. Luigi MARCHISIO (I). 2. Luigi Giacobbe (I) @ 52 secs. 3. Allegro Grandi (I). 4. Ambrogio Morelli (I) 5. Antonio Pesenti (I).
*No. of stages: 15; Distance: 3097.5 km; Av. winning speed: 26.878 kmh; No. of starters: 115; No. of finishers: 67.*

1931    1. Francesco CAMUSSO (I). 2. Luigi Glacobbe (I) @ 2.47. 3. Luigi Marchisio (I). 4. Aristide Cavallini (I). 5. Ettore Balmanion (I).
*No. of stages: 12; Distance: 3012.8 km; Av. winning speed: 29.332 kmh; No. of starters: 109; No. of finishers: 65.*

1932    1. Antonio PESENTI (I). 2. J Demuysere (B) @ 11.09. 3. Remo Bertoni (I). 4. Learco Guerra (I). 5. Kurt Stoepel (D).
*No. of stages: 13; Distance: 3234.3 km; Av. winning speed: 30.604 kmh; No. of starters: 109; No. of finishers: 66.*

1933    1. Alfredo BINDA (I) 2. J Demuysere (B) @ 12.34. 3. D Piemontesi (I) 4. Alfredo Bovet (I) 5. Allegro Grandi (I).
*No. of stages: 17; Distance: 3343 km; Av. winning speed: 30.043 kmh; No. of starters: 97; No. of finishers: 51.*

1934    1. Learco GUERRA (I). 2. Francesco Camusso (I) @ 51 secs. 3. Giovanni Cazzulani (I) 4. Giuseppe Olmo (I) 5. Giovanni Gotti (I).
*No. of stages: 17; Distance: 3706 km; Av. winning speed: 30.548; No. of starters: 105; No. of finishers: 52.*

1935    1. Vasco BERGAMASCHI (I). 2. Giuseppe Martano (I) @ 3.07. 3. Giuseppe Olma (I). 4. Learco Guerra (I). 5. Maurice Archambaud (F).
*No. of stages: 20; Distance: 3577 km; Av. winning speed: 31.363 kmh; No. of starters: 102; No. of finishers: 63.*

1936    1. Gino BARTALI (I). 2. Giuseppe Olmo (I) @ 2.33. 3. Sever Canavesi (I) 4. Aladino Mealli (I) 5. Giovanni Valetti (I)
*No. of stages: 21; Distance: 3756 km; Av. winning speed: 31.279 kmh; No. of starters: 89; No. of finishers: 45.*

1937    1. Gino BARTALI (I). 2. Giovanni Valetti (I) @ 8.18. 3. Enrico Mollo (I) 4. Severino Canavesi (I) 5. Cesare Del Cancia (I).
*No. of stages: 23; Distance: 3840 km; Av. winning speed: 31.365 kmh; No. of starters: 93; No. of finishers: 41.*

1938    1. Giovanni VALETTI (I). 2. Ezio Cecchi (I) @ 8.47. 3. Severino Canavesi (I). 4. Settimio Simonini (I) 5. Michele Benente (I).
*No. of stages: 21; Distance: 3645.8 km; Av. winning speed: 32.272 kmh; No. of starters: 94; No. of finishers: 50.*

1939    1. Giovanni VALETTI (I) 2. Gino Bartali (I) @ 2.59. 3. Mario Vicini (I). 4. Severino Canavesi (I) 5. Settimio Simonini (I).
*No. of stages: 19; Distance: 3011.4 km; Av. winning speed: 34.150 kmh; No. of starters: 89; No. of finishers: 54*

1940    1. Fausto COPPI (I). 2. Enrico Mollo (I) @ 2.40. 3. G Cottur (I). 4. Mario Vicini (I). 5. Severino Canavesi (I).
*No. of stages: 20; Distance: 3574 km; Av. winning speed: 33.240 kmh; No. of starters: 91; No. of finishers: 4.*

1946    1. Gino BARTALI (I). 2. Fausto Coppi (I) @ 47 secs. 3. Vito Ortelli (I). 4. Salvatore Crippa (I). 5. Aldo Ronconi (I).
*No. of stages: 20; Distance: 3039.5 km; Av. winning speed: 33.948 kmh; No. of starters: 79; No. of finishers: 40.*

1947    1. Fausto COPPI (I). 2. Gino Bartali (I) @ 1.43. 3. Giulio Bresci (I). 4. Ezio Cecchi (I). 5. Sylvere Maes (B).
*No. of stages: 20; Distance: 3843 km; Av. winning speed: 33.153 kmh; No. of starters: 84; No. of finishers: 50.*

1948    1. Fiorenzo MAGNI (I). 2. Ezio Cecchi (I) @ 13 secs. 3. G Cottur (I). 4. Vito Ortelli (I). 5. Primo Volpi (I).
*No. of stages: 18; Distance: 4164 km; Av. winning speed: 33.116 kmh; No. of starters: 77; No. of finishers: 41.*

1949    1. Fausto COPPI (I). 2. Gino Bartali (I) @ 23.47. 3. G Cottur (I). 4. Adolfo Leoni (I). 5. Giancarlo Astrua (I)
*No. of stages: 19; Distance: 4088 km; Av. winning speed: 32.566 kmh; No. of starters: 102; No. of finishers: 65.*

1950    1. Hugo KOBLET (SWI) 2. Gino Bartali (I) @ 5.12. 3. Alfredo Martini (I) 4. Ferdi Kübler (SWI) 5. Luciano Maggini (I).
*No. of stages: 18; Distance: 3981 km; Av. winning speed: 33.816 kmh; No. of starters: 105; No. of finishers: 75.*

*Fausto Coppi scored 5 Giro wins before his premature death*

*Felice Gimondi became a new Italian hero when he won the 1967 Giro at the age of 25. Here he climbs to Cortina in the rain*

1951    1. Fiorenzo MAGNI (I). 2. Rik Van
         Steenbergen (B) @ 1.46. 3. Ferdi Kübler (SWI).
         4. Fausto Coppi (I). 5. Giancarlo Astrua (I).
*No. of stages: 20; Distance: 4153 km; Av. winning
speed: 34.217 kmh; No. of starters: 98; No. of
finishers: 75.*

1952    1. Fausto COPPI (I). 2. Fiorenzo Magni (I)
         @ 9.48. 3. Ferdi Kübler (SWI). 4. Donato
         Zampini (I). 5. Gino Bartali (I).
*No. of stages: 20; Distance: 3964 km; Av. win: 34.560
kmh; No. of starters: 112; No. of finishers: 91.*

1953    1. Fausto COPPI (I). 2. Hugo Koblet (SWI)
         @ 1.29. 3. Pasquale Fornara (I). 4. Gino
         Bartali (I). 5. Angelo Conterno (I)
*No. of stages: 21; Distance: 4035.5 km; Av. winning
speed: 34.019 kmh; No. of starters: 112; No. of
finishers: 72.*

1954    1. Carlo CLERICI (SWI). 2. Hugo Koblet
         (SWI) @ 24.16. 3. Nino Assirelli (I). 4.
         Fausto Coppi (I). 5. Giancarlo Astrua (I).

*No. of stages: 22; Distance: 4337 km; Av. winning
speed: 33.563 kmh; No. of starters: 105; No. of
finishers: 67.*

1955    1. Fiorenzo MAGNI (I). 2. Fausto Coppi (I)
         @ 12 secs. 3. Gastone Nencini (I). 4. Raphaël
         Geminiani (F). 5. Agostino Coletto (I).
*No. of stages: 21; Distance: 3871 km; Av. winning
speed: 35.552 kmh; No. of starters: 8; No. of
finishers: 86.*

1956    1. Charly GAUL (LUX). 2. Fiorenzo
         Magni (I) @ 3.30. 3. Agostino Coletto (I).
         4. Cleto Maule (I) 5. Aldo Moser (I).
*No. of stages: 20; Distance: 3523.4 km; Av. winning
speed: 34.677 kmh; No. of starters: 105; No. of
finishers: 43.*

1957    1. Gastone NENCINI (I). 2. Louison Bobet
         (F) @ 19 secs. 3. Ercole Baldini (I). 4. Charly
         Gaul (LUX). 5. Raphaël Geminiani (F).
*No. of stages: 20; Distance: 3926.7 km; Av. winning speed:
37.488 kmh; No. of starters: 119; No. of finishers: 79.*

1958    1. Ercole BALDINI (I). 2. Jean Brankart (B) @ 4.17. 3. Charly Gaul (LUX). 4. Louison Bobet (F). 5. Gastone Nencini (I).
*No. of stages: 20; Distance: 3341.7 km; Av. winning speed: 36.274 kmh; No. of starters: 120; No. of finishers: 77.*

1959    1. Charly GAUL (LUX). 2. Jacques Anquetil (F) @ 6.12. 3. Diego Ronchini (I). 4. Rik Van Looy (B). 5. Imerio Massignan (I).
*No. of stages: 22; Distance: 3657 km; Av. winning speed: 35.909 kmh; No. of starters: 130; No. of finishers: 86.*

1960    1. Jacques ANQUETIL (F). 2. Gastone Nencini (I) @ 28 secs. 3. Charly Gaul (LUX). 4. Imerio Massignan (I). 5. J. Hoevenaers (B).
*No. of stages: 21; Distance: 3481.2 km; Av. winning speed: 37.006; No. of starters: 140; No. of finishers: 97.*

1961    1. Arnaldo PAMBIANCO (I). 2. Jacques Anquetil (F) @ 3.45. 3. Antonio Suarez (E). 4. Charly Gaul (LUX). 5. Guido Carlesi (I).
*No. of stages: 21; Distance: 4004 km; Av. winning speed: 35.934; No. of starters: 170; No. of finishers: 92.*

1962    1. Franco BALMANION (I). 2. Imerio Massignan (I) @ 2.57. 3. Nino Defilippis (I) 4. Vito Taccone (I). 5. Vittorio Adorni (I).
*No. of stages: 21; Distance: 4180 km; Av. winning speed: 33.955 kmh; No. of starters: 130; No. of finishers: 47.*

1963    1. Franco BALMANION (I). 2. Vittorio Adorni (I) @ 2.24. 3. Giorgio Zancanaro (I); 4. Guido De Rosso (I). 5. Diego Ronchini (I).
*No. of stages: 21; Distance: 4063 km; Av. winning speed: 34.774 kmh; No. of starters: 120; No. of finishers: 86*

1964    1. Jacques ANQUETIL (F). 2. Italo Zilioli (I) @ 1.22. 3. Guido De Rosso (I). 4. Vittorio Adorni (I). 5. Gianni Motta (I).
*No. of stages: 22; Distance: 4119.4 km; Av. winning speed: 35.740 kmh; No. of starters: 130; No. of finishers: 97.*

1965    1. Vittorio ADORNI (I). 2. Italo Zilioli (I) @ 11.26. 3. Felice Gimondi (I). 4. Marcello Mugniani (I). 5. Franco Balmanion (I).
*No. of stages: 22; Distance: 4151.4 km; Av. winning speed: 34.270 kmh; No. of starters: 100; No. of finishers: 81.*

1966    1. Gianni MOTTA (I). 2. Italo Zilioli (I) @ 3.57. 3. Jacques Anquetil (F). 4. Julio Jimenez (E). 5. Felice Gimondi (I).
*No. of stages: 22; Distance: 3976 km; Av. winning speed: 35.744 kmh; No. of starters: 100; No. of finishers: 83.*

1967    1. Felice GIMONDI (I). 2. F. Balmanion (I) @ 3.36. 3. Jacques Anquetil (F). 4. Vittorio Adorni (I). 5. José Perez-Frances (E).
*No. of stages: 22; Distance: 3816 km; Av. winning speed: 35.339 kmh; No. of starters: 130; No. of finishers: 70.*

1968    1. Eddy MERCKX (B). 2. Vittorio Adorni (I) @ 5.01. 3. Felice Gimondi (I). 4. Italo Adorni (I) 5. Willy Vanneste (B)
*No. of stages: 22; Distance: 3917.3 km; Av. winning speed: 36.031 kmh; No. of starters: 130; No. of finishers: 98.*

1969    1. Felice GIMONDI (I). 2. Claudio Michelotto (I) @ 3.35. 3. Italo Zilioli (I). 4. Silvano Schiavon (I). 5. Ugo Colombo (I).
*No. of stages: 23; Distance: 3731.3 km; Av. winning speed: 34.942 kmh; No. of starters: 130; No. of finishers: 81.*

1970    1. Eddy MERCKX (B). 2. Felice Gimondi (I) 3.14. 3. M Van Den Bossche (B). 4. Michele Dancelli (I). 5. Italo Zilioli (I).
*No. of stages: 20; Distance: 3292 km; Av. winning speed: 36.158 kmh; No. of starters: 130; No. of finishers: 97.*

1971    1. Gösta PETTERSSON (SWE). 2. Herman Vanspringel (B) @ 2.04. 3. Ugo Colombo (I). 4. Francisco Galdos (E). 5. Pierfranco Vianelli (I).
*No. of stages: 20; Distance: 3567 km; Av. winning speed: 36.597 kmh; No. of starters: 100; No. of finishers: 75.*

1972    1. Eddy MERCKX (B). 2. José-Manuel Fuente (E) @ 5.30. 3. Francisco Galdos (E). 4 V. Lopez-Carril (E). 5. Wladimiro Panizza (I).
*No. of stages: 20; Distance: 3725 km; Av. winning speed: 36.120 kmh; No. of starters: 100; No. of finishers: 69.*

1973    1. Eddy MERCKX (B). 2. Felice Gimondi (I) @ 7.42. 3. Giovanni Battaglin (I). 4. José Pessarodona (E). 5. Santiago Lazcano (E).
*No. of stages: 20; Distance: 3796 km; Av. winning speed: 35.506 kmh; No. of starters: 140; No. of finishers: 113.*

1974    1. Eddy MERCKX (B) 2. Gibi Baronchelli (I) @ 12 secs. 3. Felice Gimondi (I). 4. Costantino Conti (I) 5. José-Manuel Fuente (E).
*No. of stages: 22; Distance: 4001.9 km; Av. winning speed: 35.372 kmh; No. of starters: 140; No. of finishers: 96.*

1975    1. Fausto BERTOGLIO (I). 2. Francisco Galdos (E) @ 41 secs. 3. Felice Gimondi (I). 4. Roger De Vlaeminck (B). 5.Giuseppe Perletto (I)
*No. of stages: 21; Distance: 3963 km; Av. winning speed: 35.535 kmh; No. of starters: 100; No. of finishers: 70.*

1976    1. Felice GIMONDI (I). 2. Johan De Muynck (B) @ 19 secs. 3. Fausto Bertoglio (I). 4. Francesco Moser (I). 5. Gibi Baronchelli (I).
*No. of stages: 22; Distance: 4161 km; Av. winning speed: 34.683 kmh; No. of starters: 119; No. of finishers: 86.*

1977    1. Michel POLLENTIER (B). 2. Francesco Moser (I) @ 2.32. 3. Gibi Baronchelli (I). 4. Alfio Vandi (I). 5. Wladimiro Panizza (I).
*No. of stages: 22; Distance: 3868.5 km; Av. winning speed: 36.925 kmh; No. of starters: 140; No. of finishers: 121.*

1978    1. Johan DE MUYNCK (B). 2. Gibi Baronchelli (I) @ 59 secs. 3. Francesco Moser (I). 4. Wlad Panizza (I). 5. Giuseppe Saronni (I).
*No. of stages: 20; Distance: 3610.5; Av. winning speed: 35.563; No. of starters: 130; No. of finishers: 90.*

1979    1. Giuseppe SARONNI (I). 2. Francesco Moser (I) @ 2.09. 3. Bernt Johansson (SWE). 4. Michel Laurent (F). 5. Silvano Contini (I).
*No. of stages: 19; Distance: 3301 km; Av. winning speed: 36.887 kmh; No. of starters: 140. No. of finishers: 111.*

1980    1. Bernard HINAULT (F). 2. Wlad Panizza (I) @ 5.43. 3. Giovanni Battaglin (I). 4. Tommy Prim (SWE). 5. Gibi Baronchelli (I).
*No. of stages: 22; Distance: 4025.5 km; Av. winning speed: 35.897 kmh; No. of starters: 130; No. of finishers: 89.*

1981    1. Giovanni BATTAGLIN (I). 2. Tommy Prim (SWE) @ 38 secs. 3. Giuseppe Saronni (I). 4. Silvano Contini (I). 5. Josef Fuchs (SWI).
*No. of stages: 22; Distance: 3895.6 km; Av. winning speed: 37.150 kmh; No. of starters: 130; No. of finishers: 104.*

1982    1. Bernard HINAULT (F). 2. Tommy Prim (SWE) @ 2.35. 3. Silvano Contini (I). 4. Lucien Van Impe (B). 5. Gibi Baronchelli (I).
*No. of stages: 23; Distance: 4010.5 km; Av. winning speed: 36.447 kmh; No. of starters: 162; No. of finishers: 110.*

1983    1. Giuseppe SARONNI (I) 2. R Visentini (I) @ 1.07. 3. A Fernandez (E) 4. Mario Beccia (I) 5. D Thurau (D).
*No. of stages: 22; Distance: 3922 km; Av. winning speed: 38.900 kmh; No. of starters: 162; No. of finishers: 140.*

1984    1. Francesco MOSER (I). 2. Laurent Fignon (F) @ 1.03. 3. Moreno Argentin (I). 4. Marino Lejarreta (E). 5 J Van der Velde (NL).
*No. of stages: 22; Distance: 3808 km; Av. winning speed: 38.681 kmh; No. of starters: 169; No. of finishers: 143.*

1985    1. Bernard HINAULT (F) 2. Francesco Moser (I) @ 1.08. 3. Greg LeMond (USA). 4. Tommy Prim (SWE). 5. Marino Lejarreta (E).
*No. of stages: 22; Distance: 3998.6 km; Av. winning speed: 37.893 kmh; No. of starters: 199; No. of finishers: 135.*

1986    1. Roberto VISENTINI (I) 2. Giuseppe Saronni (I) @ 1.02. 3. Francesco Moser (I) 4. Greg LeMond (USA) 5. Claudio Corti (I)
*No. of stages: 22; Distance: 3858.6 km; Av. winning speed: 37.615 kmh; No. of starters: 189; No. of finishers: 143.*

1987    1. Stephen ROCHE (IRL). 2. Robert Millar (GB) @ 3.40. 3. Eric Breukink (NL). 4. Marino Lejarreta (E). 5. F Giupponi (I).
*No. of stages: 22; Distance: 3915 km; Av. winning speed: 37.045 kmh; No. of starters: 190; No. of finishers: 133.*

1988    1. Andy HAMPSTEN (USA). 2. Erik Breukink (NL) @ 1.43. 3. Urs Zimmermann (SWI). 4. F Giupponi (I). 5. F Chioccioli.
*No. of stages: 21; Distance: 3597 km; Av. winning speed: 36.788 kmh; No. of starters: 180; No. of finishers: 125.*

1989    1. Laurent FIGNON (F). 2. Flavio Giupponi (I) @ 1.15. 3. Andrew Hampsten (USA). 4. Erik Breukink (NL). 5. Franco Chioccioli (I).

*Tony Rominger dominated the 1995 Giro but the effort cost him the chance of challenging Miguel Indurain in the Tour de France*

*No. of stages: 22; Distance: 3418 km; Av. winning speed: 36.552 kmh; No. of starters: 198; No. of finishers: 141.*

1990    1. Gianni BUGNO (I) 2. Charly Mottet (F) @ 6.33. 3. Marco Giovannetti (I). 4. Vladimir Pulnikov (SU). 5. Federico Echave (E).

*No. of stages: 20; Distance: 3450 km; Av. winning speed: 37.609 kmh; No. of starters: 197; No. of finishers: 163.*

1991    1. Franco CHIOCCIOLI (I). 2. Claudio Chiappucci (I) @ 3.48. 3. Massimiliano Lelli (I). 4. Gianni Bugno (I). 5. M Lejarreta (E).

*No. of stages: 21; Distance: 3715.7 km; Av. winning speed: 37.303 kmh; No. of starters: 180; No. of finishers: 133.*

1992    1. Miguel INDURAIN (E) 2. Claudio Chiappucci (I) @ 5.12. 3. Franco Chioccioli (I). 4. Marco Giovannetti (I). 5. Andy Hampsten (USA).

*No. of stages: 22; Distance: 3843 km; Av. winning speed: 37.092 kmh; No. of starters: 180; No. of finishers: 148.*

1993    1. Miguel INDURAIN (E). 2. Piotr Ugroumov (LAT) @ 58 secs. 3. Claudio Chiappucci (I). 4. Massimiliano Lelli (I). 5. Pavel Tonkov (RUS).

*No. of stages: 21; Distance: 3702 km; Av. winning speed: 37.712 kmh; No. of starters: 180; No. of finishers: 132.*

1994    1. Evgeni BERZIN (RUS). 2. Michele Pantani (I) @ 2.51. 3. Miguel Indurain (E). 4. Pavel Tonkov (RUS) 5. Claudio Chiappucci (I).

*No. of stages: 22; Distance: 3721 km; Av. winning speed: 37.150 kmh; No. of starters: 180; No. of finishers: 99.*

1995    1. Tony ROMINGER (SWI). 2. Evgeni Berzin (RUS) @ 4.13. 3. Piotr Ugroumov (RUS). 4. Claudio Chiappucci (I). 5. Oliverio Rincon (COL).

*No. of stages: 22; Distance: 3827 km; Av. winning speed: 40.663 kmh; No. of starters: 198; No. of finishers: 122.*

# VUELTA A ESPAÑA

The Vuelta a España is the third great European road-racing tour. It is a much younger event than the Tour de France or Giro d'Italia and is now held at the end of the season in September. For this reason many of the great tour winners such as the Spanish Tour de France star Miguel Indurain have chosen to give it a miss, in order to concentrate their efforts on the one or two great tours that precede it. Nevertheless the Vuelta continues to grow in stature, with the number of stages, total distance and high mountain stages providing an event that is every bit as difficult for the riders. A total prize fund of 101 million pesetas (£505,000) was on offer for the 1995 event.

■ Robert Millar became the first British rider to wear the leader's jersey on Stage 10 of the Vuelta in 1985. He held the lead until the penultimate day's mountain stage when the Spaniard Pedro Delgado broke away and relegated Millar to second place overall. The following year the Scot was again second overall. Both Sean Yates and Malcolm Elliott won a stage in 1988. In 1989 Malcolm Elliott became the only British rider to win the points prize, having won two stages. Sean Kelly is the most successful English-speaking rider, having won the Vuelta outright in 1988.

■ In 1994 Tony Rominger became the first rider to win three years in a row. He led the 1994 Vuelta from the start at Valladolid to the finish in Madrid,

*In 1995 Laurent Jalabert capped a memorable year of Classic wins and the Tour points prize by dominating the Vuelta*

winning six stages including all three time trials.

■ In 1995 Laurent Jalabert won the Vuelta having dominated the race with five stage wins. He also won the Points and Mountains prizes and his team *Once* were first overall, giving a clean sweep. This ended a spectacular comeback season for Jalabert in which he scored 22 major victories and finished ahead of Miguel Indurain and Tony Rominger on top of the world rankings.

## Vuelta a España Results

1935    1. Gustave DELOOR (B). 2. M Canardo (E). 3. A Dignef (B).
*No. of stages: 14; Distance: 3431 km; Av. winning speed: 28.591 kmh.*

1936    1. Gustave DELOOR (B). 2. A Deloor (B). 3. A Bertola (I).
*No. of stages: 21; Distance: 4349 km; Av. winning speed: 28.967 kmh.*

1941    1. J BERRENDERO (E). 2. F Trueba (E). 3. J Jabardo (E).
*No. of stages: 22; Distance: 4442 km; Av. winning speed: 26.262 kmh.*

1942    1. J BERRENDERO (E). 2. D Chater (E). 3. A A Sancho (E).
*No. of stages: 22; Distance: 3634 km; Av. winning speed: 27.102 kmh.*

1945    1. D RODRIGUEZ (E). 2. J Berrendero (E). 3. Juan Gimeno (E).
*No. of stages: 19; Distance: 3723 km; Av. winning speed: 27.420 kmh.*

1946    1. D LANGARCIA (E). 2. J Berrendero (E). 3. J Lambrichs (NL).
*No. of stages: 19; Distance: 3847 km; Av. winning speed: 27.701 kmh.*

1947    1. E VAN DIJCK (B). 2. M Costa (E). 3. D Rodriguez (E).
*No. of stages: 24; Distance: 3818 km; Av. winning speed: 28.825 kmh.*

1948    1. Bernardo RUIZ (E). 2. E Rodriguez (E). 3. B Capo (E).
*No. of stages: 20; Distance: 4090 km; Av. winning speed: 26.358 kmh.*

1950    1. E. RODRIGUEZ (E). 2. M Rodriquez (E). 3. J Serra (E).
*No. of stages: 24; Distance: 3924 km; Av. winning speed: 29.145 kmh.*

1955    1. Jean DOTTO (F). 2. J Quilès (E). 3. Raphaël Geminiani (F).
*No. of stages: 15; Distance: 2735 km; Av. winning speed: 33.738 kmh.*

1956    1. Angelo CONTERNO (I). 2. J Lorono (E). 3. R Impanis (B).
*No. of stages: 17; Distance: 3204 km; Av. winning speed: 30.331 kmh.*

1957    1. Jesus LORONO (E). 2. Federico Bahamontes (E). 3. B Ruiz (E).
*No. of stages: 16; Distance: 2943 km; Av. winning speed: 35.035 kmh.*

1958    1. Jean STABLINSKI (F). 2. Pasquale Fornara (I). 3. F Manzaneque (E).
*No. of stages: 16; Distance: 3276 km; Av. winning speed: 35.18 kmh.*

1959    1. Antonio SUAREZ (E). 2. José Segu (E). 3. Rik Van Looy (B).
*No. of stages: 16; Distance: 3060 km; Av. winning speed: 36.009 kmh.*

1960    1. Frans DE MULDER (B). 2. A Desmet (B). 3. M Pacheco (E).
*No. of stages: 17; Distance: 3368 km; Av. winning speed: 34.537 kmh.*

1961    1. Antonio SOLER (E). 2. François Mahé (F). 3. J Perez-Frances (E).
*No. of stages: 16; Distance: 2818 km; Av. winning speed: 36.653 kmh.*

1962    1. Rudi ALTIG (D). 2. J Perez-Frances (E). 3. S Elliot (IRL).
*No. of stages: 17; Distance: 2843 km; Av. winning speed: 36.174 kmh.*

1963    1. Jacques ANQUETIL (F). 2. M Colmenarejo (E). 3. M Pacheco (E).
*No. of stages: 15; Distance: 2419 km; Av. winning speed: 37.727 kmh.*

1964    1. Raymond POULIDOR (F). 2. Luis Ocana (E). 3. J Perez-Frances (E).
*No. of stages: 17; Distance: 2865 km; Av. winning speed: 36.633 kmh.*

1965    1. Rolf WOLFSHOHL (D). 2. Raymond Poulidor (F) 3. Rik Van Looy (B).
*No. of stages: 18; Distance: 3409.8 km; Av. winning speed: 36.954 kmh.*

1966    1. F GABICA (E). 2. E Velez (E). 3. C Echevarria (E).
*No. of stages: 18; Distance: 2950.3 km; Av. winning speed: 27.605 kmh.*

1967    1. Jan JANSSEN (NL). 2. J P Ducasse (F). 3. A Gonzalez (E).
*No. of stages: 18; Distance: 2941 km; Av. winning speed: 38.724 kmh.*

1968    1. Felice GIMONDI (I). 2. J Perez-Frances (E). 3. E Velez (E).
*No. of stages: 18; Distance: 2981 km; Av. winning speed: 37.917 kmh.*

1969    1. Roger PINGEON (F). 2. Luis Ocana (E). 3. Wagtmans (NL) & Lasa (NL).
*No. of stages: 18; Distance: 2921 km; Av. winning speed: 39.843 kmh.*

1970    1. Luis OCANA (E). 2. A Tamames (E). 3. H. Vanspringel (B).
*No. of stages: 19; Distance: 3560 km; Av. winning speed: 39.831 kmh.*

1971    1. Ferdinand BRAKE (B). 2. Wilfried David (B). 3. Luis Ocana (E).
*No. of stages: 17; Distance: 2793 km; Av. winning speed: 37.829 kmh.*

1972    1. José-Manuel FUENTE (E). 2. Miguel M Lasa (E). 3. A Tamames (E).
*No. of stages: 17; Distance: 3078.6 km; Av. winning speed: 37.284 kmh.*

1973    1. Eddy MERCKX (B). 2. Luis Ocana (E). 3. Bernard Thévenet (F).
*No. of stages: 17; Distance: 3056.8 km; Av. winning speed: 36.098 kmh.*

1974    1. José-Manuel FUENTE (E). 2. Joaquim Agostinho (POR). 3. Miguel M Lasa (E).
*No. of stages: 19; Distance: 2987.9 km; Av. winning speed: 34.420 kmh.*

1975    1. A TAMAMES (E). D Perurena (E). 3. Miguel M Lasa (E).
*No. of stages: 19; Distance: 3075.7 km; Av. winning speed: 34.945 kmh.*

1976    1. J PESSARODONA (E). 2. Luis Ocana (E). 3. José Nazabal (E).
*No. of stages: 19; Distance: 3343.7 km; Av. winning speed: 35.294 kmh.*

1977    1. Freddy MAERTENS (B). 2. Miguel M
        Lasa (E). 3. K P Thaler (D).
*No. of stages: 19; Distance: 2785.1 km; Av. winning speed: 35.294 kmh.*

1978    1. Bernard HINAULT (F). 2. José
        Pesarrodona (E). 3. J R Bernaudeau (F).
*No. of stages: 19; Distance: 2990.4 km; Av. winning speed: 35.014 kmh.*

1979    1. Joop ZOETEMELK (NL). 2. F Galdos
        (E). 3. M Pollentier (B).
*No. of stages: 19; Distance: 3373.6 km; Av. winning speed: 35.529 kmh.*

1980    1. F RUPEREZ (E). 2. Pedro Torres (E). 3.
        C Criquielion (B).
*No. of stages: 19; Distance: 3216.8 km; Av. winning speed: 36.393 kmh.*

1981    1. Giovanni BATTAGLIN (I). 2. Pedro
        Munoz (E). 3. V Gelda (E).
*No. of stages: 19; Distance: 3446.1 km; Av. winning speed: 35.135 kmh.*

1982    1. Marino LEJARRETA (E). 2. M.
        Pollentier (B). 3. S A Nilsson (SWE).
*No. of stages: 19; Distance: 3456.7 km; Av. winning speed: 36.855 kmh.*

1983    1. Bernard HINAULT (F). 2. M Lejarreta
        (E). 3. A Fernandez (E).
*No. of stages: 19; Distance: 3398.8 km; Av. winning speed: 35.881 kmh.*

1984    1. Eric CARITOUX (F). 2. A Fernandez
        (E). 3. R Dietzen (D).
*No. of stages: 19; Distance: 3593.6 km; Av. winning speed: 39.869 kmh.*

1985    1. Pedro DELGADO (E). 2. Robert Millar
        (GB). 3. F Rodriguez (COL).
*No. of stages: 19; Distance: 3474.6 km; Av. winning speed: 36.417 kmh.*

1986    1. Alvaro PINO (I). 2. Robert Millar (GB).
        3. Sean Kelly (IRL).
*No. of stages: 21; Distance: 3666.5 km; Av. winning speed: 37.311 kmh.*

1987    1. Luis Herrera (COL). 2. R Dietzen (D). 3.
        Laurent Fignon (F).
*No. of stages: 22; Distance: 3921.4 km; Av. winning speed: 37.143 kmh.*

1988    1. Sean Kelly (IRL). 2. R Dietzen (D). 3. A
        Fuerte (E).

*Pedro Delgado's tally on his home tour included two wins, a second and a third before his retirement at the end of 1994*

*No. of stages: 21; Distance: 3428.4 km; Av. winning speed: 38.381 kmh.*

1989    1. Pedro DELGADO (E). 2. Fabio Parra
        (COL). 3. O Vargas (COL).
*No. of stages: 22; Distance: 3683 km; Av. winning speed: 39.589 kmh.*

1990    1. Marco GIOVANNETTI (I). 2. Pedro
        Delgado (E). 3. A Fuerte (E).
*No. of stages: 22; Distance: 3711 km; Av. winning speed: 39.224 kmh.*

1991    1. Melchor MAURI (E). 2. Miguel
        Indurain (E). 3. Marino Lejarreta (E).
*No. of stages: 21; Distance: 3212.5 km; Av. winning speed: 38.797 kmh.*

1992    1. Tony ROMINGER (SWI). 2. Jesus
        Montoya (E). 3. Pedro Delgado (E).
*No. of stages: 21; Distance: 3395.1 km; Av. winning speed: 35.275 kmh.*

1993    1. Tony ROMINGER (SWI). 2. Alex Zülle
        (SWI). 3. Laudelino Cubino (E).
*No. of stages: 21; Distance: 3605.2 km; Av. winning speed: 37.508 kmh.*

1994    1. Tony ROMINGER (SWI). 2. Mikel
        Zarrabeitia (E). 3. Pedro Delgado (E).

*No. of stages: 21; Distance: 3531km ; Av. winning speed: 38.333 kmh.*

1995    1. Laurent JALABERT (F). 2. Abraham
        Olano (E). 3. Johan Bruyneel (NL)
*No. of stages: 21; Distance: 3750 km ; Av. winning speed: 39.263 kmh.*

# PARIS—NICE

The Paris–Nice 'Race to the Sun' is the traditional first major event of the European road-race season. It was originally devised by the French journalist Jean Leulliot as a preparation race, but has now built a status which matches any of the Classics and has gained a reputation for only being won by champion riders of the present and future. It was not run between 1940 and 1945, and in 1959 was run as the Paris–Nice–Rome.

Famous Paris–Nice winners include Louison Bobet, Jacques Anquetil who won five times and then became race director, Raymond Poulidor, Eddy Merckx, Joop Zoetemelk, Freddy Maertens, Stephen Roche, Sean Kelly who holds the record of seven consecutive wins between 1982 and 1988, Miguel Indurain, Tony Rominger, Alex Zülle and Laurent Jalabert for whom it was the first of a series of major wins in 1995 after crashing out of the opening stage of the 1994 Tour de France. The only great riders who failed to win the Paris–Nice are Fausto Coppi and Bernard Hinault.

The Paris–Nice is held over eight stages in early March, following a route of approximately 1400 kilometres. Four of the eight stages feature major climbs, with the race culminating in the final afternoon time trial up the Col d'Eze above Nice. Since first being held in 1969 this has attained

major status in itself, with Sean Kelly taking a record five wins.

The only British rider to win the Paris–Nice is Tommy Simpson in 1967. He joined a break to pull out 17 minutes on team-mate and race leader Eddy Merckx on the fourth stage, to eventually win overall by 2 minutes, 17 seconds. Sean Yates led overall for the first three stages of the 1988 Paris–Nice, before being overhauled by the eventual winner Sean Kelly.

Stephen Roche of Ireland won the Paris–Nice in 1981 and came second a record four times – twice to Sean Kelly in 1984–85, and twice to Miguel Indurain in 1989–90.

**Paris–Nice Winners**

1933    1. Alfons Schepers (B) 2. L Hardiquest (B)
        3. B Faure (F)
1934    1. Gaston Rebry (B) 2. Roger Lapébie (F)
        3. M Archambaud (F)
1935    1. René Vietto (F) 2. A Dignef (B) 3. R
        Lesueur (F)
1936    1. Maurice Archambaud (F) 2. J Fontenay
        (F) 3. A Deloor (B)
1937    1. Roger Lapébie (F) 2. S Marcaillou (F) 3.
        Albert Van Schendel (NL)
1938    1. Jules Lowie (B) 2. Albert Disseaux (B) 3.
        Albert Van Schendel (NL)

*The Paris-Nice starts early in the season and snow can be expected in the mountains*

1939    1. Maurice Archambaud (F) 2. F Bonduel (B) 3. G Desmedt (B)

1946    1. Fermo Camellini (I) 2. Maurice De Muer (F) 3. Frans Bonduel (B)

1951*   1. Roger Decock (B) 2. L Teisseire (F) 3. K. Piot (F)

1952*   1. Louison Bobet (F) 2. D Zampini (I) 3. Raymond Impanis (B)

1953*   1. Jean-Pierre Munch (F) 2. R Walkowiak (F) 3. R Bertaz (F)

1954    1. Raymond Impanis (B) 2. N Lauredi (F) 3. F. Anastasi (F)

1955    1. Jean Bobet (F) 2. P Molineris (F) 3. B Gauthier (F)

1956    1. Fred Debruyne (B) 2. P Barbotin (F) 3. F Mahé (F)

1957    1. Jacques Anquetil (F) 2. D Keteleer (B) 3. J Brankart (B)

1958    1. Fred Debruyne (B) 2. P Fornara (I) 3. G Derijcke (B)

1959**  1. Jean Graczyck (F) 2. G Saint (F) 3. P Baffi (I)

1960    1. Raymond Impanis (B) 2. François Mahé (F) 3. R Cazala (F)

1961    1. Jacques Anquetil (F) 2. J Groussard (F) 3. J Planckaert (B)

1962    1. Jozef Planckaert (B) 2. T Simpson (UK) 3. Rolf Wolfshohl (DNK)

1963    1. Jacques Anquetil (F) 2. R Altig (DNK) 3. Rik van Looy (B)

1964    1. Jan Janssen (NL) 2. J-C Annaert (F) 3. J Forestier (F)

1965    1. Jacques Anquetil (F) 2. Rudi Altig (DNK) 3. I. Zilioli (I)

1966    1. Jacques Anquetil (F) 2. Raymond Poulidor (F) 3. Vito Adorni (I)

1967    1. Tom Simpson (UK) 2. B Guyot (F) 3. R Wolfshohl (DNK)

1968    1. Rolf Wolfshohl (DNK) 2. F Bracke (B) 3. J L Bodin (F)

1969    1. Eddy Merckx (B) 2. Raymond Poulidor (F) 3. Jacques Anquetil (F)

1970    1. Eddy Merckx (B) 2. Luis Ocana (E) 3. J Janssen (NL)

1971    1. Eddy Merckx (B) 2. G Petterson (SWE) 3. Luis Ocana (E)

1972    1. Raymond Poulidor (F) 2. Eddy Merckx (B) 3. Luis Ocana (E)

1973    1. Raymond Poulidor (F) 2. Joop Zoetemelk (NL) 3. Eddy Merckx (B)

1974    1. Joop Zoetemelk (NL) 2. Al Santy (F) 3. Eddy Merckx (B)

1975    1. Joop Zoetemelk (NL) 2. Eddy Merckx (B) 3. Gerrie Knetemann (NL)

1976    1. Michel Laurent (F) 2. H Kuiper (NL) 3. Luis Ocana (E)

1977    1. Freddy Maertens (B) 2. Gerrie Knetemann (NL) 3. J-L Vandenbroucke (B)

1978    1. Gerrie Knetemann (NL) 2. Bernard Hinault (F) 3. Joop Zoetemelk (NL)

1979    1. Joop Zoetemelk (NL) 2. S A Nilsson (SWE) 3. Gerrie Knetemann (NL)

1980    1. G Duclos-Lassalle (F) 2. S Mutter (SWI) 3. Gerrie Knetemann (NL)

1981    1. Stephen Roche (IRL) 2. A Van der Piel (NL) 3. Fons De Wolf (B)

1982    1. Sean Kelly (IRL) 2. G Duclos-Lassalle (F) 3. J L Vandenbroucke (B)

1983    1. Sean Kelly (IRL) 2. J M Grezet (SWI) 3. Steven Rooks (NL)

1984    1. Sean Kelly (IRL) 2. Stephen Roche (IRL) 3. Bernard Hinault (F)

1985    1. Sean Kelly (IRL) 2. Stephen Roche (IRL) 3. F Vichot (F)

1986    1. Sean Kelly (IRL) 2. U Zimmermann (SWI) 3. Greg LeMond (USA)

1987    1. Sean Kelly (IRL) 2. Jean-François Bernard (F) 3. Laurent Fignon (F)

1988    1. Sean Kelly (IRL) 2. R Pensec (F) 3. J Gorospe (E)

1989    1. Miguel Indurain (E) 2. Stephen Roche (IRL) 3. M Madiot (F)

*Raymond Poulidor, who was so often disappointed in the Tour de France, got it right in the 1973 Paris-Nice*

1990 1. Miguel Indurain (E) 2. Stephen Roche (IRL) 3. L Leblanc (F)
1991 1. Tony Rominger (SWI) 2. Laurent Jalabert (F) 3. Mart Gayant (F)
1992 1. Jean-François Bernard (F) 2. Tony Rominger (SWI) 3. Miguel Indurain (E)
1993 1. Alex Zülle (SWI) 2. Laurent Bezault (F) 3. Pascal Lance (F)

1994 1. Tony Rominger (SWI) 2. Jesus Montoya (E) 3. Viatcheslav Ekimov (RUS)
1995 1. Laurent Jalabert (F) 2. Vladislav Bobrik (RUS) 3. Alex Zülle (SWI)
* Paris–Côte d'Azur. **Paris–Nice–Rome.

**Col D'Eze Time-Trial Winners**

| Year | Winner | Distance/Time (mins) | Av. speed ( kmh) |
|---|---|---|---|
| 1969 | Eddy Merckx (B) | 9.5 km/20:40 | 27.580 |
| 1970 | Eddy Merckx (B) | 9.5 km/20:14 | 28.165 |
| 1971 | Eddy Merckx (B) | 9.5 km/20:43.9 | 27.494 |
| 1972 | Raymond Poulidor (F) | 9.5 km/20:04.2 | 28.400 |
| 1973 | Joop Zoetemelk (NL) | 9.5 km/20:44.6 | 27.478 |
| 1974 | Joop Zoetemelk (NL) | 9.5 km/20:38.9 | 27.605 |
| 1975 | Joop Zoetemelk (NL) | 9.5 km/20:59.8 | 27.147 |
| 1976 | Michel Laurent (F) | 9.5 km/20:51 | 27.438 |
| 1978 | Gerrie Knetemann (NL) | 9.5 km/20:14.26 | 28.165 |
| 1979 | Joop Zoetemelk (NL) | 11.0 km/21:22 | 30.831 |
| 1980 | Gerrie Knetemann (NL) | 11.0 km/20:28.87 | 32.224 |
| 1981 | Stephen Roche (IRL) | 11.0 km/21:09.64 | 31.189 |
| 1982 | Sean Kelly (IRL) | 11.0 km/20:50.89 | 31.657 |
| 1983 | Sean Kelly (IRL) | 11.0 km/20:19.54 | 32.471 |
| 1984 | Sean Kelly (IRL) | 11.0 km/20:41.00 | 31.898 |
| 1985 | Stephen Roche (IRL) | 11.0 km/20:52.02 | 31.508 |
| 1986 | Sean Kelly (IRL) | 10.0 km/19:45.00 | 30.379 |
| 1987 | Stephen Roche (IRL) | 10.0 km/19:47 | 30.329 |
| 1988 | Sean Kelly (IRL) | 10.0 km/20:11 | 29.727 |
| 1989 | Stephen Roche (IRL) | 10.0 km/19:51 | 30.226 |
| 1990 | Jean-François Bernard (F) | 12.0 km/22:15 | 32.341 |
| 1993 | Alex Zülle (SWI) | 12.5 km/23:05 | 32.474 |
| 1994 | Tony Rominger (SWI) | 12.5 km/22:06 | 33.926 |
| 1995 | Vladislac Bobrik (RUS) | 12.5 km/22:32 | 33.285 |

# The Great Riders

## Djamolidin ABDUZHAPAROV (USSR/Uzbekistan)

b. Tashkent, USSR, 28 February 1964

Variously known as 'Abdu' and 'The Tashkent Terror' due to his fearless and aggressive riding style and amazing sprint, Djamolidin Abduzhaparov was one of the first great riders to come out of the USSR, and made an immediate impression with three stage wins when he first appeared in the 1986 British Milk Race. Having turned professional he settled in Italy, and went on to win the points prize in the 1991 Tour de France as well as being responsible for a massive pile-up at the very end of the Tour when he crashed in the final 500m sprint on the Champs Elysées. In 1993 he won the Tour de France points prize once again, this time winning the final stage on the Champs Elysées. He went on to win the Tour de France points prize for a third time in 1994.

## Jean AERTS (Belgium)

b. Laken-Brussels, 8 September 1908; d. June 1992

The first man to win both the world amateur (1927) and professional (1935) road race championships. In the 1927 event the professionals and amateurs rode concurrently at the Nürburgring in Germany and Aerts finished fifth overall, but was the highest ranked amateur. He was an excellent sprinter which helped in the world championships, but he lacked the climbing ability needed for a high overall place in the major tours. However, he used his sprinting ability to win 11 stages of the Tour de France, including six in 1933 when his poor climbing kept his final position down to ninth. He won the Paris–Brussels in 1931.

## Rudi ALTIG (West Germany)

b. Mannheim, 18 March 1937

An outstanding pursuit cyclist, winner of world titles as an amateur in 1959 and professional in 1960 and 1961, Altig became a top road sprinter. His lack of ability as a climber limited him in the major tours, although he won the 1962 Vuelta a España. He also won the Tour of Flanders in 1964 and Milan–San Remo in 1968. His 1966 professional world road championship win came at home in Germany when he outsprinted Jacques Anquetil for the title. Altig was also the winner of 23 six-day races, won 13 German championships, and set world records at 1000m and 500m. Although he never won the Tour de France he wore the yellow jersey for a total of 18 days between 1962 and 1969 and was third in 1966.

Altig supplemented his training with yoga, often standing on his head between heats of track races. He had trained as an automobile electrician and after his racing days became a coach to the German team. He set world indoor records for five kilometres with a standing start of 6 minutes, 7.6 seconds as a pro in 1962, and for one kilometre with a flying start of 1 minute, 9.06 seconds as an amateur in 1959.

## Phil ANDERSON (Australia)

b. London, 13 March 1958

Phil Anderson rates as the most successful Australian on the European road-race circuit. His first break came at the age of 17 when he won the 1977 Dulux Tour of New Zealand. He then won the Commonwealth Games road race the following year, which led to an invitation to race in France and his first win as an amateur in Europe came at the 1979 Grand Prix de Sanary, the year in which he also won the amateur Grand Prix des Nations.

In 1980 Anderson turned professional for Peugeot. A year later he took the yellow jersey for a day in the 1981 Tour de France, becoming the first Australian to lead the Tour after a battle against Bernard Hinault at Pla D'Adet. He led the Tour for another ten days in 1982, finished the Tour five times in the top ten, and twice finished fifth overall – in 1982 and 1985. Anderson also scored victories in other stage races and the one-day Classics, taking the Amstel Gold Race in 1983, the Tour of Switzerland in 1985 (his best season with 16 wins), the Grand Prix of Frankfurt in both 1984 and 1985, the Zurich Meisterschaft in 1984, Créteil-Chaville in 1986, the Kellogg's Tour of Britain in 1991 and 1993, and the Nissan Classic of Ireland in 1992, as well as winning Tour du Pont stages in the USA in 1991 and 1992. He retired in 1994, having been a member of the Australian gold medal winning team in the Commonwealth Games team time trial.

**Phil Anderson Major Victories**

| | |
|---|---|
| 1983 | Amstel Gold Race. |
| 1984 | Grand Prix of Frankfurt; Zurich Meisterschaft. |
| 1985 | Grand Prix of Frankfurt; Tour of Switzerland. |
| 1986 | Créteil-Chaville. |
| 1991 | Kellogg's Tour of Britain. |
| 1992 | Nissan Classic of Ireland. |
| 1993 | Kellogg's Tour of Britain. |

## Jacques ANQUETIL (France)

b. Mont Saint-Aignan, 8 January 1934; d. Boos, near Rouen, 17 November 1987

One of the greatest cyclists ever, known as the man who could not be broken. His wins were never spectacular, but his major tour victories were always carefully planned and steadily ridden. Anquetil was a small man at only 5 ft 8 in tall, but his only weakness was as a road sprinter. He was an excellent climber, and his forte was as a time triallist. He had

*Jacques Anquetil was the most famous French rider of all time. He enjoyed four straight wins in the Tour de France*

five wins in the Tour de France (1957, 1961–64) and wore the *maillot jaune* for a total of 51 days, the third highest ever. He is also one of the few top professional cyclists to have won an Olympic medal, having helped France to a bronze in the 1952 team road race. The greatest disappointment of his career was that he never managed to win the world professional road race title, his lack of sprinting ability holding him back, and his best was second in 1966. In 1956 he was French champion and second in the world championships at pursuit, and set world records for the one hour with 46.159 km and for 20 km with 25:57.40. In 1967 he achieved 47.493 km in the one hour, and his last win of any repute came in 1969 in the Vuelta Al Pais Basco. Decorated as Chevalier of the Legion d'Honneur by General de Gaulle in 1966, he became president of the French professional cyclists' union and director of the French world championships team.

Anquetil did not leave racing until the end of 1969, after a track race in Antwerp. He then retired to his château and spent the rest of his life farming. He never rode a bicycle again, but retained an interest in the sport as an occasional TV commentator and technical director for a number of races, including Paris–Nice which he had won six times. In 1987 France was stunned by the news of his death from cancer at the age of 53. He had worked until the end, with few people aware that he was terminally ill. He is buried near his château outside Rouen, and his grave, like those of Fausto Coppi and Tom Simpson, is a place of pilgrimage for cyclists from all over the world.

**Jacques Anquetil Major Victories**

| | |
|---|---|
| 1952 | Amateur champion of France. |
| 1953 | Grand Prix des Nations. |
| 1954 | Grand Prix des Nations. |
| 1955 | Grand Prix des Nations. |
| 1956 | World Hour Record (46.159 km); Grand Prix des Nations. |
| 1957 | Tour de France (4 stage wins); Paris–Nice; Grand Prix des Nations; Paris Six-Day. |
| 1958 | Grand Prix des Nations; Paris Six-Day. |
| 1959 | (3rd in Tour de France; 2nd in Tour of Italy.) |
| 1960 | Tour of Italy (2 stage wins). |
| 1961 | Tour de France (2 stage wins); Paris–Nice; Grand Prix des Nations. |
| 1962 | Tour de France (2 stage wins); Baracchi Trophy (with Rudi Altig). |
| 1963 | Tour de France (4 stage wins); Tour of Spain (1 stage win); Paris–Nice. |
| 1964 | Tour de France (4 stage wins); Tour of Italy (1 stage win); Ghent–Wevelgem. |
| 1965 | Bordeaux–Paris; Paris–Nice; Grand Prix |

1966  des Nations; Baracchi Trophy (with Jean Stablinski); Manx Trophy.
1966  Liège–Bastogne–Liège; Paris–Nice; Grand Prix des Nations.

## Maurice ARCHAMBAUD (France)

b. Paris, 30 August 1906; d. Le Raincy, 3 December 1955

A solid rider who became most famous as a time triallist. He won the first ever Grand Prix, the Grand Prix des Nations of 1932. For a time this was considered to be the time-trialling championship of the world. His ability against the clock also helped him set his hour record of 45.84 km in Milan at the famed Vigorelli velodrome in 1937. He won the Paris–Nice race in 1936 and 1939.

## Lance ARMSTRONG (USA)

b. Piano, Dallas, 18 September 1971

Lance Armstrong graduated to the pro peloton after starting as a triathlete, riding for the American Motorola team in Europe. Having finished last in the 1992 San Sebastian Classic he was second at the Zurich Meisterschaft, and then in 1993 went on to win a stage of the Tour de France and take the world road race champion's rainbow jersey when he beat Miguel Indurain into second place at Oslo.

Great things were expected of this young rider who was viewed as a successor to Greg LeMond in 1994, but he failed to live up to expectations with no Classic victories. With youth on his side, he still has time to reassert himself as a winner. He started the 1995 season well by winning America's top stage race, the Tour Du Pont, which he also won in 1993, and after his first Tour de France stage victory finished with a win in the San Sebastian Classic.

## Federico BAHAMONTES (Spain)

b. Val de Santo Domingo, 9 July 1928

Bahamontes was known as a small man who was one of the greatest *grimpeurs* in cycling history. His record of six King of the Mountains titles (1954, 1958–59, 1962–64) in the Tour de France remains unbeaten, and he won the Tour in 1959. His nickname was the 'Eagle of Toledo'. The biggest disappointment of his career must be that he never won the Vuelta a España, although he was King of the Mountains in the Vuelta in 1957 and 1958.

*Lance Armstrong has been billed as the American most likely to take over where his compatriot Greg LeMond left off*

## Dave BAKER (UK)

b. Dronfield, Yorkshire, 30 December 1965

Dave Baker rates as Britain's most successful mountain-bike racer, having won the national points series in 1993–94 and the national championship title three times from 1992–94. On the international scene he was third in the 1992 UCI world championship and won one round of the Grundig World Cup series at Plymouth in 1993. A change of team from Raleigh to Scott USA spurred him to an initially impressive season in 1995. For much of the early part of the season he lay second in the World Cup series, before a broken collar bone at a national event in Britain saw him fall down the order.

## Ercole BALDINI (Italy)

b. Villanova de Forli, 26 January 1933

In 1956 Baldini had one of the greatest years in amateur cycling history. He won the world pursuit title, broke the world one-hour record twice at Milan (44.870 km and 46.39361 km), and ended the year with the Olympic gold in the individual road race. He turned professional later in 1956 and Italian cycling fans envisaged him as the next *campionissimo*. However, although he won the world professional road race title in 1958, he was never quite as successful as a professional rider. His other major wins were in the 1958 Giro d'Italia and the 1960 Grand Prix des Nations.

## Gino BARTALI (Italy)

b. Ponte a Ema, 18 July 1914

A world-class professional cyclist for 26 years, the longest career of any top rider. He was best known as a climber, and on both occasions that he won the Tour de France (1938 and 1948) he also won the King of the Mountains title. In the Giro d'Italia, which he won in 1936, 1937 and 1946, he was King of the Mountains seven times (1935–37, 1939–40 and 1946–47). He was also a good enough sprinter to record several victories in the one-day classics. He had a great rivalry with Fausto Coppi, who succeeded Bartali as the *campionissimo* among Italian cycling fans. He was also the owner of a bicycle manufacturer, Bartali International Corporation.

**Gino Bartali Major Victories**

| | |
|---|---|
| 1936 | Tour of Italy; Tour of Lombardy. |
| 1937 | Tour of Italy. |
| 1938 | Tour de France. |
| 1939 | Milan–San Remo; Tour of Lombardy. |
| 1940 | Milan–San Remo; Tour of Lombardy. |
| 1946 | Tour of Italy; Tour of Switzerland; Zurich Meisterschaft. |
| 1947 | Milan–San Remo; Tour of Switzerland. |
| 1948 | Tour de France; Zurich Meisterschaft. |
| 1950 | Milan–San Remo. |

## Alfredo BINDA (Italy)

b. Cittiglio, 11 August 1902; d. 19 July 1986

Binda succeeded Costante Girardengo as the *campionissimo* among Italian cycling fans. His greatest successes came within Italy, with wins in the Giro d'Italia in 1925, 1927–29 and 1933 (when he was also King of the Mountains), but he was also superb in the world road race championship. His record of three wins in that race (1927, 1930, 1932) is still unbeaten, and he was also third in 1929. Binda was so dominant in his day that in 1930 the organizers of the Giro d'Italia paid him the equivalent of the winner's prize not to start, because it ruined the suspense of the race. He also won the Tour of Lombardy (1925–27 and 1931).

Binda retired from racing after breaking his femur in the 1936 Milan–San Remo. Following World War Two he was appointed manager and selector of the Italian team for the world championships and Tour de France, juggling the rivalry of Gino Bartali and Fausto Coppi to give the Italians Tour victories in 1948, 1949 and 1952 with a spectacular one-two for Coppi and Bartali in 1949. During this time he was a hard taskmaster who imposed a 'no wives' policy. Binda explained that in his winning days he only allowed himself one sexual encounter a year, and the riders who didn't respect the same ascetic lifestyle weakened first when the going got tough. Thus Coppi's wife Bruna was not allowed to accompany or even telephone her husband on the 1949 Tour!

**Alfredo Binda Major Victories**

| | |
|---|---|
| 1925 | Tour of Lombardy; Tour of Italy. |
| 1926 | Tour of Lombardy. |
| 1927 | Tour of Lombardy; Tour of Italy; World Road Race Champion. |
| 1928 | Tour of Italy. |
| 1929 | Tour of Italy; Milan–San Remo. |
| 1930 | World Road Race Champion. |
| 1931 | Tour of Lombardy; Milan–San Remo. |
| 1932 | World Road Race Champion. |
| 1933 | Tour of Italy (plus King of the Mountains). |

## Chris BOARDMAN (UK)

b. Clatterbridge, Wirral, 26 August 1968

Chris Boardman won a Commonwealth bronze medal at team pursuit in 1986 and competed at the

*Chris Boardman made the transition from track champion and Olympic gold to the maillot jaune in the Tour de France*

1988 Olympics; he also won a series of national titles. However, he shot to fame when he won the Olympic 4000m pursuit title in 1992. Much attention was focused on his revolutionary Lotus bicycle, but that distracted attention from some of the greatest riding ever seen at the Olympics. From a pre-Games best of 4 minutes, 31.4 seconds, Boardman set Olympic records in the preliminary rounds with times of 4 minutes, 27.357 seconds and 4 minutes, 24.496 seconds. The latter was later recognized as the world record for the distance when the lists were rationalized in 1993. Boardman went even faster in the Olympic final, and completed 4000m in about 4 minutes, 22 seconds. By then he had eased up and the race was over, because at 4 minutes, 11 seconds he achieved the unprecedented feat of catching his opponent, Jens Lehmann of Germany, who started half a lap ahead.

In 1993 he prepared an attack on the world record for one hour. Six days before his attempt the Scot Graeme Obree smashed the record set by Francesco Moser at 51.151 km in 1984, with 51.596 km. Boardman was undaunted and powered to a distance of 52.270 km at Bordeaux on 23 July 1993. He was invited to join Miguel Indurain on the rostrum of the Tour de France which swept into the French city that day, and immediately began to receive offers to join the professional road racers. Boardman signed for the Gan team, descended from the famous Peugeot teams of French cycling history, and made his mark by winning the Grand Prix Eddy

Merckx time-trial in Belgium the same autumn. In seven time-trial starts for Gan he was first four times, second twice, and never out of the top four.

The following season was the best for Boardman so far. He lost the one-hour record to Obree, who in turn lost it to Indurain and Tony Rominger, but otherwise it was a shining season as he continued to make the transition to a road racer. He won three stages of the Dauphiné-Libéré, a time-trial stage of the Tour of Switzerland, and in Britain recorded the fastest ever ten-mile time trial at 18:21. He then made history by winning the time-trial prologue in his first Tour de France, holding the *maillot jaune* for three days and then retiring (as planned) as the Tour headed for the mountains. A month later he won two gold medals at the world championships in Sicily, taking the first ever road time-trial world title and the pursuit world title. He became the fourth Britain to win the pursuit title in a decade, following Tony Doyle (twice), Colin Sturgess and Graeme Obree. His 1995 season was effectively lost due to a major crash on the Tour de France Prologue.

**Chris Boardman Major Victories**
| | |
|---|---|
| 1991 | World amateur 5 km record – 5.47.70. |
| 1992 | Olympic Gold Medal – 4000m pursuit. |
| 1993 | World One-Hour Record – 52.270 km. |
| 1994 | World Pursuit Champion; World Time Trial Champion. |

## Louison BOBET (France)

b. St Meen-le-Grand, 13 March 1925; d. Biarritz, 13 March 1983

Bobet was a self-made rider, relying on tenacity rather than any natural abilities. He was a superb climber, but at first was a poor time triallist until he willed himself to improve in that discipline. He eventually became the first man to win the Tour de France three consecutive times (1953–55), having first worn the yellow jersey in 1948.

In the peloton Bobet was a highly respected rider, as much for his class and determination as for his skill. Once, while well behind in Liège–Bastogne–Liège during terrible weather (it was snowing), he rode on instead of quitting. At the race banquet that night he entered to a standing ovation from his fellow riders, one of whom announced 'A great champion is here.' He was world road race champion in 1954, and was second in 1957 and 1958. His retirement was typical of his style. In the 1959 Tour de France, having been sick for many days, he forced himself to ride to the highest pass in the race. He then got off his bike and bid the peloton farewell. It was said of him that there have been greater all-rounders, but no greater champions.

**Louison Bobet Major Victories**

| | |
|---|---|
| 1950 | King of the Mountains – Tour de France. |
| 1951 | King of the Mountains – Giro d'Italia. |
| 1951 | Milan–San Remo; Tour of Lombardy. |
| 1952 | Paris–Nice; Grand Prix des Nations. |
| 1953 | Tour de France. |
| 1954 | Tour de France. |
| 1954 | World Road Race Champion. |
| 1955 | Tour de France; Dauphiné-Liberé. |
| 1956 | Paris–Roubaix. |
| 1959 | Bordeaux–Paris. |

## Giovanna BONAZZI (Italy)

b. 24 July 1962

The downhill mountain-bike racer from Verona is known for her timing and superb technical bike-handling skills which brought her the senior women's downhill world championship when it was held at Il Ciocca in Italy in 1991. Two years later she repeated her success by winning the 1993 world championship at Métabief in France, as well as taking the 1993 European championship.

## Bart BRENTJENS (Holland)

b. Haelen, 10 October 1968

Bart Brentjens has been one of the most consistent cross-country mountain bike riders on the international circuit. Having started the season as an outsider he won the 1994 Grundig World Cup series with a single win and only one race lost, when his more high profile rivals could not match his points tally at the end of the season. The 1995 Grundig series did not go so well for him due to lack of form and mechanical troubles in the early season, but he bounced back to win the first ever Tour de France VTT and then took the 1995 World Championship.

## Gianni BUGNO (Italy)

b. Brugg, Switzerland, 14 February 1964

After taking third place in 1990, Gianni Bugno became the fourth man to win the world road race championship in successive years (1991–92). By then, in a professional career that started in 1985, he had achieved 48 victories in major races.

His best year as a professional was 1990 when he won the overall World Cup title, the Giro d'Italia, Milan–San Remo and the Wincanton Classic. In the Tour de France he had four stage wins, his first in 1988, but never managed to win the race, coming seventh in 1990, second in 1991, and third in 1992.

## Beryl BURTON (UK)

b. Leeds, 12 May 1937; née Charnock, married Charles Burton in 1955

Beryl Burton was chiefly renowned as a time triallist, although in the early 1960s few women could beat her at any discipline. She collected an unprecedented number of British titles during her racing career. She was all-round time trial champion 25 times between 1959 and 1983 and winner of 72 individual road time-trial titles, as well as taking 14 track-pursuit titles and 12 road-race titles up to 1986. In 1967 she covered 446.19 km in a 12-hour time trial, which was then 9.25 km beyond the British men's record, and in 1968 she rode 100 miles in 3 hours, 55 minutes, 5 seconds, 12 years after the first British man had broken four hours for that distance. At the world championships her medal collection was as follows: individual pursuit – five gold (1959–60, 1962–63, 1966), three silver, three bronze; road race – two gold (1960, 1967), one silver. She was also the first woman to be allowed to compete at the highest level against men, when she rode in the Grand Prix des Nations. She was awarded the MBE in 1964 and the OBE in 1968. Her daughter Denise (b. Jan 1956) competed with her at the 1972 world championships.

World outdoor records ratified: 3 km at 4:16.6 and 4:14.9 in 1964, 20 km at 28:58.4 in 1960.

## Connie CARPENTER (USA)

b. Madison, Wisconsin, 26 February 1957; later Carpenter-Phinney

One of the greatest athletes in American sporting history. She won 12 US cycling championships, more than any man or woman before. She also won four medals at the world championships in both the pursuit and road race, including the pursuit title in 1983. Her finest moment came in the 1984 Olympic road race, the first ever for women, when she outlasted America's Rebecca Twigg to narrowly win the gold medal. At the finish she 'threw' her bike, using a move taught by her husband, Davis Phinney, who was a bronze medallist at the 1984 Olympics in the team time-trial and later rode professionally for the 7-Eleven team.

Connie Carpenter also competed in the 1972 Olympics as a speed skater, even though she was only 15 at the time. In addition she rowed for the University of California in the national collegiate championships.

## Claudio CHIAPPUCCI (Italy)

b. 28 February 1963

Claudio Chiappucci turned professional in 1985, with his first major wins coming in 1989. He won the Milan–San Remo classic in 1991. An outstanding climber, he won the King of the Mountains title in the Tour de France in 1991 and 1992, but was not so strong at time trials. Thus he has not been able to overcome Miguel Indurain to win the overall Tour, although after 81st place in his first Tour in 1989 he wore the *maillot jaune* for eight days in 1990 and has been second, third, second and sixth in successive years but failed to finish in 1994. It has been a similar story for Chiappucci in the Giro d'Italia, in which he was second in 1991 and 1992 and third in 1993. He was also second in the 1994 world road race championship in Sicily, behind Luc Leblanc of France, and partnered Chris Boardman to second place in the Telekom 2-Up in 1993. He won the 1993 San Sebastian. Known as 'Chiappucino' by his fans, his career appeared to be fading by 1995 after ten years as a professional.

## Fausto COPPI (Italy)

b. Castellania, 15 September 1919; d. 2 January 1960 from a tropical illness contracted in Upper Volta

Probably the greatest Italian sporting hero ever, Coppi was the *campionissimo* – the champion of champions. He first raced in 1937 and turned professional in 1940, but because of World War Two his career did not begin seriously until he was 26 years old. Had he not missed the war years, his record might rival even that of Eddy Merckx.

Coppi's only weakness as a rider was as a sprinter, but he was so strong that he rarely needed that talent. In 1949 Coppi effectively ended the challenge to his supremacy of Gino Bartali with the greatest ride ever seen at the Giro d'Italia. On a mountain stage crossing the Alpine passes of Maddalena, Vars, Izoard, Montgenevre and Sestrieres, Coppi dropped Bartali shortly before the Izoard climb and won the stage by more than 20 minutes. Other monumental victories which testify to his strength were his six-minute victory margin in the 1950 Flèche–Wallonne and his 14-minute win in the 1946 Milan–San Remo. By the end of his career Coppi had won 118 road races, and the world one-hour record that he set at 45.848 km in 1942 lasted until 1956.

*Fausto Coppi rates as the greatest ever Italian rider. Here he wins the 1953 Baracchi Trophy, from Bergamo to Milan*

**Team Wins**

| Year | Team | Wins |
|---|---|---|
| 1940 | Legnano | 2 |
| 1941 | Bianchi | 5 |
| 1942 | Bianchi | 1 |
| 1945 | Bianchi | 5 |
| 1946 | Bianchi | 9 |
| 1947 | Bianchi | 13 |
| 1948 | Bianchi | 9 |
| 1949 | Bianchi | 16 |
| 1950 | Bianchi | 6 |
| 1951 | Bianchi | 8 |
| 1952 | Bianchi | 18 |
| 1953 | Bianchi | 20 |
| 1954 | Bianchi | 17 |
| 1955 | Bianchi | 11 |
| 1956 | Carpano-Coppi | 3 |
| 1957 | Carpano-Coppi | 3 |
| 1958 | Bianchi | 2 |
| 1959 | Bianchi | 2 |
| *Total* | | 150 |
| *Total (inc. amateur)* | | 158 |

**Fausto Coppi Major Victories**

| | |
|---|---|
| 1940 | Tour of Italy (1 stage win) |
| 1942 | World Hour Record (45.87 km); World 40 km Record (52.19); World 45 km Record (58.51.4); Italian National Championship. |
| 1946 | Milan–San Remo; Tour of Lombardy; Grand Prix des Nations. |
| 1947 | World Pursuit Champion; Italian National Champion; Tour of Lombardy; Tour of Italy (3 stage wins); Grand Prix des Nations. |
| 1948 | Milan–San Remo; Tour of Lombardy. |
| 1949 | World Pursuit Champion; Italian National Champion; Tour de France (3 stage wins); Tour of Italy (3 stage wins); Milan–San Remo; Tour of Lombardy. |
| 1950 | Paris–Roubaix; Flèche–Wallonne. |
| 1952 | Tour de France (5 stage wins); Tour of Italy (3 stage wins). |
| 1953 | World Professional Road Race; Tour of Italy (4 stage wins); Baracchi Trophy (with R. Filippi). |
| 1954 | Tour of Lombardy; Baracchi Trophy (with R. Filippi). |
| 1955 | Italian National Champion; Baracchi Trophy (with R. Filippi). |
| 1957 | Baracchi Trophy (with Ercole Baldini). |
| 1958 | Buenos Aires Six-day (with Jorge Batiz). |

# André DARRIGADE (France)

b. Narrosse, Landes, 24 April 1929

Darrigade, nicknamed 'Dédé', was a great road sprinter who was able to win many smaller races in Europe, but his lack of ability as a climber cost him dearly in the major tours. However, he did manage to win the first stage of the Tour de France five times, relying on his great sprint, and in all had 22 stage wins in the Tour. He was French road champion in 1955 and won the Tour of Lombardy in 1956. His greatest year was 1959 when he won the world championship and the points jersey in the Tour de France (which he also won in 1961). In the world championships he was second in 1960, third in 1957 and 1958, and fourth in 1963. Tragedy befell him at the end of the 1958 Tour when he lost control on the tour of the velodrome at the end of the final stage, killing an official and sustaining a serious head injury.

# Pedro DELGADO (Spain)

b. Segovia, 15 April 1960

'Perrico' Delgado has been one of the great riders in the major tours from the 1980s, but he has had to fight against Bernard Hinault and Greg LeMond and thus won less than perhaps was expected of him. His strength has been his ability as a climber. He is also a good time triallist, but his inability to sprint well costs him dearly and has prevented him from winning any one-day classics.

Delgado turned professional in 1982, and after taking second place in 1987 won the Tour de France in 1988, a feat which had been expected of him for years. However his victory was tarnished, because he tested positive after one stage for the masking agent, probenecid. He was not disqualified since probenecid was not prohibited by the UCI, although it was by the IOC. He was third in the Tour in 1989 and fourth in 1990. He won the Vuelta a España in 1985 and 1989, later continuing as a Banesto team rider to Miguel Indurain before retiring at the end of the 1994 season.

# Roger DE VLAEMINCK (Belgium)

b. Eeklo, 24 August 1947

One of the great riders in history, but one who had to battle Eddy Merckx for supremacy throughout his career. The younger brother of Eric de Vlaeminck, he is one of the few great professional cyclists to have also claimed cyclo-cross championships, winning the amateur cyclo-cross world title in 1968 and the professional title in 1975. Such ability enabled him to win the bone-shattering Paris–Roubaix four times (1972, 1974–75, 1977) – still a record – and defeat Merckx several times in the process, including by the race-record winning margin of 5 minutes, 21 seconds in 1970. He was second in the 1975 world professional road race.

**Roger de Vlaeminck Major Victories**

| | |
|---|---|
| 1969 | Het Volk. |
| 1970 | Liège–Bastogne–Liège. |
| 1971 | Flèche–Wallonne. |
| 1972 | Points – Tour of Italy. |
| 1973 | Milan–San Remo. |
| 1974 | Tour of Lombardy; Points – Tour of Italy. |
| 1975 | Tour of Switzerland; Zurich Meisterschaft; Points – Tour of Italy. |
| 1976 | Tour of Lombardy. |
| 1977 | Tour of Flanders. |
| 1978 | Milan–San Remo. |
| 1979 | Milan–San-Remo; Het Volk. |
| 1981 | Paris–Brussels. |

*Eric de Vlaeminck heads for the finish at the 1972 cyclo-cross world championship, taking the title for the sixth successive year*

## Eric DE VLAEMINCK (Belgium)

b. Eeklo, 23 August 1945

The most successful cyclo-cross rider of all time, Eric de Vlaeminck of Belgium won seven world championships in eight years. His first professional title came in 1966, his debut year, at the age of 20. A year later he slipped to fifth and was lapped by the winner Renato Longo of Italy. His run of six straight wins started in 1968, the year in which his brother Roger de Vlaeminck took the amateur world championship. Eric de Vlaeminck's last world championship was when the event was held in London event of 1973. Roger de Vlaeminck won the professional world championship two years later.

## Tony DOYLE (UK)

b. Woking, 19 May 1958

Having failed to be selected to ride in the amateur 4000m pursuit world championship in 1979, Tony Doyle turned professional and proved his worth by taking the 5000m pursuit world championship in 1980, a feat he repeated in 1986 as well as taking

two silvers and a bronze in this event and a silver behind Urs Freuler of Switzerland in the 1987 world championship points race. He became the most successful British rider in six-day competition, forming a winning partnership with Australian Danny Clark which scored 18 victories. He also won six-day events teamed with Francesco Moser of Italy and Belgian Etienne De Wilde, and despite a near-fatal accident at the Munich Six in 1989 came back to win the same event a year later. In 1995 he was elected President of the British Cycling Federation after a particularly acrimonious campaign.

## Henrik DJERNIS (Denmark)

b. 22 April 1966

Henrik or 'Hank' Djernis was amateur cyclo-cross world champion in 1993, but his main claim to fame is in the world of mountain biking where he was UCI world champion three years running – in 1992 at Bromont, Canada; in 1993 at Métabief, France; and in 1994 at Vail, USA. In 1994 he also won two rounds of the Grundig World Cup series and was fourth overall.

In 1995 he caused a mild sensation, leaving the

Ritchey team which he rode in with Thomas Frischknecht to ride for Pro-Flex and make the transition to racing full-suspension bikes.

**Henrik Djernis Major Victories**

| | |
|---|---|
| 1993 | World amateur Cyclo-Cross champion. |
| 1992 | UCI World Cross-Country champion. |
| 1993 | UCI World Cross-Country champion. |
| 1994 | UCI World Cross-Country champion. |

## Oscar EGG (Switzerland)

b. Schlatt, 2 March 1890; d. Nice, 9 February 1961

An exceptional all-rounder who set the world one-hour record three times, recording 42.360 km in 1912, 43.775 km in 1913 and 44.247 km in 1914. He also campaigned vigorously on behalf of his records. When his 1912 record was beaten by Richard Weise in 1913 he demanded that the track on which he had set the original record be remeasured. It was found to be longer than expected and this enabled Egg to hold on to the record! In 1933 Jan van Hout broke Egg's record and Egg demanded a measurement of the track on which van Hout rode! It was found to be short, but the record was soon broken by Maurice Richard.

Egg was Swiss track-sprint champion for 12 consecutive years, and was also superb at motor-paced races and tandem track racing. He won the 1914 Paris–Tours race and eight six day-races, and was also able to make a fortune selling Oscgear, an early *derailleur* which he had helped to invent. He later trained Switzerland's only two Tour de France winners, Ferdi Kübler (1950) and Hugo Koblet (1951).

## François FABER (Luxembourg)

b. Aulnay-sur-Iton, France, 26 January 1887, France; d. Garency, France, 9 May 1915

Faber is, with Charly Gaul, one of the two greatest riders ever produced by Luxembourg. His career victories were compressed into five great years before World War One intervened. Faber's major wins were the Tour of Lombardy in 1908, Tour de France and Paris–Brussels in 1909, Paris–Tours in 1909–10, Bordeaux–Paris in 1911 and Paris–Roubaix in 1913.

## Leandro FAGGIN (Italy)

b. Padova, 18 July 1933; d. Padova, 6 December 1970

Faggin possesses one of the greatest records ever among pursuit cyclists. After being placed successively first, third and second for the world amateur title in 1954–56, he was professional champion three times in 1963 and 1965–66, second in 1958, 1962 and 1964, and third in 1961 and 1967–68. The individual pursuit did not become an Olympic event until 1964, but he took the Olympic gold medals of 1956 at the kilometre time-trial and the team pursuit. He was Italian pursuit champion 12 times and three times set new records for the 5000m unpaced on the track, from 6 minutes, 15.4 seconds as an amateur in 1956 to 6 minutes, 2.4 seconds as a pro in 1961. He also set an amateur world record for one kilometre with 1 minute, 9.2 seconds in 1956. Shortly after his retirement from cycling he died at the age of just 37.

## Laurent FIGNON (France)

b. Tournan-en-Brie, 16 August 1960

Fignon has been called 'The Professor' because of his background. Unlike many professional cyclists, he attended college (though only briefly) where he was studying to become a veterinarian. However, the lure of the peloton was too much and he became one of the great riders in the world. He came to glory at the 1983 Tour de France when his win humbled four-time champion Bernard Hinault, and he won again in 1984.

Fignon staged a classic battle with Greg LeMond in the 1989 Tour de France, leading the Tour going into the last time-trial stage but eventually losing when LeMond made up 58 seconds to win by eight seconds, the closest finish in Tour history.

**Laurent Fignon Major Victories**

| | |
|---|---|
| 1982 | Criterium International. |
| 1983 | Tour de France. |
| 1984 | Tour de France; King of the Mountains – Tour of Italy. |
| 1986 | Flèche–Wallonne. |
| 1988 | Milan–San Remo. |
| 1989 | Milan–San Remo; Tour of Italy; Grand Prix des Nations. |
| 1990 | Criterium International. |

## Gary FOORD (UK)

b. Staffordshire, 14 September 1970

Gary Foord sprang to international prominence when riding for Scott International. He finished fourth overall in the 1993 Grundig World Cup series, winning the prestigious round at Mammoth, USA in 1994 where he was seventh overall, and continuing to put consistent performances in the 1995 series to finish 4th overall. He was second to Albert Iten of Switzerland in the 1994 European championship at Métabief, France.

## Urs FREULER (Switzerland)

b. Glarus, 6 November 1958

Prior to turning professional, Freuler, a car mechanic, was Swiss sprint champion in 1978 and finished third in the world amateur points race in 1979. He became the greatest rider in the points race on the track, winning the world professional title each year from 1981 to 1987 and also in 1989. He was also world champion in keirin in 1983 and 1985, although he has not raced professionally in Japan, the home of the event. He has also ridden on many winning six-day event teams and was the points winner in the 1984 Giro d'Italia. At one kilometre he set two world records – outdoors with a best of 1 minute, 6.091 seconds (1983) and indoors with 1 minute, 6.603 seconds (1981). He also set the 500m flying-start record indoors at 28.486 seconds in 1981.

## Thomas FRISCHKNECHT (Switzerland)

b. Ulster, Switzerland, 17 February 1970

Thomas Frischknecht dominated mountain-bike racing to win the Grundig World Cup series in 1992 and 1993. Like other leading mountain-bike racers of his time he learnt his skills in cyclo-cross where he was also world champion. His father Peter won three cyclo-cross world championship silver medals in his 14 years as a professional, giving Thomas the inspiration that led him to become junior cyclo-cross world champion in 1988 at Hagersdorf in Switzerland. Two years later Thomas was placed third at the cyclo-cross world championship in Spain, and in the same year was invited to the USA to race with the Ritchey mountain-bike team, winning his second-ever race there at Mount Snow, Vermont. The following September he finished second to American Ned Overend in the first UCI-approved world mountain bike championship held in Durango, Colorado.

In 1991 Frischknecht became world cyclo-cross champion in Holland, was unable to take part in the Grundig World Cup series due to military service, and finished second once again in the mountain bike world championship, this time behind American John Tomac in Italy. Four wins assured him of the Grundig World Cup 1992 series overall title, but once again he took second place in the mountain bike world championship, this time behind Henrik Djernis of Denmark in Bromont, Quebec. He successfully defended his Grundig World Cup series title in 1993 despite more military service, went on to win the European cross-country championship,

but failed once again in the world championship, retiring from the race with stomach cramps. In 1994 he came back to form, winning two rounds of the Grundig World Cup series. In 1995 he went on to win the series for the third time after having trailed Norway's Rune Hoydahl.

**Thomas Frischknecht Major Victories**
| | |
|---|---|
| 1988 | World junior cyclo-cross champion. |
| 1991 | World amateur cyclo-cross champion; Swiss cyclo-cross champion. |
| 1992 | Grundig World Cup overall winner. |
| 1993 | Grundig World Cup overall winner; European cross-country champion. |
| 1995 | Grundig World Cup overall winner; European cross-country champion. |

## Juli FURTADO (USA)

b. Durango, 4 April 1967

One of the set of leading American mountain-biker racers who live in Durango, Colorado, Juli Furtado first made a winning impact on international women's cross-country racing when she won the 1990 UCI world championship held in Durango. In 1992 she won the UCI world downhill championship at Bromont in Canada, paving the way for her domination of the sport. In 1993 she won all nine rounds that she entered of the 1993 Grundig World Cup series to finish first overall, as well as taking the US NORBA national series in which she won all six rounds she entered. Her domination continued in 1994 when she won the Grundig World Cup series once again with six wins, as well as claiming the UCI world championship at Vail ahead of Britain's Caroline Alexander and being US Jeep NORBA National champion. In 1995 she won the Grundig World Cup series for the third year in a row, having won six of the eight rounds.

**Juli Furtado Major Victories**
| | |
|---|---|
| 1990 | UCI World Champion. |
| 1992 | UCI Downhill World Champion. |
| 1993 | Grundig World Cup series 1st overall. |
| 1993 | NORBA national championship series 1st overall. |
| 1994 | Grundig World Cup series 1st overall. |
| 1994 | UCI World Champion. |
| 1994 | US Jeep NORBA National champion. |
| 1995 | Grundig World Cup series 1st overall. |

## François GACHET (France)

b. St Gaudens, 17 December 1965

Men's downhill mountain-bike racing was

dominated during 1994 by 30-year-old François Gachet, an ex-carpenter, rock musician and family man with a flamboyant streak who uses the unusual training technique of riding on the road for his high-speed exploits. He was first in both the 1994 world championship at Vail and the World Cup downhill series in which he won four rounds.

## Tamara GARKUSHINA (USSR)

b. Lipetsk region, USSR, 1 February 1946

From 1970 to 1974 she was unchallenged at the women's pursuit, winning five consecutive world championships on the track, having also won in 1967. She did not compete in 1968 but in 1969 she finished second in the world to her fellow countrywoman Obodovskaya. Although she occasionally rode on the roads she was never placed in the women's world road race championship in that event. In 1964 she improved the world record for three kilometres from a standing start from 4 minutes, 1.7 seconds to 3 minutes, 52.5 seconds at the Olympic velodrome in Montreal.

## Charly GAUL (Luxembourg)

b. Ash, 18 December 1932

The greatest cyclist ever produced by Luxembourg and one of the greatest climbers produced by any nation. He was also renowned for riding very well in bad weather conditions. Known as 'The Angel of the Mountain' for his skill as a *grimpeur*, he earned the nickname in the 1955 Tour de France in a mountain stage crossing the cols of Aravis, Telegraphe and Galibier when he won by 14 minutes. He was King of the Mountains in that race in 1955 and 1956, and won the Tour in 1958. He was third in the 1954 world professional road race championship and won the Giro d'Italia in 1956 and 1959, also taking the Giro King of the Mountains title in 1959.

## Felice GIMONDI (Italy)

b. Sedrina, 29 September 1942

At the time of his retirement, only Eddy Merckx and Fausto Coppi had won more international titles than Felice Gimondi in their careers. Gimondi won the Tour de l'Avenir in 1964 and then turned professional. In his first year he won the Tour de France, even though he had been included in the race only as a last-minute substitute. Gimondi was a good climber, an excellent time triallist, and a proficient road sprinter. He was later overshadowed by Merckx, but in 1973 defeated him in the finishing sprint to win his only rainbow jersey as world

*Following Fausto Coppi, Felice Gimondi became the most successful Italian rider of the post-war generation*

professional road champion, having been third in 1970 and second in 1971. He retired in 1976 to be an insurance agent and cycling manager.

**Felice Gimondi Major Victories**

| | |
|---|---|
| 1965 | Tour de France. |
| 1966 | Tour of Lombardy; Paris–Roubaix; Paris–Brussels. |
| 1967 | Tour of Italy; Grand Prix des Nations. |
| 1968 | Tour of Italy; Tour of Spain; Tour of Lombardy; Grand Prix des Nations. |
| 1973 | World Road Race Champion. |
| 1974 | Milan–San Remo. |
| 1976 | Tour of Italy; Paris–Brussels. |

## Missy GIOVE (USA)

b. 20 January 1973

Yet another American mountain-bike racer resident in Durango, Colorado, Missy 'The Missile' Giove became equally well-known in downhill competition for her bike handling, tough riding, forthright opinions and cropped hairstyle. In 1993 she took the bronze medal in the downhill world championship, and also took third overall in the World Cup series having won two rounds. In 1994 she was third in the

*A winter regime of cyclo-cross training still serves Tim Gould, a top rider on the international mountain bike circuit*

World Cup once again, but made sure of winning the world championship on home territory at Vail. After a good start to the 1995 season with two wins in the World Cup series, she crashed and broke a collar bone in the World Cup round at Mount Snow, USA.

## Costante GIRARDENGO (Italy)

b. Novi-Ligure, 18 March 1893; d. 9 February 1978.

The first *campionissimo* for Italian cycling aficionados. In addition to his major tour wins, the Giro d'Italia in 1919 and 1923 and the Tour of Lombardy in 1919 and 1921–22, he won the Milan–San Remo race seven times in 1918, 1921, 1923, 1925–26 and 1928, and was Italian road race champion from 1913–25. With a break for World War One that gave him nine consecutive national championships, a record unmatched in any country by road riders. He competed almost exclusively in Italy, but late in his career won several six-day races

in Germany. He also held the Italian one-hour record from 1917 to 1926.

## Tim GOULD (UK)

b. 30 May 1964

Tim Gould from Sheffield was the first British rider to make an impact on the international mountain-bike scene. Having changed from cyclo-cross his first big successes came in 1990 when he won the hill-climb race at the UCI world championship in Durango and was third in the cross-country. After a poor season in 1993 he returned to form with the Schwinn team in the Grundig World Cup series, finishing fifth overall in 1994 and equal seventh overall (with top US rider Tinker Juarez) in 1995 when his best result was second at Vail.

## Andy HAMPSTEN (USA)

b. Great Plains, North Dakota, 7 April 1962

Andy Hampsten first became well known in 1984 when he made the US Olympic team. Riding exclusively for 7-Eleven (now Motorola), Hampsten is best known for his toughness and ability as a climber. He won the Tour de Suisse in 1986 and 1987, but his victory in the 1988 Giro d'Italia (when he also won the King of the Mountains title) sealed his fame as the American most likely to ride alongside Greg LeMond. This victory was primarily due to a brutal ride over the Gavia Pass in a blinding snowstorm when he and Eric Breaukink broke clear of the field, giving Hampsten the pink jersey which he kept to the finish. However, four years later in 1992 Hampsten achieved probably his greatest stage victory, when he won the ride to L'Alpe d'Huez during the Tour de France. He was the top-ranked rider in the 1994 American Motorola team.

## Reg HARRIS (UK)

b. Bury, Lancashire, 31 March 1920; d. Macclesfield, Cheshire, 22 June 1992

Britain's greatest ever track sprint-cyclist. He began track racing in 1936 and in 1947 was world amateur champion, but at the 1948 Olympics was hampered by a recent recovery from a broken arm and won only silvers in the individual and tandem sprint races. He turned professional shortly afterwards, and became the first sprinter to win a world professional championship at the first attempt, going on to four sprint titles (1949–51, 1954), and was placed second in 1956 and third in 1953.

As a professional he also set two world records for the unpaced kilometre from a standing start

*Reg Harris OBE at the British Track Championships in 1975 when he was 55 years old and still racing*

outdoors, with 1 minute, 9.8 seconds in 1949 and 1 minute, 8.6 seconds in 1952, which stood for over 21 years. He set two indoor records at one kilometre with a best of 1 minute, 8.9 seconds in 1955. Seventeen years after his retirement in 1957 he made an amazing return to racing in 1974, winning the British sprint championship.

## Beth HEIDEN (USA)

b. Madison, Wisconsin, 27 September 1959

Beth Heiden was a great all-rounder who found success in speed skating, cycling and skiing. She became the first American to win the speed-skating world title in 1979 and was world junior champion in 1978 and 1979, while an ankle injury restricted her to a 3000m bronze in the 1980 Olympics. Later that year she became the first American to win the women's world road race title at cycling, and in 1983 won the NCAA cross-country skiing title. Her brother is Eric Heiden, widely considered the greatest speed-skater of all time.

## Lutz HESSLICH (GDR — East Germany)

b. Ortrand, 17 January 1959

Lutz Hesslich was Olympic sprint-cycling champion in 1980 and 1988. Had the GDR not boycotted the

1984 Olympics, he probably would have won three consecutive gold medals, bettering the record of the great Daniel Morelon. He was world junior champion in 1976 and 1977, and after third place in 1977 won senior titles in 1979, 1983, 1985 and 1987, with silver medals in 1981–82 and 1986 and bronze in 1977. He was GDR champion in 1978–80, 1982–83 and 1986. He set world records for 200m with a flying start at 10.441 sec in 1984 and 10.190 in 1985.

## Bernard HINAULT (France)

b. Yffignac, Côtes du Nord, 14 November 1954

Hinault is one of the all-time great cyclists. He was French junior champion in 1972 and turned professional in 1974, winning the French pursuit title in 1975–76. Having been brought up on a Breton farm he was incredibly tough despite his small 5 ft 7 in stature, earning the nickname 'Le Blaireau' ('The Badger').

In the Tour de France he equalled the record of Anquetil and Merckx by winning the Tour five times (1978–79, 1981–82 and 1985), and collected the second highest totals of 77 days wearing the *maillot jaune* and 28 stage wins, with the King of the Mountains title in 1986. In 1980 he was forced to retire from the Tour through injury while leading once again.

Hinault is also one of the few riders to have won all three major tours, taking the Giro d'Italia in 1980, 1982 and 1985, and the Vuelta a España in 1978 and 1983. His only weakness was that he was not a great road sprinter, but at the end of a fast, difficult race his sprint became formidable and he won many one-day races in addition to his tour victories.

Having won his first Classics in 1977 at the age of 21, and his first Tour de France at his first attempt a year later, Hinault retired on his 32nd birthday while still at the height of his powers, as he always said he would. His career record of five Tour wins, three Giros, two Vueltas, a world championship and eight Classics has only been bettered by Eddy Merckx. On his retirement he became an advisor to the Tour de France and the Look cycle components company.

**Bernard Hinault Major Victories**

| 1977 | Ghent–Wevelgem; Liège–Bastogne–Liège; Grand Prix des Nations. |
|---|---|
| 1978 | French National Champion; Tour de France (3 stage wins); Tour of Spain (5 stage wins); Grand Prix des Nations. |
| 1979 | Tour de France (7 stage wins); Tour of Lombardy; Flèche–Wallonne; Grand Prix |

*The 23-year-old Bernard Hinault takes the first of his five Tour de France victories, in 1978*

des Nations.
1980  World Professional Road Race; Tour of Italy (1 stage win); Liège–Bastogne–Liège.
1981  Tour de France (5 stage wins); Amstel Gold Race; Paris–Roubaix.
1982  Tour de France (4 stage wins); Tour of Italy (4 stage wins); Tour of Luxembourg (1 stage win); Grand Prix des Nations.
1983  Tour of Spain (2 stage wins); Flèche–Wallonne.
1984  Tour of Lombardy.
1985  Tour de France (2 stage wins); Tour of Italy.

## Rune HOYDAHL (Norway)

b. Galleberg, 10 December 1969

Racing for Giant, Rune Hoydahl came from relative obscurity to dominate the 1995 Grundig World Cup series. Following an unprecedented hat trick when he won the first three events of the series with ease, he went on to score five wins in the first seven races of the series, losing the other two due to illness and mechanical problems. His superiority was partly due

to greater downhill speed, with his principal tactic being to lead from the start while setting a pace that broke his opponents. However, the last three races went wrong for him. He opted to miss Mammoth, preferring not to race at altitude; he had a poor result at Plymouth due to a cold; and in the final round in Rome he punctured twice giving the series victory to Thomas Frischknecht.

## Miguel INDURAIN (Spain)

b. Villava, near Pamplona, Navarra, 16 July 1994

'Big Mig' made rapid progress to become the world's leading cyclist of the early 1990s, demonstrating his superb time-trialling ability and fine strength on the mountains to win the Tour de France for four successive years from 1991 to 1995.

As an amateur he was Spanish champion in 1983 and competed at the 1984 Olympics before turning professional in 1985. Indurain first contested the Tour in 1985, failing to finish then or in 1986; from 1987 he was placed successively 97th, 47th, 17th (including his first stage win) and tenth before his first win in 1991. He also won the Paris–Nice race in 1989 and 1990.

In one of the Tour de France time-trials in 1992 Indurain defeated the second-best rider by over three minutes, one of the greatest single rides in Tour history. He went on to set a record average speed for the Tour of 39.504 kmh, and then became only the sixth rider to win the Giro d'Italia and the Tour de France in the same year. He repeated this feat when he won both the Tour and the Giro again with consummate mastery in 1993. A stage-race specialist, he was third in the world professional road race in 1991, sixth in 1992 and second in 1993. In 1994 he became the third man to win the Tour de France four times in a row, but failed to win his third Tour of Italy. In September 1994 he set a new one-hour record of 53.04 kilometres, beating Graeme Obree by 327 metres and becoming the second man, after Eddy Merckx in 1972, to take both the Tour and the one hour in the same season.

In 1995 he became the first man to win the Tour de France five times in a row. He also won the Time-Trial title at the world road race championships in Colombia, but was beaten into second place in the road race for the second time in his career.

**Miguel Indurain Major Victories**
1988  Tour of Catalonia.
1989  Paris–Nice.
1990  Paris–Nice.
1991  Tour de France.
1992  Tour de France; Tour of Italy.
1993  Tour de France; Tour of Italy.

*Miguel Indurain has proved a phenomenon who has staked his career on the Tour de France*

| 1994 | Tour de France; World One-Hour Record – 53.04 km. |
| 1995 | Tour de France; World Time-Trial Champion. |

## Laurent JALABERT (France)

b. Mazamet, 30 November 1968

Having won the points jersey in both the 1992 Tour de France and Vuelta a España, Laurent Jalabert crashed out of the first stage of the 1994 Tour de France at Armentières and effectively lost the whole of the remaining season. He started the 1995 season in spectacular style with wins in the Paris–Nice, Milan–San Remo and the Criterium International to complete an unprecedented hat trick – no rider had ever managed to win all three early season Classics before. He then went on to win the Flèche Wallonne before pulling out of racing to prepare for the Tour de France in which he won the Points prize. He finished the season by winning the Vuelta a España as well as taking the Points and Mountains prizes, having chalked up 22 major victories in the season which made him the top-ranked racer of the year.

## Jan JANSSEN (Holland)

b. Nootdorp, 19 May 1940

One of the great road sprinters of all time, an ability which helped him win a lot of races. However he was only an average climber, and this prevented him from winning more major tours. His victory in the 1968 Tour de France over Joop Zoetemelk came by only 38 seconds, at the time the closest finish in Tour history. He had been Tour de France points winner in 1964, 1965 and 1967.

**Jan Janssen Major Victories**

| 1962 | Zurich Meisterschaft. |
| 1964 | World Road Race Champion; Points prize – Tour de France. |
| 1965 | Points prize – Tour de France. |
| 1966 | Bordeaux–Paris. |
| 1967 | Tour of Spain (and points); Points prize – Tour de France; Paris–Roubaix. |
| 1968 | Tour de France; Points prize – Tour of Spain. |

## Tinker JUAREZ (USA)

b. 4 March 1961

David 'Tinker' Juarez from Sugarloaf, California has built a colourful reputation in international mountain-bike racing with his helmet barely covering his long, flowing hair. Racing for the Volvo-Cannondale team he won the Mount St Anne round of the 1993 Grundig World Cup series to finish fifth overall, winning at Silver Star in 1994 when he was third overall in the series, as well as winning the 1994 US Jeep Norba national championship. In 1995 he was seventh equal in the Grundig World Cup series, and the top American in the event.

## Sean KELLY (Ireland)

b. Carrick-on-Suir, Tipperary, 24 May 1956

A professional cyclist from 1977, for much of the 1980s Sean Kelly was rated the world's best in the computer rankings, winning the points aggregate Super Prestige Pernod Trophy three years running between 1984 and 1986. This was based mainly on his many wins in one-day Classics which earnt him the title 'King of the Classics', and he also became the first World Cup series winner in 1989.

His biggest disappointment was his inability to win the Tour de France due to his average climbing talent. Although he has been green jersey points winner a record four times (1982–83, 1985, 1989) and won four stages, his best placing overall was fourth in 1985.

*With a decade of major wins in one-day races, Sean Kelly gained the unofficial title of 'King of the Classics'*

He started the Tour 14 times, retired twice, and only wore the yellow jersey for one day in 1983.

Kelly's greatest successes have come in the Paris–Nice stage race, which he won for an amazing seven consecutive years (1982–88). Together with Henri Pelissier he is the only non-Italian to claim three wins in the Tour of Lombardy which closes the Classic season. His last great win was in the 1992 Milan–San Remo. He retired from professional competition at the age of 38 during the 1994 season, winding down gradually with his last international race, the Route du Sud in the Pyrenees. He scored 193 wins in an 18-year professional career.

**Sean Kelly Major Victories**

| | |
|---|---|
| 1982 | Paris–Nice; Points Prize – Tour de France. |
| 1983 | Paris–Nice; Criterium International; Tour of Switzerland; Tour of Lombardy; Points Prize – Tour de France. |
| 1984 | Criterium International; Paris–Nice; Tour of Pays Basque; Tour of Catalonia; Paris–Roubaix; Liège–Bastogne–Liège; Blois–Chaville. (Led world rankings October 1984–May 1989.) |
| 1985 | Nissan Classic, Ireland; Tour of Lombardy; Paris–Nice. |
| 1986 | Paris–Nice; Tour of Pays Basque; Tour of Catalonia; Nissan Classic, Ireland; Paris–Roubaix; Milan–San Remo; Grand Prix des Nations; Points Prize – Tour de France. |
| 1987 | Paris–Nice; Criterium International; Tour of Pays Basque; Nissan Classic, Ireland. |
| 1988 | Tour of Spain; Paris–Nice; Semaine Catalan; Ghent–Wevelgem. |
| 1989 | Liège–Bastogne–Liège; Points Prize – Tour de France. |
| 1990 | Tour of Switzerland. |
| 1991 | Nissan Classic, Ireland; Tour of Lombardy. |
| 1992 | Milan–San Remo. |

## Hugo KOBLET (Switzerland)

b. Zurich, 21 March 1925; d. 6 November 1964

Koblet's nickname was 'The Pedaller of Charm', for the grace and ease he displayed on his bike. At the world championships he was third in the professional pursuit in 1947 and second in 1951 and 1954, but his greatest hour in a meteoric career came in the 1951 Tour de France which he won by 20 minutes. It was one particular stage, the 177 kilometres from Brive to Agen on 15 July, which established his legend. At 37 kilometres Koblet rolled off the front in a lone breakaway. Though the peloton chased and chased, he could not be caught, winning eventually by 2 minutes, 35 seconds. One of his greatest rivals, Italy's Raphael Geminiani, described his effortless ride: 'He pedalled in a state of grace. While we suffered like dogs, he rolled along like a tourist.'

His brilliance was short-lived. He travelled to Mexico later that same winter, and came down with a mysterious illness. He was never again the same sublime rider. In 1964 he took his own life by driving his car into a tree.

**Hugo Koblet Major Victories**

| 1950 | Tour of Italy; Tour of Switzerland. |
| 1951 | Tour de France; Grand Prix des Nations. |
| 1952 | Zurich Meisterschaft. |
| 1953 | Tour of Switzerland. |
| 1954 | Zurich Meisterschaft. |
| 1955 | Tour of Switzerland. |

## Frank KRAMER (USA)

b. Evansville, Indiana, 20 November 1880; d. East Orange, New Jersey, 8 October 1958

Frank Kramer contracted tuberculosis as a teenager, and his parents got him to take up cycling for his health. He became so good that he remains the greatest track sprinter ever produced by the United States, and one of the world's greatest ever.

He won the world championship when it was held in Newark, New Jersey in 1912, and would surely have won more. However, he travelled only rarely to Europe, and competed in the world championship only one other time. Kramer won the Grand Prix de Paris in 1905 and 1906, and three six-day events. He was US pro sprint champion 1901–16, 1918 and 1921, having been amateur champion in 1899.

In the 1920s, when American cycling was in its heyday, Kramer was one of the best-known athletes and was better paid than any baseball player except Babe Ruth. He had a very long career, retiring on 26 July 1922 at the age of 42 having equalled the world sprint record for one-sixth of a mile in his final race.

## Ferdi KÜBLER (Switzerland)

b. Adliswill, 24 July 1919

Kübler was nick-named 'The Swiss Cowboy' because of his penchant for wearing Stetson cowboy hats. In successive world road race championships between 1949 and 1951, he finished second, third and first.

In 1950 he was the first Swiss rider to win the Tour de France, and was also the Tour points winner in 1954. He was one of the most versatile riders ever, being Swiss champion in pursuit and cyclo-cross in addition to his road-racing successes where his

pursuit ability made him a formidable sprinter. His other successes included winning the Liège–Bastogne–Liège in 1951 and 1952.

## Octave LAPIZE (France)

b. 20 October 1987; d. 14 July 1917

One of the very few early greats of professional cycling who also competed in the Olympics, when he won a bronze medal in the 100 km track race in 1908. He is still heralded as the only person to have won Paris–Roubaix, 'The Hell of the North', three consecutive times (1909–11). He was also the winner of the Tour de France in 1910, Paris–Brussels in 1911–13 and Paris–Tours in 1911. Lapize was killed in an aerial dogfight during World War One.

## André LEDUCQ (France)

b. Paris, 27 February 1904; d. 1990

'Dédé' Leducq was world amateur road race champion in 1924, although only ninth that year at the Paris Olympics. He turned professional in 1926 and set a record with 25 stage wins in the Tour de France between 1927 and 1938, wearing the yellow jersey for 35 days and winning the race in 1930 and 1932. He made an emotional farewell to the Tour in 1938 when he rode to the finish hand in hand with his great rival Antonin Magne to win the final stage. He also won Paris–Roubaix in 1928 and Paris–Tours in 1931.

## Greg LeMOND (USA)

b. Lakewood, California, 26 June 1961

The greatest road racer ever produced by the United States was raised in California, middle class and well educated, and a very different person from the average European professional. Greg LeMond first came to prominence in 1979 when he won three gold medals at the world junior championships – the individual road race, team time-trial and individual pursuit.

He came to Europe and turned professional when he was 19 years old in 1981, riding for the Renault team with Bernard Hinault as team leader. He was an almost immediate success in the world road race championships, winning his first title in 1983 after coming second in 1982, taking second again in 1985, and winning for the second time in 1989.

He rode in his first Tour de France in 1984, finishing third, and in 1985 served as Bernard Hinault's lieutenant in the La Vie Claire team as the Breton chalked up his record-equalling fifth victory.

*Greg LeMond came back from a near-fatal accident to win his second and third Tour de France but missed out two vital years which could have put him alongside Miguel Indurain*

or two major events which he set his sights on each year – this was a single-minded approach which many fans disliked. After his third win in the Tour de France success eluded him between 1991 and 1993, by which time lead pellets lodged in his body from the hunting accident were being blamed as part of the cause of the muscular myopathy – a damaged muscle condition – which was inhibiting his riding. Having retired from the 1994 Tour de France he pulled out of racing altogether, although he indicated that he might stay in cycle racing by managing a mountain-bike team. He goes down in history as the first and only American and the first English-speaking rider to win the Tour de France.

**Greg LeMond Major Victories**

| | |
|---|---|
| 1983 | World Road Race Champion. |
| 1986 | Tour de France (1 stage win). |
| 1989 | World Road Race Champion; Tour de France (2 stage wins). |
| 1990 | Tour de France. |

## Jeannie LONGO (France)

b. Annecy, 31 October 1958

LeMond's price was the 1986 Tour de France, but he had to fight for it as the second-placed Hinault appeared to be after a sixth win. From then on he should have been unstoppable, but in the winter after his Tour victory LeMond was shot by his brother-in-law in a bizarre accident, while hunting turkey in Lincoln, California. Only a helicopter diverted from a road accident saved his life, and it seemed he would never ride again. He did, but for two years he was a shadow of his former greatness with recurring medical problems and early in 1989 LeMond considered retirement as he was often dropped on mountain climbs.

His form reappeared enabling him to win the most dramatic finish to the Tour de France ever, taking back 58 seconds in the last stage time-trial to defeat Laurent Fignon by eight seconds, the narrowest victory margin in Tour history. A month later he won his second world road race title when he out-sprinted Sean Kelly and Dimitri Konychev at Chambéry, and a third Tour de France victory came in 1990.

LeMond's strength was time-trialling, although he was also an excellent climber. He failed to win any of the one-day Classics, but attributed this to the fact that he used them as warm-up races to the one

Considered by many to be the greatest women's road cyclist ever, with great climbing talent coupled with her track ability as a pursuiter. She won a record ten world titles: pursuit (1986, 1988–89); road (1985-1987, 1989, 1995); points (1989); and road time-trial (1995). She was French champion on the road 11 times from 1979 to 1989, in pursuit from 1980–89 and 1992, and in points in 1988, 1989 and 1992. The only missing link is that she won no Olympic title; she was sixth in the road race in 1984; 21st in 1988 when she was favourite but still recovering from a hip fracture; and finally earnt a silver medal in 1992 when she came out of retirement at Barcelona.

Jeannie Longo won the women's Tour de France in 1987–89. She set numerous world records on the track from her first in 1984, with her outdoor bests (all from 1989 at the high altitude of Mexico City) being: 3 km at 3 minutes, 38.190 seconds; 5 km at 6 minutes, 14.135 seconds; 10 km at 12 minutes, 59.435 seconds; 20 km at 25 minutes, 59.883 seconds; 1 hour at 46.3527 km. Indoors her best were: 3 km at 3 minutes, 40.264 seconds (1992); 5 km at 6 minutes, 17.608 seconds (1991); 10 km at 12 minutes, 54.260 seconds; 20 km at 26 minutes, 51.222 seconds; 1 hour at 45.016 km (all 1989). She first set world records for the one hour in 1986 with 44.770 km at high altitude and 43.587 km at sea level.

She married her coach Patrice Ciprelli, a former Alpine skiing international.

## Christa LUDING (GDR — East Germany)

b. Weisswasser, 4 December 1959; née Rothenberger

Christa Luding was world champion at both sprint cycling and speed skating. She first competed at the Olympic Games at speed skating in 1980, and in 1984 won the Olympic gold at 500m, winning another gold four years later at 1000m. She had been persuaded by her coach Ernst Luding (whom she married in 1988) to take up cycling in the skating off-season, and quickly reached the top by winning the world sprint gold medal in 1986.

## Freddy MAERTENS (Belgium)

b. Nieuwpoort, 13 February 1952

Although Freddy Maertens could never quite emulate his countryman Eddy Merckx, he compiled one of the greatest records ever in one-day Classics. He was only an average climber which prevented him from winning more in the major tours, but he was one of the greatest road sprinters as his points jersey victories testify.

**Freddy Maertens Major Victories**

| 1975 | Ghent–Wevelgem. |
| --- | --- |
| 1976 | Ghent–Wevelgem; World Road Race Champion; Amstel Gold Race; Zurich Meisterschaft; Grand Prix des Nations; Points Jersey – Tour de France. |
| 1977 | Tour of Spain (also won Points Jersey); Paris–Nice. |
| 1978 | Points Jersey – Tour de France. |
| 1981 | World Road Race Champion; Points Jersey – Tour de France. |
| 1985 | Bordeaux–Paris. |

## Antonio MASPES (Italy)

b. Milan, 14 January 1932

Antonio Maspes first came to fame when he won a bronze medal in the tandem match sprint at the 1952 Olympics with Cesare Pinarello. He became one of the great professional track sprinters, winning the world title in that event seven times (1955–56, 1959–62, 1964).

*Jeannie Longo heads for victory in the 1987 Tour de France Feminin. In 1995 she was still winning, taking two world championship titles in the road race and time-trial, 10 years after her first world championship wins*

*Eddy Merckx, the all-time number one on the road. His achievements seem unlikely ever to be surpassed*

## Yvonne McGREGOR

b. Bradford, 9 April 1961

Yvonne McGregor came to cycle sport via fell running and triathlon. Injury prompted her to change to cycling, and in 1993 she scored her first successes by taking the women's 10 mile, 50 mile and 100 mile UK time-trial titles. In 1994 she won a gold medal for England in the women's 25 km points race at the Commonwealth Games in Canada, and in 1995 she set a new one-hour international women's record of 47.4111 kilometres.

## Eddy MERCKX (Belgium)

b. Meensel-Kiezegem, 17 June 1945

It is very rare in any sport that one is able to state that one man was undoubtedly the greatest ever. But such is the case in cycling with Eddy Merckx, who came from a well-educated, middle-class background which is unusual in cycling. In contrast to the short stature of riders such as

Anquetil and Hinault, Merckx was also one of the tallest in the peloton at 6 ft 4 in. He was so strong and rode hard so often that his nickname was 'The Cannibal' – the man who wanted to win everything. He had no weaknesses, for he was the strongest time triallist and climber in the world who could also outsprint all but a few rivals.

Having excelled at a number of sports, Merckx was encouraged to try competitive cycling at the age of 14. He became world amateur champion at 18, a professional at 19, and a Classic winner at 21. From then on his list of major victories was staggering, totalling 525 wins in 1800 races. He has won the most titles in the following major races: five Tour de France (1969–72, 1974), wearing the *maillot jaune* for a record 96 days and winning a record 35 stages; five Giro d'Italia (1968, 1970, 1972–74); three world professional road races (1967, 1971, 1974), as well as the amateur title in 1964; seven Milan–San Remo (1966–67, 1969, 1971–72, 1975–76); three Ghent–Wevelgem; four Flèche–Wallonne (1967, 1970, 1972, 1975); and five Liège–Bastogne–Liège (1969, 1971–73, 1975). In all he won a total of 33 classics, and 17 six-day races.

He was the first man (equalled since only by Stephen Roche) to win the Tour de France, Giro d'Italia and world professional road race in the same year (1974). He is one of only four men to have ever won all three of the major tours – France, Italy and Spain (1973) – but only Merckx also won the Tour of Switzerland (1974). At the 1969 Tour de France, Merckx performed the still unequalled feat of winning the yellow jersey (overall winner), green jersey (points winner), and polka-dot jersey (King of the Mountains). He was again King of the Mountains in 1970 and points winner in 1971–72, and in 1972 also set world records at Mexico City for 10 km at 11 minutes, 53.2 seconds, 20 km at 24 minutes, 6.8 seconds and one hour at 49.431957 km. He was voted Belgian Sportsman of the Year each year from 1969 to 1974.

Eddy Merckx surrounded himself with a team of talented riders dedicated to helping him win, an approach which was clearly followed by his counterpart in the 1990s, Miguel Indurain. He was also fanatical about his choice of cycle equipment, putting great thought into his choice of saddles, frame angles, gear ratios and the rest. In 1994, his son, the 22-year-old Axel Merckx, joined the Telekom team in his first season as a road-racing professional, while Eddy Merckx himself continues to be closely involved with the sport.

**Eddy Merckx Major Victories**

| | |
|---|---|
| 1965 | Ghent Six-day (with Patrick Sercu). |
| 1966 | Milan–San Remo. |
| 1967 | World Professional Road Race; Milan–San Remo; Ghent–Wevelgem; Flèche–Wallonne; Baracchi Trophy; Ghent Six-day (with Patrick Sercu). |
| 1968 | Tour of Italy (4 stage wins); Paris–Roubaix; Charleroi Six-day (with Ferdinand Bracke). |
| 1969 | Tour de France (6 stage wins); Paris–Nice (3 stage wins); Milan–San Remo; Tour of Flanders; Liège–Bastogne–Liège; Ghent–Wevelgem. |
| 1970 | Tour de France (8 stage wins); Tour of Italy (3 stage wins); Tour of Belgium (2 stage wins); Paris–Nice (3 stage wins); Paris–Roubaix; Flèche–Wallonne. |
| 1971 | World Professional Road Race; Tour de France (4 stage wins); Tour of Belgium (3 stage wins); Paris–Nice (3 stage wins); Milan–San Remo; Liège–Bastogne–Liège; Tour of Lombardy; Het Volk; Henninger Turm; Midi-Libre; Milan Six-day (with J. Stevens). |
| 1972 | World Hour Record (49.431 km); World 10 km Record (1153.2); World 20 km record (24.06.8); Tour de France (6 stage wins); Tour of Italy (4 stage wins); Flèche–Wallonne; Ghent–Wevelgem; Milan–San Remo; Liège–Bastogne–Liège; Tour of Lombardy. |
| 1973 | Tour of Italy (6 stage wins); Tour of Spain (6 stage wins); Paris–Roubaix; Liège–Bastogne–Liège; Paris–Brussels; Het Volk; Amstel Gold; Grand Prix des Nations; Ghent–Wevelgem; Grenoble Six-day (with Patrick Sercu); Dortmund Six-day (with Patrick Sercu). |
| 1974 | World Professional Road Race; Tour de France (8 stage wins); Tour of Italy (2 stage wins); Tour of Switzerland (3 stage wins); Antwerp Six-day. |
| 1975 | Milan–San Remo; Liège–Bastogne–Liège; Tour of Flanders; Amstel Gold; Antwerp Six-day (with Patrick Sercu); Grenoble Six-day (with Patrick Sercu); Ghent Six-day (with Patrick Sercu). |
| 1976 | Milan–San Remo; Antwerp Six-day (with Patrick Sercu); Rotterdam Six-day (with Patrick Sercu). |
| 1977 | Berlin Six-day (with Patrick Sercu); Ghent Six-day (with Patrick Sercu); Maastricht Six-day (with Patrick Sercu); Munich Six-day (with Patrick Sercu); Zurich Six-day (with Patrick Sercu). |

## Leon MEREDITH (UK)

b. St Pancras, London, 2 July 1882; d. Davos, Switzerland, 27 January 1930

The first man to win seven world championships, all in the now-defunct amateur 100 km motor-paced event (1904–05, 1907–09, 1911 and 1913). Meredith also won seven British championships (1902–08). At the 1908 Olympic Games he would have been favourite to win the individual road race, but the event was not contested for one of the few times in Olympic history; nor was he able to win the gold medal at team pursuit. Four years later he was fourth in the road race at the Stockholm Olympics. He was also British amateur roller-skating champion in 1911 and 1912. He died of a heart attack while on his annual winter holiday in Davos.

## Robert MILLAR (UK)

b. Glasgow, 13 September 1958

Robert Millar is Britain's highest-ever and most successful finisher in the Tour de France. On his first tour in 1983 he took one stage win and finished 14th overall. The following year in 1984 he took one stage win, won the King of the Mountains title – the only English-speaking rider to ever do so – and was fourth overall. His only other success in the Tour de France was one stage win and tenth overall in 1989. His last Tour de France ride was his 11th in 1993 when he finished 24th overall. He was also second overall in the 1985 and 1986 Vuelta a España and second overall in the 1987 Giro d'Italia. In 1995 he won the UK professional road race championship held on the Isle of Man.

## Daniel MORELON (France)

b. Bourg-en-Bresse, 28 July 1944
After coming third in 1965, Morelon won a record nine world amateur sprint titles (1966–67, 1969–73 and 1975), and three Olympic gold medals, sprint in 1968 and 1972 and tandem sprint in 1968, with a bronze in 1964 and silver in 1976. His tandem gold medal was won with Pierre Trentin, his great countryman with whom he had many battles, and these two also won the world tandem title in 1966. He won a total of 14 French titles, and set a world record indoors for 500 metres from a flying start at 28.75 seconds in 1976. Strictly a track sprinter, he saw no reason to turn professional. He became the French sprint-cycling coach in 1983.

## Francesco MOSER (Italy)

b. Pal' di Giovo, Trento, 19 June 1951

At the 1972 Olympic road race Moser came seventh, a rather inauspicious beginning for a man who would become recognized as one of the great professionals. Moreover, although Moser went on to win many races, taking his first Italian professional title in 1972 and world titles at pursuit in 1976 and road in 1977 (second in 1976), he disappointed the Italian cycling cognoscenti because he never won as much as Coppi who had been the greatest *campionissimo*.

Moser used his great track-pursuiting ability to win many races with his sprint. In addition, his ability to mount a long, sustained attack was legendary. He used this to break Merckx's one-hour record – which had stood for 11 years – with 50.8808423 km and then 51.15135 km at the outdoor, high-altitude track at Mexico City in January 1984, becoming the first rider to break the one-hour/50 km barrier. He also excited some controversy by using a hi-tech, low-profile, oversized rear-disc wheeled bike which was seen as a technological breakthrough that had been unavailable to Merckx. In Mexico he also set records for five kilometres at 5 minutes, 47.163 seconds and

ten kilometres at 11 minutes, 39.720 seconds at Milan in 1986. Indoors he also set seven world records, with bests of ten kilometres at 11 minutes, 50.36 seconds (1988), 20 kilometres at 24 minutes, 12.28 seconds (1987) and one hour at 50.644 km (1988).

Moser's final record lasted until 1993 when it was broken by Graeme Obree and then by Chris Boardman. In response the 43-year-old Moser came out of retirement for another crack at the record in Mexico in January 1994. Riding a new bike in the crouched 'Obree position', Moser failed magnificently, covering 51.840 kilometres in the hour which was 244 metres more than Obree but 430 metres less than Boardman had done the previous year.

**Francesco Moser Major Victories**

| | |
|---|---|
| 1974 | Paris–Tours. |
| 1975 | Tour of Lombardy. |
| 1976 | Points Jersey – Tour of Italy; World Pursuit Champion. |
| 1977 | Flèche–Wallonne; Zurich Meisterschaft; Points Jersey – Tour of Italy; World Road Race Champion. |
| 1978 | Tour of Lombardy; Paris–Roubaix; Points Jersey – Tour of Italy. |
| 1979 | Paris–Roubaix; Ghent–Wevelgem. |
| 1980 | Paris–Roubaix. |

*In 1994 at the age of 43 Francesco Moser narrowly failed in a courageous attempt to win back the one hour record*

1982     Points Jersey – Tour of Italy.
1984     Tour of Italy; Milan–San Remo; World
         One-Hour Record – 51.15135 km.

## Koichi NAKANO (Japan)

b. Kurume, Fukuoka Prefecture, 14 November 1955

Koichi Nakano was world professional sprint champion for ten successive years (1977–86), a record unmatched in any cycling event. Such was his dominance that in 1985–86 only 11 and 10 riders respectively entered against him. Nakano was very strong and ideally built at 1.72m and 89 kg. His father, Mitsuyoshi, was a professional cyclist, and the son followed by joining the Japan Bicycle Racing school in Suzenji for ten months before making his professional debut in 1970. By the time of his tenth world title win, Nakano had won 470 of his 775 races and earned 838 million yen ($5.8 million). After his retirement as a match sprinter, he continued to ride in Japanese keirin races for two more years.

## Graeme OBREE (UK)

b. Ayr, Scotland, 11 September 1965

The amateur Scottish rider Graeme Obree caused a sensation when he took the world one-hour record on 17 July 1993, in a determined effort to beat his British rival Chris Boardman to the glory of destroying Francesco Moser's record of almost 10 years' standing. Riding his home-built bike featuring ball-bearings taken from a washing machine and the unique 'Obree position' for riding, Obree extended the one-hour distance to 51.596 kilometres at the Viking Ship velodrome in Hamar, Norway, adding 0.445 km to Moser's record. Six days later Boardman replied with a new world hour record of 52.270 km set in Bordeaux, but lost it once again to Obree who set a new record distance of 52.713 km on the same Bordeaux velodrome in April 1994. A week later the UCI outlawed Obree's riding position, which had also been used by Moser in an unsuccessful record attempt earlier the same year, but they allowed the Scot's record to stand. It was later eclipsed by Miguel Indurain and Tony Rominger.

Obree also used his controversial riding position to win the 1993 4000m world pursuit championship at Hamar, which was open to both professionals and amateurs. He set a new world record of 4 minutes, 22.668 seconds in the semi-final against Chris Boardman who had recently turned professional, pushing him into third place overall. It was the first time Obree had beaten Boardman on the track for three years, and he then went on to break his own

*The great British amateur Graeme Obree bounced back to take his second world championship in 1995*

day-old record to defeat defending champion Philippe Ermenault of France. The following year he was unable to defend his pursuit title, owing to the UCI ban on his riding position, and experienced an unsatisfactory season which included an abortive trial as a professional with the Le Groupement road-race team in Europe. He planned a comeback for 1995, his main target being to regain the 4000m world pursuit title, which he successfully achieved at the world track championships in Colombia.

**Graeme Obree Major Victories**

1993     World Hour record – 51.596 km; World
         4000m Pursuit Champion.
1994     World Hour record – 52.713 km.
1995     World 4000m Pursuit Champion.

## Luis OCANA (Spain)

b. Priego, 9 June 1945; d. May 1994

A great all-rounder who was primarily known as a superb climber. As he had the misfortune to race in the same era as Eddy Merckx, he was prevented from winning more major tours by the great Belgian. Ocana lacked the sprinting ability to win one-day classics, so his primary efforts were directed towards the major tours. In 1971 Ocana wore the *maillot jaune* and led Merckx in the Tour de France until he crashed on a hairpin bend on the descent of the Col de Mente in the Pyrenees; his life was at risk but he returned to ride again. His Tour de France win in 1973 was sweet but was achieved in Merckx's absence. His best world championship placing was third in the professional road-race in 1973. He was found shot dead in his home in May 1994.

**Luis Ocana Major Victories**

| | |
|---|---|
| 1969 | King of the Mountains – Tour of Spain. |
| 1970 | Tour of Spain. |
| 1971 | Grand Prix des Nations |
| 1972 | Dauphiné-Liberé. |
| 1973 | Dauphiné-Liberé; Tour de France. |

## Sir Hubert OPPERMAN (Australia)

b. Rochester, Victoria, 2 May 1904

Hubert Ferdinand Opperman first began to develop the stamina which made him a legend by cycling around the suburb of Malvern delivering telegrams. He won his first major race at the age of 17, and later the same year joined Bruce Small's Malvern Star Cycles in what became a formidable partnership in competitive cycling as he rose to become Australia's greatest cyclist with marathon racing his speciality.

He was Australian Road Champion four times and captained the Australian Tour de France team in 1928 and 1931. In 1928 he won the 24 hour Bol d'Or race although both his bikes were sabotaged and he was forced to borrow his interpreter's machine, an old roadster fitted with lamps, mudguards and upturned brakes. He was lapped 17 times before one of his repaired bikes was ready, and then went on to take the lead in the 11th hour before going on to ride the next 12 hours non-stop. Encouraged by the 50,000-strong crowd he continued for 79 minutes after the end of the race in order to break the record for 1000 kilometres.

In 1931 he won the 1200 km Paris–Brest–Paris, the longest single-stage race in the world, in a new record time of 49 hours and 21 minutes despite torrential rain and cold winds. He then came to Britain to break the Land's End to John O'Groats record, before returning to Australia to set a variety of new records. He broke all motor-paced records in a 1000-mile ride in Sydney, and set a world record for riding 1000 miles round the Melbourne Motordrome in 24 hours. In his longest solo ride he endured atrocious conditions across the Nullabor before setting a record for Freemantle to Sydney of 13 days, 10 hours and 112 minutes, eclipsing the previous record by more than five days. He rode

from Albany to Perth in 12 hours which was two and a half hours better than the train could do, and then in 1940 broke 101 records in a 24-hour unpaced ride in Sydney at the end of almost 20 years of racing.

The Second World War ended his career as a professional cyclist. After service with the RAAF he became a federal politician, holding the Victorian seat of Corio from 1949 to 1967. He served as Chief Government Whip, Minister for Shipping and Transport and Minister for Immigration. On his retirement from politics he served as the Australian High Commissioner to Malta from 1967 to 1972. Having received the OBE in 1952 he was knighted in 1968 and made a Knight Grand Cross of Justice in 1980. He took his last cycle ride round his home town of Rochester at the age of 90 on his Malvern Star. Having ridden daily up to that time 'Oppy' transferred his energies to an exercise bike which he said at least gave him the privilege of riding without a helmet.

## Hans-Henrik ORSTED (Denmark)

b. Grena, 13 December 1954

One of the greatest professional pursuiters in history. He turned professional in 1980 and in the next seven years won three gold (1984–86), two silver, and two bronze medals at the world individual pursuit championships. He set amateur world records outdoors at 4000m at 4 minutes 40.23 seconds, 5000m at 5 minutes, 50.68 seconds, 10 km at 11 minutes 54.906 seconds, 20 km at 24 minutes, 35.63 seconds and one hour at 48.200 km at high altitude in Mexico City in 1979. Then as a professional in 1985 he improved the 5 km time to 5 minutes, 45.646 seconds, which he followed with his greatest ride – shortly after the world championships – when he broke the low-altitude world one-hour record which had stood since 1967, recording 48.144 kilometres. He also set indoor world records at 4 km, 5 km and 10 km as an amateur and twice at 5 km as a professional.

Orsted was also a strong six-day rider, but his size and lack of climbing ability hampered his efforts to challenge successfully on the road.

## Ned OVEREND (USA)

b. 20 August 1955

This veteran American mountain-bike racer, based in Durango, Colorado won the first official UCI mountain bike world championship in 1990, and in the years that followed continued to give much younger riders a hard time, finishing second overall to Bart Brentjens in the 1994 Grundig World Cup

*The Pelissier brothers were the top French riders of their generation. Francis, pictured here, was never quite as successful as Henri but gave full support to his brother*

series at the age of 39, having won two events outright; he was also second overall in the NORBA series in the USA. Overend was six-times US national Champion (1986–87, 1989–92) and twice unofficial world champion (1988–89). Rated as a senior ambassador of the sport with legendary status, Overend remained loyal to his sponsor (Specialised) throughout his racing career. His hard climbing performance earned him the nickname 'The Lung'.

## Henri PELISSIER (France)

b. Paris, 22 January 1889; d. Dampierre, 1 May 1935

A great all-round cyclist who struggled for many years before finally winning the Tour de France in 1923. At the 1919 Tour he was cautioned for dangerous riding. That night he quit the race, declaring he would not tolerate being treated like a convict. In his statement, he coined the term which is now a favoured description of members of the peloton, *forcats de la route* (convicts of the road).

His first major win, the 1911 Tour of Lombardy, was hardly planned at all. At a Paris railway station he met Lucien Petit-Breton, who talked him into

going for a week's racing in Italy. Pelissier ran home and packed his bags, winning the race ten days later. He won the race again in 1913 and 1920. His brother François Pelissier won the Paris–Tours in 1921.

**Henri Pelissier Major Victories**
1911    Tour of Lombardy.
1912    Milan–San Remo.
1913    Tour of Lombardy.
1919    Paris–Roubaix; Bordeaux–Paris; Tour de France.
1920    Tour of Lombardy; Paris–Brussels.
1921    Paris–Roubaix.
1922    Milan–San Remo; Paris–Tours; Bordeaux–Paris
1924    Bordeaux–Paris.

## Paola PEZZO (Italy)

b. 8 January 1969

Paola Pezzo from Boscochiesanuova was Italy's women's mountain national champion in 1993 when she went on to win the UCI world championship at Métabief in France. The following year she won the 1994 European championship at the same location and took two rounds of the Grundig World Cup series.

## Hugh PORTER (UK)

b. Wolverhampton, 27 January 1940

Until the advent of Chris Boardman, Hugh Porter has been considered the finest ever British pursuit cyclist. In addition to his four world professional titles (1968, 1970, 1972–73), he was second in 1967 and 1969, and third in 1971. As an amateur he won a bronze medal at the 1963 world championships in the pursuit, but had difficulty at the 1964 Olympics, losing in the quarter-finals at Tokyo, before winning the 1966 Commonwealth gold. He competed on the road as well, including the 1968 Tour de France (he did not finish), but with less success. Porter married British swimming gold medallist Anita Lonsbrough on 1 June 1965. He was awarded the MBE.

## Raymond POULIDOR (France)

b. Masbaraud-Merignat, 15 April 1936

The most popular rider of his time and one of the best-loved French cyclists ever. His acclaim was mostly for his grace in defeat, for he rarely won the major victories often expected of him. It was his bad fortune to ride in the same era as Anquetil and then Merckx. In the Tour de France, Poulidor started 14 times between 1962 and 1976, and was placed second three times (1964–65, 1974) and third five times (1962, 1966, 1969, 1972, 1976). He won seven stages in his 14 Tours, but despite this never wore the yellow jersey for even a day. In the world professional road race he was second in 1974 and third in 1961, 1964 and 1966.

**Raymond Poulidor Major Victories**
1961    Milan–San Remo.
1963    Flèche–Wallonne; Grand Prix des Nations.
1964    Tour of Spain.
1966    Dauphiné-Liberé.
1972    Paris–Nice.
1973    Paris–Nice.

## Yvonne REYNDERS (Belgium)

b. Schaarbeek-Brussels, 4 August 1937

With Beryl Burton of Britain, Reynders was one of the two great women road riders of the 1960s. She won 12 medals at the women's world championships, including four golds in the road race (1959, 1961, 1963, 1966), and three golds in the pursuit (1961, 1964–65).

## Roger RIVIERE (France)

b. Saint-Etienne, 23 February 1936

Roger Rivière was world professional pursuit champion from 1957 to 1959. When he turned to the road in 1959, French cycling fans turned to him, looking for a hero they could embrace. Though they had Jacques Anquetil, he was never loved by them.

After Rivière had broken Anquetil's world one-hour record with 46.2342 km in 1957 and then 47.3469 km in 1958, setting records en route at 10 km and 20 km on both occasions, great things were expected of him. In the Tour de France he finished third in 1959 behind Anquetil (who, in second place to Federico Bahamontes, lost his only Tour), and Rivière was favourite in 1960 when Anquetil opted to race in the Giro instead. Rivière was on course to win, with several of his favourite time trials remaining, when he crashed off the side of the Col de Perjuret in the Tarn Gorges. The broken back he sustained ended his promising career and he never raced again.

*Sean Kelly and Stephen Roche, the two greats of Irish cycling*

## Stephen ROCHE (Republic of Ireland)

b. Dublin, 20 November 1959

Roche had a record year in 1987 that has been matched by only one rider ever – the great Eddy Merckx. He won both the Tour de France and Giro d'Italia, and also won the rainbow jersey as world road race champion. His Tour de France win was the stuff of high drama. In second place entering the Alps with Pedro Delgado close behind in third, Roche fell off the pace as Delgado attacked up the Villard de Lans. Delgado took over the race, and was the leader on the road as he opened up a huge margin, but Roche countered and closed to within four seconds at the finish. It was an almost superhuman effort which earned him the yellow jersey, and also put him in hospital overnight. He recovered enough to race the next day and keep the *maillot jaune* into Paris, becoming the first and only Irishman and the second English-speaking rider (with American Greg LeMond who won in 1986, 1989 and 1990) to win the Tour de France.

Roche's career was hampered by knee problems both before 1987 and in the ensuing years. After finishing 45th in the Olympic road race in 1980 he turned professional in 1981, winning the Paris–Nice and the Tour of Corsica in his first season. He was third in the world professional road race in 1983 and in the Tour de France in 1985. For Roche 1987 was the one and only year in which everything happened.

**Stephen Roche Major Victories**
1981    Paris–Nice; Tour of Corsica.
1987    Tour de France; Tour of Italy; World Road
         Race Champion.

## Aleksandr ROMANOV (USSR)

b. Moscow, 11 May 1953

A superb track rider who was best known as a motor-paced time-triallist. Oddly, he never competed in the amateur motor-paced event at the world championships. He did compete in the individual pursuit, and was third in the world juniors in 1983.

Romanov set the following world records while paced behind a motorbike, with all his best times coming in 1987. Outdoors he set three 50 km world records, his best being 35 minutes, 21.108 seconds; three 100 km world records to a best time of 1 hour, 10 minutes, 50.940 seconds; and three one-hour world records to a best distance of 84.710 km. Indoors he set eight world records over 50 km (best: 32 minutes, 56.746 seconds); six at 100 km to a best of 1 hour, 5 minutes, 58.031 seconds; and six at one hour to a best distance of 91.131 kilometres.

## Tony ROMINGER (Switzerland)

b. Velje, 27 March 1961

Tony Rominger blew the one-hour record wide apart in 1994, and as one of the most successful stage race

*In 1995 Tony Rominger dominated the Giro and saw his one-hour record survive the attentions of Miguel Indurain*

riders of his time with great time-trial and mountain-climbing ability was also rated as the man most likely to beat Miguel Indurain in the big tours.

Rominger's first Classic win came in the 1989 Tirreno Adriatico which he also won the following year. In 1991 he won the Paris–Nice, the Tour de Romande and Grand Prix des Nations time-trial race, and then in 1992 added the Tour of Lombardy, the Vuelta al Pais Vasco and the Tour of Spain, winning the last two tours again the next year when he finished second to Miguel Indurain in the Tour de France, 4 minutes and 59 seconds behind.

In 1994 Rominger won the Paris–Nice, the Tour of the Pays-Basque, and the Tour of Spain in which as well as overall victory he won the prologue, the two time trials and three mountain stages. He abandoned the Tour de France at the 13th stage due to illness, leaving the race to Indurain, but took his revenge at the Bordeaux velodrome in October when he smashed the one-hour record with a distance of 53.832 km. Two weeks later he hoisted the record past 55 kilometres to 55.291 km, recording the greatest increase on the record since 1894. For the 1995 season Rominger's main targets were the Giro d'Italia and Tour de France. He dominated the Giro by taking the Points prize and the InterGiro award as well as winning overall, but was well below form for the Tour de France in which he was eighth overall.

**Tony Rominger Major Victories**
1989    Tirreno Adriatico.
1990    Tirreno Adriatico.
1991    Paris–Nice; Tour de Romande; Grand Prix
         des Nations.
1992    Tour of Lombardy; Vuelta al Pais Vasco; Tour
         of Spain.
1993    Vuelta al Pais Vasco; Tour of Spain.
1994    Paris–Nice; Tour of the Pays-Basque; Tour of
         Spain; Grand Prix des Nations; World
         One-Hour Record – 55.291 km.
1995    Giro d'Italia.

## Erika SALYUMAE (USSR/Estonia)

b. Pärnu, 11 June 1962

While competing for the USSR Erika Salyuumae became the first Estonian woman to win an Olympic gold medal, taking the sprint title in 1988. She won again in 1992, this time in the colours of Estonia which was competing at the Games in its own right for the first time since 1936. She was also world sprint champion in 1987 and 1989, and runner-up in 1984 and 1986. In USSR championships she won ten gold, three silver and three bronze medals.

She came to the sport late, taking up cycling in 1981 and making the Soviet national team in 1984.

She has set 17 world records with her outdoor flying start 1 km record of 1 minute, 10.463 seconds lasting from 1984, and her indoor records for unpaced flying starts for the 500m of 29.655 seconds and for the 1 km of 1 minute, 5.232 seconds lasting from 1987. Her 1 km standing start bests are 1 minute, 14.249 seconds outdoors in 1984 and 1 minute, 13.377 seconds indoors in 1983.

## Jef SCHERENS (Belgium)

b. Wercher, 7 February 1909; d. 1988

Known as having the greatest acceleration ever in track sprinting, 'The Cat' was the first cyclist to win six consecutive world championships (1932–37) in the same event before coming second to Dutchman Arie van Vliet in 1938. He had also been third in 1931. He had a very long career, winning his last world title in 1947, 15 years after his first, and but for World War Two might have won several more.

## Briek SCHOTTE (Belgium)

b. Canegem, 7 September 1919

Schotte was primarily known for his great sprinting ability, which enabled him to win a number of one-day classics. His lack of ability in time trials and the mountains prevented him from being a factor in the major tours. Most of his victories came in his native Belgium, although he did win the world road championship two years out of three on foreign ground (1948 and 1950). Other major victories included the Tour of Flanders in 1942 and 1948; Ghent–Wevelgem in 1950 and 1955; Paris–Brussels in 1946 and 1952; and Paris–Tours in 1946 and 1947.

## Patrick SERCU (Belgium)

b. 27 June 1944 Roeselare

Patrick Sercu began his career as a great track sprinter, winning the world amateur title in 1963, the Olympic gold for the kilometre time-trial in 1964, and the world professional sprint in 1967 and 1969, with second places in 1965 and 1968. He set indoor world records for 1 kilometre with a flying start of 1 minute, 1.23 seconds in 1967 and with a standing start of 1 minute, 7.35 seconds in 1972, and an outdoor kilometre record of 1 minute, 2.46 seconds in 1973.

Later in his career he finished the Tour de France twice and was points winner in 1974, but he will be remembered as one of the greatest six-day racers ever. From 1964 to 1983 he won a record 88 out of 233 six-day races with several different partners. He

coached the Belgian Olympic team in 1984. His father Albert Sercu won the Het Volk and was second in the world professional road race in 1947.

## Tommy SIMPSON (UK)

b. Co Durham, 30 November 1937; d. Mont Ventoux, France; 13 July 1967

Tommy Simpson was the first truly great British road professional, and until the advent of Robert Millar and Chris Boardman remained the greatest produced by the British Isles. He turned professional in 1960 after an amateur career which included an Olympic bronze medal in the 1956 team pursuit and a silver in the individual pursuit at the 1958 Commonwealth Games. He lacked only the ability to climb strongly, which made him more of a factor in one-day Classics than in the major tours.

In 1962 he became the first Briton to wear the *maillot jaune* at the Tour de France, though he held it for only a day. His greatest year was 1965 when he won the Tour of Lombardy and the world professional road race. Those wins occurred after a disastrous fall in the Tour de France when doctors feared they might need to amputate his arm.

In 1967, Simpson was ascending Mont Ventoux in the Tour de France when he collapsed and fell from his bike. He could not be revived and died that day. He was later found to have been quite heavily drugged with stimulants, and his death was directly responsible for many of the anti-drug regulations put in place by international sporting organizations.

**Tommy Simpson Major Victories**
1961   Tour of Flanders.
1963   Bordeaux–Paris.
1964   Milan–San Remo.

*Tommy Simpson ranked as the most popular British rider of all time. His untimely death shocked the cycling world and prompted new standards for drug-testing*

1965  Tour of Lombardy; World Road Race Champion.
1967  Paris–Nice.

## Jean STABLINSKI (France)

b. Thun-Saint-Ammand, 21 May 1932

A superb all-round cyclist whose record would have been better had Jacques Anquetil not been riding at the same time. He was world professional road champion in 1962 after his close friend Seamus Elliott had broken away. When Jos Hoevenaars chased Elliott, Stablinski went with him and eventually dropped the other two. Shortly before the finish Stablinski punctured, but was allowed to borrow a spectator's bike and rode it across the line to win his only world title.

**Jean Stablinski Major Victories**

1958  Tour of Spain.
1962  World Road Race Champion.
1963  Paris–Brussels.
1965  Tour of Henninger Tower.
1966  Amstel Gold Race.

## 'Major' TAYLOR (USA)

Marshall Walter Taylor. b. Indianapolis, 26 November 1878; d. Chicago; 6 July 1932

Marshall Taylor, a black cyclist from Worcester, Massachusetts, beat Nat and Tom Butler to win the one-mile world professional sprint championship at Queen's Park in Montreal on 10 August 1899 when he was 21 years old. It was a landmark in the sporting world, a victory for the black people of America. He became the second black world champion in any sport after the boxer George Dixon, and of the first five black world champions he was the only one to beat whites in a non-contact sport. He was also probably the first black athlete to be commercially sponsored.

Beginning in 1893, Marshall 'Major' Taylor won consistently in the north-east, later travelling widely to display his talents. His world amateur sprint title of 1899 was followed in 1900 by the US national professional championship, after at least two previous titles were believed to have been taken from him by conspiracy because of his colour. When 'Major' Taylor was given second place by the judges after a near dead-heat in the half-mile sprint championship of 1899, the crowd hissed and booed to show their contempt and the police had to be called to restore order.

'Major' Taylor raced in Europe from 1901 to 1904, winning many championships and the acclaim

*'Major' Taylor, a brilliant rider from the early days of cycle racing, whose career was dogged by racial prejudice*

of the Europeans. He lived strictly by the mores of his era, neither smoking nor drinking, and in his spare time he became a published poet. He retired in 1910 at the age of 32 having saved a substantial amount of money, but his finest days were over. He was refused entry to the Worcester Polytechnic Institute to study engineering because he was coloured, he lost money on his investments, he separated from his wife, and eventually he became destitute and lived at the YMCA. In between times he had been going door to door, attempting to sell his autobiography *The Fastest Rider in the World, The Story of a Colored Boy's Indomitable Courage and Success Against Great Odds.*

In 1932 Taylor died from heart disease and was buried in an unmarked pauper's grave. In 1948 he was re-buried with a plaque commemorating a 'God-fearing, clean-living, gentlemanly athlete, a credit to his race, who came up the hard way without hatred in his heart'. The Indianapolis velodrome was later named after him.

## Phillippe THIJS (Belgium)

b. Anderlecht-Brussels, 8 October 1890; d. Brussels, 16 January 1972

Phillipe Thijs was the first man to win the Tour de France three times (1913–14 and 1920). He rode almost exclusively in France and had no major wins outside his homeland.

In the 1913 Tour, Thijs was helped by the rules which required all riders to make their own repairs. Going over the Pyrenees, Eugene Christophe was leading the race when he broke his front fork. He carried his bike to the nearest town, found a blacksmith's shop, and fixed the bike himself. The three-hour delay handed the lead to Thijs who went on to win the race, while Eugene Christophe suffered an additional penalty due to accepting the 'outside help' of the boy who worked the blacksmith's bellows.

## Lothar THOMS (GDR)

b. Guben, 18 May 1956

Usually considered to be the greatest track kilometre time-triallist ever. In addition to his four world titles (1977–79, 1981 as well as second in 1982), his Olympic victory in 1980 was achieved in a time of 1 minute, 2.955 seconds which stood as a world record until 1989. His victory margin in that stunning performance was almost two seconds – the most dominant ever in the Olympics.

## Guillermo TIMONER (Spain)

b. Felanitx, 24 March 1926

Timoner has the best record ever in the professional motor-paced cycling event. In addition to his six world championships (1955, 1959–60, 1962, 1964–65), he twice finished second in 1956 and 1958. He was a masterful competitor, as he never set a world motor-paced record against the clock but was almost unbeatable in head-to-head races.

## John TOMAC (USA)

b. 3 November 1967

John Tomac or 'Farmer John' is, like Ned Overend, a resident of Durango, Colorado, and in the early 1990s rated as the mountain-bike racer with the greatest celebrity status in the world. His best year on the international scene came in 1991 when he won the UCI world cross-country championship held in Italy, and also finished second in the downhill. In 1993 he finished second overall in both the Grundig World Cup cross-country and downhill series, underlining his all-round ability and fearless bike-handling skills.

## Galina TSAREVA (USSR)

b. Velikiye-Luki, 19 April 1950

Tsareva first made the Soviet national team in 1969, and was still considered for the 1988 Olympic team at the close of an amazingly long career. She was world sprint champion six times (1969–71, 1977–79), and Soviet national champion (1969–71, 1973, 1975–77). She set a world record outdoors for 500 metres with a flying start at 31.70 seconds in 1978, and indoors recorded a series of records: 5 km with a standing start at 6 minutes, 42.237 seconds (1982), 10 km at 13 minutes, 41.519 seconds (1983) and 20 km at 27 minutes, 46.73 seconds (1983); with a flying start, four at 200m from 12.163 seconds in 1980 to 11.361 seconds in 1987, 500m at 32.302 seconds (1980), and 1 km at 1 minute, 9.077 seconds (1980).

## Rebecca TWIGG (USA)

b. Honolulu, Hawaii, 26 March 1963

Probably the best-known woman rider produced by America during the cycling explosion of the 1980s. She was at her best as a track pursuiter, becoming world champion in 1982, 1984, 1985 and 1988. She was forced to turn to the road race when it was the only event chosen for women's cycling at the 1984 Olympics, and narrowly missed winning a gold medal when Connie Carpenter-Phinney outsprinted her. After the Games she smashed the 10-year-old 3 km standing start world record of 3 minutes, 52.5 seconds with a time of 3 minutes, 49.78 seconds in

*Rebecca Twigg-Whitehead has been the most successful woman rider from the USA. She took her sixth world championship pursuit title in 1995*

Barcelona. She was also popular for her good looks and brilliant mind – she skipped high school completely, matriculating at the University of Washington when only 14. Twigg retired in 1987 but returned to cycle sport in late 1991 and won a bronze medal in the individual pursuit at the 1992 Olympics in Barcelona. She went on to win the world track pursuit title for a fifth and sixth time in 1993 and 1995.

## Gintautas UMARAS (USSR/Lithuania)

b. Klaipeda, 20 May 1963

One of the greatest ever pursuit cyclists. He first made the Soviet national team in 1981 and would have been a favourite at the 1984 Olympics, had the USSR not boycotted the Games. He was USSR champion from 1984 to 1987 and world individual (and team) pursuit champion in 1987, after taking second places in 1985 and 1986. After the 1988 Olympics, when he won gold medals at both individual and team pursuit, Umaras was one of several prominent Soviet riders allowed to turn professional. He also set amateur world records at 4 km unpaced with a standing start twice, outdoors in 1985 and 1987 (4 minutes, 31.160 seconds) and once indoors.

*Rik Van Looy was the most successful Belgian rider before Eddy Merckx, winning virtually all the major Classics over a 12-year period between 1955 and 1967*

## Rik VAN LOOY (Belgium)

b. Grobbendon, 20 December 1932

Prior to Eddy Merckx, van Looy won more Classics than any professional cyclist ever. This was mainly due to his tremendous ability as a road sprinter, unmatched in the peloton at the time. Only the Grand Prix des Nations (a time trial) and the Bordeaux–Paris are missing from his list of major Classic victories.

Having been third in the 1953 world road race championship as an amateur, he won the professional title twice (1960–61), and was second in 1956 and 1963. His lack of strength as a time triallist was his greatest weakness, as he had 38 stage wins in the three big tours but did not win any of them. He was not considered a great climber, though he won the King of the Mountains title in the Giro d'Italia 1960. Van Looy also won 11 six-day races, nine of them teamed with Peter Post.

**Rik van Looy Major Victories**

| | |
|---|---|
| 1955 | Ghent–Wevelgem. |
| 1956 | Ghent–Wevelgem; Paris–Brussels. |
| 1957 | Ghent–Wevelgem. |
| 1958 | Paris–Brussels; Milan–San Remo. |
| 1959 | Paris–Tours; Tour of Lombardy; Tour of Flanders; Points Jersey – Tour of Spain. |
| 1960 | World Road Race Champion; King of the Mountains – Tour of Italy. |
| 1961 | World Road Race Champion; Paris–Roubaix; Liège–Bastogne–Liège. |
| 1962 | Ghent–Wevelgem; Tour of Flanders; Paris–Roubaix. |
| 1963 | Points Jersey – Tour de France |
| 1965 | Paris–Roubaix. Points Jersey – Tour of Spain. |
| 1967 | Paris–Tours. |

## Keetie VAN OOSTEN-HAGE (Holland)

b. Maartensdijk, 1949; now know as van Oosten

Keetie van Oosten-Hage was rated as one of the strongest woman cyclists in the world. In her brilliant career she collected six world and 22 national titles. At pursuit she was world champion in 1975, 1976, 1978 and 1979, second in 1971 and 1973, and third in 1968, 1969 and 1974. She was also world road race champion in 1968 and 1976, as well as second in 1966, 1973 and 1978, and third in 1971, 1974 and 1975. In the Munich Olympic stadium in 1978 she added nearly two kilometres to the women's one-hour record with a distance of 43.08292 km, setting records en route at 5 km (6 minutes, 44.75 seconds), 10 km (13 minutes, 34.39 seconds) and 20 km (27 minutes, 26.66 seconds). She was Dutch national pursuit champion each year from 1966 to 1977, and road champion from 1969 to 1976 and again in 1978.

## Rik VAN STEENBERGEN (Belgium)

b. Oud-Turnhout, Arendonck, 9 September 1924

Van Steenbergen had a 24-year career as a top cyclist, retiring at the age of 42 in 1966. He equalled the record of three victories in the world professional road race (1949, 1956–57) and was also third in 1946. He rode almost continually, taking only a short midsummer break. On the track he won 1314 events, and his record of 40 victories in six-day races stood for almost 20 years. His track ability allowed him to win many one-day Classics because of his ability as a road sprinter, but his difficulty in climbing usually prevented him from being a factor in the major stage races.

**Rik van Steenbergen Major Victories**
1944   Tour of Flanders.
1946   Tour of Flanders.
1948   Paris–Roubaix.
1949   Flèche–Wallonne; World Road Race Champion.
1950   Paris–Brussels.
1952   Paris–Roubaix.
1954   Milan–San Remo.
1956   World Road Race Champion.
1957   World Road Race Champion.
1958   Flèche–Wallonne.

## Sean YATES (UK)

b. 18 May 1960

Sean Yates started every Tour de France between 1984 and 1995, finishing nine times and becoming the third Briton to wear the *maillot jaune* when he took it for one day in the early stages of the 1994 tour. His other Tour de France success was winning a time-trial stage in record time in 1988; his best result was 45th overall in 1989.

## Vyacheslav YEKIMOV (USSR)

b. Vyborg, 4 February 1966

Yekimov first took up cycling in 1980 and immediately made his name as a great pursuiter, with a record-equalling three world titles – as an amateur in 1985, 1986 and 1989 (second in 1987), to which he added another as a professional in 1990. He was world junior champion at points and team pursuit

and runner-up in the individual pursuit in 1984. In 1988 in Seoul he won an Olympic gold medal at team pursuit, but was not chosen for the individual event due to the availability of team-mate Gintautas Umaras. In late 1989, Yekimov made history when he was allowed to turn professional. Riding for Panasonic from 1990, he immediately became known as one of the fastest road sprinters and added a further world title with the points event in 1991.

Yekimov has set many world records on the track, including indoor records for the one-hour of 49.672 km in 1986, 4 km at 4 minutes, 28.900 seconds (1986), 5 km at 5 minutes, 43.514 seconds (1987) and, as a professional, 5 minutes, 40.872 seconds (1990), 10 km at 11 minutes, 31.968 seconds (1989) and 20 km at 23 minutes, 14.553 seconds (1989).

## Galina YERMOLEYEVA (USSR)

b. Tula, 4 February 1937

The most successful woman sprint cyclist at the world championships, where between 1958 and 1973 she won 14 medals: six gold (1958–61, 1963, 1972), five silver, and three bronze. She failed to win a medal only in 1962 and 1966. She set a 1 km standing start record with 1 minute, 16.2 seconds in 1965.

## Sheila YOUNG (USA)

b. Birmingham, Michigan, 14 October 1950; later known as Ochowicz

World sprint champion at two sports, speed skating in 1973 and cycling and 1976, winning the championship again at speed skating in 1975 and at cycling in 1981. At speed skating she also won three Olympic medals in 1976: gold at 500m, silver at 1500m, and bronze at 1000m. After marriage to US Olympic cyclist Jim Ochowicz in 1976, she raced for a while under this name, but reverted to her maiden name out of courtesy to announcers.

## Joop ZOETEMELK (Holland)

b. The Hague, 3 Dec 1946

Joop Zoetemelk is the only winner of the Tour de France to have also won an Olympic gold medal, which came in the 100 km team time-trial in 1968. He had a very long career, retiring after the 1987 season.

Zoetemelk was a great all-rounder who was frequently prevented from winning by either Merckx or Hinault. In the Tour de France, which he contested until 1986, he had ten stage wins and set a

*Two decades of winning gave Joop Zoetemelk an Olympic gold at the age of 22, the Tour de France at 34, the world road race championship at 39, and a last Classic win at 41*

record by finishing the race 16 times and being placed 11 times in the first five, wearing the *maillot jaune* for 22 days in 1971. His 1980 win came when Hinault was forced to retire with knee problems. In 1985 Zoetemelk capped his career by out-sprinting Greg LeMond to win the rainbow jersey of world professional road champion.

### Joop Zoetemelk Major Victories
1971 Tour of Spain – King of the Mountains.
1974 Paris–Nice.
1975 Paris–Nice.
1976 Flèche–Wallonne.
1977 Paris–Tours.
1979 Paris–Tours; Paris–Nice; Tour of Spain.
1980 Tour de France.
1985 World Road Race Champion.
1987 Amstel Gold Race.

# WHO WAS THE GREATEST ROAD RACER?

Attempting to compare the top winners over a selection of Classic races is something of a lottery when it comes to choosing both riders and events. The scores would also read differently if each of the three great Tours were weighted to count more points than the one-day Classics. However, what this table does clearly show is the majestic stature of Eddy Merckx as an all-rounder, and how the more recent big race winners such as Miguel Indurain, Tony Rominger and in particular Greg LeMond have opted to specialize and target a very few major events which gives them low scores, rather than the more liberal approach favoured by racers of old who liked to win everything in the calendar.

Key: VL – Rik van Looy; H – Bernard Hinault; C – Fausto Coppi; A – Jacques Anquetil, M – Eddy Merckx; K – Sean Kelly; LeM – Greg LeMond; I – Miguel Indurain; R – Tony Rominger; B – Alfredo Binda; de V – Roger de Vlaeminck; Ba – Gino Bartali; G – Felice Gimondi; VS –Rik Van Steenbergen; Bo – Louison Bobet

|  | VL | H | C | A | M | K | LeM | I | R | B | deV | Ba | G | VS | Bo |
|---|---|---|---|---|---|---|---|---|---|---|---|---|---|---|---|
| World Championships | 2 | 1 | 1 | 0 | 3 | 0 | 2 | 1 | 0 | 3 | 0 | 0 | 1 | 3 | 1 |
| Milan–San Remo | 1 | 0 | 3 | 0 | 7 | 2 | 0 | 0 | 0 | 2 | 3 | 4 | 1 | 1 | 1 |
| Tour of Flanders | 2 | 0 | 0 | 0 | 2 | 0 | 0 | 0 | 0 | 0 | 1 | 0 | 0 | 2 | 1 |
| Paris–Roubaix | 3 | 1 | 1 | 0 | 3 | 2 | 0 | 0 | 0 | 0 | 4 | 0 | 1 | 2 | 1 |
| Liège–Bastogne–Liège | 1 | 2 | 0 | 1 | 5 | 2 | 0 | 0 | 0 | 0 | 1 | 0 | 0 | 0 | 0 |
| Amstel Gold Race | 0 | 1 | 1 | 0 | 2 | 0 | 0 | 0 | 0 | 0 | 0 | 0 | 0 | 0 | 0 |
| Tour of Lombardy | 1 | 0 | 5 | 0 | 2 | 3 | 0 | 0 | 1 | 4 | 3 | 3 | 2 | 0 | 1 |
| GP des Nations | 0 | 5 | 2 | 9 | 1 | 1 | 0 | 0 | 2 | 0 | 0 | 0 | 2 | 0 | 1 |
| Ghent–Wevelgem | 3 | 1 | 0 | 1 | 3 | 1 | 0 | 0 | 0 | 0 | 0 | 0 | 0 | 0 | 0 |
| Flèche–Wallonne | 1 | 2 | 1 | 0 | 3 | 0 | 0 | 0 | 0 | 1 | 0 | 0 | 2 | 0 |  |
| Tour de France | 0 | 5 | 2 | 5 | 5 | 0 | 3 | 5 | 0 | 0 | 0 | 2 | 1 | 0 | 3 |
| Giro d'Italia | 0 | 3 | 5 | 2 | 5 | 0 | 0 | 2 | 1 | 5 | 0 | 3 | 2 | 0 | 0 |
| Vuelta a España | 0 | 2 | 0 | 1 | 1 | 1 | 0 | 0 | 3 | 0 | 0 | 0 | 1 | 0 | 0 |
| Paris–Nice | 0 | 0 | 0 | 5 | 3 | 7 | 0 | 2 | 2 | 0 | 0 | 0 | 0 | 0 | 0 |
| Tour of Switzerland | 0 | 0 | 0 | 0 | 1 | 2 | 0 | 0 | 0 | 0 | 1 | 2 | 0 | 0 | 0 |
| TOTAL | 14 | 23 | 20 | 24 | 46 | 21 | 5 | 10 | 9 | 14 | 14 | 14 | 11 | 10 | 9 |
|  | VL | H | C | A | M | K | LeM | I | R | B | deV | Ba | G | VS | Bo |

# How dangerous is cycle racing?

Cycling is perceived as a dangerous leisure pastime, but this is almost totally due to the threat of motor traffic which is involved in the vast majority of cycle road accidents. In professional cycling the threat of motor traffic is usually but not always absent, but the speeds achieved by the racers riding in close company mean that most professionals experience crashes during their careers.

If one rider goes down, following riders may have difficulty avoiding him, and multiple crashes can be caused by collisions with over-zealous fans or race-support motorcycles getting too close to the action. Amazingly, the resulting injuries are seldom more serious than cuts and bruises, though broken collar bones are more common amongst top racers of the track. Many top road racers still opt not to wear helmets during major events, and in the 1994 Tour de France the riders 'went on strike' when the organizers last attempted to force the issue.

Mountain bike racers are becoming increasingly prone to injury, particularly in the downhill discipline. At the European Downhill Championship in 1994 Pierre Lollo of France crashed when his front forks collapsed and was reported dead. It was later announced that he had survived the accident in a critical condition. However, despite the dangers, fatalities amongst racing pros are mercifully infrequent.

## Major Fatalities on road and track

1935    During the Tour de France Francisco Cepeda fell into a ravine near Bour d'Oisans. He died three days later.

1937    The 1936 world motor-paced champion André Reynaud (France) died on the track at Antwerp.

1950    Camille Danguillaume of France was knocked over by a motorbike and fatally injured during the French road championship at Monthléry.

1951    Serge Coppi, brother of Fausto, crashed when one kilometre from the finish of the Tour of Piedmont. He rode on over the line, but died the same night.

1956    Stan Ockers of Belgium, the 1955 World Road Race Champion, was fatally injured after fracturing his skull while track racing in Antwerp.

1967    Tom Simpson collapsed and died while climbing Mont Ventoux during the Tour de France. His death led to a crackdown on the use of stimulants.

*Despite the ever-present danger of spills on track or road, cycle racing has had an excellent safety record over the years which belies the speed and aggression of its participants*

1969    José Samyn of France hit a programme seller during a race in Belgium and was fatally injured.

1971    Jean-Pierre Monséré of Belgium, World Road Race Champion in 1970, was fatally injured due to a collision with a car during the Grand Prix de Retje.

1972    Manuel Galera of Spain suffered a fatal crash during the Tour of Andalucia.

1976    Juan-Manuel Santisteban of Spain hit a guardrail during the Tour of Italy and was killed instantly.

1984    Joaquim Agostinho of Portugal was fatally injured having fractured his skull after colliding with a dog during the Tour of Portugal.

1986    Emilio Ravasio of Italy suffered fatal head injuries in the Tour of Italy.

1987    Vincente Mata of Spain died after a collision with a car in the Luis Puig Trophy.

1987    Michel Goffin of Belgium crashed during the Tour du Haut Var and was fatally injured.

1995    Fabio Casartelli of Italy, winner of the amateur road race at the Barcelona Olympics in 1992, suffered fatal head injuries after crashing with other riders on the descent from Col de Portet d'Aspet during a Pyrenean stage of the Tour de France.

# National Road Race Championships

## UNITED KINGDOM

*(UK unless stated)*

| 1947 | 1. D Jaggard | 2. B Whitmore | 3. A Bailey |
|------|--------------|---------------|-------------|
| 1948 | 1. Harold Johnson | 2. J Raine | 3. Ted Jones |
| 1949 | 1. Bob Thom | 2. Len West | 3. Mike Peers |
| 1950 | 1. Len West | 2. Ted Jones | 3. Ken Russell |
| 1951 | 1. Dave Bedwell | 2. Les Scales | 3. Bob Thom |
| 1952 | 1. Tan Steel | 2. Bob Maitland | 3. Tiny Thomas & Les Scales |
| 1953 | 1. Bob Maitland | 2. Tan Stell | 3. Tiny Thomas & Ken Jowett |
| 1954 | 1. Arthur Ilsley | 2. Fred Krebs | 3. Bob Maitland |
| 1955 | 1. Graham Vines | 2. Bob Maitland | 3. Ken Russell |
| 1957 | 1. Ron Coe | 2. Richard Baltrop | 3. Brian Haskell |
| 1958 | 1. Ron Coe | 2. Brian Haskell | 3. Tom Oldfield |
| 1959 | 1. Ron Coe | 2. Owen Blowe | 3. John Geddess |
| 1961 | 1. Dave Bedwell | 2. Tony Mills | 3. Ron Jowers |
| 1962 | 1. John Harvey | 2. Dave Bedwell | 3. Ged Coles |
| 1963 | 1. Albert Hitchen | 2. Ken Nuttall | 3. Alan Jacobs |
| 1964 | 1. Keith Butler | 2. Albert Hitchen | 3. Ged Coles |
| 1965 | 1. Albert Hitchen | 2. Mick Coupe | 3. Keith Butler |
| 1966 | 1. R Goodman | 2. Bernard Burns | 3. Roger Newton |
| 1967 | 1. Colin Lewis | 2. Roger Newton | 3. Peter Hill |
| 1968 | 1. Colin Lewis | 2. John Aslin | 3. Reg Smith |
| 1969 | 1. Bill Lawrie (AUS) | 2. Dave Nie | 3. Mick Cowley |
| 1970 | 1. Les West | 2. Brian Jolly | 3. Colin Lewis |
| 1971 | 1. Danny Horton | 2. Sid Barras | 3. Albert Hitchen |
| 1972 | 1. Gary Crewe | 2. Les West | 3. Derek Harrison |
| 1973 | 1. Brian Jolly | 2. Les West | 3. Billy Bilsland |
| 1974 | 1. Keith Lambert | 2. William Bilsland | 3. Phil Bayton |
| 1975 | 1. Leslie West | 2. Keith Lambert | 3. Danny Horton |
| 1976 | 1. Geoff Wiles | 2. Sid Barras | 3. Phil Corley |
| 1977 | 1. Phil Edwards | 2. Paul Medhurst | 3. Geoff Wiles |
| 1978 | 1. Phil Corley | 2. Bill Nickson | 3. Reg Smith |
| 1979 | 1. Sid Barras | 2. Barry Hoban | 3. Dudley Hayton |
| 1980 | 1. Keith Lambert | 2. Bill Nickson | 3. Dudley Hayton |
| 1981 | 1. Bill Nickson | 2. Nigel Dean | 3. Graham Jones |
| 1982 | 1. John Herety | 2. Sean Yates | 3. Bill Nickson |
| 1983 | 1. Phil Thomas | 2. Keith Lambert | 3. M Morrison |
| 1984 | 1. Steve Joughin | 2. W Nickson | 3. M Elliott |
| 1985 | 1. Tan Banbury | 2. D Hayton | 3. M Bell |
| 1986 | 1. Mark Bell | 2. A Timmis | 3. St Joughin |
| 1987 | 1. Paul Sherwen | 2. J Herety | 3. J Kershaw |
| 1988 | 1. Steve Joughin | 2. N Barnes | 3. C Lillywhite |
| 1989 | 1. Timothy Harris | 2. M Walsham | 3. N Barnes |
| 1990 | 1. Colin Sturgess | 2. Beni Luckwell | 3. Harry Lodge |
| 1991 | 1. Brian Smith | 2. Keith Reynolds | 3. David Rayner |
| 1992 | 1. Sean Yates | 2. Brian Smith | 3. Chris Walker |

| 1993 | 1. Malcolm Elliott | 2. Brian Smith | 3. Shane Sutton |
| 1994 | 1. Brian Smith | 2. Malcolm Elliott | 3. Mark Walsham |
| 1995 | 1. Robert Millar | 2. Chris Walker | 3. Pierre Painaud (France) |

# USA

*(USA unless stated)*

| 1985 | 1. Eric Heiden | 2. Tom Broznowski | 3. Tom Schuler |
| 1986 | 1. Thomas Prehn | 2. Doug Shapiro | 3. Thurlow Rogers |
| 1987 | 1. Thom Schuler | 2. Roy Knickman | 3. Garry Fornes |
| 1988 | 1. Ron Kiefel | 2. Doug Shapiro | 3. Karl Maxon |
| 1989 | 1. Greg Oravetz | 2. Mike Engleman | 3. Alexi Grewal |
| 1990 | 1. Kurt Stockton | 2. Andy Bishop | 3. Kenny Adams |
| 1991 | 1. Davis Phinney | 2. Kurt Stockton | 3. Greg Oravetz |
| 1992 | 1. Bart Bowen | 2. Andy Bishop | 3. Jamie Paolinetti |
| 1993 | 1. Lance Armstrong | 2. Scott McKinley | 3. Jamie Paolinnetti |
| 1994 | 1. Steve Hegg | 2. Scott Fortner | 3. Mike Engelman |
| 1995 | 1. Chann McRae | 2. Fred Rodriguez | 3. Jeff Evanshine |

*Held as the Philadelphia G.P. from 1985-92*

# AUSTRALIA

*(Australian unless stated)*

| 1950 | Keith Rowley | 1965 | Matt Martino | 1980 | John Trevorrow |
| 1951 | John Beasley | 1966 | Kerry Hoole | 1981 | Clyde Sefton |
| 1952 | Neil Peadon | 1967 | Graeme Gilmore | 1982 | Wayne Hildred |
| 1953 | Alby Saunders | 1968 | Barry Waddell | 1983 | Terry Hammond |
| 1954 | Eddy Smith | 1969 | Rob Whretters | 1984 | Peter Besanko |
| 1955 | Eddy Smith | 1970 | Graham McVilly | 1985 | Laurie Venn |
| 1956 | Russell Mockridge | 1971 | Graham McVilly | 1986 | Wayne Hildred |
| 1957 | Russell Mockridge | 1972 | Kevin Spencer | 1987 | Allan Dipple |
| 1958 | Russell Mockridge | 1973 | Kerry Hoole | 1988 | Paul Miller |
| 1959 | Fred Roche | 1974 | Graham Rowley | 1989 | Garry Clively |
| 1960 | Fred Roche | 1975 | Donald Wilson | 1990 | Dean McDonald |
| 1961 | Neville Veale | 1976 | Peter Desanko | 1991 | Neil Stephens |
| 1962 | John O'Sullivan | 1977 | Donald Wilson | 1992 | David McFarlane |
| 1963 | Warwick Dalton (NZ) | 1978 | John Trevorrow | 1993 | Eddie Salas |
| 1964 | Barry Waddell | 1979 | John Trevorrow | 1994 | n/a |
| | | | | 1995 | Neil Stephens |

# MAJOR STAGE RACES IN THE UK AND USA

## AMATEUR/OPEN TOUR OF BRITAIN

The Tour of Britain cycle race was first held in 1951 when it was sponsored by the Daily Express. After a two year lay-off it was sponsored by the Milk Marketing Board from 1958 onwards and became known as the Milk Race, becoming one of the most important amateur events in the international calendar. In 1983 it became an open event, and was last held in 1993 after which it lost its Milk Marketing Board sponsorship.

■ Four riders have won the Tour of Britain (Milk Race) twice each – Bill Bradley (UK) 1959, 1960; Les West (UK) 1965, 1967; Fedor den Hertog (NL) 1969, 1971; and Yuri Kashurin (USSR) 1979, 1982.

*Racing beneath Big Ben in the 1987 professional Tour of Britain. The event was last held in 1994 and seems unlikely to be revived in the near future*

■ The closest race ever was in 1976 when after 1665.67 km (1035 miles) and 14 days (30 May – 12 June) Bill Nickson (b. UK, 1953) beat Joe Waugh (UK) by five seconds.

■ The fastest average speed in the Tour of Britain is 48.185 kmh (26.213 mph) by Joey McLoughlin (b. UK, 3 December 1964) in the 1714 km (1065 mile) 1986 race.

■ The longest ever Tour of Britain was 2624.84 kilometres (1631 miles) in 1953, starting and finishing in London.

### Amateur Tour of Britain Winners

| | |
|---|---|
| 1951 | Ian Steel (UK) |
| 1952 | Ken Russell (UK) |
| 1953 | Gordon Thomas (UK) |
| 1954 | Eugene Tamburlini (F) |
| 1955 | Anthony Hewson (UK) |
| 1958 | Anthony Hewson (UK) |
| 1959 | Richard Durlacher (A) |
| 1960 | Richard Durlacher (A) |
| 1961 | Billy Holmes (UK) |
| 1962 | Eugen Pokorny (POL) |
| 1963 | Peter Chisman (UK) |
| 1964 | Arthur Metcalfe (UK) |
| 1965 | Les West (UK) |
| 1966 | Josef Gawliczek (POL) |
| 1967 | Les West (UK) |
| 1968 | Gösta Pettersson (SWE) |
| 1969 | Fedor Den Hertog (NL) |
| 1970 | Jiri Mainus (CZ) |
| 1971 | Fedor Den Hertog (NL) |
| 1972 | Hennie Kuiper (NL) |
| 1973 | Piet van Katwijk (NL) |
| 1974 | Roy Schuiten (NL) |
| 1975 | Bernt Johansson (SWE) |
| 1976 | Bill Nickson (UK) |
| 1977 | Said Gusseinov (USSR) |
| 1978 | Jan Brzezny (POL) |
| 1979 | Yuriy Kashirin (USSR) |
| 1980 | Ivan Mitchtenko (USSR) |
| 1981 | Sergey Krivocheyev (USSR) |
| 1982 | Yuri Kashirin (USSR) |
| 1983 | Matt Eaton (USA) |
| 1984 | Oleg Czougeda (USSR) |
| 1985 | Eric van Lancker (B) |
| 1986 | Joey McLoughlin (UK) |
| 1987 | Malcolm Elliott (UK) |
| 1988 | Vasiliy Zhdanov (USSR) |
| 1989 | Brian Walton (CDN) |
| 1990 | Shane Sutton (AUS) |
| 1991 | Chris Walker (UK) |
| 1992 | Conor Henry (IRL) |
| 1993 | Chris Lillywhite (UK) |

## TOUR OF GREAT BRITAIN
## (Professional)

The 1994 Tour sponsored by Kelloggs was marred by an accident when a motorist ignored police signals to stop and drove his car into the bunch near Kirkstone Pass in the Lake District on the second stage. Among the injured riders was Dutchman Adri Van Der Poel who had won the previous day's city centre criterium in Glasgow and was forced to pull out. The riders staged a 20-minute stoppage in protest. Owing to lack of sponsorship there was no professional Tour of Britain in 1995.

**Professional Tour of Britain Winners**

| | |
|---|---|
| 1987 | 1. Joey McLoughlin (UK) 2. S Rooks (NL) 3. S Finazzi (I) |
| 1988 | 1. Malcolm Elliott (UK) 2. J McLoughlin (UK) 3. Sean Kelly (IRL) |
| 1989 | 1. Robert Millar (UK) 2. Mauro Gianetti (SWI) 3. Remig Stumpf (D) |
| 1990 | 1. Michel Dernies (B) 2. Robert Millar (UK) 3. Maurizio Fondriest (I) |
| 1991 | 1. Phil Anderson (AUS) 2. Rudy Verdonck (B) 3. H Imboden (SWI) |
| 1992 | 1. Maximillian Sciandri (I) 2. Adri Van der Poel (NL) 3. Hendrick Redant (B) |
| 1993 | 1. Phil Anderson (AUS) 2. Wladimir Belli (I) 3. Bo-André Namdvedt (NOR) |
| 1994 | 1. Maurizio Fondriest (I). 2. Vyacheslav Ekimov (RUS). 3. Olaf Ludwig (D). |

*Joey McLoughlin kisses his trophy after victory in the first professional Tour of Britain. Malcolm Elliott and Robert Millar followed, after which there were no British winners*

**Tour Du Pont Winners**

| | |
|---|---|
| 1991 | 1. Erik Breukink (NL) 2. Atle Kvalsvoll (NOR) 3. Rolf Aldag (D) |
| 1992 | 1. Greg LeMond (USA) 2. Atle Kvalsvoll (NOR) 3. Stephan Swart (NZ) |
| 1993 | 1. Raul Alcala (MEX) 2. Lance Armstrong (USA) 3. Atle Kvalsvoll (NOR) |
| 1994 | Viatcheslav Ekimov (RUS). 2. Lance Armstrong (USA). 3. Andrea Peron (I) |
| 1995 | 1. Lance Armstrong (USA). 2. Vjatcheslav Ekimov (RUS). 3. Andrea Peron (I). |

## TOUR DU PONT

The principal American stage race is the Tour Du Pont which was preceded by the Tour de Trump (named after Donald Trump) in 1989 and 1990. The only riders to take part in all seven tours between 1989 and 1995 were Americans Ron Kiefel and Steve Hegg.

■ In 1995 Lance Armstrong became the first American to lead the Tour du Pont since Greg LeMond in 1992. Both riders went on to win. In 1995 Lance Armstrong overtook Davis Phinney's record of 12 stage wins.

■ The 1995 tour was broadcast to a potential TV audience of 750 million viewers in 137 countries.

■ Briton Malcolm Elliott wore the race leader's jersey into Richmond in both the 1984 and 1985 tours. Richmond is the only city to have hosted a stage in all seven tours.

*Lance Armstrong in action on the 1994 Tour du Pont. After finishing second that year and in 1993, he dominated the event to win overall in 1995*

# MAJOR ROAD-RACING POINTS COMPETITIONS

## DESGRANGE—COLOMBO CHALLENGE

The Desgrange–Colombo Challenge was the first points competition based on finishing positions in specified classics including the major Tours. It was established in memory of Henri Desgrange, the French founder of the Tour de France, and Emilio Colombo, the Italian editor of *Gazzetta dello Sport*. The Challenge eventually came to an end in 1958 due to disagreements over which races should be included.

Desgrange–Colombo Challenge Winners

| | |
|---|---|
| 1948 | Briek Schotte (B) |
| 1949 | Fausto Coppi (I) |
| 1950 | Ferdi Kübler (SWI) |
| 1951 | Louison Bobet (F) |
| 1952 | Ferdi Kübler (SWI) |
| 1953 | Loretto Perucci (I) |
| 1954 | Ferdi Kübler (SWI) |
| 1955 | Stan Ockers (B) |
| 1956 | Fred de Bruyne (B) |
| 1957 | Fred de Bruyne (B) |
| 1958 | Fred de Bruyne (B) |

Most wins

| | |
|---|---|
| 3 | Fred de Bruyne, Ferdi Kübler |

## SUPER PRESTIGE PERNOD TROPHY

The Super Prestige Pernod Trophy first started in 1958 when it was only open to French riders. For the next two years it was open to all professional road racers, but only events on French soil (including the Tour de France) counted. Then in 1961 it was changed to include major European one-day and stage races, with a steady increase in the number of events counting for points. This peaked at 33 events in the last year of the Super Prestige Pernod Trophy in 1987.

Criticisms of the Trophy included too many events, overlapping events, and an unfair distribution of points for different races and different positions. However, primarily because of the French government's ban of alcohol advertising in sports promotion, the series came to an end in 1987.

Super Prestige Pernod Trophy Winners

| | |
|---|---|
| 1958 | Forestier (F) |
| 1959 | Anglade (F) |
| 1960 | Graczyk (F) |
| 1961 | Jacques Anquetil (F) |
| 1962 | Jo de Roo (NL) |
| 1963 | Jacques Anquetil (F) |
| 1964 | Raymond Poulidor (F) |
| 1965 | Jacques Anquetil (F) |
| 1967 | Jan Janssen (NL) |
| 1968 | Herman Vanspringel (B) |
| 1969 | Eddy Merckx (B) |
| 1970 | Eddy Merckx (B) |
| 1971 | Eddy Merckx (B) |
| 1972 | Eddy Merckx (B) |
| 1973 | Eddy Merckx (B) |
| 1974 | Eddy Merckx (B) |
| 1975 | Eddy Merckx (B) |
| 1976 | Freddy Maertens (B) |
| 1977 | Freddy Maertens (B) |
| 1978 | Francesco Moser (I) |
| 1979 | Bernard Hinault (F) |
| 1980 | Bernard Hinault (F) |
| 1981 | Bernard Hinault (F) |
| 1982 | Bernard Hinault (F) |
| 1983 | Greg LeMond (USA) |
| 1984 | Sean Kelly (IRL) |
| 1985 | Sean Kelly (IRL) |
| 1986 | Sean Kelly (IRL) |
| 1987 | Stephen Roche (IRL) |

Most wins

| | |
|---|---|
| 7 | Eddy Merckx |
| 4 | Bernard Hinault |
| 3 | Jacques Anquetil, Sean Kelly |

Between 1958 and 1984 Briton Tom Simpson was the only rider from an English-speaking country to have achieved a top three placing in the Super Prestige Pernod Trophy. He finished second in 1965. From 1983 until the final year of the Super Prestige Pernod Trophy the top places were dominated by riders from English-speaking countries.

| | |
|---|---|
| 1983 | 1. Greg LeMond (USA). 2. Sean Kelly (IRL). 3. Giuseppe Saronni (I) & Jan Raas (NL). |
| 1984 | 1. Sean Kelly (IRL). 2. Bernard Hinault (F). 3. Phil Anderson (AUS). |
| 1985 | 1. Sean Kelly (IRL). 2. Phil Anderson (AUS). 3. Greg LeMond (USA). |
| 1986 | 1. Sean Kelly (IRL). 2 Greg LeMond (USA). 3 Claude Criquielion (B). |
| 1987 | 1. Stephen Roche (IRL). 2. Sean Kelly. 3. Claude Criquielion (B). |

In 1989 Sean Kelly (left) took up where he had left off, winning the first year of the World Cup after winning the Super Prestige Pernod Trophy in 1984, 1985 and 1986, giving second best to fellow countryman Stepehen Roche (right) in 1987

## WORLD CUP

There was no points series in 1988, and the first World Cup of road racing, sponsored by Perrier, was introduced in 1989. In this series riders amass points in a set number of 12 or so major one-day races throughout the year. There have been a few changes in events included over the years which have been built around the Milan–San Remo, Tour of Flanders, Paris–Roubaix, Liège–Bastogne–Liège, Amstel Gold Race, Leeds Classic, San Sebastian, Meisterschaft von Zurich, Paris–Tours and Tour of Lombardy.

**World Cup Winners**
| | |
|---|---|
| 1989 | Sean Kelly (IRL) |
| 1990 | Gianni Bugno (I) |
| 1991 | Maurizio Fondriest (I) |
| 1992 | Olaf Ludwig (D) |
| 1993 | Maurizio Fondriest (I) |
| 1994 | Gianluca Bortolami (I) |
| 1995 | Johan Museeuw (NL) |

# The Olympic Games

Cycling was included in the first Olympics of 1896 and has been at every Games since, except in 1904 when there were no official events. A women's road race was first introduced in 1984, followed by the women's sprint in 1988 and the women's individual pursuit in 1992. Mountain biking, in the form of cross-country racing, will be introduced for the first time in the 1996 Olympics.

**Early medal winners**
The first Olympic cycling champion was Léon Flameng of France who won the 100 km race on 8 April 1896 in Athens. The event was held on a 333.33m cement track and involved 300 circuits. Four men have won a record three gold medals: Paul Masson of France (1874–1945) in 1896, Francisco Verri of Italy (1885–1945) in 1906, Frenchman Robert Charpentier (1916–66) in 1936, and Daniel Morelon, also of France, who won two in 1968 and one in 1972. Of these only Morelon won other medals, a bronze in 1964 and a silver in 1976, both in the 1000m sprint. He also won a record seven world amateur titles.

*The British team of Payne, Jones, Meredith and Kingsbury took the gold medal in the first ever team pursuit at the 1908 Olympics in London*

■ The cycling events held at St Louis in 1904 were not accepted as official Olympic events but it should be noted that Marcus Hurley (USA) won four of them at 1/4, 1/3, 1/2 and one mile; Burton Down (USA 1885–1929) won at two miles and 25 miles; and Charles Schlee (USA) won at five miles. In addition to two gold medals, Burton Down won three silver and one bronze, making six medals in all.

■ The first pair of brothers to win a medal was the Götze duo, Bruno and Max, of Germany who won the tandem silver in 1906. The greatest family performance in Olympic cycling is that by the Pettersson brothers of Sweden – Gösta, Sture, Erik and Tomas. The first three brothers, together with Sven Hamrin, won a bronze medal in the 1964 team road race. Then in 1968 they included their younger brother in the team and all four won the silver, only 99.54 seconds behind the gold medal team over the 102 km course.

**Drugs and Sportsmanship**
Although it is known that a number of athletes, particularly distance runners, were taking stimulants in the early Olympic Games, one of the first cases in the era following World War Two came to light in cycling. In the 1960 100 km race two Danish riders collapsed. One, Knut Jensen, later died from what was diagnosed as sunstroke. It was then reported that both riders had taken overdoses of a blood-circulation stimulant.

■ The sport has also furnished two extremes in the field of bad and good Olympic sportsmanship. In 1936 Robert Charpentier beat his team-mate Guy Lapébie by 0.2 seconds at the end of the 100 km road race, when the latter inexplicably slowed down just before the line. It was later discovered, in a photograph of the finish, that Charpentier had pulled Lapébie back by his shirt. At the other end of the credit scale was the action of another Frenchman, Léon Flameng, who was far ahead of the only other competitor, a Greek, left in the 1896 100 km track race, when his opponent's cycle broke down. Flameng sportingly stopped and waited until it was replaced, before continuing to win by six laps.

■ Excellent facilities have been built for many of the Olympic cycling programmes since the special track constructed around the athletics circuit at the White City for the 1908 Games in London. One of the most remarkable sites was the magnificent Jachioji velodrome in Tokyo used for the 1964 events. Built at a cost of $840,000 and used for only four days during the Games, it was demolished within a year as part of another building scheme. In 1968 the short-distance events, as in other sports, benefited greatly from the altitude of Mexico City. In the tandem race Daniel Morelon and Pierre Trentin of France achieved the greatest speed ever in Olympic Games cycling when they clocked 9.83 seconds for the last 200 metres, an average speed of 73.24 kmh (45.51 mph). Sergey Kopylov (USSR) set a new record for an individual rider at 68.76 kmh (42.73 mph) in Moscow in 1980, when he was timed at 10.47 sec for the last 200 metres in the 1000m time-trial at the Krylatskoye stadium. The longest race ever in the Games was the 1912 road race which was held over a 320 km (198.8 miles) course.

■ Relatively few top professional cyclists competed at the Olympics as amateurs. Eddy Merckx, five times winner of the Tour de France and arguably one of the greatest road racers of all time, competed in the Games only once, in 1964. Unfortunately he was involved in an accident not far from the finish and came 12th, although only 0.11 seconds behind the winner. Coincidentally, the man with whom he shares the record of five wins in the Tour de France, Jacques Anquetil, also finished in 12th place in the Olympic road race in 1952. Patrick Sercu, gold medallist in the 1964 1000m time-trial, also holds the record for professional six-day racing events.

■ The youngest rider to win a gold medal was Franco Giorgetti (Italy) in the 1920 team pursuit event when he was aged 17 years and 304 days. The oldest gold medallist was Maurice Peeters (Holland) who won the 1000m sprint in 1920 aged 38 years and 99 days. Four years later he gained a bronze in the tandem event aged 42 years and 83 days to become the oldest-ever medallist in Olympic cycling. The only American woman to win a cycling gold medal is Connie Carpenter-Phinney who won the individual road race in 1984, which was the first Olympic cycling event to be held for women. In the same Games her husband Davis won a bronze medal in the 100 km team event. She also became the first woman to compete in both the Winter and Summer Olympics, as, when aged 14, she had competed as a speed skater in 1972.

## Hosts of the Olympic Games

| | |
|---|---|
| 1896 | Athens |
| 1900 | Paris |
| 1904 | St Louis, USA (unofficial – not recognized) |
| 1906 | Athens |
| 1908 | London |
| 1920 | Antwerp |
| 1924 | Paris |
| 1928 | Amsterdam |
| 1932 | Los Angeles |
| 1936 | Berlin |
| 1948 | London |
| 1952 | Helsinki |
| 1956 | Melbourne |
| 1960 | Rome |
| 1964 | Tokyo |
| 1968 | Mexico |
| 1972 | Munich |
| 1976 | Montreal |
| 1980 | Moscow |
| 1984 | Los Angeles |
| 1988 | Seoul |
| 1992 | Barcelona |

## MEN'S OLYMPIC MEDAL RESULTS

### Sprint

*In 1896 and 1900 the sprint was held over 2000 metres. Since then it has been held over 1000 metres, with the best of three races counting. From 1924 onwards only the time in seconds over the last 200 metres has been recorded.*

| | |
|---|---|
| 1896 | G: Paul Masson (F) 4:56.0. S: Stamatios Nikolopoulos (GRE). B: Léon Flameng (F). |
| 1900 | G: Georges Taillandier (F) 2:52.0. Taillandier covered the last 200m in 13 seconds. S: Fernand Sanz (F). B: John Lake (USA). |
| 1906 | G: Francesco Verri (I) 1:42.2. S: H.C. Bouffler (GB). B: Eugène Debougnie (B). |
| 1908 | Declared void as the riders exceeded the time limit in spite of repeated warnings. |
| 1920 | G: Maurice Peeters (NL) 1:38.3. S: H. Thomas Johnson (GB). B: Harry Ryan (GB). |
| 1924 | G: Lucien Michard (F) 12.8. S: Jacob Meijer (NL). B: Jean Cugnot (F). |
| 1928 | G: Roger Beaufrand (F) 13.2. S: Antoine Mazairac (NL). B: Willy Falck-Hansen (DNK). |
| 1932 | G: Jacobus van Egmond (NL) 12.6. S: Louis Chaillot (F). B: Bruno Pellizzari (I). |
| 1936 | G: Toni Merkens (D) 11.8. S: Arie van Vliet (NL). B: Louis Chaillot (F). |
| 1948 | G: Mario Ghella (I) 12.0. S: Reginald |

Harris (GB). B: Axel Schandorff (DNK).

1952   G: Enzo Sacchi (I) 12.0. S: Lionel Cox (AUS). B: Werner Potzernheim (D).

1956   G: Michel Rousseau (F). 11.4. S: Guglielmo Pesenti (I). B: Richard Ploog (AUS).

1960   G: Sante Gaiardoni (I) 11.1. S: Leo Sterckz (B). B: Valentina Gasparella (I).

1964   G: Giovanni Pettenella (I) 13.69. S: Sergio Bianchetto (I). B: Daniel Morelon (F).

1968   G: Daniel Morelon (F) 10.68. S: Giordano Turrini (I). B: Pierre Trentin (F).

1972   G: Daniel Morelon (F) 11.25. S: John Nicholson (AUS). B: Omarc Pchakadze (URS).

1976   G: Anton Tkac (CZ) 10.78. S: Daniel Morelon (F). B: Hans-Jurgen Geschke (GDR).

1980   G: Lutz Hesslich (GDR) 11.40. S: Yave Cahard (F). B: Sergey Kopylov (USSR).

1984   G: Mark Gorski (USA). S: Nelson Vails (USA). B: Tsutomu Sakamoto (JPN).

1988   G: Lutz Hesslich (GDR). S: Nikolay Kovche (USSR). B: Gary Neiwand (AUS).

1992   G: Jens Fiedler (D). S: Gary Neiwand (AUS). B: Curtis Harnett (CDN).

## 1000m Time Trial

*In 1896 and 1906 this event was raced over a distance of 333.33 metres. Between 1908 and 1924 it was not held.*

1896   G: Paul Masson (F) 24.0. S: Stamatios Nikolopoulos (GRE) 25.4. B: Adolf Schmal (A) 26.6.

1906   G: Francesco Verri (I) 22.8. S: Herbert Crowther (GB) 22.8. B: Menjou (F) 23.2.

1928   G: Willy Falck-Hansen (DNK) 1:14.4. S: Gerard Bosch van Drakestein (NL) 1:15:2. B: Edgar Gray (AUS) 1:15:6.

1932   G: Edgar Gray (AUS) 1:13.0. S: Jacobus van Egmond (NL) 1:13:3. B: Charles Rampelberg (F) 1:13:4.

1936   G: Arie van Vliet (NL) 1:12.0. S: Pierre Georget (F) 12:8. B: Rudolf Karsch (D) 1:13:2.

1948   G: Jacques Dupont (F) 1:13.5. S: Pierre Nihant (B) 1:14.5. B: Thomas Godwin (GB) 1:15.0.

1952   G: Russell Mockridge (AUS) 1:11.1. S: Marino Morettini (I) 1:12:7. B: Raymond Robinson (SA) 1:13:0.

1956   G: Leandro Faggin (I) 1:09.8. S: Ladislav Foucek (CZ) 1:11:4. B: J. Alfred Swift (SA) 1:11:6.

1960   G: Sante Gaiardoni (I) 1:07.27. S: Dieter Gieseler (D) 1:08:75. B: Rotislav

Vargashkin (USSR) 1:08:86.

1964   G: Patrick Sercu (B) 1:09.59. S: Giovanni Pettenella (I) 1:10.09. B: Pierre Trentin (F) 1:10.42.

1968   G: Pierre Trentin (F) 1:03.91. S: Niels-Christian Fredborg (DNK) 1:04.61. B: Janusz Kierzkowski (POL) 1:04.63.

1972   G: Niels-Christian Fredborg (DNK) 1:06.44. S: Daniel Clark (AUS) 1:06.87. B: Jürgen Schuetze (GDR) 1:07.02.

1976   G: Klaus-Jürgen Grunke (GDR) 1:05.93. S: Michel Vaarten (B) 1:07.52. B: Niels-Christian Fredborg (DNK) 1:07.62.

1980   G: Lothar Thoms (GDR) 1:02.955. S: Aleksandr Pantilov (USSR) 1:04.845. B: David Weller (JAM) 1:05.241.

1984   G: Freddy Schmidtke (FRG) 1:06.10. S: Curtis Harnett (CDN) 1:06.44. B: Fabrice Colas (F) 1:06.65.

1988   G: Aleksandre Kirichenko (USSR) 1:04.499. S: Martin Vinnicombe (AUS) 1:04.784. B: Robert Lechner (FRG) 1:05.114.

1992   G: José Manuel Moreno (E) 1:03.342. S: Shane Kelly (AUS) 1:04.288. B: Eric Hartwell 1:04.753.

## 4000m Individual Pursuit

*This event was first held in 1964. In 1992 Chris Boardman caught his opponent Jens Lehmann a lap from the finish, having recorded a new record time of 4 minutes, 24.496 seconds in a preliminary round.*

1964   G: Jiri Daler (CZ) 5:04.75. S: Giorgio Ursi (I) 5:05.96. B: Preben Isaksson (DNK) 5:01.90.

1968   G: Daniel Rebillard (F) 4:41.71. S: Morgens Frey Jensen (DNK) 4:42.43. B: Xavier Kurmann (SWI) 4:39.42.

1972   G: Knut Knudsen (NOR) 4:45.74. S: Xavier Kurmann (SWI) 4:51.96. B: Hans Lutz (FRG) 4:50.80.

1976   G: Gregor Braun (GDR) 4:47.61. S: Herman Ponsteen (NL) 4:49.72. B: Thomas Huschke (GDR) 4:52.71.

1980   G: Robert Dill-Bundi (SWI) 4:35.66. S: Alain Bondue (F) 4:42.96. B: Hans-Henrik Orsted (DNK) 4:36.54.

1984   G: Steve Hegg (USA) 4:39.55. S: Rolf Gölz (FRG) 4:43:82. B: Leonard Nitz (USA) 4:44.03.

1988   G: Gintautas Umaras (USSR) 4:32.00. S: Dean Woods (AUS) 4:35.00. B: Bernd Dittert (GDR) 4:34.17.

1992   G: Chris Boardman (GB). S: Jens Lehmann (DNK). B: Gary Anderson (NZ).

## 50 km Points Race
*First held in 1984.*

1984    G: Roger Ilegems (B) 37 pts. S: Uwe Messerschmidt (FRG). B: José Youshimatz (MEX).

1988    G: Dan Frost (DNK) 38 pts. S: Leo Peelen (NL). B: Marat Ganeyev (USSR).

1992    G: Giovanni Lombardi (I) 44 pts. S: Leon van Bon (NL). B: Cédric Mathy (B).

## Individual Road Race
*Between 1912 and 1928 this event was held as a time trial. The road race distance in kilometres is shown for each year.*

1896    G: Aristidis Konstantinidis (GRE) 3:22:31.0 – 87 km. S: August Goedrick (DNK) 3:42:18.0. B: F. Battel (GB).

1906    G: Fernand Vast (F) 2:41:28.0 – 84 km. S: Maurice Bardonneau (F) 2:41:28.4. B: Edmund Lugnet (F) 2:41:28.6.

1912    G: Rudolph Lewis (SA) 10:42:39.0 – 320 km. S: Frederick Grubb (GB) 10:51:24.2. B: Carl Schutte (USA) 10:52:38.8.

1920    G: Harry Stenqvist (SWE) 4:40:01.8 – 175 km. S: Henry Kaltenbrun (SA) 4:41:26.6. B: Fernand Canteloube (F) 4:42:54.4.

1924    G: Armand Blanchonnet (F) 6:20:48.0 – 188 km. S: Henry Hoevenaers (B) 6:30:27.0. B: René Hamel (F) 6:40:51.6.

1928    G: Henry Hansen (DNK) 4:47:18.0 – 168 km. S: Frank Southall (GB) 4:55:06.0. B: Gösta Carlsson (SWE) 5:00:17.0.

1932    G: Attillo Pavesi (I) 2:28:05.6 – 100 km. S: Guglielmo Segato (I) 2:29:21.4. B: Bernhard Britz (SWE) 2:29:45:2.

1936    G: Robert Charpentier (F) 2:33:05.0 – 100 km. S: Guy Lapébie (F) 2:33:05.2. B: Ernst Nievergeit (SWI) 2:33:05.8.

1948    G: José Beyaert (F) 5:18:12.6 – 194.63 km. S: Gerardus Voorting (NL) 5:18:16.2. B: Lode Wouters (B) 5:18:16.2.

1952    G: André Noyelle (B) 5:06:03.4 – 190.40 km. S: Robert Grondelaers (B) 5:06:51.1. B: Edi Ziegler (D) 5:07:47.5.

1956    G: Ercole Baldini (I) 5:21:17.0 – 187.73 km. S: Arnaud Gevre (F) 5:23:16.0. B: Alan Jackson (GB) 5:23:16.0.

1960    G: Viktor Kapitonov (USSR) 4:20:37.0 – 175.38 km. S: Livio Trape (I) 4:20:37.0. B: Willy van den Berghen (B) 4:20:57.0.

1964    G: Mario Zanin (I) 4:39:51.0 – 194.83 km. S: Kjell Rodian (DNK) 4:39:51.65. B: Walter Godefroot (B) 4:39:51.74.

1968    G: Pierfranco Vianelli (I) 4:14:37.0 – 196.20 km. S: Leif Mortensen (DNK) 4:42:49.71. B: Gösta Pettersson (SWE) 4:43:15.24.

1972    G: Hennie Kuiper (NL) 4:14:37.0 – 182.40 km. S: Kevin Sefton (AUS) 4:15:04.0. (Jaime Huelamo [E] finished third but medal withdrawn following a drug test.)

1976    G: Bernt Johansson (SWE) 4:46:52.0 – 175.00 km. S: Giuseppe Martinelli (I) 4:47:23.0. B: Mieczyslaw Nowicki (POL) 4:47:23.0.

1980    G: Sergey Sukhoruchenkov (USSR) 4:48:28.9 – 189.00 km. S: Czeslaw Lang (POL) 4:51:26.9. B: Yuriy Barinov (USSR) 4:51:26.9.

1984    G: Alexi Grewal (USA) 4:59:57.0 – 196.00 km. S: Steve Bauer (CDN) 4:59:57.0. B: Dag Otto Lauritzen (NOR) 5:00:18.0.

1988    G: Olaf Ludwig (GDR) 4:32:22.0 – 196.80 km. S: Bernd Gröne (FRG) 4:32:25.0. B: Christian Henn (FRG) 4:32:46.0.

1992    G: Fabio Casarteli (I) 4:35:21.00 – 195 km. S: Erik Dekker (NL). B: Dainis Ozols (LAT).

## Team Road Race
*In 1912 and 1920 this event was decided on the combined times of the best four riders from each country in the individual road race. From 1924 to 1952 it was decided on the combined times of the best three riders. In 1956, the last year this event was held, it was based on placings.*

1912    G: Sweden 44:35:33.6. S: Great Britain 44:44:39.2. B: United States 44:47:55.5.

1920    G: France 19:16:43.2. S: Sweden 19:23:10.0. B: Belgium 19:28:44:4.

1924    G: France 19:13:14.0. S: Belgium 19:46:55.4. B: Sweden 19:59:41.6.

1928    G: Denmark 15:09:14.0. S: Great Britain 15:14:49.0. B: Sweden 15:27:49.0.

1932    G: Italy 7:27:15.2. S: Denmark 7:38:50:2. B: Sweden 7:39:12.6.

1936    G: France 7:39:16.2. S: Switzerland 7:39:20.4. B: Belgium 7:39:21.0.

1948    G: Belgium 15:58:17.4. S: Great Britain 16:03:31.6. B: France 16:08:19.4.

1952    G: Belgium 15:20.46.6. S: Italy 15:33:27.3. B: France 15:38:58.1.

1956    G: France 22 points. S: Great Britain 23 points. B: Germany 27 points.

## 4000m Team Pursuit
*This event was first held over 1810.5 metres in 1908. It was not held in 1912. In 1968 the Federal Republic of Germany team finished first but were disqualified for illegal assistance. However, after the Games ended the International Cycling Federation*

*Ben Jones, winner of the 5000m race at the 1908 Olympics, on a bike that is not dissimilar to racing machines of today*

*awarded them the silver medal. In 1980 Italy finished third, but were disqualified.*

1908    G: Great Britain 2:18.6. S: Germany 2:28.6. B: Canada 2:29.6.

1920    G: Italy 5:20.0. S: Great Britain. B: South Africa.

1924    G: Italy 5:15.0. S: Poland. B: Belgium.

1928    G: Italy 5:01:8 S: Netherlands 5:06.2. B: Great Britain.

1932    G: Italy 4:53.0. S: France 4:55.7. B: Great Britain 4:56.0.

1936    G: France 4:45.0. S: Italy 4:51.0. B: Great Britain 4:52.6.

1948    G: France 4:57.8. S: Italy 4:36.7. B: Great Britain 4:55.8.

1952    G: Italy 4:46.1. S: South Africa 4:53.6. B: Great Britain 4:51.5.

1956    G: Italy 4:37.4. S: France 4:39.4. B: Great Britain 4:42.2.

1960    G: Italy 4:30.90. S: FRG 4:35.78. B: Soviet Union 4:34.05.

1964    G: FRG 4:35.67. S: Italy 4:35.74. B: Netherlands 4:38.99.

1968    G: Denmark 4:22.44. S: FRG 4:18.94. B: Italy 4:18.35.

1972    G: FRG 4:22.14. S: GDR 4:25.25. B: Great Britain 4:23.78.

1976    G: FRG 4:21.06. S: Soviet Union 4:27.15. B: Great Britain 4:22.41.

1980    G: USSR 4:15.70. S: GDR 4:19.67. B: Czechoslovakia*.

1984    G: Australia 4:25.99. S: United States 4:29.85. B: FRG 4:25.60.

1988    G: USSR 4:13.31. S: GDR 4:14.09. B: Australia 4:16.02.

1992    G: Germany 4:08.791. S: Australia 4:10.218. B: Denmark 4:18.291.

* Bronze awarded to Czechoslovakia after Italy were disqualified from third place.

## 100 km Road Team Time-Trial
*Held over 109.89 km in 1964, 102 km in 1968 and 101 km in 1980.*

1960    G: Italy 2:14:33.53. S: Germany 2:16:56.31. B: Soviet Union 2:18:41.67.

1964    G: Netherlands 2:26:31.19. S: Italy 2:26:55.39. B: Sweden 2:27:11.52.

1968    G: Netherlands 2:07:49.06. S: Sweden 2:09:26.60. B: Italy 2:10:18.74.

1972    G: USSR 2:11:17.8. S: Poland 2:11:47.5. (The Dutch team finished third, but were disqualified after drug tests).

1976    G: USSR 2:08:53.0. S: Poland 2:09:13.0. B: Denmark 2:12:20.0.

1980    G: USSR 2:01:21.7. S: GDR 2:02:53.2. B: Czechoslovakia 2:02:53.9.

1984    G: Italy 1:58:28.0. S: Switzerland 2:02:38.0. B: United States 2:02:46.0.

1988    G: GDR 1:57:47.7. S: Poland 1:57:54.2. B: Sweden 1:59:47.3.

1992    G: Germany 2:01:39. S: Italy. B: France.

## Discontinued Men's Track Events

### 660 Yards Sprint
1908    G: Victor Johnson (GB) 51.2. S: Emile Demangel (F) close. B: Karl Neumer (D) 1 length.

### 5000m
1906    G: Francesco Verri (I) 8:35.0. S: Herbert Crowther (GB). B: Fernand Vast (F).

1908    G: Benjamin Jones (GB) 8:36:2. S: Maurice Schilles (F). B: André Auffray (F).

### 10,000m
1896    G: Paul Masson (F) 17:54.2. S: Léon Flameng (F). B: Adolf Schmal (A).

### 20,000m
1906    G: William Pett (GB) 29:00.0. S: Maurice Bardonneau (F) 29:30:0. B: Fernand Vast (F) 29:32.0.

1908    G: Charles Kingsbury (GB) 34:13.6. S: Benjamin Jones (GB). B: Joseph Werbrouck (B).

### 50,000m
1920    G: Henry George (B) 1:16:43.2. S: Cyril Alden (GB). B: Petrus Ikelaar (NL).

1924    G: Jacobus Willems (NL) 1:18:24.0. S: Cyril Alden (GB). B: Frederick Wyld (GB).

### 100 km
1896    G: Léon Flameng (F) 3:08:19.2. S: G. Kolettis (GRE) 6 laps.

1908    G: Charles Bartlett (GB) 2:41:48.6. S: Charles Denny (GB). B: Octave Lapize (F).

**12 Hours**
1896    G: Adolf Schmal (A) 314.997 km. S: F. Keeping (GB) 314.664 km. B: Georgios Paraskeveopoulos (GRE) 13.330 km.

**Men's 2000m Tandem**
*From 1924 to 1972 times were recorded only over the last 200 metres.*
1906    G: John Matthews & Arthur Rushen (GB) 2:57.0. S: Germany. B: Germany.
1908    G: Maurice Schilles & André Auffray (F) 3:07.8. S: Great Britain. B: Great Britain.
1920    G: Harry Ryan & Thomas Lance (GB) 2:49.4. S: South Africa. B: Holland.
1924    G: Lucien Choury & Jean Cugnot (F) 12.6. S: Denmark. B: Holland.
1928    G: Bernhard Leene & Daan van Dijk (NL) 11.8. S: Great Britain. B: Germany.
1932    G: Maurice Perrin & Louis Chaillot (F) 12.0. S: Great Britain. B: Denmark.
1936    G: Ernst Ihbe & Carl Lorenz (D) 11.8 S: Holland B: France
1948    G: Renato Perona & Ferdinando Terruzzi (I) 11.3. S: Great Britain. B: France.
1952    G: Lionel Cox & Russell Mockridge (AUS) 11.0 S: South Africa. B: Italy.
1956    G: Ian Browne & Anthony Marchant (AUS) 10.8. S: Czechoslovakia. B: Italy.
1960    G: Giuseppe Beghetto & Sergio Bianchetto (I) 10.7. S: Germany. B: USSR.
1964    G: Sergio Bianchetto & Angelo Damiano (I) 10.75. S: USSR. B: Germany.
1968    G: Daniel Morelon & Pierre Trentin (F) 9.83. S: Holland. B: Belgium.
1972    G: Vladimir Semenets & Igor Tselovalnikov (USSR) 10.52. S: GDR. B: Poland.

## WOMEN'S OLYMPIC MEDAL RESULTS

**Road Race**
1984    G: Connie Carpenter-Phinney (USA) 2:11:11.0 – 79.2 km. S: Rebecca Twigg (USA) 2:11:14.0. B: Sandra Schumacher (FRG) 2:11:14.0.
1988    G: Monique Knol (NL) 2:00:52.0 – 82.0 km. S: Jutta Niehaus (FRG) close. B: Laima Zilporiteye (USSR) close.
1992    G: Kathryn Watt (AUS) 2:04:42 – 81.0 km. S: Jeannie Longo (F). B: Monique Knol (NL).

**Sprint (1000m)**
1988    G: Erika Salumyae (USSR). S: Christa Rothenburger-Luding (GDR). B: Connie Young (USA).

1992    G: Erika Salumyae (EST). S: Annett Neumann (D). B: Ingrid Haringa (NL).

**3000m Individual Pursuit**
1992    G: Petra Rossner (D). S: Kathryn Watt (AUS). B: Rebecca Twigg (USA).

## Record Holders

*The Most Gold Medals*
Three gold medals have each been won by Paul Masson (France) in 1896, Francisco Verri (Italy) in 1906, Robert Charpentier (France) in 1936 and Daniel Morelon (France) between 1968 and 1972.

*The Most Medals*
Five medals have been won by Daniel Morelon, who as well as three golds also won a silver in 1976 and bronze in 1964, both in the sprint.

## Cycling Medals — Totals

|  | Men | | | Women | | | Total |
|---|---|---|---|---|---|---|---|
| *Country* | G | S | B | G | S | B |  |
| France | 27 | 15 | 21 | - | 1 | - | 64 |
| Italy | 28 | 15 | 6 | - | - | - | 49 |
| Great Britain | 9 | 21 | 14 | - | - | - | 44 |
| United States* | 10 | 9 | 13 | 1 | 1 | 2 | 36 |
| Germany (FRG) | 8 | 12 | 12 | 1 | 2 | 1 | 36 |
| USSR | 10 | 4 | 8 | 1 | - | 1 | 24 |
| Holland | 8 | 13 | 4 | 1 | - | 2 | 28 |
| Belgium | 6 | 6 | 10 | - | - | - | 22 |
| Denmark | 7 | 6 | 8 | - | - | - | 21 |
| GDR | 7 | 5 | 4 | - | 1 | - | 17 |
| Australia | 5 | 9 | 4 | 1 | 1 | - | 20 |
| Sweden | 3 | 2 | 8 | - | - | - | 13 |
| South Africa | 1 | 4 | 3 | - | - | - | 8 |
| Poland | - | 5 | 3 | - | - | - | 8 |
| Czechoslovakia | 2 | 2 | 2 | - | - | - | 6 |
| Switzerland | 1 | 3 | 2 | - | - | - | 6 |
| Greece | 1 | 3 | 1 | - | - | - | 5 |
| Austria | 1 | - | 2 | - | - | - | 3 |
| Canada | - | 2 | 2 | - | - | - | 4 |
| Norway | 1 | - | 1 | - | - | - | 2 |
| Jamaica | - | - | 1 | - | - | - | 1 |
| Japan | - | - | 1 | - | - | - | 1 |
| Mexico | - | - | 1 | - | - | - | 1 |
| Spain | 1 | - | - | - | - | - | 1 |
| New Zealand | - | - | 1 | - | - | - | 1 |
| Latvia | - | - | 1 | - | - | - | 1 |
| Estonia | - | - | - | 1 | - | - | 1 |
| *Total* | 136 | 136 | 133** | 6 | 6 | 6 |  |

* Includes seven events in 1904 in USA formerly excluded.
** No bronzes in 1896 100 km, 1972 road team-trial and individual road race.

# COMMONWEALTH GAMES

**1966    Kingston, Jamaica**
*1000m Sprint:* R. Gibbon (Trinidad)
*1000m Time-Trial:* R. Gibbon (Trinidad)
*10 miles Scratch:* I. Alsop (England)
*4000m Individual Pursuit:* Hugh Porter (England)
*120 miles Road Race:* P. Buckley (Isle of Man)

**1970    Edinburgh, Scotland**
*1000m Sprint:* J. Nicholson (Australia)
*1000m Time-Trial:* H. Kent (New Zealand)
*10 miles Scratch:* J. Lovell (Canada)
*2000m Tandem:* G. Johnson and R. Jonker
          (Australia)
*4000m Individual Pursuit:* Ian Hallam (England)
*120 miles Road Race:* B. Biddle (NZ)

**1974    Christchurch, New Zealand**
*1000m Sprint:* J. Nicholson (Australia)
*1000m Time-Trial:* D. Paris (Australia)
*10 miles Scratch:* S. Hefferman (England)
*2000m Tandem:* G. Cooke and E. Crutchlow (England)
*4000m Individual Pursuit:* I. Hallam (England)
*4000m Team Pursuit:* I. Hallam, W. Moore, R.
          Evans, M. Bennett (England)
*120 miles Road Race:* C. Sefton (Australia)

**1978    Edmonton, Canada**
*1000m Sprint:* K. Tucker (Australia)
*1000m Time-Trial:* J. Lovell (Canada)
*10 miles Scratch:* J. Lovell (Canada)
*2000m Tandem:* J. Lovell and G. Singleton (Canada)
*4000m Individual Pursuit:* M. Richards (New Zealand)
*4000m Team Pursuit:* Australia
*120 miles Road Race:* Phil Anderson (Australia)

**1982    Brisbane, Australia**
*1000m Sprint:* K. Tucker (Australia)
*1000m Time-Trial:* C. Adair (New Zealand)
*10 miles Scratch:* K. Nichols (Australia)
*4000m Individual Pursuit:* M. Turner (Australia)
*4000m Team Pursuit:* Australia
*100 km Team Time-Trial:* R. Downs, M. Elliot, S.
          Lawrence, J. Waugh (England)
*120 miles Road Race:* M. Elliott (England)

**1986    Edinburgh, Scotland**
*1000m Sprint:* G. Neiwand (Australia)
*1000m Time-Trial:* M. Vinnicombe (Australia)
*10 miles Scratch:* W. McCarney (Australia)
*4000m Individual Pursuit:* D. Woods (Australia)
*4000m Team Pursuit:* Australia
*100 km Team Time-Trial:* P. Curran, D. Davie, A.
          Gornall, K. Reynolds (England)
*105 miles Road Race:* P. Curran (England)

**1990    Auckland, New Zealand**
*1000m Sprint:* G. Neiwand (Australia)
*1000m Time-Trial:* M. Vinicombe (Australia)
*10 miles Scratch:* G. Anderson (New Zealand)
*50 km Points:* R. Burns (Australia)
*4000m Individual Pursuit:* G. Anderson (New
          Zealand)
*4000m Team Pursuit:* N. Donnelly, G. McLeay, S.
          Williams, G. Anderson (New Zealand)
*1000m Women's Sprint:* L. Jones (Wales)
*3000m Women's Pursuit:* M. Harris (New Zealand)
*100 km Team Time-Trial:* G. Miller, I. Richards, B.
          Fowler, G. Stevens (New Zealand)
*107 miles Road Race:* G. Miller (New Zealand)
*45 miles Women's Road Race:* K. Watt (Australia)

**1994    Victoria, Canada**
*1000m Sprint:* Gary Neiwand (Australia)
*1000m Time-Trial:* Shane Kelly (Australia)
*10-miles Scratch:* Stuart O'Grady (Australia)
*40 km Points:* Brett Aitken (Australia)
*4000m Individual Pursuit:* Bradley McGee
          (Australia)
*4000m Team Pursuit:* Australia
*1000m Women's Sprint:* Tanya Dubnicoff (Canada)
*3000m Women's Pursuit:* Kathryn Watt (Australia)
*25 km Women's Points Race:* Yvonne McGregor
          (England)

*The British team in action at the 1994 Commonwealth Games held in Victoria, Canada. The medals were again dominated by Australia*

# UK Track Records

## MEN'S RECORDS

### Bicycles – Unpaced Standing Start

| Event | min:sec | Cyclist | Location | Date |
|---|---|---|---|---|
| 500m | 33.8 | P Medhurst | Herne Hill | 1976 |
| 1 km | 1:04.297 | S Wallace | Quito | 1995 |
| 4 km | 4:20.894 | G Obree | Hamar | 1993 |
| 5 km | 5:35.026 | C Sturgess | Stuttgart | 1991 |
| 10 km | 11:18.13 | G Obree | Bordeaux | 1994 |
| 20 km | 22:39.03 | G Obree | Bordeaux | 1994 |
| 1 hr | 52.713 km | G Obree | Bordeaux | 1994 |
| 4 km Team | 4:13.522 | M Illingworth B Steel S Lillistone C Newton | Bogota | 1995 |

### Bicycles – Unpaced Flying Start

| | | | | |
|---|---|---|---|---|
| 200m | 10.704 | E Alexander | Vienna | 1987 |
| 500m | 27.984 | S Wallace | Manchester | 1995 |
| 1 km | 58.995 | S Wallace | Colorado | 1986 |

### Bicycles – Motor Paced Standing Start

| | | | | |
|---|---|---|---|---|
| 10 km | 8:30.4 | M Coles | Leicester | 1981 |
| 25 km | 20:49 | M Coles | Leicester | 1981 |
| 50 km | 41:46 | M Coles | Leicester | 1981 |
| 1 hr | 70.506 km | R Notley | Leicester | 1976 |

## WOMEN'S RECORDS

### Bicycles – Unpaced Standing Start

| | | | | |
|---|---|---|---|---|
| 500m | 36.266 | W Everson | Bogota | 1995 |
| 1 km | 1:14.18 | S Boyden | Manchester | 1995 |
| 3 km | 3:40.916 | Y McGregor | Bogota | 1995 |
| 5 km | 6:20.573 | Y McGregor | Manchester | 1995 |
| 10 km | 12:36.044 | Y McGregor | Manchester | 1995 |
| 20 km | 25:08.530 | Y McGregor | Manchester | 1995 |
| 1 hr | 47.411 km | Y McGregor | Manchester | 1995 |

### Bicycles – Unpaced Flying Start

| | | | | |
|---|---|---|---|---|
| 200m | 11.651 | W Everson | Bogota | 1995 |
| 500m | 33.245 | S Boyden | Manchester | 1995 |
| 1 km | 1:09.91 | S Boyden | Manchester | 1995 |

## JUNIOR MEN'S RECORDS

**Bicycles – Unpaced Standing Start**

| | | | | |
|---|---|---|---|---|
| 1 km | 1:05.518 | G Sadler | Leicester | 1980 |
| 3 km | 3:29.549 | R Prince | Leicester | 1982 |
| 4 km Team | 4:29.21 | C Newton | Colorado | 1991 |
| | | R Hayles | | |
| | | A Forbes | | |
| | | P Jennings | | |

**Bicycles – Unpaced Flying Start**

| | | | | |
|---|---|---|---|---|
| 200m | 11.730 | J Taylor | Leicester | 1993 |
| 500m | 30.80 | C Hoy | Meadowbank | 1994 |

## JUNIOR WOMEN'S RECORDS

**Bicycles – Unpaced Standing Start**

| | | | | |
|---|---|---|---|---|
| 500m | 37.453 | M Hughes | Manchester | 1995 |
| 2 km | 2:41.107 | E Davies | Manchester | 1995 |

**Bicycles – Unpaced Flying Start**

| | | | | |
|---|---|---|---|---|
| 200m | 12.503 | M Hughes | Manchester | 1995 |
| 500m | 33.772 | E Davies | Manchester | 1994 |

## JUVENILE (under 16) MEN'S RECORDS

**Bicycles – Unpaced Standing Start**

| | | | | |
|---|---|---|---|---|
| 500m | 35.757 | K Niblett | Leicester | 1992 |
| 2 km | 2:26.982 | S Jones | Manchester | 1995 |

**Bicycles – Unpaced Flying Start**

| | | | | |
|---|---|---|---|---|
| 200m | 11.754 | J Taylor | Leicester | 1992 |
| 500m | 32.397 | S Jones | Manchester | 1995 |

## JUVENILE (under 16) MEN'S RECORDS

**Bicycles – Unpaced Standing Start**

| | | | | |
|---|---|---|---|---|
| 500m | 41.014 | E Davies | Manchester | 1994 |
| 2 km | 2:51.13 | E Davies | Manchester | 1994 |

**Bicycles – Unpaced Flying Start**

| | | | | |
|---|---|---|---|---|
| 200m | 13.593 | C Gross | Manchester | 1995 |
| 500m | 35.61 | E Davies | Leicester | 1994 |

## BRITISH ALLCOMERS' RECORDS

**Bicycles – Unpaced Standing Start**

| | | | | |
|---|---|---|---|---|
| 500m | 33.4 | G Singleton | Leicester | 1982 |
| 1 km | 1:05.8 | F Schmidtke | Leicester | 1982 |

**Bicycles – Unpaced Flying Start**

| | | | | |
|---|---|---|---|---|
| 200m | 10.7 | G Singleton | Leicester | 1982 |
| 500m | 28.333 | G Singleton | Leicester | 1982 |

# UK Road Records

## The Roads Records' Association

The Road Records' Association was formed on 11 April 1888, at a meeting at Freemason's Tavern, Great Queen Street, London. Sidney A. Chalk was appointed Hon. Secretary and Treasurer. Records already passed by the National Cyclists' Union were placed on the book for 50 miles, 100 miles, 24 hours and Land's End to John O'Groats. In 1889 place-to-place records were recognized for London to Bath and back, London to York, London to Edinburgh, and London to Liverpool.

In 1890 London to Brighton and back was added to the records list, using the coach route from Piccadilly to the Old Ship Hotel. A Liverpool–Edinburgh record route was also added. In 1893 all restrictions on the popular London–Brighton route were lifted, with new start and turn-round points at Hyde Park Corner and the Brighton Aquarium. Record Challenge Shields were presented for the 50- and 100-mile bicycle records, the 12- and 24-hour bicycle records, the 24-hour tricycle record, and for the London to Bath and back and London to Brighton and back records. In 1894 a record challenge shield was presented for the Land's End to John O'Groats record.

## The Police Intervene

Interest in record breaking soon began to tail off due to police opposition. Only four claims to records were passed in 1896 compared to a high of 37 in 1890. However the 1000-mile and Edinburgh-to-York records were added in 1897, when unpaced records were also added as a separate class. The first unpaced record was recorded by A.A. Chase a year later when he cycled 50 miles in 2 hours, 5 minutes, 8 seconds. Record routes were added for London to Portsmouth and back and Land's End to London in 1899.

In 1900 motor pacing was banned, but as the RRA entered the 20th century the number of affiliated clubs was reduced to five with many changing their allegiances from road to track. The activities of the Association were then suspended during World War One, and in 1919 only one new claim to a record was passed, which until then was the lowest figure ever.

In 1920 the use of motor vehicles was permitted for all purposes except pacing and in 1923 the rule prohibiting Sunday records was rescinded, both moves intended to help popularize the RRA. On 20 March 1945, the Association lost its founder and first President (1890–1924), Arthur James Wilson, who died at the age of 87. Another prominent member, Harry Green, died in June 1950. During his career he broke 15 records at distances from 50 to 800 miles, six of which stood for more than 20 years.

## The RRA Today

Despite the changes to Britain's roads and the huge growth in traffic, the RRA still attracts a steady number of would-be record breakers. Place-to-place records follow definitive routes, while mileage records, such as 50 or 100 miles, can be attempted in any part of Great Britain provided there are easily distinguishable landmarks for the starting, turning and finishing points. However an attempt cannot be made by riding up and down the same stretch of road. To make it a true 'road record', the RRA rules state that a rider covering any portion of a road more than twice shall not be credited with the distance covered on the third and subsequent occasions except in unforeseen circumstances.

## The Women's Roads Records' Association

On 4 October 1934 the inaugural meeting of the Women's Road Records' Association was held at Craven Hill, London W2. Mrs Evelyn Parkes was appointed President, and 13 record routes and distances with standard times were adopted for bicycle, tandem, tricycle, and tricycle tandem, with a further 12 records being recognized over the years. In 1977 the rule recognizing separate amateur and professional classes was rescinded. The first proposal to merge with the Road Records' Association was defeated in 1981, but by 1987 both associations were keen to combine forces. Eventually on 1 January 1989 the trophies, records and assets of the Women's RRA were formally transferred to the Road Records' Association. A total of 177 records had been recorded during the 54 years of the Women's RRA as an independent association.

## 'ORDINARY' BICYCLE RECORDS

*(Pacing was permitted in these records.)*

**50 Miles**

| | Hrs:Mins.Sec |
|---|---|
| 1888  A Pellant | 3:14.13 |

| | | |
|---|---|---|
| 1888 | A Pellant | 3:14.07 |
| 1888 | G R White | 2:57.47 |
| 1890 | R J Ilsley | 2:56.46 |
| 1890 | J F Walsh | 2:51.10 |
| 1890 | H J Howard (Best on solid tyres) | 2:49.17 |
| 1891 | R J Ilsley | 2:46.20 |
| 1891 | S C Houghton | 2:45.55 |

## 100 Miles

| | | |
|---|---|---|
| 1888 | F H Williams | 7:06.18 |
| 1888 | G R White | 6:48.14 |
| 1890 | J F Walsh (Best on solid tyres) | 6:47.15 |
| 1890 | R C Nesbitt | 6:27.30 |
| 1981 | J F Walsh | 6:22.15 |

## 12 Hours

| | | Miles |
|---|---|---|
| 1889 | G T Langridge | 154 |
| 1890 | R C Nesbitt | 155.5 |
| 1890 | J F Walsh (Best on solid tyres) | 164 |
| 1891 | J F Walsh | 175.5 |

## 24 Hours

| | | |
|---|---|---|
| 1885 | G P Mills | 259 |
| (Best on solid tyres) | | |
| 1891 | J F Walsh | 312 |

## Land's End to John O'Groats

| | | Days:Hrs:Mins |
|---|---|---|
| 1885 | J Lennox | 6:16:07 |
| 1886 | G P Mills | 5:01:45 |

## London to Bath and back

| | | Hrs:Mins.Sec |
|---|---|---|
| 1891 | R C Nesbitt | 15:40.34 |

## London to Brighton and back

| | | |
|---|---|---|
| 1892 | R C Nesbitt | 7:42.50 |

# MEN'S UNPACED BICYCLE RECORDS

## 25 Miles

| | | Mins.Sec |
|---|---|---|
| 1970 | D A Cottington | 47.55 |
| 1971 | P W Crofts | 47.00 |
| 1977 | A S Richards | 46.23 |
| 1982 | D C Lloyd | 42.37 |
| 1991 | I S Cammish | 41.21 |

## 50 Miles

| | | Hrs:Mins.Sec |
|---|---|---|
| 1898 | A A Chase | 2:07.08 |
| 1906 | H Green | 2:06.46 |
| 1909 | H Green | 2:01.02 |
| 1922 | L Meredith | 2:00.32 |
| 1928 | L Cave | 1:57.13 |

| | | |
|---|---|---|
| 1928 | J Lauterwasser | 1:54.47 |
| 1934 | F W Southall | 1:46.31 |
| 1938 | H H Hill | 1:44.30 |
| 1939 | H Earnshaw | 1:39.42 |
| 1970 | P D Smith | 1:39.29 |
| 1970 | D A Cottington | 1:39.23 |
| 1974 | D C Lloyd | 1:35.45 |
| 1990 | I S Cammish | 1:34.22 |
| 1990 | P Longbottom | 1:30.14 |
| 1991 | I S Cammish | 1:24.32 |

## 100 Miles

| | | |
|---|---|---|
| 1900 | R N Cary | 5:26.06 |
| 1900 | H Green | 5:03.43 |
| 1902 | H Green | 4:36.22 |
| 1924 | L Meredith | 4:35.16 |
| 1924 | J W Rossiter | 4:33.38 |
| 1927 | C Marshall | 4:32.03 |
| 1928 | J Lauterwasser | 4:13.35 |
| 1928 | C Marshall | 4:06.30 |
| 1934 | F W Southall | 3:55.44 |
| 1938 | H James | 3:45.51 |
| 1953 | K H Joy | 3:45.12 |
| 1956 | R C Booty | 3:28.40 |
| 1990 | I S Cammish | 3:16.56 |
| 1993 | I S Cammish | 3:11.11 |

## 1000 Miles

| | | Days:Hrs:Mins |
|---|---|---|
| 1907 | G A Olley | 4:09:03 |
| 1907 | W Welsh | 4:07:41 |
| 1908 | T A Fisher | 3:19:01 |
| 1909 | W Welsh | 3:15:57 |
| 1930 | J W Rossiter | 3:11:58 |
| 1934 | H Opperman | 3:01:52 |
| 1937 | S H Ferris | 2:22:40 |
| 1956 | A Render | 2:16:50 |
| 1960 | R F Randall | 2:10:40 |

## 12 Hours

| | | Miles |
|---|---|---|
| 1898 | A F Ilsley | 187 |
| 1898 | E Gould | 191 |
| 1898 | E Gould | 201.5 |
| 1900 | H Green | 226.5 |
| 1926 | J W Rossiter | 242 |
| 1934 | H Opperman | 243 |
| 1934 | F W Southall | 253 |
| 1938 | H James | 259.25 |
| 1939 | H Earnshaw | 276.25 |
| 1989 | P G Wells | 283.63 |
| 1991 | P G Wells | 292.63 |

## 24 Hours Bicycle

| | | Miles |
|---|---|---|
| 1900 | T G King | 346.5 |

| | | |
|---|---|---|
| 1901 | T G King | 357 |
| 1901 | H Green | 394 |
| 1922 | M G Selbach | 397.25 |
| 1923 | C F Davey | 402.5 |
| 1931 | E B Brown | 416.5 |
| 1934 | H Opperman | 431.5 |
| 1934 | F W Southall | 454 |
| 1935 | H Opperman | 461.75 |
| 1938 | C Heppleston | 464.75 |
| 1938 | S H Ferris | 465.75 |
| 1939 | C Heppleston | 467.75 |
| 1954 | K H Joy | 475.75 |
| 1982 | M Coupe | 482.5 |
| 1982 | P J Woodburn | 494.5 |

## LAND'S END TO JOHN O'GROATS

*Days:Hrs:Mins.Sec*

**Paced**

| | | |
|---|---|---|
| 1891 | G P Mills | 4:11:17 |
| 1892 | T A Edge | 4:00:40 |
| 1892 | L Fletcher | 3:23:55 |
| 1894 | R H Carlisle | 3:14:15 |
| 1894 | G P Mills | 3:05:49 |

**Unpaced**

| | | |
|---|---|---|
| 1903 | C J Mather | 5:05:12 |
| 1904 | F W Wesley | 4:07:25 |
| 1905 | G A Olley | 3:20:15 |
| 1907 | T Peck | 3:12:53 |
| 1907 | W Welsh | 3:08:04 |
| 1908 | G A Olley | 3:05:20 |
| 1908 | T Peck | 2:22:42 |
| 1908 | H Green | 2:19:50 |
| 1929 | J W Rossiter | 2:13:22 |
| 1934 | H Opperman | 2:09:01 |
| 1937 | S H Ferris | 2:06:33 |
| 1958 | D J Keeler | 2:03:09 |
| 1958 | R F Randall | 2:01:58 |
| 1965 | R W E Poole | 1:23:46.35 |
| 1979 | P A Carbutt | 1:23:23.01 |
| 1982 | M Coupe | 1:22:39.49 |
| 1982 | P J Woodburn | 1:21:03.16 |
| 1990 | A Wilkinson | 1:21:02.18 |

## WOMEN'S UNPACED BICYCLE RECORDS

**25 Miles**

*(Out and Home until 1981)*

*Hrs:Mins.Sec*

| | | | |
|---|---|---|---|
| 1936 | T M Biggs | Am | 1:13.18 |
| 1937 | M Ball | Am | 1:09.29 |
| 1940 | M Wilson | Pro | 1:06.16 |
| 1947 | S M Farrell | Am | 1:05.31 |
| 1947 | J Dean | Am | 1:03.29 |
| 1954 | E Sheridan | Pro | 1:03.58 |

| | | | |
|---|---|---|---|
| 1960 | J Bowers | Am | 1:02.01 |
| 1960 | J Kershaw | Am | 1:01.39 |
| 1961 | B Burton | Am | 1:00.31 |
| 1966 | B Burton | Am | 59.32 |
| 1981 | P J Strong | Am | 56.05 |
| 1989 | S E Wright | Am | 47.46 |

**50 Miles**

| | | | |
|---|---|---|---|
| 1935 | J M Springall | Am | 2:13.09 |
| 1939 | M Wilson | Pro | 2:09.36 |
| 1940 | A Briercliffe | Am | 2:09.29 |
| 1940 | M Wilson | Pro | 2:07.59 |
| 1940 | A Briercliffe | Am | 1:59.14 |
| 1941 | M Wilson | Pro | 1:56.33 |
| 1954 | E Sheridan | Pro | 1:55.00 |
| 1989 | S E Wright | Am | 1:36.46 |

**100 Miles**

| | | | |
|---|---|---|---|
| 1936 | T M Biggs | Am | 5:14.11 |
| 1938 | T M Biggs | Am | 4:48.07 |
| 1938 | M Wilson | Am | 4:31.08 |
| 1952 | E Sheridan | Pro | 4:16.01 |
| 1965 | L J Partington | Am | 4:27.06 |
| 1990 | S E Wright | Am | 3:50.39 |
| 1991 | P J Strong | Am | 3:49.42 |

**1000 Miles**

*Days:Hrs:Mins*

| | | | |
|---|---|---|---|
| 1938 | L Dredge | Pro | 4:19:14 |
| 1939 | M Wilson | Pro | 3:11:44 |
| 1953 | W Wrightson | Am | 3:15:53 |
| 1954 | E Sheridan | Pro | 3:01:00 |

*Time to be beaten*

**12 Hours**

*Miles*

| | | | |
|---|---|---|---|
| 1937 | R Wright | Am | 205.25 |
| 1938 | P Wellington | Am | 211 |
| 1938 | M Wilson | Am | 215 |
| 1939 | M Wilson | Pro | 230 |
| 1952 | E Sheridan | Pro | 231 |
| 1953 | E Atkins | Am | 234.75 |
| 1953 | E Sheridan | Pro | 238 |
| 1953 | E Sheridan | Pro | 250.5 |
| 1970 | A Horswell | Am | 259 |
| 1992 | P J Strong | Am | 259.5 |

**24 Hours**

| | | | |
|---|---|---|---|
| 1936 | L Dredge | Pro | 339.75 |
| 1938 | F Wren | Am | 355.5 |
| 1938 | P Wellington | Am | 377.25 |
| 1939 | M Wilson | Pro | 396 |
| 1953 | E Atkins | Am | 422 |
| 1953 | E Sheridan | Pro | 442.75 |
| 1954 | E Sheridan | Pro | 446.25 |

# UK Time-Trial Road Records

The first National Cyclists' Union time-trial championships were held in 1878 when A.A. Weir won in a time of 1 hour, 27 minutes, 47 seconds on a high Ordinary. These early events were not like the time trials of today where riders race against the clock alone and are not allowed to pace one another. They were held as mass participation road races with non-competitiors sometimes riding parts of the course to give assistance to those racing, and by the 1880s they had fallen foul of the police who were known to charge the racers on horses and throw sticks into their wheels. This drove time trials off the roads and onto tracks by the mid-1890s, but by the turn of the century they were back on the roads where competitors had resorted to dressing in black tights with black alpaca jackets so as to be inconspicuous, as well as holding their events early in the mornings in underpopulated areas. No prior publicity of events was allowed, in order to evade the attentions of the police.

■ In 1895 F.T. Bidlake had devised the system of sending competitors off alone at fixed intervals and timing them over the course. His idea was that competitors would appear to be ordinary cyclists riding along the road and would therefore escape the attentions of the police. This helped to earn him the title of 'Father of Time Trialling'. The North Road CC ran the first of these new-style events – 100 years later a centenary 50-Mile Time-Trial was held using exactly the same course.

■ In 1930 the magazine *Cycling* announced a British Best All-Rounder (BBAR) competition with a 25-guinea award to each year's winner. This was to be a season-long competition for the best combined average speed for each rider's best qualifying ride at 50 miles, 100 miles and 12 hours. Frank Southall of Norwood Paragon CC won the first four years of the BBAR competition between 1930 and 1933, his best average being 21.852 mph in 1931. In 1944 the rules of the competition were changed to include 25, 50 and 100 miles and exclude 12 hours. Ian Cammish of Manchester Wheelers won the BBAR a record six times between 1980 and 1985, and still holds the BBAR record average of 27.355 set in 1983. He also held the 50-mile record for 11 years between 1983 and 1993, and has held the 100-mile record since 1983 at 3 hours, 31 minutes, 53 seconds at an average of 28.317 mph.

*In 1895 F.T. Bidlake became the 'Father of Time-Trialling'. A hundred years later modern time-triallists rode the same 50-mile course in honour of his pioneering work*

■ Gethin Butler won the BBAR for the second time in 1995, becoming the second man to top 27 mph with an average of 27.148. His father Keith Butler was national amateur road champion in 1962 and professional road champion in 1964. His grandfather Stan Gethin rode in the 1932 Olympics.

■ Modern time-trialling dates from the first meeting of the Road Racing Council at the Cyclists' Touring offices in Euston Road, London on 27 June 1922. F.T. Bidlake was elected Chairman. At one time he was holder of the 50-mile, 100-mile, 12-hour and

24-hour tricycle records, but his life was cut short when he was killed by a car in 1933. The Road Racing Council later evolved into the Road Time Trials Council which held its first meeting in the Strand, London on 16 November 1937.

■ The principal rules of time-trialling have stayed the same for more than 50 years:

● The interval between starters should not be less than one minute.
● Competitors start at an allotted time or lose the time by which they are late.
● Having started, a competitor is not allowed a second start.
● Competitors must ride alone and unassisted. No shelter can be taken from another rider or any vehicle.

■ Despite steadily increasing problems with road traffic, road time-trialling has proved the most healthy aspect of cycle sport in the UK. In 1938 the RTTC calendar listed 429 time trials, and its first handbook sold 5564 copies. Fifty years later there were 2069 time trials in the 1987 calendar and 11,500 copies of the handbook were sold.

■ Having taken his first 25-mile competition record in 1959, Alf Engers of Polytechnic CC was first to break the 50-minute/30mph barrier for 25 miles with a time of 49 minutes, 24 seconds set in August 1978. He held the record until 1990. He won the 25-mile national championship a record six times in 1969 and 1972–76; Chris Boardman has come closest to this achievement, winning the title five times between 1989 and 1993.

■ Medium gear 25-mile time trials using gears limited to 72 inches enjoyed a period of popularity. A total of 13 riders have ridden a 25 in less than 60 minutes using a medium gear, led by Tony Doyle who achieved a record time of 56 minutes, 30 seconds in February 1980 at an average pedalling speed of 124 rpm.

■ Every 25-mile national championship between the inaugural event in 1944 and 1960 was won by riders using a fixed rear-wheel gear. In 1961 John Woodburn of Barnet CC became the first rider to win the championship using a freewheel and multiple gearing, and the event has never been won by a fixed-gear bike since.

■ Beryl Burton dominated women's time-trials over 25 years. She won 25 consecutive British All-Rounder championships, 72 individual time-trial national championships and held 50 women's time-trial competition records from 10 miles to 24 hours. She held the 10-mile record for eight years; the 15-mile record three times and held it with a time of 32 minutes, 56 seconds set in 1981 until it was beaten

*Beryl Burton combined international cycling success on road and track with her total domination of UK time-trialling, in which she was frequently ahead of both women and men*

in 1995; the 25-mile record since 1959 with a best time of 53 minutes, 21 seconds; the 30-mile record five times; the 50-mile record 11 times and still holds it with a time of 1 hour, 51 minutes, 30 seconds set in 1976; the 100-mile record ten times and still holds it with a time of 3 hours, 55 minutes, 5 seconds set in 1968; and the 12-hour record of 277.25 miles since 1967 when she became the fifth rider ever to exceed 270 miles. On that 277.25-mile ride she also caught and beat M McNamara who won the men's event with a distance of 276.52 miles, a record which he held until 1969.

■ John Watson of Clifton CC became the first rider to pass 280 miles (281.87) in 12 hours in 1970. In the same year he broke the 50-mile record with 1 hour, 43 minutes, 46 seconds, and remained unbeaten over 50 miles for 13 years. Also in 1969 Roy Cromack set a 24-hour record of 507 miles. In the 26 years to 1995 four other solo riders and one tandem pair exceeded 500 miles, but none of them beat Cromack's record. Glenn Longland of Antelope Racing Team became the first rider to exceed 290 miles in 12 hours in 1985 with a distance of 291.85 miles. In 1991 he pushed the record past 300 miles with a distance of 300.08 miles.

# MEN'S BICYCLE RECORDS

## 10 Miles

|  |  |  | *Time*<br>*Hrs:Mins.Sec* |
|---|---|---|---|
| 1972 | W Moore | Merseyside Wheelers | 20.36 |
| 1975 | I R White | Hull Coureurs CRC | 20.27 |
| 1978 | S Denton | Rockingham CC | 20.26 |
| 1979 | S Yates | 34th Nomads | 20.07 |
| 1980 | D Akam | Gemini Bicycle Club | 19.50 |
| 1980 | S Yates | 34th Nomads | 19.44 |
| 1981 | M Pyne | CC Breckland | 19.41 |
| 1981 | D Lloyd | Manchester Wheelers Club | 19.11 |
| 1988 | C Sturgess | Team Haverhill | 18.48 |
| 1992 | M Illingworth | G S Strada | 18.34 |
| 1993 | G Obree | Leo Road Club | 18.27 |

## 10 Miles – Team

| 1973 | West Kent RC (M Ballard, J Mummery, D Osborn) | 1:05.31 |
|---|---|---|
| 1973 | Rockingham CC (M L Johnson, J Burnham, J Nixon) | 1:05.21 |
| 1975 | Marlboro AC (G West, M Amey, D G Mee) | 1:04.43 |
| 1976 | Unity CC (M Haynes, J Lyons, D Smith) | 1:04.39 |
| 1979 | Velo Club Slough (R J Queen, S G Hunt, B M Parsons) | 1:04.30 |
| 1980 | 34th Nomads (S Yates, T Stevens, R Keeble) | 1:03.38 |
| 1980 | C C Breckland (M D Pyne, R J Bradley, S C Warren) | 1:03.07 |
| 1980 | C C Breckland (M D Pyne, R J Bradley, S C Warren) | 1:02.33 |
| 1980 | C C Breckland (M D Pyne, R J Bradley, S C Warren) | 1:02.04 |
| 1981 | C C Breckland (M D Pyne, R J Bradley, S C Warren) | 1:01.11 |
| 1982 | Charnwood Cycle R C (G T Platts, S R Pike, K W Platts) | 1:00.13 |
| 1991 | Leo RC (S Dangerfield, W Moore, M St Leger) | 59.28 |
| 1991 | Leo RC (M Illingworth, S Dangerfield, W Moore) | 58.02 |

## 25 Miles

| 1944 | C Cartwright | Manchester Clarion C&AC | 59.18 |
|---|---|---|---|
| 1946 | B B Francis | Solihull CC | 58.49 |
| 1946 | B B Francis | Solihull CC | 58.35 |
| 1949 | G F Fell | Becontree Wheelers CC | 58.00 |
| 1951 | R Inman | Mercury Road Club | 57.17 |
| 1951 | D J Keeler | Vegetarian C&AC | 57.15 |
| 1951 | D J Keeler | Vegetarian C&AC | 57.11 |
| 1952 | S F Higginson | Halesowen A&CC | 57.08 |
| 1953 | S F Higginson | Halesowen A&CC | 56.32 |
| 1953 | S F Higginson | Halesowen A&CC | 56.29 |
| 1955 | W Holmes | Hull Thursday RC | 56.05 |
| 1955 | N Sheil | Molyneux RC | 55.51 |
| 1955 | W Holmes | Hull Thursday RC | 55.49 |
| 1958 | D S Evans | Acme Wheelers (Rhondda) | 55.45 |
| 1959 | A Shackleton | North Lancs RC | 55.38 |
| 1959 | A R Engers | Barnet CC | 55.11 |
| 1961 | C McCoy | Melling Wheelers | 55.01 |
| 1962 | D C Bonner | Old Portlians CC | 54.28 |
| 1964 | B Breedon | Conisbrough Ivanhoe CC | 54.23 |
| 1965 | M J V Burrow | Crest CC | 54.04 |
| 1965 | P A Bennett | Barnet CC | 53.31 |
| 1966 | D Dungworth | Rutland CC | 53.18 |

| 1966 | T Morgan | Barnet CC | 52.56 |
|---|---|---|---|
| 1966 | D Dungworth | Rutland CC | 52.28 |
| 1969 | A R Engers | Polytechnic CC | 51.59 |
| 1969 | A R Engers | Polytechnic CC | 51.00 |
| 1978 | E J Adkins | Velo Club Slough | 50.50 |
| 1978 | A R Engers | Unity CC | 49.24 |
| 1990 | P Longbottom | Manchester Wheelers' Club | 49.13 |
| 1991 | J Pritchard BEM | Polytechnic CC | 48.28 |
| 1991 | G Dighton | Manchester Wheelers' Club | 48.07 |
| 1992 | C Boardman | G S Strada | 47.19 |
| 1993 | C Boardman MBE | North Wirral Velo | 45.57 |

## 25 Miles – Team

| 1938 | Monkton CC (H Earnshaw, E Larkin, A Martin) | 3:05.34 |
|---|---|---|
| 1946 | Hemsworth Wheelers CC (J Simpson, R Ventom, E Larkin) | 3:05.33 |
| 1946 | Kingston Road CC (W C Whitbourn, W Hubbard, P Crook) | 3:03.24 |
| 1947 | Manchester Wheelers' Club (C Cartwright, W B Chapman, A R Potter) | 3:02.25 |
| 1949 | Becontree Wheelers (G F Fell, L Eshouse, N Clarke) | 3:00.53 |
| 1951 | Bec CC (GK Bentley, J A Pentecost, D H Hathway) | 3:00.09 |
| 1951 | Mercury Road Club (R Inman, I P Sirett, J A Bell) | 2:57.16 |
| 1952 | Halesowen A&CC (S F Higginson, B J Higginson, K Sparks) | 2:57.01 |
| 1953 | Halesowen A&CC (S F Higginson, B J Higginson, K Sparks) | 2:56.21 |
| 1955 | Hull Thursday RC (W Holmes, J M Dawson, B Underwood) | 2:55.26 |
| 1957 | Clarence Wheelers (M J Gambrill, A L Killick, C R Gambrill) | 2:55.03 |
| 1957 | Silchester CC (P C Brown, RC Hutchins, R J Hawkins) | 2:53.42 |
| 1959 | Nottingham Wheelers (G Ian, R Shaw, R E Hallam) | 2:52.54 |
| 1959 | Melling Wheelers (C McCoy, B A Richards, J P McLean) | 2:51.42 |
| 1962 | Old Portlians CC (D C Bonner, P R Burgess, J R Jewell) | 2:47.19 |
| 1965 | Barnett CC (P A Bennett, A Rochford, J Mummery) | 2:42.30 |
| 1968 | Polytechnic CC (A R Engers, J Burnham, J R Cornillie) | 2:40.43 |
| 1969 | Rockingham CC (M L Johnson, G B Huck, J G Blacker) | 2:40.26 |
| 1969 | Clifton CC, (P D Smith, D Pickard, P L Watson) | 2:39.43 |
| 1969 | Polytechnic CC, (A R Engers, J Burnham, J R Cornillie) | 2:36.34 |
| 1978 | Velo Club Slough (E J Adkins, R J Queen, J Burnham) | 2:36.09 |
| 1987 | Polytechnic CC (J Pritchard BEM, S Barnes, W Rowe) | 2:34.16 |
| 1991 | Polytechnic CC (M Pyne, R van Looy, W Rowe) | 2:34.02 |
| 1991 | Leo RC (S Dangerfield, W Moore, G Taylor) | 2:31.58 |
| 1991 | Polytechnic CC (J Pritchard BEM, C Brooks, D McKellow) | 2:31.32 |
| 1991 | Manchester Wheelers' Club (G Dighton, E Adkins, J Woodburn) | 2:29.07 |

## 30 Miles

| 1938 | G H Fleming | Belle Vue CC | 1:13.01 |
|---|---|---|---|
| 1945 | C Cartwright | Manchester Clarion C & AC | 1:12.51 |
| 1947 | W C Whitbourn | Kingston Road CC | 1:12.44 |
| 1947 | C Cartwright | Manchester Wheelers' Club | 1:12.10 |
| 1948 | J Nightingale | Abbotsford Park RC | 1:11.35 |
| 1949 | G F Fell | Becontree Wheelers CC | 1:11.15 |
| 1951 | T H A Withers | North Road CC | 1:10.39 |
| 1951 | V A Gibbons | Brentwood Road Club | 1:10.11 |
| 1951 | D J Keeler | Vegetarian C & AC | 1:09.20 |
| 1954 | V A Gibbons | Brentwood Road Club | 1:08.22 |
| 1955 | R Jowers | Twickenham CC | 1:07.30 |
| 1963 | B Green | Port Sunlight Wheelers | 1:07.25 |
| 1966 | D Dungworth | Rutland CC | 1:05.21 |
| 1967 | D Dungworth | Rutland CC | 1:04.56 |

| | | | |
|---|---|---|---|
| 1975 | A R Engers | Woolwich CC | 1:02.27 |
| 1978 | R J Queen | Velo Club Slough | 1:02.07 |
| 1981 | J Oakes | Bedouin CC | 1:01.46 |
| 1981 | M Pyne | CC Breckland | 1:00.11 |
| 1991 | G Empson | CC Breckland | 59.56 |
| 1991 | E Adkins | Manchester Wheelers' Club | 59.22 |

## 30 Miles – Team

| | | |
|---|---|---|
| 1942 | Clarence Wheelers CC (D Perrin, R Watson, G Royston) | 3:49.45 |
| 1947 | Marsh RC (L Oldfield, W Siggins, D Ockmore) | 3:47.27 |
| 1947 | Becontree Wheelers (G F Fell, L Eshouse, N Clarke) | 3:46.04 |
| 1948 | Abbotsford Park Road Club (J Nightingale, E R Brown, L Cooke) | 3:45.14 |
| 1948 | Yiewsley Road Club (D S Burrows, A C J Green, E E Smith) | 3:45.04 |
| 1949 | Norwood Paragon CC (D H Chamberlain, G A Nightingale, R Tugwell) | 3:42.43 |
| 1950 | Solihull CC (B B Francis, A Hobson, V Rudd) | 3:40.04 |
| 1950 | Becontree Wheelers (G F Fell, L Eshouse, C J Jepson) | 3:39.19 |
| 1951 | North Road CC (T H A Withers, A C Kennedy, E Blackman) | 3:36.06 |
| 1954 | Willesden CC (P L Baulch, J R Blunsden, G J Love) | 3:32.54 |
| 1963 | Edgware RC (P A Bennett, A G Adams, R C Back) | 3:28.39 |
| 1963 | Port Sunlight Wheelers (B Green, J Kennedy, M Whyard) | 3:26.18 |
| 1968 | Cleveleys RC (M Gadd, P Shuttleworth, B Scarisbrick) | 3:26.04 |
| 1968 | Oldbury & District CC (B Hayes, R Iddles, D J Blount) | 3:24.16 |
| 1968 | Oldbury & District CC (B Hayes, A Boden, D J Blount) | 3:20.11 |
| 1978 | Velo Club Slough (R J Queen, J Burnham, J W Webb) | 3:15.46 |
| 1978 | Velo Club Slough (R J Queen, J Burnham, D A Smith) | 3:14.13 |
| 1978 | Velo Club Slough (R J Queen, E J Adkins, J Burnham) | 3:08.37 |
| 1981 | CC Breckland (M D Pyne, R J Bradley, S C Warren) | 3:06.10 |

## 50 Miles

| | | | |
|---|---|---|---|
| 1937 | L Thorpe | Barnet CC | 2:03.28 |
| 1946 | A E G Derbyshire | Calleva Road Club | 2:02.32 |
| 1946 | B B Francis | Solihull CC | 2:02.19 |
| 1947 | G H Fleming | Belle Vue CC | 2:01.32 |
| 1947 | G H Fleming | Belle Vue CC | 1:59.14 |
| 1951 | G K Bentley | Bec CC | 1:58.29 |
| 1952 | G K Bentley | Bec CC | 1:57.46 |
| 1952 | G K Bentley | Bec CC | 1:56.44 |
| 1955 | V A Gibbons | Brentwood RC | 1:56.24 |
| 1957 | R Jowers | Twickenham CC | 1:55.44 |
| 1957 | R Jowers | Twickenham CC | 1:55.28 |
| 1957 | W Holmes | Hull Thursday RC | 1:55.14 |
| 1959 | G Ian | Nottingham Wheelers | 1:55.09 |
| 1959 | G Ian | Nottingham Wheelers | 1:55.07 |
| 1959 | B F Wiltcher | Zeus RC | 1:53.56 |
| 1960 | B F Wiltcher | Zeus RC | 1:53.40 |
| 1962 | C J Munford | Barnet CC | 1:53.28 |
| 1962 | R F Colden | Camberley Wheelers | 1:52.38 |
| 1964 | D Reay | Gosforth RC | 1:52.36 |
| 1964 | M McNamara | Rockingham CC | 1:51.49 |
| 1964 | P Hill | Askern CC | 1:51.39 |
| 1964 | B Breedon | Conisbrough Ivanhoe CC | 1:50.03 |
| 1966 | P Smith | Clifton CC | 1:49.22 |
| 1967 | P Smith | Clifton CC | 1:48.33 |

| 1969 | D Whitehouse | Shirley RC | 1:47.38 |
| 1970 | I White | Clifton CC | 1:47.34 |
| 1970 | E J Watson | Clifton CC | 1:43.46 |
| 1983 | D Lloyd | Manchester Wheelers' Club | 1:40.52 |
| 1983 | I S Cammish | G S Strada | 1:39.51 |
| 1993 | G Obree | Leo Road Club | 1:39.01 |

## 50 Miles – Team

| 1937 | Monkton CC (H Earnshaw, E Larkin, C Brian) | 6:18.38 |
| 1946 | Calleva Road Club (A E G Derbyshire, D S Burrows, J Simmons) | 6:18.35 |
| 1947 | Solihull CC (R J Maitland, E Jones, R W Bowes) | 6:16.39 |
| 1950 | Brentwood Road Club (V A Gibbons, D Haxell, D W Brunwin) | 6:13.30 |
| 1951 | Brentwood Road Club (V A Gibbons, D Haxell, E Cook) | 6:13.12 |
| 1952 | Medway Wheelers (K H Joy, B F Hawkes, L L Hitch) | 6:12.52 |
| 1952 | Leicestershire RC (D E Lewin, O G Blower, G F Smith) | 6:10.35 |
| 1952 | Brentwood RC (V A Gibbons, B L Shaw, R T Spanton) | 6:08.10 |
| 1953 | Brentwood RC (V A Gibbons, R T Spanton, B L Shaw) | 6:06.18 |
| 1953 | Mersey RC (H E Roberts, J C Hulme, D J Russell) | 6:06.00 |
| 1955 | Brentwood RC (V A Gibbons, J Styles, R T Spanton) | 6:05.49 |
| 1955 | Hull Thursday RC (W Holmes, J M Dawson, B Trotter) | 6:04.20 |
| 1958 | Acme Wheelers (Rhondda) (D S Evans, C Hughes, D J Hughes) | 6:00.59 |
| 1958 | Crescent Wheelers (K Craven, E Beauchamp, D Minall) | 5:57.29 |
| 1958 | Crescent Wheelers (K Craven, D Minall, E Beauchamp) | 5:54.52 |
| 1962 | Camberley Wheelers (R F Colden, A W Stone, K J Fairhead) | 5:48.42 |
| 1964 | Askern CC (J P Hill, A Robson, D Brunt) | 5:44.09 |
| 1964 | Kirkby CC (K Boardman, H D Middleton, J V Oakley) | 5:44.03 |
| 1965 | Rockingham CC (B N Breedon, M McNamara, D Wood) | 5:43.19 |
| 1966 | Clifton CC (P D Smith, I R White, P T Taylor) | 5:40.06 |
| 1966 | Clifton CC (P D Smith, E J Watson, P T Taylor) | 5:33.48 |
| 1970 | Clifton CC (E J Watson, I R White, K Mitchell) | 5:33.12 |
| 1970 | Clifton CC (E J Watson, I R White, D Pickard) | 5:20.40 |
| 1990 | Manchester Wheelers' Club (C Boardman, G Dighton, P Longbottom) | 5:18.26 |
| 1991 | Manchester Wheelers' Club (C Boardman, C Dighton, P Longbottom) | 5:14.46 |
| 1995 | Optimum Performance RT (K Dawson, W Randle, P Curran) | 5:10.50 |

## 100 Miles

| 1938 | H Earnshaw | Monkton CC | 4:20.48 |
| 1946 | A E G Derbyshire | Calleva Road Club | 4:20.23 |
| 1946 | A C Harding | Middlesex Road Club | 4:17.46 |
| 1947 | R Firth | Altrincham Ravens CC | 4:17.02 |
| 1950 | K H Joy | Medway Wheelers | 4:14.30 |
| 1950 | V A Gibbons | Brentwood Road Club | 4:12.49 |
| 1950 | L V Willmott | Midland C & AC | 4:12.22 |
| 1952 | K H Joy | Medway Wheelers CC | 4:06.52 |
| 1953 | V A Gibbons | Brentwood RC | 4:06.31 |
| 1955 | R C Booty | Ericsson Wheelers | 4:04.30 |
| 1956 | R C Booty | Ericsson Wheelers | 4:01.52 |
| 1956 | R C Booty | Ericsson Wheelers | 3:58.28 |
| 1962 | R F Colden | Camberley Wheelers | 3:54.23 |
| 1968 | M C Roach | Hounslow & District Wheelers | 3:01.41 |
| 1969 | P D Smith | Clifton CC | 3:50.20 |
| 1969 | A Taylor | Oldbury & District CC | 3:46.37 |
| 1976 | P W Griffiths | G S Strada | 3:46.22 |
| 1978 | P W Griffiths | G S Strada | 3:45.28 |
| 1979 | P W Griffiths | G S Strada | 3:41.43 |
| 1980 | I S Cammish | Edgware RC | 3:41.41 |

| 1981 | I S Cammish | G S Strada | 3:41.32 |
| 1981 | I S Cammish | G S Strada | 3:38.39 |
| 1983 | I S Cammish | G S Strada | 3:31.53 |

## 100 Miles – Team

| 1939 | Bronte Wheelers (R Firth, N Hey, B Rangeley) | 13:24.19 |
| 1947 | Altrincham Ravens CC (R Firth, C Farebrother, E Wooley) | 13:13.23 |
| 1948 | Medway Wheelers (K H Joy, P Beardsmore, R Enfield) | 13:05.54 |
| 1949 | Medway Wheelers (R Enfield, K H Joy, P Beardsmore) | 13:03.32 |
| 1952 | Medway Wheelers (K H Joy, F N Jackson, B F Hawkes) | 12:49.40 |
| 1958 | Midland Clarion C & AC (J P Ogden, C J Clarke, G A Morris) | 12:43.42 |
| 1959 | Camberley Wheelers (J Rogers, R E Colden, R L Agar) | 12:36.17 |
| 1962 | Camberley Wheelers (R F Colden, K J Fairhead, A W Stone) | 12:11.08 |
| 1967 | Clifton CC (P D Smith, R Cromack, E J Watson) | 12:09.10 |
| 1968 | Hounslow & District Wheelers (M C Roach, K J Fairhead, J E Marshall) | 11:55.08 |
| 1969 | Clifton CC (P D Smith, E J Watson, R Cromack) | 11:37.47 |
| 1986 | Manchester Wheelers' Club (I Cammish, S Potts, P Guy) | 11:26.58 |
| 1988 | Manchester Wheelers' Club (I Cammish, S Potts, P Guy) | 11:24.09 |
| 1989 | Manchester Wheelers' Club (I Cammish, E Adkins, P J Woodburn) | 11:17.10 |
| 1989 | Manchester Wheelers' Club (I Cammish, D Smith, D Ardern) | 11:17.10 |
| 1990 | Manchester Wheelers' Club ( G J Dighton, A J Gornall, E J Adkins) | 11:04.16 |

## 12 Hours

| | | | Miles |
|---|---|---|---|
| 1937 | C Heppleston | Yorkshire Road Club | 251.62 |
| 1945 | A Overton | Kingston Road Club | 251.87 |
| 1950 | A R J Hill | Kentish Wheelers | 259.23 |
| 1951 | K H Joy | Medway Wheelers | 260.02 |
| 1952 | E Britton | Yorkshire RC | 262.16 |
| 1952 | K H Joy | Medway Wheelers | 264.87 |
| 1956 | R C Booty | Ericsson Wheelers | 265.66 |
| 1957 | R C Booty | Army Cycling Union | 266.00 |
| 1958 | O G Blower | Leicestershire RC | 271.80 |
| 1967 | M McNamara | Rockingham CC | 276.52 |
| 1968 | M C Roach | Hounslow & District Wheelers | 277.17 |
| 1969 | E J Watson | Clifton CC | 281.87 |
| 1979 | P J Woodburn | Velo Club Slough | 285.51 |
| 1979 | P Wells | Edgware Road Club | 286.85 |
| 1983 | G N Longland | Antelope Racing Team | 287.28 |
| 1986 | G N Longland | Antelope Racing Team | 291.72 |
| 1991 | G N Longland | Antelope Racing Team | 300.08 |

## 12 Hours – Team

| 1937 | Yorkshire Road Club (C Heppleston, N Read, J T Wilkinson) | 728.25 |
| 1948 | Medway Wheelers (P Beardsmore, R Enfield, K H Joy) | 732.27 |
| 1948 | Norwood Paragon CC (B J Brown, P H Kitchiner, V Callanan) | 740.09 |
| 1951 | Kentish Wheelers (A R J Hill, B W Apperley, R Robbins) | 755.26 |
| 1955 | Rutland CC (S Thompson, R Coukham, G Fouldes) | 756.52 |
| 1957 | Middlesex RC (D W Stokes, A C Harding, F A Burrell) | 767.15 |
| 1958 | Leicestershire RC (O G Blower, D L Bowman, T H Jobson) | 772.70 |
| 1963 | Selby CC (R Charles, G K Wood, J L West) | 780.05 |
| 1967 | Clifton CC (R Cromack, P D Smith, E J Watson) | 800.28 |
| 1971 | Hounslow & District Wheelers (M C Roach, K F Clapton, J E Marshall) | 804.73 |
| 1986 | Antelope Racing Team (G Longland, P Pickers, J Short) | 820.77 |

**24 Hours**

| 1935 | E B Seeley | Calleva Road Club | 444.75 |
|------|------------|-------------------|--------|
| 1948 | G H Basham | Wessex Road Club | 454.20 |
| 1950 | E Mundy | Addiscombe CC | 455.91 |
| 1950 | S M Butler | Northwood Paragon CC | 458.18 |
| 1950 | R F Mynott | North Road CC | 459.50 |
| 1951 | G Andrews | Addiscombe CC | 461.31 |
| 1952 | G A T Laws | Catford CC | 463.29 |
| 1952 | E Mundy | Addiscombe CC | 467.52 |
| 1954 | S Thompson | Rutland CC | 469.66 |
| 1955 | S Thompson | Rutland CC | 474.12 |
| 1955 | K Price | Cardiff 100 Miles RC | 478.55 |
| 1956 | D H White | Swindon Wheelers | 484.64 |
| 1958 | D H White | Swindon Wheelers | 484.75 |
| 1964 | E Matthews | Altrincham RC | 490.03 |
| 1966 | N Carline | Morley CC | 496.37 |
| 1969 | R Cromack | Clifton CC | 507.00 |

**24 Hours – Team**

| 1937 | Vegetarian C & AC (F N Robertson, E G Guy, A G Oxbrow) | 1254.62 |
|------|--------------------------------------------------------|---------|
| 1947 | Luton Wheelers CC (R Goodman, E S Ellington, H Walker) | 1283.50 |
| 1949 | Vegetarian C & AC (J Purves, W A E Shillibeer, E G Guy) | 1284.19 |
| 1950 | Addiscombe CC (C C Mundy, S E Harvey, S E Armstrong) | 1341.95 |
| 1951 | Addiscombe CC (G Andrews, S E Harvey, J F Watts) | 1351.92 |
| 1952 | Addiscombe CC (E Mundy, G Andrews, S E Harvey) | 1361.94 |
| 1955 | Rutland CC (S Thompson, R Coukham, G Fouldes) | 1397.13 |
| 1958 | Rutland CC (R Coukham, S Thompson, G Steers) | 1402.69 |
| 1960 | Middlesex RC (F A Burrell, A C Harding, R W E Poole) | 1407.23 |
| 1979 | North Staffs St Christophers CCC (M Coupe, J D Cahill, M J Parker) | 1417.39 |
| 1980 | North Staffs St Christophers CCC (J D Cahill, M Coupe, T Finney) | 1441.59 |

# GLOSSARY

**Audax** International association which promotes long-distance group rides, primarily at distances of 200, 300, 400 and 600 kilometres. The most famous Audax ride is the 1200 km Paris–Brest–Paris, held every four years.

**balloon tyres** The old name for fat section tyres.

**ball race** A metal ring which holds the ball bearings for the bottom bracket, headset or pedals.

**BCF** The British Cycling Federation administers cycle competition in Britain.

**BMX** Single gear stunt bikes with small wheels and frames more formally known as Bicycle Motor-Cross. BMX racing is held on hard dirt tracks with bumps ('whoops'), banks ('berms') and steep drops ('drop-offs').

**bonk** Term used for exhaustion. Also called 'knock'.

**boss** Metal fitting on a bicycle frame to hold items such as gear levers and drink-bottle cages.

**bottom bracket** The hole in the base of the frame where the axle unit is attached.

**brake blocks** The rubber blocks which are squeezed against the wheel rim.

**brake cables** The wire cables which connect the handles to the brakes. Some are Gore-Tex coated to help them slide more easily. Alternative hydraulic brakes are sometimes used by tourists, tandems and mountain bikes.

**brazing** A method of hot welding when assembling steel-frame tubes.

**break** One or more riders accelerating away from the main group in a race.

**bunch** Main group of riders in a race. Also called the *pack* or *peloton* in a road race.

**butted tubing** Frame tubing that is thicker at one (single) or both (double) ends to improve the strength-to-weight ratio.

**cadence** The number of times the pedals revolve in a minute.

**Campagnolo** Classic long established Italian groupset manufacturer widely favoured by road racers.

**caliper brakes** Inverted U-shape rim brakes that close like a pair of scissors. The best have two pivot points and are favoured for all road racing.

**cantilever brakes** A type of brake system with two separate arms favoured for mountain bikes.

**cro-moly** Chrome molybendum alloy steel tubing used in the manufacture of bicycle frames.

**cross-country** A mountain bike or cyclo-cross race round a natural circuit.

**chainset** The chainwheels, chain and rear cogs or sprockets.

**chainstays** The two horizontal parts of the frame that join the bottom bracket to the rear wheel.

**chainwheels** The big toothed rings that drive the chain via the pedals and cranks. Also called 'chainrings'.

**cleats** Fittings on the bottom of cycling shoes which hold them firmly on the pedals.

**clipless pedals** A system which allows cycling shoes to be locked into the pedals.

**commissaire** An official who controls a road race.

**cranks** The arms which drive the chainwheels. Cotterless cranks are bolted straight to the bottom bracket axle for all high performance cycling.

**criterium** A road race held on a short circuit, usually in a town or village.

**cycleway** A purpose-built cycle route.

**cyclo-cross** A racing competition that involves running and riding on a mixed course which includes hard sections, very steep hills, grass and frequently mud.

**cyclometer** A handlebar mounted unit which can display information such as speed, distance, average speed and time. It can also be combined with a heart monitor and cadence recorder.

**deep rim wheels** Road race wheels with deep carbon rims for added rigidity.

**derailleur** The modern style of gear system which moves the chain from side to side across the geared rear cogs (sprockets) and front chainwheels. The alternative is a hub gear.

**derny** A small motorbike used for paced racing on the track.

**devil take the hindmost** An elimination track race.

**directeur sportif** The manager of a road or track race team.

**disc brakes** Occasionally used with hydraulic systems for tandems and by downhill mountain bike racers who require the best possible stopping power. The drawbacks are cost and weight.

**disc wheel** A solid wheel for improved aerodynamic performance. Mainly used on tracks.

*domestique* A 'worker' in a road race team. The *domestiques* will support the best riders in the team, helping to pace them while tactically undermining the leaders of rival teams.

**downhill** A downhill mountain bike race is a high-speed event from the top to the bottom of a hill. Riders are normally sent one at a time, with the rider with the lowest aggregate time winning.

**down tube** The diagonal tube connecting the bottom bracket to the head tube.

**drafting** Being paced by another rider.

**drop-outs** Cut-outs in the front forks and chainstays where the wheel axles fit into the frame.

**drops** The bottom part of drop handlebars. When the peloton sees Miguel Indurain go onto the drops, they know they are in for trouble.

**echelon** A group of riders who spread out in a diagonal line to help deal with a cross wind in a road race.

**fixed wheel** A single gear rear-wheel hub which drives the chain as the wheel rotates. All track bikes are fixed wheel since it is the most effective means of producing maximum power over short distances.

**forks** The two front forks hold the front wheel.

**fork rake** The amount the forks are curved from a straight line. The straighter the forks, the more direct the handling will be.

**frameset** The set of tubes that are used to make a frame. Well known manufacturers include Reynolds, Columbus and Ritchey.

**freewheel** A device which fits into the rear wheel hub, allowing the chain to drive the wheel forwards without the wheel driving the chain forwards. With a few exceptions all road bikes have a freewheel.

**gear measurement (UK/USA)** In the UK and USA gears are measured in inches using the following formula:

*Diameter of rear wheel in inches, multiplied by the number of teeth on the chainwheel, divided by the number of teeth on the rear cog = gear in inches.* The lower the gear number, the easier it will be to spin the pedals while riding uphill. It is also possible to calculate speed using the following formula:

*Gear in inches, multiplied by cadence, divided by 336 = speed mph*

**gear measurement (Europe)** In France and other European countries gearing is expressed as the distance in metres travelled for one complete revolution of the pedals. This system is called 'gear development'.

**gear ratios** The gear ratios are determined by the number of teeth on each sprocket and chainwheel.

**general classification** Overall positions in a stage race.

**Gore-Tex** Trade-name for a breathable, waterproof clothing material.

**grimpeur** A hill climb or hill climber.

**Gripshift** Trade-name for a type of twist-grip gear changer.

**groupset** The collection of moving components that are attached to a frame. The best known groupset manufacturer is Shimano, followed by Sachs and Campagnolo.

**headset** The internal unit which allows the handlebars and front forks to pivot while being held rigid inside the head tube.

**head tube** The small tube that connects with the down tube and seat tube, as well as supporting the headset and front forks.

**head-tube angle** The angle between the head tube and horizontal. This can have a marked effect on performance.

**high gears** Gears for going downhill, using the biggest chainwheel and smallest rear sprocket for the highest gear.

**honking** Standing on the pedals and swaying the bike from side to side while climbing a hill.

**hub gears** A gear system enclosed in the rear hub unit. Popular for many years as a recreational gear system made by Sturmey Archer, and more recently updated by Sachs and Shimano.

**indexed gears** Gear shifters which click precisely from gear to gear.

**inner tube** The lightweight rubber tube which is inflated inside the tyre.

**jockey wheels** The small wheels mounted on the *derailleur* arm that guide the chain onto the rear sprockets.

**keirin** A track discipline which originally evolved in Japan. The riders are paced to top speed before an unpaced sprint to the finish.

**King of the Mountains** Prize for the best climber in a stage race.

**knobblies** Mountain bike tyres.

**low gears** Gears for going uphill, or riding over difficult surfaces. The lowest gear uses the smallest chainwheel and largest rear sprocket.

**low profile** A cycle frame with the top tube sloping down towards the front to create a low front profile to reduce drag. Mainly used for time-trial and track racing and commonly known as 'low pro'.

**lugs** Steel sleeves used to join tubes in frame construction.

**madison** A track discipline in which teams of two riders race in relays. Originated from six-day racing at Madison Square Gardens in New York.

*maillot jaune* Yellow jersey worn by leader of Tour de France.

**monocoque** A bicycle frame which is made as one complete unit. Usually refers to specialist carbon fibre track bikes.

**motor paced** Track race in which each rider is paced by a motor cycle.

**Moulton** Small wheel bicycle invented by Sir Alex Moulton.

**mountain bike** Bicycle for use on rough surfaces. Also more accurately called an ATB (All Terrain Bike).

**NORBA** The National Off-Road Bicycling Association is the national governing body for mountain biking in the USA.

**open** A race open to both amateur and professional riders.

**ordinary** Correct name for the Penny-Farthing style of cycle.

**oxygen debt** Over-stretching your physical capabilities and gasping for air.

**pace line** A line of road racers who take turns to go in front to set the pace.

**panniers** Bags carried on either side of the wheels for long distance touring.

**peloton** The main pack of riders in a road race.

**prime** A prize awarded at an intermediate stage of a race, often for hill climbs.

**prologue** The opening stage in a long distance event such as one of the great Tours. Usually held as a time-trial to select the first overall leader.

**pursuit** Track race in which two riders (or teams) pursue one another over a set distance having started from opposite sides of the track.

**quick release** A lever used to let off wheel hubs.

**ram bars** Extensions attached to the handlebars of a mountain bike.

**randonée** The French word for a group ride. A hard riding tourist, often with a competitive edge, is known as a *randonneur*.

**recumbent** A bike in which the rider pedals in a horizontal position. It may be the same as an HPV (Human Powered Vehicle).

**roadster** Traditional bicycle for leisure use, often featuring straight handlebars and balloon tyres.

**rollers** Rolling cylinders used for static cycling. Mainly of use for winter training or warming up.

**rolling resistance** The friction caused by the tyres. In general terms fat tyres have more resistance than thin tyres, but tyre construction and flexibility are also important factors.

**safety** The forerunner of the modern bicycle which was developed with conventional size wheels and a rear-drive chain in place of the ordinary or Penny-Farthing.

**sag wagon** A vehicle that follows a road race and collects any riders who drop out.

**sealed bearings** Most modern bicycles have sealed bearings designed to keep the grease in and the water out.

**seatpost** The post which supports the saddle.

**seat stays** The two narrow tubes connecting the chainstays to the seat tube.

**seat tube** The tube connecting the bottom bracket to the saddle end of the seat tube.

**seat-tube angle** The angle between the seat tube and the horizontal.

**Shimano** The world's leading manufacturer of groupsets, based in Japan. Particularly favoured for mountain bike use.

**sidewalls** The sides of a tyre.

**six-day race** A track race for two-man teams held over six days. They were originally non-stop events, but are now usually held on successive afternoons or evenings.

**skinsuit** An all-in-one garment for better streamlining when track racing.

**slalom** Off-road mountain bike competition usually featuring two or four riders.

**soigneur** Racing team masseur or coach.

**SPD** The Shimano system which allows cycling shoes to be locked into the pedals. Also called 'clipless' pedals available in a variety of designs from different manufacturers.

**sprint**[1] A track discipline in which the final sprint over approximately 200 metres is all that matters.

**sprint**[2] Many road races end in a sprint to victory, when the leading group come within sight of the finish line.

**sprint**[3] Term sometimes used for a tubular tyre.

**sprockets** The rear cogs on a bicycle.

**stage race** A series of road races in which the winner is the rider with the lowest total time. Stage racing has also been introduced for mountain bike competition.

**stem** The bar which connects the handlebars to the head tube.

**STI** Shimano system which combines brake and gear levers for road use. A similar system is made by Campagnolo.

**stoker** The rear rider on a tandem.

**Sustrans** A charity dedicated to building cycle paths and planning cycle-friendly routes in Britain. Founded by John Grimshaw.

**tandem** Bicycle with two seats and two sets of pedals and cranks with one rider behind the other.

**TIG welding** Tungsten Inert Gas welding. A sophisticated method of joining frame tubes – particularly favoured with aluminium.

**toe-in** The amount the brake blocks are set at an angle to prevent them squealing when the brakes are applied.

**toe-straps** Straps and clips which hold the feet to the pedals. Still used for touring, but replaced by clipless pedals for competition use.

**time-trial** A race against the clock, with riders leaving the start one at a time, usually held over a fixed distance or fixed time.

**tri-bars** Extension bars to enable a road racer to adopt a more aerodynamic position when riding on flat ground.

**tricycle/trike** A cycle with two rear wheels.

**tubeset** The collection of tubes which makes up a frame.

**tubs** Also called 'tubulars'. Very light road racing tyres in a tubular section which completely encloses the inner tube. The tub is attached to the wheel rim using a sticky tape.

**turbo trainer** Sophisticated winter training device for static cycling.

**UCI** The Union Cycliste Internationale is the governing body of international cycle competition.

**USCF** The United States Cycling Federation is the governing body of road and track racing in the USA.

**velodrome** A banked, oval shaped racing track which may be indoors or outdoors depending on the climate.

**wheelbase** The distance between the centres of the front and rear wheels.

**wheelbase** The horizontal distance between the two wheel hubs.

**wire-ons** The conventional type of tyre which is held on the wheel rim by two rigid beads made of wire or kevlar.

**yellow jersey** The *maillot jaune* worn by the leader of the Tour de France.

# Useful Addresses

**Adventure Cycling Association**
PO Box 8308, Missoula, MT59807, USA.
Tel: 406 721 1776.
A national, non-profit making
organization dedicated to bicycle travel.

**American Bicycle Association**
PO Box 718, Chandler, AZ8524, USA.
Tel: 602 961 1903.
A leading BMX racing organization.

**Audax UK**
Secretary: Ben Steven, Coniston View,
Redhills Road, Arnside, Carnforth LA5
0AN, UK. Tel: 01524 761869.
AUK is one of the largest cycling clubs in
Britain. It promotes non-competitive
long-distance cycling as the British
representative of 'Randonneurs
Mondiaux'.

**Bicycle Federation of America**
1506 21st St, NW, Suite 200,
Washington DC, 20036-1008. Tel: 202
463 6622.
A national, non profit-making
organization promoting bicycle use.

**Bicycle Mobile Hams of America**
Box 4009-B, Boulder, Co 80306. Tel:
303 494 6559.
A national, non profit-making
organization whose members
communicate by miniature radios while
pedalling.

**British Cycling Federation**
National Cycling Centre, 1 Stuart Street,
Manchester
M11 4DQ. Tel: 0161 223 2244.
The governing body for cycle racing in
the UK.

**Environmental Transport Association**
The Old Post House, Heath Road,
Weybridge KT13 8RS, UK.
Tel: 0193 282 8882.
The ETA lobbies for increased cycle use
and public transport.

**European Cyclists Federation**
Postbus 2150, Nl-3440 DD Woerden,
Netherlands.
Tel: (31) 3480 23119.
'Cities for Cyclists' is an ECF project
working towards more bike-friendly
cities and comparing experiences across
Europe.

**Classic Bicycle & Whizzer Club of
America**
35892 Parkdale, Livonia, MI 48150, USA.
Tel: 810 791 5594.
Cycle enthusiasts whose interests lie in
collecting and restoring bikes of the
1930–1960s period.

**Cyclists' Touring Club**
Cotterell House, 39 Meadrow, Godalming,
Surrey GU7 3HS, UK. Tel: 01483 417217.
The CTC is Britain's leading club for
cycle tourists. It campaigns for cyclists'
rights, provides various legal and
insurance services, and publishes its own
bi-monthly magazine.

**English Schools' Cycling Association**
157 Kingsclere Avenue, Weston,
Southampton SO92 9JR.
Tel: 0703 442912.
The ESCA has award schemes for
schools for cycle touring and racing.

**International Human-Powered Vehicle
Association**
PO Box 51255, Indianapolis, IN 46251,
USA.
Tel: 317 876 9478.
A non profit-making organization
promoting innovation in the design of
human powered transport on land, water
and in the air.

**International Mountain Bicycling
Association**
PO Box 412043, Los Angeles, CA
90041-9043, USA.
Tel: 818 792 8830.
Promotes the safe and responsible use of
mountain bikes.

**International Randonneurs**
Old Engine House No2, 727 North
Salina Street, Syracuse,
NY 13208, USA.
A touring organization for *randonneurs*.

**League of American Bicyclists**
190 West Ostend St, Suite 120,
Baltimore, MD 21230, USA. Tel: 301
539 3399.
A national organization working to make
bicycling safer and more enjoyable.

**London Cycling Campaign**
Tress House, 3 Stamford Street, London
SE1 9NT.

Tel: 0171 928 7220
A coordinating body for cycling action
groups in London, lobbying for a better
deal for the cyclists.

**National Bicycle History Archive of
America**
Leon Dixon, Box 28242, Santa Ana, CA
92799. USA.
Tel: 714 647 1949.
A bicycle history archive.

**National Bicycle League**
3958 Brown Park Drive, Suite D,
Hilliard, OH 43026, USA. Tel: 614 777
1625.
Sanctions BMX racing across America.

**National Off-Road Bicycling Association**
Tel: 719 578 4717.
National governing body of mountain
biking in the USA.

**Ordre des Cols Durs**
Secretary: John Partington, 20 Spencer
Gate, St Albans, Herts AL1 4AD.
A club for riders who like nothing better
than cycling up and down mountain passes.

**Pickwick Bicycle Club**
Secretary: Michael Radford Esq (Mr.
Brooks), Kingsmere, Shawford,
Winchester, Hampshire SO21 2BL.
The world's oldest cycle club. Each
member takes the name of a character
from Dickens's *Pickwick Papers* which
limits the numbers who can join.

**Road Records Association**
Secretary: H. Hargraves, 133 Colcot
Road, Barry, South Glamorgan CF62 8UJ.
Tel: 0446 747609.
The RRA administers every kind of
place-to-place and timed road record in
Britain.

**Road Time Trials Council**
National Secretary: Philip Heaton,
77 Arlington Drive, Pennington, Leigh
WN7 3QP.
Tel: 0942 603976.
The RTTC administers time-trials held
on roads in Britain.

**Rough Stuff Fellowship**
Secretary: R. Callow, Belle Vue,
Marnhilad, Pontypool, Gwent.
The RSF was founded for off-road riders
long before mountain bikes. It attracts a

loyal membership composed of tourists who want to be a little different.

**Royal Society for the Prevention of Accidents**
Cannon House, The Priory Queensway, Birmingham B4 6BS.
Tel: 0121 200 2461.
RoSPA produces a wide range of information and educational material on all aspects of cycling safety.

**Sustrans**
The Railway Path and Cycle Route Construction Company, 35 King Street, Bristol BS1 4DZ.
Tel: 0272 268893.
Sustrans is a charity which is dedicated to creating a magnificent network of long-distance cycle routes throughout Britain, starting with the Dover–Inverness route.

**Tandem Club**
Secretary: Peter Hallowell, 25 Hendred Way, Abingdon, Oxon OX14 2AN.
The TC supplies information and postal spares for tandem owners.

**Tandem Club of America**
Secretary: Bob & Terri Gorman, PO Box 2176, Los Gatos, CA 95031, USA.
Sponsors rallies for tandems.

**The Recumbent Bicycle Club of America**
PO Box 58755, Renton, WA 98058-1755, USA.

Publishes newsletter and buyers' guide.

**Unicycling Society of America**
Box 40534, Redford, MI 48240, USA.
Send sae for information.

**UK Bicycle Association**
Starley House, Eaton Road, Coventry CV1 2FH. Tel: 01203 559823.
A trade association for the UK bike industry.

**United States Cycling Federation**
1 Olympic Plaza, Colorado Springs, CO 80909. Tel: 719 578 4581.
The governing body for cycle racing in the USA.

# INDEX

*Index compiled by Jeremy Evans*

# Acknowledgements for illustrations

Adventure Cycling (photo by Dan Burden) *p* 31
Adventure Cycling (photo by Greg Siple) *p* 23
Allsport *pp* 77, 137, 152
Allsport Historical Collection *pp* 5, 7 (top), 7 (bottom), 8, 17, 18, 20 (left), 20 (right), 39, 54, 56, 60, 89, 90, 97, 105, 110, 114, 122, 125, 135, 138, 144, 149, 153, 155, 157, 165, 169, 178
Allsport–Simon Bruty *p* 158
Allsport–Russell Cheyne *pp* 161, 162 (top)
Allsport–Chris Cole *pp* 66, 128
Allsport–Tony Duffy *pp* 63, 154
Allsport–Jim Gensheimer *p* 30
Allsport–David Leah *pp* 67, 146
Allsport–Fred Mons *p* 108
Allsport–Mike Powell *pp* 22, 50, 59, 109, 126, 139, 151, 162 (bottom), 171
Allsport–Pascal Rondeau *pp* 47, 52, 147
Allsport–Agence Vandystadt *pp* 68, 69, 74, 82, 95 (left), 95 (right), 96, 98, 100, 102, 121, 143
Cycling Weekly *pp* 14, 29, 86, 92, 177
Graham Watson *pp* 55, 78, 84, 88, 117, 118, 150
Hemistour (photo by Greg Siple) *pp* 24, 32
Hulton-Deutsch Collection *pp* 10, 11, 12, 21, 44, 71, 80, 130, 132
Phil O'Connor *pp* 41, 42, 43, 73, 107, 120, 136, 140, 142, 164